The Writings
of
Matthew Prior

MATTHEW PRIOR

Born 1664
Died 1721

MATTHEW PRIOR

POEMS

ON
SEVERAL OCCASIONS

THE TEXT EDITED BY
A. R. WALLER, M.A.

CAMBRIDGE:
at the University Press
1941

CAMBRIDGE
UNIVERSITY PRESS
LONDON: BENTLEY HOUSE
NEW YORK, TORONTO, BOMBAY
CALCUTTA, MADRAS: MACMILLAN
TOKYO: MARUZEN COMPANY LTD

First Edition 1905
Reprinted 1941

PRINTED IN GREAT BRITAIN

NOTE.

IN 1718 a folio edition of Prior's poems was published by subscription, containing all the poems previously issued by him which he wished to acknowledge and preserve, carefully revised, and accompanied by others then printed for the first time. This folio was issued in three sizes. It will be remembered that a passage in Prior's will runs thus :—'To the College of St. John the Evangelist, in Cambridge, I leave Such and so many of my Books, as shall be judged to amount unto the Value of Two Hundred Pounds: These Books, with my own Poems in the greatest Paper, to be kept in the Library, together with the Books which I have already given.' Of these eighteenth-century examples of large-paper issues Mr Austin Dobson remarks, 'with the small copy of 1718, Johnson might have knocked down Osborne the bookseller; with the same work in its tallest form....Osborne the bookseller might have laid prostrate the "Great Lexicographer" himself.' Those who have seen the 'greatest' copy will not doubt the truth of this statement. Desirous of being suitably equipped in this 'Battle of the Books,' I have used a medium copy as the basis of the present text, a copy measuring $16\frac{3}{8}$ ins. $\times$ $10\frac{3}{4}$ ins. Even this is a handsome folio, with engraved initial letters, head-pieces and tail-pieces, of the usual mythological nature. 'The Names of the Subscribers' who received the volume in

NOTE

1719 in exchange for some four thousand guineas are duly given. These names occupy twenty double-columned pages, and it did not seem desirable to reprint them here. *The Reverend Dr* Peter Drelincourt, *Dean of* Armagh, known to students of Defoe, in connection with 'The Apparition of Mrs Veal,' is a subscriber ; William Congreve, *Esq.*, *Sir* Godfrey Kneller, *Bar.*, *Sir* Isaac Newton, each take a copy, and so does Alexander Pope, *Esq.*; while Jonathan Swift, *D.D.*, *Dean of* St. Patricks, Dublin, subscribes for '*Five Books*,' and, low down on the list, appears the name of *Sir* John Vanbrugh, architect and dramatist.

Two or three previous collections of Prior's poems had appeared. In 1707 a volume entitled 'Poems on Several Occasions : consisting of Odes, Satyrs and Epistles; With some Select *Translations* and *Imitations*,' was published bearing the imprint, 'London : Printed for R. Burrough, and J. Baker, at the *Sun* and *Moon* in *Cornhill*, and E. Curll, at the *Peacock* without *Temple-Bar*,' with three lines from Roscommon on the title-page :

> '*Be not too Rigidly Censorious ;*
> *A String may Jarr, in the Best Master's Hand,*
> *And the most Skilful Archer miss his Aim.*'

Its Contents are given in the Appendix to the present edition (p. 362). Two years later, Prior published a volume of 'Poems on *Several Occasions*. London : Printed for *Jacob Tonson*, within *Grays-Inn* Gate next *Grays-Inn* Lane,' in the Preface to which, referring to the issue of 1707, he says : '*a Collection of Poems has lately appeared under my Name, tho' without my Knowledge, in which the Publisher has given me the Honour of some Things that did not belong to me, and has Transcribed others so imperfectly, that I hardly knew them to be mine.*'

NOTE

(See p. xxiii, the Preface and Dedication of the 1709 volume forming a part of the edition of 1718.) Since all the poems in the 1707 edition save the first two ('A Satyr, on the Modern Translators of Ovid's Epistles' and 'The Seventh Satyr of Juvenal, imitated') are known to be by Prior, the first portion of the above disclaimer must refer to these two. They will be included in the second volume of the present edition, and they need not, therefore, be discussed here. A collation of the earlier issues of Prior's publications with his later collected versions induces the belief that the second portion of the above disclaimer may also be regarded in a diplomatic or Pickwickian sense. A reference to the variants given in the Appendix to this volume will show that Prior's final forms, especially in his State Odes, differ as greatly from their earlier acknowledged versions as do the texts of the poems of 1709 from the 'imperfectly...Transcribed' copies of 1707, and it will be seen that, in the case of the 'Prologue, spoken at Court before the Queen, On Her Majesty's Birth-Day, 1704,' Prior's first version of 1704 is practically identical with the 1707 'unauthorised' version, though greatly altered when he issued, in 1709, the 'indifferent Collection of Poems, for fear of being thought the Author of a worse.'

On the whole, therefore, it seemed best to give in the present volume, the text of Prior's last collected issue, following the folio of 1718, and in the Appendix to give not only the variants of the acknowledged edition of 1709, but also (a) those of the separate early states of the poems where possible, (b) those of the repudiated collection of 1707, and (c) those of 'A Second Collection of Poems on Several Occasions. By Matthew Prior, Esq.,' which was published in London in 1716, 'Printed for J. Roberts near the Oxford Arms in *Warwick-Lane.* Price One Shilling.' The four collections are distinguished in the Notes by the letters A (= 1707), B (= 1709), C (= 1716) and D (= 1718). The 1716 edition also was disowned, in the London Gazette, March 24, 1716. There can be little doubt, however, of the truth of Pope's statement (*Letters*, ed. Elwin and Courthope, iii. 194–5) that 'Mr Prior himself thought it prudent to disown' certain poems, i.e. the two Satires above referred to, which also appear in the 1716 volume. For the contents of C see Appendix, p. 362.

The original spelling and punctuation, etc., of the folio of 1718 have been preserved, and the few misprints corrected are noted. The folio is excellently printed, the errors of the press are remarkably few, and there is no doubt that it presents the final form of those poems which at the date of its publication Prior wished to preserve.

I have not reprinted the Latin version of the *Carmen Seculare*, by Tho. Dibben, of Trinity College, Cambridge, referred to in the Preface (p. xxiii), nor *The Nut-brown Maid. A Poem, written Three Hundred Years Since,* upon which Prior's *Henry and Emma* (pp. 138—158) was modelled. Mrs Elizabeth Singer's *Pastoral* (see pp. 26 and 27) has been printed in smaller type to differentiate it from Prior's own work, and the same course has been adopted in a few other similar cases.

It is a pleasure to acknowledge the help given me by Mr George A. Brown in the collation of some of the early editions.

The second volume of the present edition is in the press. It will contain the remainder of Prior's writings in prose and verse, the poems published before the

viii

NOTE

folio of 1718 but not included therein, the poems
published between 1718 and 1721, the date of Prior's
death, and those posthumously published. Through
the kindness of the Marquis of Bath it will also contain
the Prose Dialogues of Prior, hitherto unpublished,
from the Longleat MSS.

A. R. WALLER.

CAMBRIDGE,
25 *June*, 1905.

POEMS

ON

SEVERAL OCCASIONS.

LONDON:

Printed for JACOB TONSON at *Shakespear's-Head* over
against *Katharine-Street* in the *Strand*, and JOHN
BARBER upon *Lambeth-Hill.* MDCCXVIII.

To the Right Honorable

LIONEL,

Earl of

DORSET and *MIDDLE-SEX.*

IT looks like no great Compliment to Your Lordship, that I prefix Your Name to this Epistle; when, in the Preface, I declare the Book is publish'd almost against my Inclination. But, in all Cases, My Lord, You have an Hereditary Right to whatever may be called Mine. Many of the following Pieces were written by the Command of Your Excellent Father; and most of the rest, under His Protection and Patronage.

The particular Felicity of Your Birth, My Lord; The natural Endowments of Your Mind, (which, without suspicion of Flattery) I may tell You, are very Great; The good Education with which these Parts have been improved; and Your coming into the World, and seeing Men very early; make Us expect from Your Lordship all the Good, which our Hopes can form in Favour of a young Nobleman. *Tu Marcellus eris,*— Our Eyes and our Hearts are turned on You. You must be a Judge and Master of Polite Learning; a Friend and Patron to Men of Letters and Merit; a faithful and able Counsellor to Your Prince; a true Patriot to your Countrey; an Ornament and Honor to the Titles You possess; and in one Word, a Worthy Son to the Great Earl of Dorset.

It is as impossible to mention that Name, without desiring to Commend the Person; as it is to give Him the Commendations which His Virtues deserved. But I assure my self, the most agreeable Compliment I can bring Your Lordship, is to

DEDICATION

pay a grateful Respect to Your Father's Memory. And my own Obligations to Him were such; that the World must pardon my Endeavoring at His Character, however I may miscarry in the Attempt.

A Thousand Ornaments and Graces met in the Composition of this Great Man; and contributed to make Him universally Belov'd and Esteem'd. The Figure of His Body was Strong, Proportionable, Beautiful : and were His Picture well Drawn, it must deserve the Praise given to the Pourtraits of RAPHAEL; and, at once, create Love and Respect. While the Greatness of His Mein inform'd Men, they were approaching the Nobleman; the Sweetness of it invited them to come nearer to the Patron. There was in His Look and Gesture something that is easier conceived than described; that gain'd upon You in His Favor, before He spake one Word. His Behavior was Easie and Courteous to all; but Distinguished and Adapted to each Man in particular, according to his Station and Quality. His Civility was free from the Formality of Rule, and flowed immediately from His good Sense.

Such were the Natural Faculties and Strength of His Mind, that He had occasion to borrow very little from Education : and He owed those Advantages to His own Good Parts, which Others acquire by Study and Imitation. His Wit was Abundant, Noble, Bold. Wit in most Writers is like a Fountain in a Garden, supply'd by several Streams brought thro' artful Pipes, and playing sometimes agreeably. But the Earl of DORSET's was a Source rising from the Top of a Mountain, which forced it's own way, and with inexhaustible Supplies, delighted and inriched the Country thro' which it pass'd. This extraordinary Genius was accompany'd with so true a Judgment in all Parts of fine Learning, that whatever Subject was before Him, He Discours'd as properly of it, as if the peculiar Bent of His Study had been apply'd That way; and He perfected His Judgment by Reading and Digesting the best Authors, tho' He quoted Them very seldom.

Contemnebat potiùs literas, quàm nesciebat:

and rather seem'd to draw His Knowledge from His own Stores, than to owe it to any Foreign Assistance.

The Brightness of His Parts, the Solidity of His Judgment,

xiv

DEDICATION

and the Candor and Generosity of His Temper distinguish'd Him in an Age of great Politeness, and at a Court abounding with Men of the finest Sense and Learning. The most eminent Masters in their several Ways appeal'd to His Determination. WALLER thought it an Honor to consult Him in the Softness and Harmony of his Verse: and Dr. SPRAT, in the Delicacy and Turn of his Prose. DRYDEN determines by Him, under the Character of *Eugenius*; as to the Laws of Dramatick Poetry. BUTLER ow'd it to Him, that the Court tasted his *Hudibras*: WICHERLEY, that the Town liked his *Plain Dealer*: and the late Duke of BUCKINGHAM deferr'd to publish his *Rehearsal*; 'till He was sure (as He expressed it) that my Lord DORSET would not *Rehearse* upon Him again. If We wanted Foreign Testimony; LA FONTAINE and St. EVREMONT have acknowledg'd, that He was a Perfect Master in the Beauty and Fineness of their Language, and of All that They call *les Belles Lettres*. Nor was this Nicety of His Judgement confined only to Books and Literature; but was the Same in Statuary, Painting, and all other Parts of Art. BERNINI would have taken His Opinion upon the Beauty and Attitude of a Figure; and King CHARLES did not agree with LELY, that my Lady CLEVELAND's Picture was Finished, 'till it had the Approbation of my Lord BUCKEHURST.

As the Judgement which He made of Others Writings, could not be refuted; the Manner in which He wrote, will hardly ever be Equalled. Every one of His Pieces is an Ingot of Gold, intrinsically and solidly Valuable; such as, wrought or beaten thinner, would shine thro' a whole Book of any other Author. His Thought was always New; and the Expression of it so particularly Happy, that every body knew immediately, it could only be my Lord DORSET's: and yet it was so Easy too, that Every body was ready to imagine himself capable of writing it. There is a Lustre in His Verses, like That of the Sun in CLAUDE LORAINE's Landskips; it looks Natural, and is Inimitable. His Love-Verses have a Mixture of Delicacy and Strength: they convey the Wit of PETRONIUS in the Softness of TIBULLUS. His Satyr indeed is so severely Pointed, that in it He appears, what His Great Friend the Earl of ROCHESTER (that other Prodigy of the Age) says He was;

The best good Man, with the worst-natur'd Muse.

DEDICATION

Yet even here, That Character may justly be Applied to Him, which PERSIUS gives of the best Writer in this Kind, that ever lived:

Omne vafer vitium ridenti Flaccus *amico*
Tangit, & *admissus circum præcordia ludit.*

And the Gentleman had always so much the better of the Satyrist, that the Persons touched did not know where to fix their Resentments; and were forced to appear rather Ashamed than Angry. Yet so far was this great Author from Valuing himself upon His Works, that He cared not what became of them, though every body else did. There are many Things of His not Extant in Writing, which however are always repeated: like the Verses and Sayings of the Ancient DRUIDS, they retain an Universal Veneration; tho' they are preserved only by Memory.

As it is often seen, that those Men who are least Qualified for Business, love it most; my Lord DORSET's Character was, that He certainly understood it, but did not care for it.

Coming very Young to the Possession of two Plentiful Estates, and in an Age when Pleasure was more in Fashion than Business; He turned his Parts rather to Books and Conversation, than to Politicks, and what more immediately related to the Public. But whenever the Safety of His Countrey demanded His Assistance, He readily entred into the most Active Parts of Life; and underwent the greatest Dangers, with a Constancy of Mind, which shewed, that He had not only read the Rules of Philosophy, but understood the Practice of them.

In the first *Dutch* War He went a Voluntier under the Duke of YORK: His Behavior, during That Campaigne, was such, as distinguish'd the SACKVILLE descended from that HILDEBRAND of the Name, who was one of the greatest Captains that came into ENGLAND with the Conqueror. But His making a Song the Night before the Engagement (and it was one of the prettiest that ever was made) carries with it so sedate a Presence of Mind, and such an unusual Gallantry, that it deserves as much to be Recorded, as ALEXANDER's jesting with his Soldiers, before he passed the GRANICUS: or WILLIAM the First of ORANGE, giving Order over Night for a Battel, and

xvi

DEDICATION

desiring to be called in the Morning, lest He should happen to Sleep too long.

From hence, during the remaining Part of King CHARLES's Reign, He continued to Live in Honorable Leisure. He was of the Bed-chamber to the King; and Possessed not only His Master's Favor, but (in a great Degree) His Familiarity; never leaving the Court, but when He was sent to That of FRANCE, on some short Commissions and Embassies of Compliment: as if the King designed to show the FRENCH, (who would be thought the Politest Nation) that one of the Finest Gentlemen in EUROPE was His Subject; and that We had a Prince who understood His Worth so well, as not to suffer Him to be long out of His Presence.

The succeeding Reign neither relish'd my Lord's Wit, nor approved His Maxims: so He retired altogether from Court. But as the irretrievable Mistakes of That unhappy Government, went on to Threaten the Nation with something more Terrible than a *Dutch* War: He thought it became Him to resume the Courage of His Youth, and once more to Engage Himself in defending the Liberty of His Countrey. He entred into the Prince of ORANGE's Interest; and carried on His Part of That great Enterprise here in LONDON, and under the Eye of the Court; with the same Resolution, as His Friend and Fellow-Patriot the late Duke of DEVONSHIRE did in open Arms at NOTTINGHAM; 'till the Dangers of those Times increased to Extremity; and just Apprehensions arose for the Safety of the Princess, our present Glorious Queen: then the Earl of DORSET was thought the properest Guide of Her necessary Flight, and the Person under whose Courage and Direction the Nation might most safely Trust a Charge so Precious and Important.

After the Establishment of Their late Majesties upon the Throne, there was Room again at Court for Men of my Lord's Character. He had a Part in the Councils of those Princes; a great Share in their Friendship; and all the Marks of Distinction, with which a good Government could reward a Patriot. He was made Chamberlain of their Majesties Houshold; a Place which He so eminently Adorn'd, by the Grace of His Person, the Fineness of His Breeding, and the Knowledge and Practice of what was Decent and Magnificent; that He

DEDICATION

could only be Rivalled in these Qualifications by one great Man, who has since held the same Staff.

The last Honors He received from His Soveraign, (and indeed they were the Greatest which a Subject could receive) were, that He was made Knight of the Garter, and constituted One of the Regents of the Kingdom, during His Majesty's Absence. But his Health, about that time, sensibly Declining; and the Public Affairs not Threatned by any Imminent Danger; He left the Business to Those who delighted more in the State of it; and appeared only sometimes at Council, to show his Respect to the Commission: giving as much Leisure as He could to the Relief of those Pains, with which it pleased God to Afflict Him; and Indulging the Reflexions of a Mind, that had looked thro' the World with too piercing an Eye, and was grown weary of the Prospect. Upon the whole; it may very justly be said of this Great Man, with Regard to the Public, that thro' the Course of his Life, He Acted like an able Pilot in a long Voyage; contented to sit Quiet in the Cabin, when the Winds were allayed, and the Waters smooth; but Vigilant and Ready to resume the Helm, when the Storm arose, and the Sea grew Tumultuous.

I ask Your Pardon, My Lord, if I look yet a little more nearly into the late Lord DORSET's Character: if I examine it not without some Intention of finding Fault; and (which is an odd way of making a Panegyric) set his Blemishes and Imperfections in open View.

The Fire of His Youth carried Him to some Excesses: but they were accompanied with a most lively Invention, and true Humour. The little Violences and easie Mistakes of a Night too gayly spent, (and That too in the Beginning of Life) were always set Right, the next Day, with great Humanity, and ample Retribution. His Faults brought their Excuse with them, and his very Failings had their Beauties. So much Sweetness accompanied what He said, and so great Generosity what He did; that People were always prepossess'd in his Favor: and it was in Fact true, when the late Earl of ROCHESTER said, in Jest, to King CHARLES; That He did not know how it was, but my Lord DORSET might do any thing, yet was never to Blame.

He was naturally very subject to Passion; but the short

xviii

DEDICATION

Gust was soon over, and served only to set off the Charms of his Temper, when more Compos'd. That very Passion broke out with a Force of Wit, which made even Anger agreeable: While it lasted, He said and forgot a thousand Things, which other Men would have been glad to have studied and wrote: but the Impetuosity was Corrected upon a Moment's Reflection; and the Measure altered with such Grace and Delicacy, that You could scarce perceive where the Key was Changed.

He was very Sharp in his Reflections; but never in the wrong Place. His Darts were sure to Wound; but they were sure too to hit None but those whose Follies gave Him very fair Aim. And when He allowed no Quarter; He had certainly been provoked by more than common Error: by Men's tedious and circumstantial Recitals of their Affairs; or by their multiply'd Questions about his own: by extreme Ignorance and Impertinence; or the mixture of these, an ill-judg'd and never-ceasing Civility: or lastly, by the two Things which were his utter Aversion; the Insinuation of a Flatterer, and the Whisper of a Tale-bearer.

If therefore, We set the Piece in it's worst Position; if it's Faults be most exposed, the Shades will still appear very finely join'd with their Lights; and every Imperfection will be diminished by the Lustre of some Neighb'ring Virtue. But if We turn the great Drawings and wonderful Colourings to their true Light; the Whole must appear Beautiful, Noble, Admirable.

He possessed all those Virtues in the highest Degree, upon which the Pleasure of Society, and the Happiness of Life depend: and He exercised them with the greatest Decency, and best Manners. As good Nature is said, by a great *Author, to belong more particularly to the ENGLISH, than any other Nation; it may again be said, that it belonged more particularly to the late Earl of DORSET, than to any other ENGLISH Man.

A kind Husband He was, without Fondness: and an indulgent Father without Partiality. So extraordinary good a Master, that This Quality ought indeed to have been number'd among his Defects: for He was often worse served than became his Station; from his Unwillingness to assume an Authority too Severe. And, during those little Transports of Passion, to

* Sprat, *Hist. of the Royal Society.*

DEDICATION

which I just now said He was subject; I have known his Servants get into his way, that They might make a Merit of it immediately after: for He that had the good Fortune to be Chid, was sure of being Rewarded for it.

His Table was one of the Last, that gave Us an Example of the Old House-keeping of an ENGLISH Nobleman. A Freedom reigned at it, which made every one of his Guests think Himself at Home: and an Abundance, which shewed that the Master's Hospitality extended to many More, than Those who had the Honor to sit at Table with Him.

In his Dealings with Others; his Care and Exactness, that every Man should have his Due, was such, that You would think He had never seen a Court: the Politeness and Civility with which this Justice was administred, would convince You He never had lived out of One.

He was so strict an Observer of his Word, that no Consideration whatever, could make him break it: yet so cautious, lest the Merit of his Act should arise from that Obligation only; that He usually did the greatest Favors, without making any previous Promise. So inviolable was He in his Friendship; and so kind to the Character of Those, whom He had once Honored with a more intimate Acquaintance; that nothing less than a Demonstration of some Essential Fault, could make Him break with Them: and then too, his good Nature did not consent to it, without the greatest Reluctance and Difficulty. Let me give one Instance of this amongst many. When, as Lord Chamberlain, He was obliged to take the King's Pension from Mr. DRYDEN, who had long before put Himself out of a Possibility of Receiving any Favor from the Court: my Lord allowed Him an Equivalent, out of his own Estate. However displeased with the Conduct of his old Acquaintance, He relieved his Necessities; and while He gave Him his Assistance in Private; in Public, He extenuated and pitied his Error.

The Foundation indeed of these Excellent Qualities, and the Perfection of my Lord DORSET's Character, was, That unbounded Charity which ran through the whole Tenor of his Life; and sat as visibly Predominant over the other Faculties of his Soul; as She is said to do in Heaven, above Her Sister Virtues.

Crouds of Poor daily thronged his Gates, expecting thence

DEDICATION

their Bread: and were still lessened by His sending the most proper Objects of his Bounty to Apprenticeships, or Hospitals. The Lazar and the Sick, as He accidentally saw them, were removed from the Street to the Physician: and Many of Them not only restored to Health; but supplied with what might enable Them to resume their former Callings, and make their future Life happy. The Prisoner has often been released, by my Lord's paying the Debt; and the Condemned has been saved by his Intercession with the Sovereign; where He thought the Letter of the Law too rigid. To Those whose Circumstances were such as made Them ashamed of their Poverty; He knew how to bestow his Munificence, without offending their Modesty: and under the Notion of frequent Presents, gave Them what amounted to a Subsistance. Many yet alive know This to be true, though He told it to None, nor ever was more uneasy, than when any one mentioned it to Him.

We may find among the *Greeks* and *Latins*, TIBULLUS, and GALLUS; the Noblemen that writ Poetry: AUGUSTUS and MÆCENAS; the Protectors of Learning: ARISTIDES, the good Citizen; and ATTICUS, the well-bred Friend: and bring Them in, as Examples, of my Lord DORSET's Wit; His Judgment; His Justice; and His Civility. But for His Charity, My Lord, We can scarce find a Parallel in History it self.

TITUS was not more the *Deliciæ Humani generis*, on this Account, than my Lord DORSET was. And, without any Exageration, that Prince did not do more good in Proportion, out of the Revenue of the *Roman* Empire, than Your Father, out of the Income of a private Estate. Let this, my Lord, remain to You and Your Posterity a Possession for ever, to be Imitated, and if possible, to be Excelled.

As to my own Particular, I scarce knew what Life was, sooner than I found my self obliged to His Favor; nor have had Reason to feel any Sorrow, so sensibly as That of His Death.

> *Ille dies—quem semper acerbum*
> *Semper honoratum (sic Dî voluistis) habebo.*

ÆNEAS could not reflect upon the Loss of His own Father with greater Piety, my Lord, than I must recall the Memory of Your's: and when I think whose Son I am writing to, the

DEDICATION

least I promise my self from Your Goodness is an uninterrupted
Continuance of Favor, and a Friendship for Life. To which
that I may with some Justice Intitle my self, I send Your Lord-
ship a Dedication, not filled with a long Detail of Your Praises,
but with my sincerest Wishes, that You may Deserve them;
That You may Imploy those extraordinary Parts and Abilities,
with which Heaven has blessed You, to the Honor of Your
Family, the Benefit of Your Friends, and the Good of Your
Country; That all Your Actions may be Great, Open, and
Noble, such as may tell the World, whose Son, and whose
Successor You are.

What I now offer to Your Lordship is a Collection of
Poetry, a kind of Garland of Good Will. If any Verses of My
Writing should appear in Print, under another Name and
Patronage, than That of an Earl of DORSET; People might
suspect them not to be Genuine. I have attained my present
End, if these Poems prove the Diversion of some of Your
Youthful Hours, as they have been occasionally the Amusement
of some of Mine; and I humbly hope, that as I may hereafter
bind up my fuller Sheaf, and lay some Pieces of a very different
Nature (the Product of my severer Studies) at Your Lordship's
Feet, I shall engage Your more serious Reflection: Happy, if
in all my Endeavors I may contribute to Your Delight, or to
Your Instruction. I am, with all Duty and Respect,

MY LORD,

Your Lordship's

most Obedient, and

most Humble Servant,

MAT. PRIOR.

PREFACE.

THE Greatest Part of what I have Written having already been Published, either singly or in some of the Miscellanies; it would be too late for Me to make any Excuse for appearing in Print: But a Collection of Poems has lately appeared under my Name, tho' without my Knowledge, in which the Publisher has given Me the Honor of some Things that did not belong to Me; and has Transcribed others so imperfectly, that I hardly knew them to be Mine. This has obliged Me, in my own Defence, to look back upon some of those lighter Studies, which I ought long since to have quitted, and to Publish an indifferent Collection of Poems, for fear of being thought the Author of a worse.

Thus I beg Pardon of the Public for Reprinting some Pieces, which, as they came singly from their first Impression, have (I fancy) lain long and quietly in Mr. TONSON's Shop; and adding others to them, which were never before Printed, and might have lain as quietly, and perhaps more safely, in a Corner of my own Study.

The Reader will, I hope, make Allowance for their having been written at very distant Times, and on very different Occasions; and take them as they happen to come, Public Panegyrics, Amorous Odes, Serious Reflections, or Idle Tales, the Product of his leisure Hours, who had Business enough upon his Hands, and was only a Poet by Accident.

I take this Occasion to thank my good Friend and School-fellow Mr. DIBBEN, for his excellent Version of the Carmen Seculare; though my Gratitude may justly carry a little Envy with it: for I believe the most accurate Judges will find the Translation exceed the Original.

I must likewise own my self obliged to Mrs. SINGER, who has given Me Leave to Print a Pastoral of Her Writing; That Poem having produced the Verses immediately following it. I wish She might be prevailed with to publish some other Pieces of that Kind, in which the Softness of Her Sex, and the Fineness of Her Genius, conspire to give Her a very distinguishing Character.

POSTSCRIPT.

I Must help my Preface by a Postscript, to tell the Reader, that there is Ten Years Distance between my writing the One and the Other; and that (whatever I thought then, and have somewhere said, that I would publish no more Poetry) He will find several Copies of Verses scattered through this Edition, which were not printed in the First. Those relating to the Publick stand in the Order They did before, and according to the several Years, in which They were written; however the Disposition of our National Affairs, the Actions, or the Fortunes of some Men, and the Opinions of others may have changed. Prose, and other Human Things may take what Turn they can; but Poetry, which pretends to have something of Divinity in it, is to be more permanent. Odes once printed cannot well be altered, when the Author has already said, that He expects His Work should Live for Ever. And it had been very foolish in my Friend HORACE, if some Years after His Exegi Monumentum, He should have desired to see his Building taken down again.

The Dedication likewise is Reprinted to the Earl of DORSET, in the foregoing Leaves, without any Alteration; though I had the fairest Opportunity, and the strongest Inclination to have added a great deal to it. The blooming Hopes, which I said the World expected from my then very Young Patron, have been confirmed by most Noble and distinguished First-Fruits; and His Life is going on towards a plentiful Harvest of all accumulated Virtues. He has in Fact exceeded whatever the Fondness of my Wishes could invent in His Favor: His equally Good and Beautiful Lady enjoys in Him an Indulgent, and Obliging Husband; His Children, a Kind, and Careful Father; and His Acquaintance, a Faithful, Generous, and Polite Friend. His Fellow-Peers have attended to the Perswasion of His Eloquence; and have been convinced by the Solidity of His Reasoning. He has long since deserved and attained

POSTSCRIPT

the Honor of the Garter. He has managed some of the greatest Charges of the Kingdom with known Ability; and laid them down with entire Disinteressment. And as He continues the Exercises of these eminent Virtues (which that He may do to a very old Age, shall be my perpetual Wish) He may be One of the Greatest Men that our Age, or possibly our Nation has bred; and leave Materials for a Panegyric, not unworthy the Pen of some future PLINY.

From so Noble a Subject as the Earl of DORSET, to so mean a one as my self, is (I confess) a very Pindaric Transition. I shall only say one Word, and trouble t[h]e Reader no further. I published my Poems formerly, as Monsieur JOURDAIN sold his Silk: He would not be thought a Tradesman; but ordered some Pieces to be measured out to his particular Friends. Now I give up my Shop, and dispose of all my Poetical Goods at once: I must therefore desire, that the Public would please to take them in the Gross; and that every Body would turn over what He does not like.

POEMS

ON

SEVERAL OCCASIONS.

On *Exodus* iii. 14. *I am that I am.*

An ODE.

Written in 1688, *as an Exercise at* St. JOHN's *College,*
CAMBRIDGE.

I.

MAN! Foolish Man!
   Scarce know'st Thou how thy self began:
Scarce hast Thou Thought enough to prove Thou art:
Yet steel'd with study'd Boldness, Thou dar'st try
To send thy doubting Reason's dazled Eye
Through the mysterious Gulph of vast Immensity.
Much Thou canst there discern, much thence impart.
  Vain Wretch! suppress thy knowing Pride:
    Mortifie thy learned Lust:
Vain are thy Thoughts; while Thou thy self are Dust.

II.

Let Wit her Sails, her Oars let Wisdom lend:
The Helm let Politick Experience guide:
Yet cease to hope thy short-liv'd Bark shall ride
Down spreading Fate's unnavigable Tide.
  What, tho' still it farther tend?
    Still 'tis farther from it's End;
And, in the Bosom of that boundless Sea,
Still finds it's Error lengthen with it's Way.

III.

With daring Pride and insolent Delight
Your Doubts resolv'd you boast, your Labours crown'd ;
And, ΕΥΡΗΚΑ ! your GOD, forsooth, is found
Incomprehensible and Infinite.
But is He therefore found ? Vain Searcher ! no :
Let your imperfect Definition show,
That nothing You, the weak Definer, know.

IV.

Say, why should the collected Main
It self within it self contain ?
Why to its Caverns should it sometimes creep,
And with delighted Silence sleep
On the lov'd Bosom of it's Parent Deep ?
Why shou'd it's num'rous Waters stay
In comely Discipline, and fair Array,
'Till Winds and Tides exert their high Command[s] ?
Then prompt and ready to obey,
Why do the rising Surges spread
Their op'ning Ranks o'er Earth's submissive Head,
Marching thro' different Paths to different Lands ?

V.

Why does the constant Sun
With measur'd Steps his radiant Journeys run ?
Why does He order the Diurnal Hours
To leave Earth's other Part, and rise in Our's ?
Why does He wake the correspondent Moon,
And fill her willing Lamp with liquid Light,
Commanding Her with delegated Pow'rs
To beautifie the World, and bless the Night ?
Why does each animated Star
Love the just Limits of it's proper Sphere ?
Why does each consenting Sign
With prudent Harmony combine
In Turns to move, and subsequent appear
To gird the Globe, and regulate the Year ?

VI.

Man does with dangerous Curiosity
  These unfathom'd Wonders try :
With fancy'd Rules and arbitrary Laws
Matter and Motion He restrains ;
And study'd Lines, and fictious Circles draws :
  Then with imagin'd Soveraignty
  Lord of his new *Hypothesis* He reigns.
He reigns ? How long ? 'till some Usurper rise :
And He too, mighty thoughtful, mighty wise,
Studies new Lines, and other Circles feigns.
  From this last Toil again what Knowledge flows ?
    Just as much, perhaps, as shows,
    That all his Predecessor's Rules
  Were empty *Cant*, all *Jargon* of the Schools ;
  That he on t'other's Ruin rears his Throne ;
And shows his Friend's Mistake, and thence confirms his own.

VII.

  On Earth, in Air, amidst the Seas and Skies,
    Mountainous Heaps of Wonders rise ;
    Whose tow'ring Strength will ne'er submit
To Reason's Batt'ries, or the Mines of Wit :
Yet still enquiring, still mistaking Man,
Each Hour repuls'd, each Hour dare onward press ;
And levelling at GOD his wand'ring Guess
(That feeble Engine of his reasoning War,
Which guides his Doubts, and combats his Despair)
Laws to his Maker the learn'd Wretch can give ;
Can bound that Nature, and prescribe that Will,
  Whose pregnant Word did either Ocean fill ;
Can tell us whence all BEINGS are, and how they move and
    live.
    Thro' either Ocean (foolish Man !)
    That pregnant Word sent forth again,
  Might to a World extend each ATOM there ;
For every Drop call forth a Sea, a Heav'n for every Star.

MATTHEW PRIOR

VIII.

Let cunning Earth her fruitful Wonders hide;
And only lift thy stagg'ring Reason up
To trembling CALVARY's astonish'd Top:
Then mock thy Knowledge, and confound thy Pride,
Explaining how Perfection suffer'd Pain;
Almighty languish'd; and Eternal dy'd:
How by her Patient Victor Death was slain;
And Earth prophan'd, yet bless'd with Deicide.
Then down with all thy boasted Volumes, down:
  Only reserve the Sacred One:
    Low, reverently low,
  Make thy stubborn Knowledge bow;
Weep out thy Reason's, and thy Body's Eyes;
    Deject thy self, that Thou may'st rise;
To look to Heav'n, be blind to all below.

IX.

Then Faith, for Reason's glimmering Light, shall give
  Her Immortal Perspective;
And Grace's Presence Nature's Loss retrieve:
Then thy enliven'd Soul shall see,
That all the Volumes of Philosophy,
With all their Comments, never cou'd invent
  So politick an Instrument,
To reach the Heav'n of Heav'ns, the high Abode,
Where MOSES places his Mysterious GOD,
As was that Ladder which old JACOB rear'd,
When Light Divine had human Darkness clear'd;
And his enlarg'd Ideas found the Road,
Which Faith had dictated, and Angels trod.

TO THE

COUNTESS of EXETER,

Playing on the LUTE.

WHAT Charms You have, from what high Race You
sprung,
Have been the pleasing Subjects of my Song:
Unskill'd and young, yet something still I writ,
Of CA'NDISH Beauty join'd to CECIL's Wit.
But when You please to show the lab'ring MUSE,
What greater Theme Your Musick can produce;
My babling Praises I repeat no more;
But hear, rejoice, stand silent, and adore.

The PERSIANS thus, first gazing on the Sun,
Admir'd, how high 'twas plac'd, how bright it shone:
But, as his Pow'r was known, their Thoughts were rais'd;
And soon They worship'd, what at first They prais'd.

ELIZA's Glory lives in SPENCER's Song;
And COWLEY's Verse keeps Fair ORINDA young.
That as in Birth, in Beauty You excell,
The MUSE might dictate, and the Poet tell:
Your Art no other Art can speak; and You,
To show how well You play, must play anew:
Your Musick's Pow'r Your Musick must disclose;
For what Light is, 'tis only Light that shows.

5

MATTHEW PRIOR

Strange Force of Harmony, that thus controuls
Our Thoughts, and turns and sanctifies our Souls:
While with it's utmost Art Your Sex could move
Our Wonder only, or at best our Love:
You far above Both these Your GOD did place;
That Your high Pow'r might worldly Thoughts destroy;
That with Your Numbers You our Zeal might raise,
And, like Himself, communicate Your Joy.

When to Your Native Heav'n You shall repair,
And with Your Presence crown the Blessings there;
Your Lute may wind it's Strings but little higher,
To tune their Notes to that immortal Quire.
Your Art is perfect here: Your Numbers do,
More than our Books, make the rude Atheist know,
That there's a Heav'n, by what He hears below.

As in some Piece, while LUKE his Skill exprest,
A cunning Angel came, and drew the rest:
So, when You play, some Godhead does impart
Harmonious Aid; Divinity helps Art:
Some Cherub finishes what You begun,
And to a Miracle improves a Tune.

To burning ROME when frantick NERO play'd,
Viewing that Face, no more He had survey'd
The raging Flames; but struck with strange Surprize,
Confest them less than Those of ANNA's Eyes:
But had He heard Thy Lute, He soon had found
His Rage eluded, and his Crime atton'd:
Thine, like AMPHION's Hand, had wak'd the Stone,
And from Destruction call'd the rising Town:
Malice to Musick had been forc'd to yield;
Nor could He Burn so fast, as Thou could'st Build.

Picture *of* Seneca *dying in a Bath.*

By Jordain.

At the Right Honorable the Earl *of* Exeter's *at* Burleigh-House.

WHILE cruel Nero only drains
    The moral Spaniard's ebbing Veins,
By Study worn, and slack with Age;
How dull, how thoughtless is his Rage!
Heighten'd Revenge He should have took:
He should have burnt his Tutor's Book;
And long have reign'd supream in Vice.
One nobler Wretch can only rise:
'Tis He whose Fury shall deface
The Stoick's Image in this Piece:
For while unhurt, divine Jordain,
Thy Work and Seneca's remain:
He still has Body, still has Soul,
And lives and speaks, restor'd and whole.

MATTHEW PRIOR

An ODE.

I.

WHILE blooming Youth, and gay Delight
    Sit on thy rosey Cheeks confest ;
Thou hast, my Dear, undoubted Right
    To triumph o'er this destin'd Breast.
My Reason bends to what thy Eyes ordain ;
For I was born to Love, and Thou to Reign.

II.

    But would You meanly thus rely
        On Power, You know I must Obey ?
    Exert a Legal Tyranny,
        And do an Ill ; because You may ?
Still must I Thee, as Atheists Heav'n adore ;
Not see thy Mercy, and yet dread thy Power ?

III.

    Take Heed, my Dear : Youth flies apace :
        As well as CUPID, TIME is blind :
    Soon must those Glories of thy Face
        The Fate of vulgar Beauty find :
The Thousand LOVES, that arm thy potent Eye,
Must drop their Quivers, flag their Wings, and die.

IV.

    Then wilt Thou sigh ; when in each Frown
        A hateful Wrinkle more appears ;
    And putting peevish Humours on,
        Seems but the sad Effect of Years :
Kindness it self too weak a Charm will prove,
To raise the feeble Fires of aged Love.

V.

Forc'd Compliments, and formal Bows
 Will show Thee just above Neglect:
The Heat, with which thy Lover glows,
 Will settle into cold Respect:
A talking dull *Platonic* I shall turn;
Learn to be civil, when I cease to burn.

VI.

Then shun the Ill, and know, my Dear,
 Kindness and Constancy will prove
The only Pillars fit to bear
 So vast a Weight as that of Love.
If Thou can'st wish to make My Flames endure;
Thine must be very fierce, and very pure.

VII.

Haste, CELIA, haste, while Youth invites;
 Obey kind CUPID's present Voice;
Fill ev'ry Sense with soft Delights,
 And give thy Soul a Loose to Joys:
Let Millions of repeated Blisses prove,
That Thou all Kindness art, and I all Love.

VIII.

Be Mine, and only Mine: take care
 Thy Looks, thy Thoughts, thy Dreams to guide
To Me alone; nor come so far,
 As liking any Youth beside:
What Men e'er court Thee, fly 'em, and believe,
They're Serpents all, and Thou the tempted EVE.

IX.

So shall I court thy dearest Truth;
 When Beauty ceases to engage:
So thinking on thy charming Youth,
 I'll love it o'er again in Age:
So TIME it self our Raptures shall improve;
While still We wake to Joy, and live to Love.

MATTHEW PRIOR

AN

EPISTLE

TO

FLEETWOOD SHEPHARD, Esq;

Burleigh, May 14, 1689.

SIR,

AS once a Twelvemonth to the Priest,
    Holy at ROME, here Antichrist,
The SPANISH King presents a Jennet,
To show his Love :——That's all that's in it :
For if his Holiness would thump
His reverend Bum 'gainst Horse's Rump ;
He might b' equipt from his own Stable
With one more White, and eke more Able.

Or as with *Gondola's* and Men, His
Good Excellence the Duke of VENICE
(I wish, for Rhime, 't had been the King)
Sails out, and gives the Gulph a Ring ;
Which Trick of State, He wisely maintains,
Keeps Kindness up 'twixt old Acquaintance :
For else, in honest Truth, the Sea
Has much less need of Gold than He.

Or, not to rove, and pump one's Fancy
For Popish Similies beyond Sea ;
As Folks from Mud-wall'd Tenement
Bring Landlords Pepper-corn for Rent ;

Present a Turkey, or a Hen
To Those might better spare Them Ten:
Ev'n so with all Submission, I
(For first Men instance, then apply)
Send You each Year a homely Letter,
Who may return Me much a better.

Then take it, Sir, as it was writ,
To pay Respect, and not show Wit:
Nor look askew at what it saith:
There's no Petition in it——'Faith.

Here some would scratch their Heads, and try
What They should write, and How, and Why:
But I conceive, such Folks are quite in
Mistakes, in Theory of Writing.
If once for Principle 'tis laid,
That Thought is Trouble to the Head;
I argue thus: The World agrees,
That He writes well, who writes with Ease:
Then He, by Sequel Logical,
Writes best, who never thinks at all.

Verse comes from Heav'n, like inward Light;
Meer human Pains can ne'er come by't:
The God, not We, the Poem makes:
We only tell Folks what He speaks.
Hence, when Anatomists discourse,
How like Brutes Organs are to Our's;
They grant, if higher Powers think fit,
A Bear might soon be made a Wit;
And that, for any thing in Nature,
Pigs might squeak Love-Odes, Dogs bark Satyr.

MEMNON, tho' Stone, was counted vocal;
But 'twas the God, mean while, that spoke all.
ROME oft has heard a Cross haranguing,
With prompting Priest behind the Hanging:
The Wooden Head resolv'd the Question;
While You and PETTIS help'd the Jest on.

MATTHEW PRIOR

Your crabbed Rogues, that read LUCRETIUS,
Are against Gods, You know; and teach us,
The God makes not the Poet; but
The Thesis, *vice-versâ* put,
Should *Hebrew-wise* be understood;
And means, The Poet makes the God.

ÆGYPTIAN Gard'ners thus are said to
Have set the Leeks they after pray'd to;
And ROMISH Bakers praise the Deity
They chipp'd, while yet in it's *Paniety.*

That when You Poets swear and cry,
The God inspires! I rave! I die!
If inward Wind does truly swell Ye,
'T must be the Cholick in your Belly:
That Writing is but just like Dice;
And lucky Mains make People Wise:
That jumbled Words, if Fortune throw 'em,
Shall, well as DRYDEN, form a Poem;
Or make a Speech, correct and witty,
As You know who——at the Committee.

So Atoms dancing round the Center,
They urge, made all Things at a Venture.

But granting Matters should be spoke
By Method, rather than by Luck;
This may confine their younger Styles,
Whom DRYDEN pedagogues at WILL'S:
But never could be meant to tye
Authentic Wits, like You and I:
For as young Children, who are try'd in
Go-Carts, to keep their Steps from sliding;
When Members knit, and Legs grow stronger,
Make use of such Machine no longer;
But leap *pro Libitu,* and scout
On Horse call'd Hobby, or without:
So when at School we first declaim,
Old BUSBEY walks us in a Theme,
Whose Props support our Infant Vein,
And help the Rickets in the Brain:

But when our Souls their Force dilate,
And Thoughts grow up to Wit's Estate;
In Verse or Prose, We write or chat,
Not Six-Pence Matter upon what.

'Tis not how well an Author says;
But 'tis how much, that gathers Praise.
TONSON, who is himself a Wit,
Counts Writers Merits by the Sheet.
Thus each should down with all he thinks,
As Boys eat Bread, to fill up Chinks.

Kind Sir, I should be glad to see You;
I hope Y' are well; so God be wi' You;
Was all I thought at first to write:
But Things, since then, are alter'd quite;
Fancies flow in, and Muse flies high:
So God knows when my Clack will lye:
I must, Sir, prattle on, as afore,
And beg your Pardon yet this half Hour.

So at pure Barn of loud NON-CON,
Where with my *Granam* I have gone,
When LOBB had sifted all his Text,
And I well hop'd the Pudding next;
Now to apply, has plagu'd me more,
Than all his Villain *Cant* before.

For your Religion, first, of Her
Your Friends do sav'ry Things aver:
They say, She's honest, as your Claret,
Not sowr'd with *Cant*, nor stum'd with Merit:
Your Chamber is the sole Retreat
Of Chaplains ev'ry SUNDAY Night:
Of Grace, no doubt, a certain Sign,
When Lay-Man herds with Man Divine:
For if their Fame be justly great,
Who would no Popish *Nuncio* treat;
That His is greater, We must·grant,
Who will treat *Nuncio's* Protestant.
One single *Positive* weighs more,
You know, than *Negatives* a Score.

MATTHEW PRIOR

In Politicks, I hear, You're stanch,
Directly bent against the FRENCH;
Deny to have your free-born Toe
Dragoon'd into a Wooden Shoe:
Are in no Plots; but fairly drive at
The Publick Welfare in your Private:
And will, for ENGLAND's Glory, try
Turks, Jews, and Jesuits to defy,
And keep your Places 'till You die.

For me, whom wand'ring Fortune threw
From what I lov'd, the Town and You;
Let me just tell You how my Time is
Past in a Country-Life.——*Imprimis*,
As soon as PHOEBUS' Rays inspect us,
First, Sir, I read; and then I Breakfast;
So on, 'till foresaid God does set,
I sometimes Study, sometimes Eat.
Thus, of your Heroes and brave Boys,
With whom old HOMER makes such Noise,
The greatest Actions I can find,
Are, that They did their Work, and din'd.

The Books of which I'm chiefly fond,
Are such, as You have whilom con'd;
That treat of CHINA's Civil Law,
And Subjects Rights in GOLCONDA;
Of Highway-Elephants at CEYLAN,
That rob in Clans, like Men o' th' HIGHLAND;
Of Apes that storm, or keep a Town,
As well almost, as Count LAUZUN;
Of Unicorns and Alligators,
Elks, Mermaids, Mummies, Witches, Satyrs,
And twenty other stranger Matters;
Which, tho' they're Things I've no Concern in,
Make all our Grooms admire my Learning.

Criticks I read on other Men,
And *Hypers* upon Them again;
From whose Remarks I give Opinion
On twenty Books, yet ne'er look in One.

Then all your Wits, that flear and sham,
Down from DON QUIXOTE to TOM TRAM;
From whom I Jests and Punns purloin,
And slily put 'em off for Mine:
Fond to be thought a Country Wit:
The rest,——when Fate and You think fit.

Sometimes I climb my Mare, and kick her
To bottl'd Ale, and neighb'ring Vicar;
Sometimes at STAMFORD take a Quart,
'Squire SHEPHARD's Health——With all my Heart.

Thus, without much Delight, or Grief,
I fool away an idle Life;
'Till SHADWELL from the Town retires
(Choak'd up with Fame and Sea-coal Fires)
To bless the Wood with peaceful *Lyric*;
Then hey for Praise and Panegyric,
Justice restor'd, and Nations freed,
And Wreaths round WILLIAM's glorious Head.

TO THE

COUNTESS of DORSET.

Written in her MILTON.

By Mr. *BRADBURY.*

SEE here, how bright the first-born Virgin shone;
And how the first fond Lover was undone.
Such charming Words our beauteous Mother spoke,
As MILTON wrote; and such as Your's Her Look.
Your's the best Copy of th' Original Face,
Whose Beauty was to furnish all the Race:
Such Chains no Author could escape but He:
There's no Way to be safe, but not to See.

15

TO THE

LADY *DURSLEY*

On the same Subject.

HERE reading how fond ADAM was betray'd ;
    And how by Sin EVE's blasted Charms decay'd ;
Our common Loss unjustly You complain ;
So small that Part of it, which You sustain.

You still, fair Mother, in your Offspring trace
The Stock of Beauty destin'd for the Race :
Kind Nature, forming Them, the Pattern took
From Heav'n's first Work, and EVE's Original Look.

You, happy Saint, the Serpent's Pow'r controul :
Scarce any actual Guilt defiles your Soul :
And Hell does o'er that Mind vain Triumph boast,
Which gains a Heav'n, for Earthly EDEN lost.

With Virtue strong as Your's had EVE been arm'd,
In vain the Fruit had blush'd, or Serpent charm'd :
Nor had our Bliss by Penitence been bought :
Nor had frail ADAM fall'n, nor MILTON wrote.

TO

My LORD *BUCKHURST*,

Very Young,

Playing with a CAT.

THE am'rous Youth, whose tender Breast
Was by his darling Cat possest,
Obtain'd of VENUS his Desire,
Howe'er irregular his Fire :
Nature the Pow'r of Love obey'd :
The Cat became a blushing Maid ;
And, on the happy Change, the Boy
Imploy'd his Wonder and his Joy.

Take care, O beauteous Child, take care,
Lest Thou prefer so rash a Pray'r :
Nor vainly hope, the Queen of Love
Will e'er thy Fav'rite's Charms improve.
O ! quickly from her Shrine retreat ;
Or tremble for thy Darling's Fate.

The Queen of Love, who soon will see
Her own ADONIS live in Thee,
Will lightly her first Loss deplore ;
Will easily forgive the Boar :
Her Eyes with Tears no more will flow:
With jealous Rage her Breast will glow :
And on her tabby Rival's Face
She deep will mark her new Disgrace.

An ODE.

I.

WHILE from our Looks, fair Nymph, You guess
The secret Passions of our Mind;
My heavy Eyes, You say, confess
A Heart to Love and Grief inclin'd.

II.

There needs, alas! but little Art,
To have this fatal Secret found:
With the same Ease You threw the Dart,
'Tis certain, You may show the Wound.

III.

How can I see You, and not love;
While You as op'ning East are fair?
While cold as Northern Blasts You prove;
How can I love, and not despair?

IV.

The Wretch in double Fetters bound
Your Potent Mercy may release:
Soon, if my Love but once were crown'd,
Fair Prophetess, my Grief would cease.

A SONG.

IN vain You tell your parting Lover,
   You wish fair Winds may waft Him over.
Alas! what Winds can happy prove,
That bear Me far from what I love?
Alas! what Dangers on the Main
Can equal Those that I sustain,
From slighted Vows, and cold Disdain?

  Be gentle, and in Pity choose
To wish the wildest Tempests loose:
That thrown again upon the Coast,
Where first my Shipwrackt Heart was lost,
I may once more repeat my Pain;
Once more in dying Notes complain
Of slighted Vows, and cold Disdain.

THE

DESPAIRING SHEPHERD.

ALEXIS shun'd his Fellow Swains,
   Their rural Sports, and jocund Strains:
  (Heav'n guard us all from CUPID's Bow!)
He lost his Crook, He left his Flocks;
And wand'ring thro' the lonely Rocks,
  He nourish'd endless Woe.

The Nymphs and Shepherds round Him came:
His Grief Some pity, Others blame:
  The fatal Cause All kindly seek.
He mingled his Concern with Their's:
He gave 'em back their friendly Tears:
  He sigh'd, but would not speak.

CLORINDA came among the rest:
And She too kind Concern exprest,
  And ask'd the Reason of his Woe:
She ask'd, but with an Air and Mein,
That made it easily foreseen,
  She fear'd too much to know.

The Shepherd rais'd his mournful Head:
And will You pardon Me, He said,
  While I the cruel Truth reveal?
Which nothing from my Breast should tear;
Which never should offend .Your Ear;
  But that You bid Me tell.

'Tis thus I rove, 'tis thus complain;
Since You appear'd upon the Plain:
  You are the Cause of all my Care:
Your Eyes ten thousand Dangers dart:
Ten thousand Torments vex My Heart:
  I love, and I despair.

Too much, ALEXIS, I have heard:
'Tis what I thought; 'tis what I fear'd:
  And yet I pardon You, She cry'd:
But You shall promise ne'er again
To breath your Vows, or speak your Pain:
  He bow'd, obey'd, and dy'd.

To the Honorable

CHARLES MONTAGUE, Esq;

I.

HOWE'ER 'tis well, that while Mankind
  Thro' Fate's perverse *Mæander* errs,
He can imagin'd Pleasures find,
  To combat against real Cares.

II.

Fancies and Notions He pursues,
 Which ne'er had Being but in Thought:
Each, like the GRÆCIAN Artist, woo's
 The Image He himself has wrought.

III.

Against Experience He believes:
 He argues against Demonstration,
Pleas'd, when his Reason He deceives;
 And sets his Judgment by his Passion.

IV.

The hoary Fool, who many Days
 Has struggl'd with continu'd Sorrow,
Renews his Hope, and blindly lays
 The desp'rate Bett upon To-morrow.

V.

To-morrow comes: 'tis Noon: 'tis Night:
 This Day like all the former flies:
Yet on He runs to seek Delight
 To-morrow, 'till To-night He dies.

VI.

Our Hopes, like tow'ring Falcons, aim
 At Objects in an airy height:
The little Pleasure of the Game
 Is from afar to view the Flight.

VII.

Our anxious Pains We, all the Day,
 In search of what We like, employ:
Scorning at Night the worthless Prey,
 We find the Labour gave the Joy.

VIII.

At Distance thro' an artful Glass
 To the Mind's Eye Things well appear:
They lose their Forms, and make a Mass
 Confus'd and black, if brought too near.

21

IX.

If We see right, We see our Woes:
    Then what avails it to have Eyes?
From Ignorance our Comfort flows:
    The only Wretched are the Wise.

X.

We wearied should lie down in Death:
    This Cheat of Life would take no more;
If You thought Fame but empty Breath;
    I, PHYLLIS but a perjur'd Whore.

HYMN to the SUN.

Set by Dr. *PURCEL*,

And Sung before their MAJESTIES

On New-Years-Day, 1694.

I.

LIGHT of the World, and Ruler of the Year,
    With happy Speed begin Thy great Career;
And, as Thou dost thy radiant Journeys run,
    Through every distant Climate own,
        That in fair ALBION Thou hast seen
        The greatest Prince, the brightest Queen,
    That ever sav'd a Land, or blest a Throne,
Since first Thy Beams were spread, or Genial Power was
        known.

II.

So may Thy Godhead be confest;
So the returning Year be blest;
As His Infant Months bestow
Springing Wreaths for WILLIAM's Brow;

As His Summer's Youth shall shed
Eternal Sweets around MARIA's Head.
From the Blessings They bestow,
Our Times are dated, and our *Æra's* move:
They govern, and enlighten all Below,
As Thou dost all Above.

III.

Let our Hero in the War
Active and fierce, like Thee, appear:
Like Thee, great Son of JOVE, like Thee,
When clad in rising Majesty,
Thou marchest down o'er DELOS' Hills confest,
With all Thy Arrows arm'd, in all Thy Glory drest.
Like Thee, the Hero does his Arms imploy,
The raging PYTHON to destroy,
And give the injur'd Nations Peace and Joy.

IV.

From fairest Years, and Time's more happy Stores,
Gather all the smiling Hours;
Such as with friendly Care have guarded
Patriots and Kings in rightful Wars;
Such as with Conquest have rewarded
Triumphant Victors happy Cares;
Such as Story has recorded
Sacred to NASSAU's long Renown,
For Countries sav'd, and Battels won.

V.

March Them again in fair Array,
And bid Them form the happy Day,
The happy Day design'd to wait
On WILLIAM's Fame, and EUROPE's Fate.
Let the happy Day be crown'd
With great Event, and fair Success;
No brighter in the Year be found,
But That which brings the Victor home in Peace.

23

MATTHEW PRIOR

VI.

Again Thy Godhead We implore,
    Great in Wisdom as in Power;
Again, for good MARIA's Sake, and Our's,
    Chuse out other smiling Hours,
Such as with Joyous Wings have fled,
    When happy Counsels were advising;
Such as have lucky Omens shed
    O'er forming Laws, and Empires rising;
Such as many Courses ran,
Hand in Hand, a goodly Train,
To bless the great ELIZA's Reign;
And in the *Typic* Glory show,
What fuller Bliss MARIA shall bestow.

VII.

    As the solemn Hours advance,
    Mingled send into the Dance
Many fraught with all the Treasures,
    Which Thy Eastern Travels views;
Many wing'd with all the Pleasures,
    Man can ask, or Heav'n diffuse:
That great MARIA all those Joys may know,
Which, from Her Cares, upon Her Subjects flow.

VIII.

For Thy own Glory sing our Soveraign's Praise,
    God of Verses and of Days:
Let all Thy tuneful Sons adorn
    Their lasting Work with WILLIAM's Name:
Let chosen Muses yet unborn
Take great MARIA for their future Theme:
Eternal Structures let Them raise,
On WILLIAM's and MARIA's Praise:
Nor want new Subject for the Song;
    Nor fear they can exhaust the Store;
'Till Nature's Musick lyes unstrung;
'Till Thou, great God, shalt lose Thy double Pow'r;
And touch Thy Lyre, and shoot Thy Beams no more.

THE

LADY's LOOKING-GLASS.

CELIA and I the other Day
  Walk'd o'er the Sand-Hills to the Sea:
The setting Sun adorn'd the Coast,
His Beams entire, his Fierceness lost:
And, on the Surface of the Deep,
The Winds lay only not asleep:
The Nymph did like the Scene appear,
Serenely pleasant, calmly fair:
Soft fell her words, as flew the Air.
With secret Joy I heard Her say,
That She would never miss one Day
A Walk so fine, a Sight so gay.

But, oh the Change! the Winds grow high:
Impending Tempests charge the Sky:
The Lightning flies: the Thunder roars:
And big Waves lash the frighten'd Shoars.
Struck with the Horror of the Sight,
She turns her Head, and wings her Flight;
And trembling vows, She'll ne'er again
Approach the Shoar, or view the Main.

Once more at least look back, said I;
Thy self in That large Glass descry:
When Thou art in good Humour drest;
When gentle Reason rules thy Breast;
The Sun upon the calmest Sea
Appears not half so bright as Thee:
'Tis then, that with Delight I rove
Upon the boundless Depth of Love:
I bless my Chain: I hand my Oar;
Nor think on all I left on Shoar.

MATTHEW PRIOR

But when vain Doubt, and groundless Fear
Do That Dear Foolish Bosom tear;
When the big Lip, and wat'ry Eye
Tell Me, the rising Storm is nigh:
'Tis then, Thou art yon' angry Main,
Deform'd by Winds, and dash'd by Rain;
And the poor Sailor that must try
Its Fury, labours less than I.

Shipwreck'd, in vain to Land I make;
While Love and Fate still drive Me back:
Forc'd to doat on Thee thy own Way,
I chide Thee first, and then obey:
Wretched when from Thee, vex'd when nigh,
I with Thee, or without Thee, die.

LOVE and *FRIENDSHIP:*

A

PASTORAL.

By Mrs. Elizabeth Singer.

AMARYLLIS.

WHILE from the Skies the ruddy Sun descends;
And rising Night the Ev'ning Shade extends:
While pearly Dews o'erspread the fruitful Field;
And closing Flowers reviving Odors yield:
Let Us, beneath these spreading Trees, recite
What from our Hearts our Muses may indite.
Nor need We, in this close Retirement, fear,
Lest any Swain our am'rous Secrets hear.

SILVIA.

To ev'ry Shepherd I would Mine proclaim;
Since fair Aminta is my softest Theme:
A Stranger to the loose Delights of Love,
My Thoughts the nobler Warmth of Friendship prove:
And while it's pure and sacred Fire I sing;
Chast Goddess of the Groves, Thy Succour bring.

26

POEMS ON SEVERAL OCCASIONS

AMARYLLIS.

Propitious God of Love, my Breast inspire
With all Thy Charms, with all Thy pleasing Fire:
Propitious God of Love, Thy Succour bring;
Whilst I Thy Darling, Thy ALEXIS sing;
ALEXIS, as the ope'ning Blossoms fair,
Lovely as Light, and soft as yielding Air.
For Him each Virgin sighs; and on the Plains
The happy Youth above each Rival reigns.
Nor to the Ecchoing Groves, and whisp'ring Spring,
In sweeter Strains does artful CONON sing;
When loud Applauses fill the crowded Groves;
And PHOEBUS the superior Song approves.

SILVIA.

Beauteous AMINTA is as early Light,
Breaking the melancholy Shades of Night.
When She is near, all anxious Trouble flies;
And our reviving Hearts confess her Eyes.
Young Love, and blooming Joy, and gay Desires,
In ev'ry Breast the beauteous Nymph inspires:
And on the Plain when She no more appears;
The Plain a dark and gloomy Prospect wears.
In vain the Streams roll on: the Eastern Breeze
Dances in vain among the trembling Trees.
In vain the Birds begin their Ev'ning Song,
And to the silent Night their Notes prolong:
Nor Groves, nor chrystal Streams, nor verdant Field
Does wonted Pleasure in Her Absence yield.

AMARYLLIS.

And in His Absence, all the pensive Day,
In some obscure Retreat I lonely stray;
All Day to the repeating Caves complain,
In mournful Accents, and a dying Strain.
Dear lovely Youth! I cry to all around:
Dear lovely Youth! the flatt'ring Vales resound.

SILVIA.

On flow'ry Banks, by ev'ry murm'ring Stream,
AMINTA is my Muse's softest Theme:
'Tis She that does my artful Notes refine:
With fair AMINTA's Name my noblest Verse shall shine.

AMARYLLIS.

I'll twine fresh Garlands for ALEXIS' Brows,
And consecrate to Him eternal Vows:
The charming Youth shall my APOLLO prove:
He shall adorn my Songs, and tune my Voice to Love.

MATTHEW PRIOR

TO THE

AUTHOR

OF THE

Foregoing PASTORAL.

BY SILVIA if thy charming Self be meant;
If Friendship be thy Virgin Vows Extent;
O! let me in AMINTA's Praises join:
Her's my Esteem shall be, my Passion Thine.
When for Thy Head the Garland I prepare;
A second Wreath shall bind AMINTA's Hair:
And when my choicest Songs Thy Worth proclaim;
Alternate Verse shall bless AMINTA's Name:
My Heart shall own the Justice of Her Cause;
And Love himself submit to Friendship's Laws.

But if beneath thy Numbers soft Disguise,
Some favor'd Swain, some true ALEXIS lyes;
If AMARYLLIS breaths thy secret Pains;
And thy fond Heart beats Measure to thy Strains:
May'st thou, howe'er I grieve, for ever find
The Flame propitious, and the Lover kind:
May VENUS long exert her happy Pow'r,
And make thy Beauty, like thy Verse, endure:
May ev'ry God his friendly Aid afford;
PAN guard thy Flock, and CERES bless thy Board.

But if by chance the Series of thy Joys
Permit one Thought less chearful to arise;
Piteous transfer it to the mournful Swain,
Who loving much, who not belov'd again,
Feels an ill-fated Passion's last Excess;
And dies in Woe, that Thou may'st live in Peace.

To a LADY:

She refusing to continue a DISPUTE *with me, and leaving me in the* ARGUMENT.

An ODE.

I.

SPARE, Gen'rous Victor, spare the Slave,
  Who did unequal War pursue;
That more than Triumph He might have,
  In being overcome by You.

II.

In the Dispute whate'er I said,
  My Heart was by my Tongue bely'd;
And in my Looks You might have read,
  How much I argu'd on your side.

III.

You, far from Danger as from Fear,
  Might have sustain'd an open Fight:
For seldom your Opinions err:
  Your Eyes are always in the right.

IV.

Why, fair One, would You not rely
  On Reason's Force with Beauty's join'd?
Could I their Prevalence deny;
  I must at once be deaf and blind.

V.

Alas! not hoping to subdue,
  I only to the Fight aspir'd:
To keep the beauteous Foe in view
  Was all the Glory I desir'd.

VI.

But She, howe'er of Vict'ry sure,
  Contemns the Wreath too long delay'd;
And, arm'd with more immediate Pow'r,
  Calls cruel Silence to her Aid.

VII.

Deeper to wound, See shuns the Fight:
  She drops her Arms, to gain the Field:
Secures her Conquest by her Flight;
  And triumphs, when She seems to yield.

VIII.

So when the PARTHIAN turn'd his Steed,
  And from the Hostile Camp withdrew;
With cruel Skill the backward Reed
  He sent; and as He fled, He slew.

SEEING THE

DUKE of *ORMOND*'s

PICTURE,

AT

Sir *GODFREY KNELLER*'s.

OUT from the injur'd Canvas, KNELLER, strike
  These Lines too faint: the Picture is not like.
Exalt thy Thought, and try thy Toil again:
Dreadful in Arms, on LANDEN's glorious Plain
Place Ormond's Duke: impendent in the Air
Let His keen Sabre, Comet-like, appear,

Where-e'er it points, denouncing Death: below
Draw routed Squadrons, and the num'rous Foe
Falling beneath, or flying from His Blow:
'Till weak with Wounds, and cover'd o'er with Blood,
Which from the Patriot's Breast in Torrents flowed,
He faints: His Steed no longer hears the Rein;
But stumbles o'er the Heap, His Hand had slain.
And now exhausted, bleeding, pale He lyes;
Lovely, sad Object! in His half-clos' Eyes
Stern Vengeance yet, and Hostile Terror stand:
His Front yet threatens; and His Frowns command:
The GALLICK Chiefs their Troops around Him call;
Fear to approach Him, tho' they see Him fall.——

O KNELLER, could Thy Shades and Lights express
The perfect Hero in that glorious Dress;
Ages to come might ORMOND's Picture know;
And Palms for Thee beneath His Lawrels grow:
In spight of Time Thy Work might ever shine;
Nor HOMER's Colors last so long as Thine.

CELIA

TO

DAMON.

Atque in Amore mala hæc proprio, summéque secundo
Inveniuntur——   Lucret. Lib. 4.

WHAT can I say? What Arguments can prove
My Truth? What Colors can describe my Love?
If it's Excess and Fury be not known,
In what Thy CELIA has already done.

Thy Infant Flames, whilst yet they were conceal'd
In tim'rous Doubts, with Pity I beheld;
With easie Smiles dispell'd the silent Fear,
That durst not tell Me, what I dy'd to hear:
In vain I strove to check my growing Flame,
Or shelter Passion under Friendship's Name:

31

MATTHEW PRIOR

You saw my Heart, how it my Tongue bely'd;
And when You press'd, how faintly I deny'd——

E'er Guardian Thought could bring it's scatter'd Aid;
E'er Reason could support the doubting Maid;
My Soul surpriz'd, and from her self disjoin'd,
Left all Reserve, and all the Sex behind:
From your Command her Motions She receiv'd;
And not for Me, but You, She breath'd and liv'd.

But ever blest be CYTHEREA's Shrine;
And Fires Eternal on Her Altars shine;
Since Thy dear Breast has felt an equal Wound;
Since in Thy Kindness my Desires are crown'd.
By Thy each Look, and Thought, and Care 'tis shown,
Thy Joys are center'd All in Me Alone;
And sure I am, Thou would'st not change this Hour
For all the white Ones, Fate has in it's Pow'r.——

Yet thus belov'd, thus loving to Excess;
Yet thus receiving and returning Bliss;
In this great Moment, in this golden Now,
When ev'ry Trace of What, or When, or How
Should from my Soul by raging Love be torn,
And far on Swelling Seas of Rapture born;
A melancholy Tear afflicts my Eye;
And my Heart labours with a sudden Sigh:
Invading Fears repel my Coward Joy;
And Ills foreseen the present Bliss destroy.

Poor as it is, This Beauty was the Cause,
That with first Sighs Your panting Bosom rose:
But with no Owner Beauty long will stay,
Upon the Wings of Time born swift away:
Pass but some fleeting Years, and These poor Eyes
(Where now without a Boast some Lustre lyes)
No longer shall their little Honors keep;
Shall only be of use to read, or weep:
And on this Forehead, where your Verse has said,
The LOVES delighted, and the GRACES play'd;
Insulting Age will trace his cruel Way,
And leave sad Marks of his destructive Sway.

Mov'd by my Charms, with them your Love may cease,
And as the Fuel sinks, the Flame decrease:
Or angry Heav'n may quicker Darts prepare;
And Sickness strike what Time awhile would spare.
Then will my Swain His glowing Vows renew:
Then will His throbbing Heart to Mine beat true;
When my own Face deters Me from my Glass;
And KNELLER only shows what CELIA was.

Fantastic FAME may sound her wild Alarms:
Your Country, as You think, may want your Arms.
You may neglect, or quench, or hate the Flame,
Whose Smoke too long obscured your rising Name:
And quickly cold Indiff'rence will ensue;
When You Love's Joys thro' Honor's Optic view.

Then CELIA's loudest Pray'r will prove too weak,
To this abandon'd Breast to bring You back;
When my lost Lover the tall Ship ascends,
With Musick gay, and wet with Jovial Friends:
The tender Accents of a Woman's Cry
Will pass unheard, will unreguarded die;
When the rough Seaman's louder Shouts prevail;
When fair Occasion shows the springing Gale;
And Int'rest guides the Helm; and Honor swells the Sail.

Some wretched Lines from this neglected Hand,
May find my Hero on the foreign Strand,
Warm with new Fires, and pleas'd with new Command:
While She who wrote 'em, of all Joy bereft,
To the rude Censure of the World is left;
Her mangl'd Fame in barb'rous Pastime lost,
The Coxcomb's Novel, and the Drunkard's Toast.

But nearer Care (O pardon it!) supplies
Sighs to my Breast, and Sorrow to my Eyes.
Love, Love himself (the only Friend I have)
May scorn his Triumph, having bound his Slave.
That Tyrant God, that restless Conqueror
May quit his Pleasure, to assert his Pow'r;
Forsake the Provinces that bless his Sway,
To vanquish Those which will not yet obey.

MATTHEW PRIOR

Another Nymph with fatal Pow'r may rise,
To damp the sinking Beams of CELIA's Eyes;
With haughty Pride may hear Her Charms confest;
And scorn the ardent Vows that I have blest:
You ev'ry Night may sigh for Her in vain;
And rise each Morning to some fresh Disdain:
While CELIA's softest Look may cease to Charm;
And Her Embraces want the Pow'r to warm:
While these fond Arms, thus circling You, may prove
More heavy Chains, than Those of hopeless Love.

Just Gods! All other Things their Like produce:
The Vine arises from her Mother's Juice:
When feeble Plants, or tender Flow'rs decay;
They to their Seed their Images convey:
Where the old Myrtle her good Influence sheds;
Sprigs of like Leaf erect their Filial Heads:
And when the Parent Rose decays, and dies;
With a resembling Face the Daughter-Buds arise.
That Product only which our Passions bear,
Eludes the Planter's miserable Care:
While blooming Love assures us Golden Fruit; ⎫
Some inborn Poison taints the secret Root: ⎬
Soon fall the Flow'rs of Joy: soon Seeds of Hatred shoot.⎭

Say, Shepherd, say: Are these Reflections true? ⎫
Or was it but the Woman's Fear, that drew ⎬
This cruel Scene, unjust to Love and You? ⎭
Will You be only, and for ever Mine?
Shall neither Time, nor Age our Souls disjoin?
From this dear Bosom shall I ne'er be torn?
Or You grow cold, respectful, and forsworn?
And can You not for Her You love do more,
Than any Youth for any Nymph before?

An ODE.

Presented to the KING, *on his* MAJESTY's *Arrival in* HOLLAND,

AFTER

THE QUEEN's DEATH. 1695.

Quis desiderio sit pudor aut modus
Tam cari capitis? præcipe lugubres
Cantus, Melpomene.

I.

AT MARY's Tomb, (sad, sacred Place!)
   The Virtues shall their Vigils keep:
And every Muse, and every Grace
   In solemn State shall ever weep.

II.

The future, pious, mournful Fair,
   Oft as the rolling Years return,
With Fragrant Wreaths, and flowing Hair,
   Shall visit Her distinguish'd Urn.

III.

For Her the Wise and Great shall mourn;
   When late Records her Deeds repeat:
Ages to come, and Men unborn
   Shall bless her Name, and sigh her Fate.

IV.

Fair ALBION shall, with faithful Trust,
   Her holy Queen's sad Reliques guard;
'Till Heav'n awakes the precious Dust,
   And gives the Saint her full Reward.

V.

But let the King dismiss his Woes,
  Reflecting on his fair Renown;
And take the Cypress from his Brows,
  To put his wonted Lawrels on.

VI.

If prest by Grief our Monarch stoops;
  In vain the BRITISH Lions roar:
If He, whose Hand sustain'd them, droops;
  The BELGIC Darts will wound no more.

VII.

Embattl'd Princes wait the Chief,
  Whose Voice should rule, whose Arm should lead;
And, in kind Murmurs, chide That Grief,
  Which hinders EUROPE being freed.

VIII.

The great Example They demand,
  Who still to Conquest led the Way;
Wishing Him present to Command,
  As They stand ready to Obey.

IX.

They seek That Joy, which us'd to glow,
  Expanded on the Hero's Face;
When the thick Squadrons prest the Foe,
  And WILLIAM led the glorious Chace.

X.

To give the mourning Nations Joy,
  Restore Them Thy auspicious Light,
Great Sun : with radiant Beams destroy
  Those Clouds, which keep Thee from our Sight.

XI.

Let Thy sublime Meridian Course
  For MARY's setting Rays attone :
Our Lustre, with redoubl'd Force,
  Must now proceed from Thee alone.

XII.

See, Pious King, with diff'rent Strife
    Thy struggling ALBION's Bosom torn:
So much She fears for WILLIAM's Life,
    That MARY's Fate She dare not mourn.

XIII.

Her Beauty, in thy softer Half
    Bury'd and lost, She ought to grieve:
But let her Strength in Thee be safe:
    And let Her weep; but let Her live.

XIV.

Thou, Guardian Angel, save the Land
    From thy own Grief, her fiercest Foe;
Lest BRITAIN, rescu'd by Thy Hand,
    Should bend and sink beneath Thy Woe.

XV.

Her former Triumphs all are vain,
    Unless new Trophies still be sought;
And hoary Majesty sustain
    The Battels, which Thy Youth has tought.

XVI.

Where now is all That fearful Love,
    Which made Her hate the War's Alarms?
That soft Excess, with which She strove
    To keep her Hero in her Arms?

XVII.

While still She chid the coming Spring,
    Which call'd Him o'er His subject Seas:
While, for the Safety of the King,
    She wish'd the Victor's Glory less.

XVIII.

'Tis chang'd: 'tis gone: sad BRITAIN now
    Hastens her Lord to Foreign Wars:
Happy! if Toils may break His Woe;
    Or Danger may divert His Cares.

MATTHEW PRIOR

XIX.

In Martial Din She drowns her Sighs,
　　Lest He the rising Grief should hear:
She pulls her Helmet o'er her Eyes,
　　Lest He should see the falling Tear.

XX.

Go, mighty Prince, let FRANCE be taught,
　　How constant Minds by Grief are try'd;
How great the Land, that wept and fought,
　　When WILLIAM led, and MARY dy'd.

XXI.

Fierce in the Battel make it known,
　　Where Death with all his Darts is seen,
That He can touch Thy Heart with None,
　　But That which struck the Beauteous Queen.

XXII.

BELGIA indulg'd her open Grief,
　　While yet her Master was not near;
With sullen Pride refus'd Relief,
　　And sat Obdurate in Despair.

XXIII.

As Waters from her Sluces, flow'd
　　Unbounded Sorrow from her Eyes:
To Earth her bended Front She bow'd,
　　And sent her Wailings to the Skies.

XXIV.

But when her anxious Lord return'd;
　　Rais'd is her Head; her Eyes are dry'd:
She smiles, as WILLIAM ne'er had mourn'd:
　　She looks, as MARY ne'er had dy'd.

XXV.

That Freedom which all Sorrows claim,
　　She does for Thy Content resign:
Her Piety itself would blame;
　　If Her Regrets should waken Thine.

XXVI.

To cure Thy Woe, She shews Thy Fame;
    Lest the great Mourner should forget,
That all the Race, whence ORANGE came,
    Made Virtue triumph over Fate.

XXVII.

WILLIAM His Country's Cause could fight,
    And with His Blood Her Freedom seal:
MAURICE and HENRY guard that Right,
    For which Their pious Parents fell.

XXVIII.

How Heroes rise, how Patriots set,
    Thy Father's Bloom and Death may tell:
Excelling Others These were Great:
    Thou, greater still, must These excell.

XXIX.

The last fair Instance Thou must give,
    Whence NASSAU's Virtue can be try'd;
And shew the World, that Thou can'st live
    Intrepid, as Thy Consort dy'd.

XXX.

Thy Virtue, whose resistless Force
    No dire Event could ever stay,
Must carry on it's destin'd Course;
    Tho' Death and Envy stop the Way.

XXXI.

For BRITAIN's Sake, for BELGIA's, live:
    Pierc'd by Their Grief forget Thy own:
New Toils endure; new Conquest give;
    And bring Them Ease, tho' Thou hast None.

XXXII.

Vanquish again; tho' She be gone,
    Whose Garland crown'd the Victor's Hair:
And Reign; tho' She has left the Throne,
    Who made Thy Glory worth Thy Care.

39

XXXIII.

Fair BRITAIN never yet before
    Breath'd to her King a useless Pray'r:
Fond BELGIA never did implore,
    While WILLIAM turn'd averse His Ear.

XXXIV.

But should the weeping Hero now
    Relentless to Their Wishes prove;
Should He recall, with pleasing Woe,
    The Object of his Grief and Love;

XXXV.

Her Face with thousand Beauties blest,
    Her Mind with thousand Virtues stor'd,
Her Pow'r with boundless Joy confest,
    Her Person only not ador'd:

XXXVI.

Yet ought his Sorrow to be checkt;
    Yet ought his Passions to abate:
If the great Mourner would reflect,
    Her Glory in her Death compleat.

XXXVII.

She was instructed to command,
    Great King, by long obeying Thee:
Her Scepter, guided by Thy Hand,
    Preserv'd the Isles, and Rul'd the Sea.

XXXVIII.

But oh! 'twas little, that her Life
    O'er Earth and Water bears thy Fame:
In Death, 'twas worthy WILLIAM's Wife,
    Amidst the Stars to fix his Name.

XXXIX.

Beyond where Matter moves, or Place
    Receives it's Forms, Thy Virtues rowl:
From MARY's Glory, Angels trace
    The Beauty of her Part'ner's Soul.

XL.

Wise Fate, which does it's Heav'n decree
  To Heroes, when They yield their Breath,
Hastens Thy Triumph. Half of Thee
  Is Deify'd before thy Death.

XLI.

Alone to thy Renown 'tis giv'n,
  Unbounded thro' all Worlds to go :
While She great Saint rejoices Heav'n ;
  And Thou sustain'st the Orb below.

IN
IMITATION
OF
ANACREON.

LET 'em Censure : what care I ?
    The Herd of Criticks I defie.
Let the Wretches know, I write
Regardless of their Grace, or Spight.
No, no : the Fair, the Gay, the Young
Govern the Numbers of my Song.
All that They approve is sweet :
And All is Sense, that They repeat.

  Bid the warbling Nine retire :
VENUS, String thy Servant's Lyre :
Love shall be my endless Theme :
Pleasure shall triumph over Fame :
And when these Maxims I decline,
APOLLO, may Thy Fate be Mine :
May I grasp at empty Praise ;
And lose the Nymph, to gain the Bays.

An ODE.

I.

THE Merchant, to secure his Treasure,
  Conveys it in a borrow'd Name:
EUPHELIA serves to grace my Measure;
  But CLOE is my real Flame.

II.

My softest Verse, my darling Lyre
  Upon EUPHELIA's Toylet lay;
When CLOE noted her Desire,
  That I should sing, that I should play.

III.

My Lyre I tune, my Voice I raise;
  But with my Numbers mix my Sighs:
And whilst I sing EUPHELIA's Praise,
  I fix my Soul on CLOE's Eyes.

IV.

Fair CLOE blush'd: EUPHELIA frown'd:
  I sung and gaz'd: I play'd and trembl'd:
And VENUS to the LOVES around
  Remark'd, how ill We all dissembl'd.

ODE

Sur la Prise

De *NAMUR*,

Par les ARMES *du* ROY,

L'Année 1692.

Par Monsieur BOILEAU DESPREAUX.

I.

QUELLE doête & Sainte yvresse
Aujourd'huy me fait la loy?
Chastes Nymphes du *Permesse*,
N'est-ce pas vous que je voy?
Accourez, Troupe Sçavante:
Des sons que ma Lyre enfante;
Ces Arbres sont réjoüis:
Marquez en bien la cadence:
Et vous, Vents, faites Silence:
Je vais Parler de LOUIS.

II.

Dans ses chansons immortelles,
Comme un Aigle audacieux,
PINDARE étendant ses aisles,
Fuit loin des Vulgaires yeux.
Mais, ô ma fidele Lyre,
Si, dans l'ardeur qui m'inspire,
Tu peux suivre mes Transports;
Les chesnes de Monts de *Thrace*
N'ont rien oüi, que n'efface
La douceur de tes accords.

43

III.

Est-ce APOLLON & NEPTUNE,
Qui sur ces Rocs Sourcilleux
Ont, compagnons de Fortune,
Basti ces Murs orgueilleux?
De leur enceinte fameuse
La *Sambre* unie à la *Meuse*,
Deffend la fatal abord;
Et par cent bouches horribles
L'airain sur ces Monts terribles
Vomit le Fer, & la Mort.

IV.

Dix mille vaillans ALCIDES
Les bordant de toutes parts,
D'éclairs au loin homicides
Font petiller leurs Remparts:
Et dans son Sein infidele
Par tout la Terre y recele
Un feu prest à s'élancer,
Qui soudain perçant son goufre,
Ouvre un Sepulchre de soufre
A quiconque ose avancer.

V.

Namur, devant tes murailles
Jadis la *Grece* eust vingt Ans
Sans fruit veu les funerailles
De ses plus fiers Combattans.
Quelle effroyable Puissance
Aujourd-huy pourtant s'avance,
Preste à foudroyer tes monts?
Quel bruit, quel feu l'environne?
C'est JUPITER en Personne;
Ou c'est le Vainqueur de *Mons*.

VI.

N'en doute point: c'est luy-mesme.
Tout brille en luy; Tout est Roy.
Dans *Bruxelles* NASSAU blême
Commence à trembler pour Toy.
En vain il voit le *Batàve*,
Desormais docile Esclâve,
Rangé Sous ses étendars:
En vain au Lion *Belgique*
Il voit l'Aigle *Germanique*
Uni Sous les Leopards.

VII.

Plein de la frayeur nouvelle,
Dont ses sens sont agités,
A son secours il appelle
Les Peuples les plus vantéz.
Ceux-là viennent du rivage,
Ou s'enorgueillit le *Tage*
De l'or, qui roule en ses eaux ;
Ceux-ci des champs, où la neige
Des marais de la *Norvége*
Neuf mois couvre les roseaux.

VIII.

Mais qui fait enfler la *Sambre?*
Sous les *Jumeaux* effrayéz,
Des froids Torrens de *Decembre*
Les Champs par tout sont noyéz.
CERES s'enfuit, éplorée
De voir en proye à BOREE
Ses guerets d'epics chargéz,
Et Sous les Urnes fangeuses
Des *Hyades* orageuses
Tous ses Trésors submergéz.

IX.

Déployez toutes vos rages,
Princes, Vents, Peuples, Frimats ;
Ramassez tous vos nuages ;
Rassamblez tous vos Soldats.
Malgré vous *Namur* en poudre
S'en va tomber Sous la foudre
Qui domta *Lille, Courtray,*
Gand la Superbe Espagnole,
Saint Omer, Bezançon, Dole,
Ypres, Mastricht, & *Cambray.*

X.

Mes présages s'accomplissent :
Il commence à chanceler :
Sous les coups qui retentissent
Ses Murs s'en vont s'écrouler.
MARS en feu qui les domine,
Souffle à grand bruit leur ruine ;
Et les Bombes dans les airs
Allant chercer le tonnere,
Semblent tombant sur la Terre,
Vouloir s'ouvrir les Enfers.

45

MATTHEW PRIOR

XI.

Accourez, NASSAU, BAVIERE,
De ces Murs l'unique espoir :
A couvert d'une Riviere
Venez : vous pouvez tout voir.
Considerez ces approches :
Voyez grimper sur ces roches
Ces Athletes belliqueux ;
Et dans les Eaux, dans la Flame,
LOUIS à tout donnant l'ame,
Marcher, courir avecque eux.

XII.

Contemplez dans la tempeste,
Qui sort de ces Boulevars,
La Plume qui sur sa teste
Attire tous les regards.
A cet Astre redoutable
Toûjours un sort favorable
S'attache dans les Combats :
Et toûjours avec la Gloire
MARS amenant la Victoire
Vôle, & le suit à grands pas.

XIII.

Grands Deffenseurs de l'*Espagne*,
Montrez-vous : il en est temps :
Courage ; vers la *Mahagne*
Voilà vos Drapeaux flottans.
Jamais ses ondes craintives
N'ont veû sur leurs foibles rives
Tant de guerriers s'amasser.
Courez donc : Qui vous retarde ?
Tout l'Univers vous regarde.
N'osez-vous la traverser ?

XIV.

Loin de fermer la passage
A vos nombreux bataillons,
LUXEMBOURG a du rivage
Reculé ses pavillons.
Quoy ? leur seul aspect vous glace ?
Où sont ces chefs pleins d'audace,
Jadis si prompts à marcher,
Qui devoient de la *Tamise*,
Et de la *Drâve* Soûmise,
Jusqu' à *Paris* nous chercher ?

XV.

Cependant l'effroy redouble
Sur les Remparts de *Namur*.
Son Gouverneur qui se trouble
S'enfuit sous son dernier mur.
Déja jusques à ses portes
Je voy monter nos cohortes,
La Flame & le Fer en main :
Et sur les Monceaux de piques,
De Corps morts, de Rocs, de Briques,
S'ouvrir un large chemin.

XVI.

C'en est fait. Je viens d'entendre
Sur ces Rochers éperdus
Battre un Signal pour se rendre :
Le Feu cesse. Ils sont rendus.
Dépoüillez vôtre arrogance,
Fiers Ennemis de la *France*,
Et desormais gracieux,
Allez à *Liege*, à *Bruxelles*,
Porter les humbles nouvelles
De *Namur* pris à vox yeux.

An *English* BALLAD,

On the Taking of

NAMUR

By the KING *of* GREAT BRITAIN,

1695.

Dulce est desipere in loco.

I *and* II.

SOME Folks are drunk, yet do not know it :
 So might not BACCHUS give You Law ?
Was it a Muse, O lofty Poet,
 Or Virgin of St. CYR, You saw ?

MATTHEW PRIOR

Why all this Fury? What's the Matter,
   That Oaks must come from *Thrace* to dance?
Must stupid Stocks be taught to flatter?
   And is there no such Wood in *France*?
Why must the Winds all hold their Tongue?
   If they a little Breath should raise;
Would that have spoil'd the Poet's Song;
   Or puff'd away the Monarch's Praise?

PINDAR, that Eagle, mounts the Skies;
   While Virtue leads the noble Way:
Too like a Vultur BOILEAU flies,
   Where sordid Interest shows the Prey.
When once the Poet's Honour ceases,
   From Reason far his Transports rove:
And BOILEAU, for eight hundred Pieces,
   Makes LOUIS take the Wall of JOVE.

III.

NEPTUNE and SOL came from above,
   Shap'd like MEGRIGNY and VAUBAN:
They arm'd these Rocks; then show'd old JOVE
   Of *Marli* Wood, the Wond'rous Plan.
Such Walls, these three wise Gods agreed,
   By Human Force could ne'er be shaken:
But You and I in HOMER read
   Of Gods, as well as Men, mistaken.
Sambre and *Maese* their Waves may join;
   But ne'er can WILLIAM's Force restrain:
He'll pass them Both, who pass'd the *Boyn*:
   Remember this, and arm the *Sein*.

IV.

Full fifteen thousand lusty Fellows
   With Fire and Sword the Fort maintain:
Each was a HERCULES, You tell us;
   Yet out they march'd like common Men.
Cannons above, and Mines below
   Did Death and Tombs for Foes contrive:
Yet Matters have been order'd so,
   That most of Us are still alive.

V.

If *Namur* be compar'd to *Troy*;
 Then BRITAIN'S Boys excell'd the GREEKS:
Their Siege did ten long Years employ:
 We've done our Bus'ness in ten Weeks.
What Godhead does so fast advance,
 With dreadful Pow'r those Hills to gain?
'Tis little WILL, the Scourge of *France*;
 No Godhead, but the first of Men.
His mortal Arm exerts the Pow'r,
 To keep ev'n *Mons*'s Victor under:
And that same JUPITER no more
 Shall fright the World with impious Thunder.

VI.

Our King thus trembles at *Namur*,
 Whilst VILLEROY, who ne'er afraid is,
To *Bruxelles* marches on secure,
 To bomb the Monks, and scare the Ladies.
After this glorious Expedition,
 One Battle makes the Marshal Great:
He must perform the King's Commission:
 Who knows, but ORANGE may retreat?
Kings are allow'd to feign the Gout,
 Or be prevail'd with not to Fight:
And mighty LOUIS hop'd, no doubt,
 That WILLIAM wou'd preserve that Right.

VII.

From *Seyn* and *Loyre*, to *Rhone* and *Po*,
 See every Mother's Son appear:
In such a Case ne'er blame a Foe,
 If he betrays some little Fear.
He comes, the mighty VILL'ROY comes;
 Finds a small River in his Way:
So waves his Colours, beats his Drums;
 And thinks it prudent there to stay.
The *Gallic* Troops breath Blood and War:
 The Marshal cares not to march faster:
Poor VILL'ROY moves so slowly here,
 We fancy'd all, it was his Master.

P.   D   49

VIII.

Will no kind Flood, no friendly Rain
  Disguise the Marshal's plain Disgrace?
No Torrents swell the low *Mehayne*?
  The World will say, he durst not pass.
Why will no *Hyades* appear,
  Dear Poet, on the Banks of *Sambre*?
Just as they did that mighty Year,
  When You turn'd *June* into *December*.
The Water-*Nymphs* are too unkind
  To VILL'ROY; are the Land-*Nymphs* so?
And fly They All, at Once Combin'd
  To shame a General, and a Beau?

IX.

Truth, Justice, Sense, Religion, Fame
  May join to finish WILLIAM's Story:
Nations set free may bless his Name;
  And *France* in Secret own his Glory.
But *Ipres*, *Mastrich*, and *Cambray*,
  Besançon, *Ghent*, St. *Omers*, *Lysle*,
Courtray, and *Dole*——Ye Criticks, say,
  How poor to this was PINDAR's Style?
With Eke's and Also's tack thy Strain,
  Great Bard; and sing the deathless Prince,
Who lost *Namur* the same Campaign,
  He bought *Dixmude*, and plunder'd *Deynse*.

X.

I'll hold Ten Pound, my Dream is out:
  I'd tell it You, but for the Rattle
Of those confounded Drums: no doubt
  Yon' bloody Rogues intend a Battel.
Dear me! a hundred thousand *French*
  With Terror fill the neighb'ring Field;
While WILLIAM carries on the Trench,
  'Till both the Town and Castle yield.
VILL'ROY to BOUFFLERS should advance,
  Says MARS, thro' Cannons Mouths in Fire;
Id est, one Mareschal of *France*
  Tells t'other, He can come no nigher.

XI.

Regain the Lines the shortest Way,
   VILL'ROY; or to *Versailles* take Post:
For, having seen it, Thou can'st say
   The Steps, by which *Namur* was lost.
The Smoke and Flame may vex thy Sight:
   Look not once back: but as thou goest,
Quicken the Squadrons in their Flight;
   And bid the D——l take the slowest.
Think not what Reason to produce,
   From LOUIS to conceal thy Fear:
He'll own the Strength of thy Excuse;
   Tell him that WILLIAM was but there.

XII.

Now let us look for LOUIS' Feather,
   That us'd to shine so like a Star:
The Gen'rals could not get together,
   Wanting that Influence, great in War.
O Poet! Thou had'st been discreeter,
   Hanging the Monarch's Hat so high;
If Thou had'st dubb'd thy Star, a Meteor,
   That did but blaze, and rove, and die.

XIII.

To animate the doubtful Fight,
   Namur in vain expects that Ray:
In vain *France* hopes, the sickly Light
   Shou'd shine near WILLIAM's fuller Day.
It knows *Versailles*, it's proper Station;
   Nor cares for any foreign Sphere:
Where You see BOILEAU's Constellation,
   Be sure no Danger can be near.

XIV.

The *French* had gather'd all their Force;
   And WILLIAM met them in their Way:
Yet off they brush'd, both Foot and Horse.
   What has Friend BOILEAU left to say?

When his high Muse is bent upon't,
  To sing her King, that Great Commander,
Or on the Shores of *Hellespont*,
  Or in the Valleys near *Scamander* ;
Wou'd it not spoil his noble Task,
  If any foolish *Phrygian* there is,
Impertinent enough to ask,
  How far *Namur* may be from *Paris* ?

XV.

Two Stanza's more before we end,
  Of Death, Pikes, Rocks, Arms, Bricks, and Fire :
Leave 'em behind You, honest Friend :
  And with your Country-Men retire.
Your Ode is spoilt ; *Namur* is freed ;
  For *Dixmuyd* something yet is due :
So good Count GUISCARD may proceed ;
  But BOUFFLERS, Sir, one Word with you.——

XVI.

'Tis done. In Sight of these Commanders,
  Who neither Fight, nor raise the Siege,
The Foes of *France* march safe thro' *Flanders* ;
  Divide to *Bruxelles*, or to *Liege*.
Send, FAME, this News to *Trianon* ;
  That BOUFFLERS may new Honours gain :
He the same Play by Land has shown,
  As TOURVILLE did upon the Main.
Yet is the Marshal made a Peer :
  O WILLIAM, may thy Arms advance ;
That He may lose *Dinant* next Year,
  And so be Constable of *France.*

Presented to the

KING,

AT HIS

ARRIVAL in *HOLLAND*,

AFTER THE

DISCOVERY *of the* CONSPIRACY

1696.

Serus in cælum redeas; *diuque*
Lætus intersis populo Quirini :
Neve Te nostris vitiis iniquum
     Ocyor aura
Tollat—   Hor. ad Augustum.

YE careful Angels, whom eternal Fate
 Ordains, on Earth and human Acts to wait ;
Who turn with secret Pow'r this restless Ball,
And bid predestin'd Empires rise and fall :
Your sacred Aid religious Monarchs own ;
When first They merit, then ascend the Throne :
But Tyrants dread Ye, lest your just Decree
Transfer the Pow'r, and set the People free :
See rescu'd BRITAIN at your Altars bow :
And hear her Hymns your happy Care avow :
That still her Axes and her Rods support
The Judge's Frown, and grace the awful Court :
That Law with all her pompous Terror stands,
To wrest the Dagger from the Traitor's Hands ;
And rigid Justice reads the fatal Word ;
Poises the Ballance first, then draws the Sword.

53

MATTHEW PRIOR

BRITAIN Her Safety to your Guidance owns,
That She can sep'rate Parricides from Sons;
That, impious Rage disarm'd, She lives and Reigns,
Her Freedom kept by Him, who broke Her Chains.

And Thou, great Minister, above the rest
Of Guardian Spirits, be Thou for ever blest:
Thou, who of old wert sent to ISRAEL's Court,
With secret Aid great DAVID's strong Support;
To mock the frantick Rage of cruel SAUL;
And strike the useless Jav'lin to the Wall.
Thy later Care o'er WILLIAM's Temples held,
On BOYN's propitious Banks, the heav'nly Shield;
When Pow'r Divine did Sov'reign Right declare;
And Cannons mark'd, Whom They were bid to spare.

Still, blessed Angel, be thy Care the same;
Be WILLIAM's Life untouch'd, as is his Fame:
Let Him own Thine, as BRITAIN owns His Hand:
Save Thou the King, as He has sav'd the Land.

We Angels Forms in pious Monarchs view:
We reverence WILLIAM; for He acts like You;
Like You, Commission'd to chastize and bless,
He must avenge the World, and give it Peace.

Indulgent Fate our potent Pray'r receives;
And still BRITANNIA smiles, and WILLIAM lives:
The Hero dear to Earth, by Heav'n belov'd,
By Troubles must be vex'd, by Dangers prov'd:
His Foes must aid to make his Fame compleat,
And fix his Throne secure on their Defeat.

So, tho' with sudden Rage the Tempest comes;
Tho' the Winds roar; and tho' the Water foams;
Imperial BRITAIN on the Sea looks down,
And smiling sees her Rebel Subject frown:
Striking her Cliff the Storm confirms her Pow'r:
The Waves but whiten her Triumphant Shore:
In vain They wou'd advance, in vain retreat:
Broken They dash, and perish at her Feet.

POEMS ON SEVERAL OCCASIONS

For WILLIAM still new Wonders shall be shown:
The Pow'rs that rescu'd, shall preserve the Throne.
Safe on his Darling BRITAIN's joyful Sea,
Behold, the Monarch plows his liquid Way:
His Fleets in Thunder thro' the World declare,
Whose Empire they obey, whose Arms they bear.
Bless'd by aspiring Winds He finds the Strand   )
Blacken'd with Crowds; He sees the Nations stand }
Blessing his Safety, proud of his Command.   )
In various Tongues He hears the Captains dwell
On their great Leader's Praise: by Turns They tell,
And listen, each with emulous Glory fir'd,
How WILLIAM conquer'd, and how FRANCE retir'd;
How BELGIA freed the Hero's Arm confess'd,
But trembl'd for the Courage which She blest.

O LOUIS, from this great Example know,
To be at once a Hero, and a Foe:
By sounding Trumpets, Hear, and ratl'ing Drums,
When WILLIAM to the open Vengeance comes:
And See the Soldier plead the Monarch's Right,
Heading His Troops, and Foremost in the Fight.

Hence then, close Ambush and perfidious War,
Down to your Native Seats of Night repair.
And Thou, BELLONA, weep thy cruel Pride
Restrain'd, behind the Victor's Chariot ty'd
In brazen Knots, and everlasting Chains.
(So EUROPE's Peace, so WILLIAM's Fate ordains.)
While on the Iv'ry Chair, in happy State
He sits, Secure in Innocence, and Great
In regal Clemency; and views beneath
Averted Darts of Rage, and pointless Arms of Death.

MATTHEW PRIOR

To CLOE *Weeping.*

SEE, whilst Thou weep'st, fair CLOE, see
   The World in Sympathy with Thee.
The chearful Birds no longer sing,
Each drops his Head, and hangs his Wing.
The Clouds have bent their Bosom lower,
And shed their Sorrows in a Show'r.
The Brooks beyond their Limits flow;
And louder Murmurs speak their Woe.
The Nymphs and Swains adopt Thy Cares:
They heave Thy Sighs, and weep Thy Tears.
Fantastic Nymph! that Grief should move
Thy Heart, obdurate against Love.
Strange Tears! whose Pow'r can soften All,
But That dear Breast on which they fall.

TO

Mr. *HOWARD:*

An ODE.

I.

DEAR HOWARD, from the soft assaults of Love,
   Poets and Painters never are Secure:
Can I untouch'd the Fair ones Passions move?
   Or Thou draw Beauty, and not feel it's Pow'r?

II.

To Great APELLES when Young AMMON brought
   The darling Idol of his Captive Heart;
And the pleas'd Nymph with kind Attention sat,
   To have Her Charms recorded by His Art:

III.

The am'rous Master own'd Her potent Eyes;
   Sigh'd when He look'd, and trembl'd as He drew:
Each flowing Line confirm'd his first Surprize;
   And as the Piece advanc'd, the Passion grew.

IV.

While PHILIP's Son, while VENUS' Son was near,
   What different Tortures does his Bosom feel?
Great was the Rival, and the God severe:
   Nor could He hide his Flame, nor durst reveal.

V.

The Prince, renown'd in Bounty as in Arms,
   With Pity saw the ill-conceal'd Distress;
Quitted His Title to CAMPASPE's Charms,
   And gave the Fair one to the Friend's Embrace.

VI.

Thus the more beauteous CLOE sat to Thee,
   Good HOWARD, emu'lous of the GRÆCIAN Art:
But happy Thou, from CUPID's Arrow free,
   And Flames that pierc'd Thy Predecessor's Heart.

VII.

Had Thy poor Breast receiv'd an equal Pain;
   Had I been vested with the Monarch's Pow'r;
Thou must have sigh'd, unlucky Youth, in vain;
   Nor from My Bounty hadst Thou found a Cure.

VIII.

Tho' to convince Thee, that the Friend did feel
   A kind Concern for Thy ill-fated Care,
I would have sooth'd the Flame, I could not heal;
   Giv'n Thee the World; tho' I with-held the Fair.

MATTHEW PRIOR

LOVE Disarm'd.

BENEATH a Myrtle's verdant Shade
As CLOE half asleep was laid,
CUPID perch'd lightly on Her Breast,
And in That Heav'n desir'd to rest:
Over her Paps his Wings He spread:
Between He found a downy Bed,
And nestl'd in His little Head.

Still lay the God: The Nymph surpriz'd,
Yet Mistress of her self, devis'd,
How She the Vagrant might inthral,
And Captive Him, who Captives All.

Her Boddice half way She unlac'd:
About his Arms She slily cast
The silken Bond, and held Him fast.

The God awak'd; and thrice in vain
He strove to break the cruel Chain;
And thrice in vain He shook his Wing,
Incumber'd in the silken String.

Flutt'ring the God, and weeping said,
Pity poor CUPID, generous Maid,
Who happen'd, being Blind, to stray,
And on thy Bosom lost his Way:
Who stray'd, alas! but knew too well,
He never There must hope to dwell.
Set an unhappy Pris'ner free,
Who ne'er intended Harm to Thee.

To Me pertains not, She replies,
To know or care where CUPID flies;
What are his Haunts, or which his Way;
Where He would dwell, or whither stray:
Yet will I never set Thee free:
For Harm was meant, and Harm to Me.

Vain Fears that vex thy Virgin Heart!
I'll give Thee up my Bow and Dart:
Untangle but this cruel Chain,
And freely let Me fly again.

Agreed : Secure my Virgin Heart :
Instant give up thy Bow and Dart :
The Chain I'll in Return unty ;
And freely Thou again shalt fly.

Thus She the Captive did deliver :
The Captive thus gave up his Quiver.

The God disarm'd, e'er since that Day
Passes his Life in harmless Play ;
Flies round, or sits upon her Breast,
A little, flutt'ring, idle Guest.

E'er since that Day the beauteous Maid
Governs the World in CUPID's stead ;
Directs his Arrow as She wills ;
Gives Grief, or Pleasure ; spares, or kills.

CLOE HUNTING.

BEHIND her Neck her comely Tresses ty'd,
    Her Iv'ry Quiver graceful by her Side,
A-Hunting CLOE went : She lost her Way,
And thro' the Woods uncertain chanc'd to stray.
APOLLO passing by beheld the Maid ;
And, Sister Dear, bright CYNTHIA turn, He said :
The hunted Hind lyes close in yonder Brake.
Loud CUPID laugh'd, to see the God's Mistake ;
And laughing cry'd, Learn better, great Divine,
To know Thy Kindred, and to honour Mine.
Rightly advis'd, far hence Thy Sister seek,
Or on MEANDER's Bank, or LATMUS' Peak.
But in This Nymph, My Friend, My Sister know :
She draws My Arrows, and She bends My Bow :
Fair THAMES She haunts, and ev'ry neighb'ring Grove
Sacred to soft Recess, and gentle Love.
Go, with Thy CYNTHIA, hurl the pointed Spear
At the rough Boar ; or chace the flying Deer :
I and My CLOE take a nobler Aim :
At human Hearts We fling, nor ever miss the Game.

59

MATTHEW PRIOR

CUPID and *GANYMEDE.*

IN Heav'n, one Holy-day, You read
   In wise *Anacreon*, GANYMEDE
Drew heedless CUPID in, to throw
A Main, to pass an Hour, or so.
The little Trojan, by the way,
By HERMES taught, play'd All the Play.

   The God unhappily engag'd,
By Nature rash, by Play enrag'd,
Complain'd, and sigh'd, and cry'd, and fretted;
Lost ev'ry earthly thing He betted:
In ready Mony, all the Store
Pick'd up long since from DANAE's Show'r;
A Snush-Box, set with bleeding Hearts,
Rubies, all pierc'd with Diamond Darts;
His Nine-pins, made of Myrtle Wood;
(The Tree in IDA's Forest stood)
His Bowl pure Gold, the very same
Which PARIS gave the CYPRIAN Dame;
Two Table-Books in Shagreen Covers;
Fill'd with good Verse from real Lovers;
Merchandise rare! A Billet-doux,
It's Matter passionate, yet true:
Heaps of Hair Rings, and cypher'd Seals;
Rich Trifles; serious Bagatelles.

   What sad Disorders Play begets!
Desp'rate and mad, at length He sets
Those Darts, whose Points make Gods adore
His Might, and deprecate his Pow'r:
Those Darts, whence all our Joy and Pain
Arise: those Darts——come, Seven's the Main,
Cries GANYMEDE: The usual Trick:
Seven, slur a Six; Eleven: A Nick.

Ill News goes fast: 'Twas quickly known,
That simple CUPID was undone.
Swifter than Lightning VENUS flew:
Too late She found the thing too true.
Guess how the Goddess greets her Son:
Come hither, Sirrah; no, begon;
And, hark Ye, is it so indeed?
A Comrade You for GANYMEDE?
An Imp as wicked, for his Age,
As any earthly Lady's Page;
A Scandal and a Scourge to TROY:
A Prince's Son? A Black-guard Boy:
A Sharper, that with Box and Dice
Draws in young Deities to Vice.
All Heav'n is by the Ears together,
Since first That little Rogue came hither:
JUNO her self has had no Peace:
And truly I've been favour'd less:
For JOVE, as FAME reports, (but FAME
Says things not fit for Me to name)
Has acted ill for such a God,
And taken Ways extreamly odd.

And Thou, unhappy Child, She said
(Her Anger by her Grief allay'd)
Unhappy Child, who thus hast lost
All the Estate We e'er could boast;
Whither, O whither wilt Thou run,
Thy Name despis'd, thy Weakness known?
Nor shall thy Shrine on Earth be crown'd:
Nor shall thy Pow'r in Heav'n be own'd;
When Thou, nor Man, nor God can'st wound.

Obedient CUPID kneeling cry'd,
Cease, dearest Mother, cease to chide:
GANY's a Cheat, and I'm a Bubble:
Yet why this great Excess of Trouble?
The Dice were false: the Darts are gone:
Yet how are You, or I undone?

The Loss of These I can supply
With keener Shafts from CLOE's Eye:
Fear not, We e'er can be disgrac'd,
While That bright Magazine shall last:
Your crowded Altars still shall smoke;
And Man your Friendly Aid invoke:
JOVE shall again revere your Pow'r,
And rise a Swan, or fall a Show'r.

CUPID *Mistaken.*

I.

AS after Noon, one Summer's Day,
    VENUS stood bathing in a River;
CUPID a-shooting went that Way,
    New strung his Bow, new fill'd his Quiver.

II.

With Skill He chose his sharpest Dart:
    With all his Might his Bow He drew:
Swift to His beauteous Parent's Heart
    The too well-guided Arrow flew.

III.

I faint! I die! the Goddess cry'd:
    O cruel, could'st Thou find none other,
To wreck thy Spleen on? Parricide!
    Like NERO, Thou hast slain thy Mother.

IV.

Poor CUPID sobbing scarce could speak;
    Indeed, Mamma, I did not know Ye:
Alas! how easie my Mistake?
    I took You for your Likeness, CLOE.

VENUS *Mistaken*.

I.

WHEN CLOE's Picture was to VENUS shown;
　　Surpriz'd, the Goddess took it for Her own.
And what, said She, does this bold Painter mean?
When was I Bathing thus, and Naked seen?

II.

Pleas'd CUPID heard, and check'd His Mother's Pride:
And who's blind now, Mamma? the Urchin cry'd.
'Tis CLOE's Eye, and Cheek, and Lip, and Breast:
Friend HOWARD's Genius fancy'd all the rest.

A SONG.

IF Wine and Musick have the Pow'r,
　　To ease the Sickness of the Soul;
Let PHOEBUS ev'ry String explore;
And BACCHUS fill the sprightly Bowl.
Let Them their friendly Aid imploy,
To make my CLOE's Absence light;
And seek for Pleasure, to destroy
The Sorrows of this live-long Night.

　But She to Morrow will return:
VENUS, be Thou to Morrow great;
Thy Myrtles strow, Thy Odours burn;
And meet Thy Fav'rite Nymph in State.
Kind Goddess, to no other Pow'rs
Let Us to Morrow's Blessings own:
Thy darling LOVES shall guide the Hours;
And all the Day be Thine alone.

63

MATTHEW PRIOR

The DOVE.

——Tantæne animis cælestibus Iræ? Virg.

I.

IN VIRGIL's Sacred Verse we find,
  That Passion can depress or raise
The Heav'nly, as the Human Mind:
  Who dare deny what VIRGIL says?

II.

But if They shou'd; what our Great Master
  Has thus laid down, my Tale shall prove.
Fair VENUS wept the sad Disaster
  Of having lost her Fav'rite DOVE.

III.

In Complaisance poor CUPID mourn'd;
  His Grief reliev'd his Mother's Pain;
He vow'd he'd leave no Stone unturn'd,
  But She shou'd have her DOVE again.

IV.

Tho' None, said He, shall yet be nam'd,
  I know the Felon well enough:
But be She not, Mamma, condemn'd
  Without a fair and legal Proof.

V.

With that, his longest Dart he took,
  As Constable wou'd take his Staff:
That Gods desire like Men to look,
  Wou'd make ev'n HERACLITUS laugh.

VI.

LOVES Subaltern, a Duteous Band,
  Like Watchmen round their Chief appear:
Each had his Lanthorn in his Hand:
  And VENUS mask'd brought up the Rear.

VII.

Accouter'd thus, their eager Step
    To CLOE's Lodging They directed:
(At once I write, alas! and weep,
    That CLOE is of Theft suspected.)

VIII.

Late They set out, had far to go:
    St. DUNSTAN'S, as They pass'd, struck One.
CLOE, for Reasons good, You know,
    Lives at the sober End o'th' Town.

IX.

With one great Peal They rap the Door,
    Like Footmen on a Visiting-Day.
Folks at Her House at such an Hour!
    Lord! what will all the Neighbours say?

X.

The Door is open'd: up They run:
    Nor Prayers, nor Threats divert their Speed:
Thieves, Thieves! cries SUSAN; We're undone;
    They'll kill my Mistress in her Bed.

XI.

In Bed indeed the Nymph had been
    Three Hours: for all Historians say,
She commonly went up at Ten,
    Unless *Picquet* was in the Way.

XII.

She wak'd, be sure, with strange Surprize.
    O CUPID, is this Right or Law,
Thus to disturb the brightest Eyes,
    That ever slept, or ever saw?

XIII.

Have You observ'd a sitting Hare,
    List'ning, and fearful of the Storm
Of Horns and Hounds, clap back her Ear,
    Afraid to keep, or leave her Form?

XIV.

Or have You mark'd a Partridge quake,
  Viewing the tow'ring Faulcon nigh?
She cuddles low behind the Brake:
  Nor wou'd she stay: nor dares she fly.

XV.

Then have You seen the Beauteous Maid;
  When gazing on her Midnight Foes,
She turn'd each Way her frighted Head,
  Then sunk it deap beneath the Cloaths.

XVI.

VENUS this while was in the Chamber
  Incognito: for SUSAN said,
It smelt so strong of Myrrh and Amber—
  And SUSAN is no lying Maid.

XVII.

But since We have no present Need
  Of VENUS for an Episode;
With CUPID let us e'en proceed;
  And thus to CLOE spoke the God:

XVIII.

Hold up your Head: hold up your Hand:
  Wou'd it were not my Lot to show ye
This cruel *Writ*, wherein you stand
  Indicted by the Name of CLOE:

XIX.

For that by secret Malice stirr'd,
  Or by an emulous Pride invited,
You have purloin'd the fav'rite Bird,
  In which my Mother most delighted.

XX.

Her blushing Face the lovely Maid
  Rais'd just above the milk-white Sheet.
A Rose-Tree in a Lilly Bed,
  Nor glows so red, nor breathes so sweet.

XXI.

Are You not He whom Virgins fear,
  And Widows court? Is not your Name
CUPID? If so, pray come not near—
  Fair Maiden, I'm the very same.

XXII.

Then what have I, good Sir, to say,
  Or do with Her, You call your Mother?
If I shou'd meet Her in my Way,
  We hardly court'sy to each other.

XXIII.

DIANA Chaste, and HEBE Sweet,
  Witness that what I speak is true:
I wou'd not give my Paroquet
  For all the DOVES that ever flew.

XXIV.

Yet, to compose this Midnight Noise,
  Go freely search where-e'er you please:
(The Rage that rais'd, adorn'd Her Voice)
  Upon yon' Toilet lie my Keys.

XXV.

Her Keys He takes; her Doors unlocks;
  Thro' Wardrobe, and thro' Closet bounces;
Peeps into ev'ry Chest and Box;
  Turns all her Furbeloes and Flounces.

XXVI.

But DOVE, depend on't, finds He none;
  So to the Bed returns again:
And now the Maiden, bolder grown,
  Begins to treat Him with Disdain.

XXVII.

I marvel much, She smiling said,
  Your Poultry cannot yet be found:
Lies he in yonder Slipper dead,
  Or, may be, in the Tea-pot drown'd?

MATTHEW PRIOR

XXVIII.

No, Traytor, angry Love replies,
    He's hid somewhere about Your Breast;
A Place, nor God, nor Man denies,
    For VENUS' DOVE the proper Nest.

XXIX.

Search then, She said, put in your Hand,
    And CYNTHIA, dear Protectress, guard Me:
As guilty I, or free may stand,
    Do Thou, or punish, or reward Me.

XXX.

But ah! what Maid to Love can trust?
    He scorns, and breaks all Legal Power:
Into her Breast his Hand He thrust;
    And in a Moment forc'd it lower.

XXXI.

O, whither do those Fingers rove,
    Cries CLOE, treacherous Urchin, whither?
O VENUS! I shall find thy DOVE,
    Says He; for sure I touch his Feather.

A LOVER's ANGER.

AS CLOE came into the Room t'other Day,
    I peevish began; Where so long cou'd You stay?
In your Life-time You never regarded your Hour:
You promis'd at Two; and (pray look Child) 'tis Four.
A Lady's Watch needs neither Figures nor Wheels:
'Tis enough, that 'tis loaded with Baubles and Seals.
A Temper so heedless no Mortal can bear——
Thus far I went on with a resolute Air.
Lord bless Me! said She; let a Body but speak:
Here's an ugly hard Rose-Bud fall'n into my Neck:
It has hurt Me, and vext Me to such a Degree——
See here; for You never believe Me; pray see,
On the left Side my Breast what a Mark it has made.
So saying, her Bosom She careless display'd.
That Seat of Delight I with Wonder survey'd;
And forgot ev'ry Word I design'd to have said.

MERCURY and CUPID.

IN sullen Humour one Day Jove
  Sent HERMES down to IDA's Grove,
Commanding CUPID to deliver
His Store of Darts, his total Quiver;
That HERMES shou'd the Weapons break,
Or throw 'em into LETHE'[s] Lake.

  HERMES, You know, must do his Errand:
He found his Man, produc'd his Warrant:
CUPID, your Darts——this very Hour——
There's no contending against Power.

  How sullen JUPITER, just now
I think I said: and You'll allow,
That CUPID was as bad as He:
Hear but the Youngster's Repartée.

  Come Kinsman (said the little God)
Put off your Wings; lay by your Rod;
Retire with Me to yonder Bower;
And rest your self for half an Hour:
'Tis far indeed from hence to Heav'n:
And You fly fast: and 'tis but Seven.
We'll take one cooling Cup of Nectar;
And drink to this Celestial Hector——

  He break my Darts, or hurt my Pow'r!
He, LEDA's Swan, and DANAE's Show'r!
Go, bid him his Wife's Tongue restrain;
And mind his Thunder, and his Rain.——
My Darts? O certainly I'll give 'em:
From CLOE's Eyes He shall receive 'em.
There's One, the Best in all my Quiver,
Twang! thro' his very Heart and Liver.
He then shall Pine, and Sigh, and Rave:
Good Lord! what Bustle shall We have!
NEPTUNE must straight be sent to Sea;
And FLORA summon'd twice a-day:

One must find Shells, and t'other Flow'rs,
For cooling Grotts, and fragrant Bow'rs,
That CLOE may be serv'd in State:
The HOURS must at Her Toilet wait:
Whilst all the reasoning Fools below,
Wonder their Watches go too slow.
LYBS must fly South, and EURUS East,
For Jewels for Her Hair and Breast:
No Matter tho' their cruel Haste
Sink Cities, and lay Forrests waste.
No Matter tho' This Fleet be lost;
Or That lie wind-bound on the Coast.
What whis'pring in my Mother's Ear!
What Care, that JUNO shou'd not hear!
What Work among You Scholar Gods!
PHŒBUS must write Him am'rous Odes:
And Thou, poor Cousin, must compose
His Letters in submissive Prose:
Whilst haughty CLOE, to sustain
The Honour of My mystic Reign,
Shall all his Gifts and Vows disdain;
And laugh at your Old Bully's Pain.

  Dear Couz, said HERMES in a Fright,
For Heav'n sake keep Your Darts: Good Night.

On *BEAUTY*.

A RIDDLE.

RESOLVE Me, CLOE, what is THIS:
    Or forfeit me One precious Kiss.
'Tis the first Off-spring of the Graces;
Bears diff'rent Forms in diff'rent Places;
Acknowledg'd fine, where-e'er beheld;
Yet fancy'd finer, when conceal'd.
'Twas FLORA's Wealth, and CIRCE's Charm;
PANDORA's Box of Good and Harm:

'Twas MARS's Wish, ENDYMION's Dream;
APELLES' Draught, and OVID's Theme.
THIS guided THESEUS thro' the Maze;
And sent Him home with Life and Praise.
But THIS undid the PHRYGIAN Boy;
And blew the Flames that ruin'd TROY.
THIS shew'd great Kindness to old GREECE,
And help'd rich JASON to the Fleece.
THIS thro' the East just Vengeance hurl'd,
And lost poor ANTHONY the World.
Injur'd, tho' LUCRECE found her Doom;
THIS banish'd Tyranny from ROME.
Appeas'd, tho' LAIS gain'd her Hire;
THIS set PERSEPOLIS on Fire.
For THIS ALCIDES learn'd to Spin;
His Club laid down, and Lion's Skin.
For THIS APOLLO deign'd to keep,
With servile Care, a Mortal's Sheep.
For THIS the Father of the Gods,
Content to leave His high Abodes,
In borrow'd Figures loosely ran,
EUROPA's Bull, and LEDA's Swan.
For THIS He reassumes the Nod;
(While SEMELE commands the God)
Launces the Bolt, and shakes the Poles;
Tho' MOMUS laughs, and JUNO scolds.

Here list'ning CLOE smil'd, and said;
Your Riddle is not hard to read:
I Guess it——Fair one, if You do;
Need I, alas! the Theme pursue?
For THIS, Thou see'st, for THIS I leave,
Whate'er the World thinks Wise or Grave,
Ambition, Business, Friendship, News,
My useful Books, and serious Muse.
For THIS I willingly decline
The Mirth of Feasts, and Joys of Wine;
And chuse to sit and talk with Thee,
(As Thy great Orders may decree)
Of Cocks and Bulls, of Flutes and Fiddles,
Of Idle Tales, and foolish Riddles.

71

MATTHEW PRIOR

The QUESTION, *to* LISETTA.

WHAT Nymph shou'd I admire, or trust,
But CLOE Beauteous, CLOE Just?
What Nymph should I desire to see,
But Her who leaves the Plain for Me?
To Whom shou'd I compose the Lay,
But Her who listens, when I play?
To Whom in Song repeat my Cares,
But Her who in my Sorrow shares?
For Whom should I the Garland make,
But Her who joys the Gift to take,
And boasts She wears it for My Sake?
In Love am I not fully blest?
LISETTA, pr'ythee tell the rest.

LISETTA'*s* REPLY.

SURE CLOE Just, and CLOE Fair
Deserves to be Your only Care:
But when You and She to Day
Far into the Wood did stray,
And I happen'd to pass by;
Which way did You cast your Eye?
But when your Cares to Her You sing,
Yet dare not tell Her whence they spring;
Does it not more afflict your Heart,
That in those Cares She bears a Part?
When You the Flow'rs for CLOE twine,
Why do You to Her Garland join
The meanest Bud that falls from Mine?
Simplest of Swains! the World may see,
Whom CLOE loves, and Who loves Me.

The GARLAND.

I.

THE Pride of ev'ry Grove I chose,
    The Violet sweet, and Lilly fair,
The dappl'd Pink, and blushing Rose,
    To deck my charming CLOE's Hair.

II.

At Morn the Nymph vouchsaft to place
    Upon her Brow the various Wreath;
The Flow'rs less blooming than Her Face,
    The Scent less fragrant than Her Breath.

III.

The Flow'rs She wore along the Day:
    And ev'ry Nymph and Shepherd said,
That in her Hair they lookt more gay,
    Than glowing in their Native Bed.

IV.

Undrest at Evening, when She found
    Their Odours lost, their Colours past;
She chang'd her Look, and on the Ground
    Her Garland and her Eye She cast.

V.

That Eye dropt Sense distinct and clear,
    As any MUSE's Tongue cou'd speak;
When from it's Lid a pearly Tear
    Ran trickling down her beauteous Cheek.

VI.

Dissembling, what I knew too well,
    My Love, my Life, said I, explain
This Change of Humour: pr'ythee tell:
    That falling Tear—What does it mean?

73

VII.

She sigh'd ; She smil'd : and to the Flow'rs
  Pointing, the Lovely Moralist said :
See ! Friend, in some few fleeting Hours,
  See yonder, what a Change is made.

VIII.

Ah Me ! the blooming Pride of MAY,
  And That of Beauty are but One :
At Morn Both flourish bright and gay,
  Both fade at Evening, pale, and gone.

IX.

At Dawn poor STELLA danc'd and sung ;
  The am'rous Youth around Her bow'd :
At Night her fatal Knell was rung ;
  I saw, and kiss'd Her in her Shrowd.

X.

Such as She is, who dy'd to Day ;
  Such I, alas ! may be to Morrow :
Go, DAMON, bid Thy Muse display
  The Justice of thy CLOE's Sorrow.

The LADY *who offers her Looking-Glass to* VENUS.

VENUS, take my Votive Glass :
  Since I am not what I was ;
What from this Day I shall be,
VENUS, let Me never see.

CLOE JEALOUS.

I.

FORBEAR to ask Me, why I weep;
  Vext CLOE to her Shepherd said :
'Tis for my Two poor stragling Sheep
  Perhaps, or for my Squirrel dead.

II.

For mind I what You late have writ?
  Your subtle Questions, and Replies ;
Emblems, to teach a Female Wit
  The Ways, where changing CUPID flies.

III.

Your Riddle, purpos'd to rehearse
  The general Pow'r that Beauty has :
But why did no peculiar Verse
  Describe one Charm of CLOE's Face?

IV.

The Glass, which was at VENUS' Shrine,
  With such Mysterious Sorrow laid :
The Garland (and You call it Mine)
  Which show'd how Youth and Beauty fade.

V.

Ten thousand Trifles light as These
  Nor can my Rage, nor Anger move :
She shou'd be humble, who wou'd please :
  And She must suffer, who can love.

VI.

When in My Glass I chanc'd to look;
  Of VENUS what did I implore?
That ev'ry Grace which thence I took,
  Shou'd know to charm my DAMON more.

75

VII.

Reading Thy Verse ; who heeds, said I,
  If here or there his Glances flew ?
O free for ever be His Eye,
  Whose Heart to Me is always true.

VIII.

My Bloom indeed, my little Flow'r
  Of Beauty quickly lost it's Pride :
For sever'd from it's Native Bow'r,
  It on Thy glowing Bosom dy'd.

IX.

Yet car'd I not, what might presage
  Or withering Wreath, or fleeting Youth :
Love I esteem'd more strong than Age,
  And Time less permanent than Truth.

X.

Why then I weep, forbear to know :
  Fall uncontroll'd my Tears, and free :
O DAMON, 'tis the only Woe,
  I ever yet conceal'd from Thee.

[XI.]

The secret Wound with which I bleed
  Shall lie wrapt up, ev'n in my Herse :
But on my Tomb-stone Thou shalt read
  My Answer to Thy dubious Verse.

ANSWER to *CLOE* JEALOUS,

in the same STILE.

The AUTHOR *sick.*

I.

YES, fairest Proof of Beauty's Pow'r,
  Dear Idol of My panting Heart,
Nature points This my fatal Hour :
  And I have liv'd ; and We must part.

II.

While now I take my last Adieu,
　　Heave Thou no Sigh, nor shed a Tear;
Lest yet my half-clos'd Eye may view
　　On Earth an Object worth it's Care.

III.

From Jealousy's tormenting Strife
　　For ever be Thy Bosom free'd:
That nothing may disturb Thy Life,
　　Content I hasten to the Dead.

IV.

Yet when some better-fated Youth
　　Shall with his am'rous Parly move Thee;
Reflect One Moment on His Truth,
　　Who dying Thus, persists to love Thee.

A BETTER ANSWER.

I.

DEAR CLOE, how blubber'd is that pretty Face?
　　Thy Cheek all on Fire, and Thy Hair all uncurl'd:
Pr'ythee quit this Caprice; and (as old FALSTAF says)
　　Let Us e'en talk a little like Folks of This World.

II.

How can'st Thou presume, Thou hast leave to destroy
　　The Beauties, which VENUS but lent to Thy keeping?
Those Looks were design'd to inspire Love and Joy:
　　More ord'nary Eyes may serve People for weeping.

III.

To be vext at a Trifle or two that I writ,
　　Your Judgment at once, and my Passion You wrong:
You take that for Fact, which will scarce be found Wit:
　　Od's Life! must One swear to the Truth of a Song?

IV.

What I speak, my fair CLOE, and what I write, shews
　　The Diff'rence there is betwixt Nature and Art:
I court others in Verse; but I love Thee in Prose:
　　And They have my Whimsies; but Thou hast my Heart.

77

V.

The God of us Verse-men (You know Child) the Sun,
   How after his Journeys He sets up his Rest:
If at Morning o'er Earth 'tis his Fancy to run;
   At Night he reclines on his Thetis's Breast.

VI.

So when I am weary'd with wand'ring all Day;
   To Thee my Delight in the Evening I come:
No Matter what Beauties I saw in my Way:
   They were but my Visits; but Thou art my Home.

VII.

Then finish, Dear Cloe, this Pastoral War;
   And let us like Horace and Lydia agree:
For Thou art a Girl as much brighter than Her,
   As He was a Poet sublimer than Me.

PALLAS and *VENUS*.

AN

EPIGRAM.

THE Trojan Swain had judg'd the great Dispute;
   And Beauty's Pow'r obtain'd the Golden Fruit;
When Venus, loose in all Her naked Charms,
Met Jove's great Daughter clad in shining Arms.
The wanton Goddess view'd the Warlike Maid
From Head to Foot, and Tauntingly She said:

   Yield, Sister; Rival, yield; Naked, You see,
I vanquish: Guess how Potent I should be;
If to the Field I came in Armour drest;
Dreadful, like Thine, my Shield, and terrible my Crest.

   The Warrior Goddess with Disdain reply'd;
Thy Folly, Child, is equal to thy Pride:
Let a brave Enemy for once advise,
And Venus (if 'tis possible) be Wise.
Thou to be strong must put off every Dress:
Thy only Armour is thy Nakedness:
And more than once, (or Thou art much bely'd)
By Mars himself That Armour has been try'd.

TO A

Young Gentleman *in* Love.

A

TALE.

FROM publick Noise and factious Strife,
From all the busie Ills of Life,
Take me, My CELIA, to Thy Breast;
And lull my wearied Soul to Rest:
For ever, in this humble Cell,
Let Thee and I, my Fair One, dwell;
None enter else, but LOVE——and He
Shall bar the Door, and keep the Key.

To painted Roofs, and shining Spires
(Uneasie Seats of high Desires)
Let the unthinking Many croud,
That dare be Covetous and Proud:
In golden Bondage let Them wait,
And barter Happiness for State:
But Oh! My CELIA, when Thy Swain
Desires to see a Court again;
May Heav'n around This destin'd Head
The choicest of it's Curses shed:
To sum up all the Rage of Fate,
In the Two Things I dread and hate;
May'st Thou be False, and I be Great.

Thus, on his CELIA's panting Breast,
Fond CELADON his Soul exprest;
While with Delight the lovely Maid
Receiv'd the Vows, She thus repaid:

Hope of my Age, Joy of my Youth,
Blest Miracle of Love and Truth!
All that cou'd e'er be counted Mine,
My Love and Life long since are Thine:
A real Joy I never knew;
'Till I believ'd Thy Passion true:
A real Grief I ne'er can find;
'Till Thou prov'st Perjur'd or Unkind.
Contempt, and Poverty, and Care,
All we abhor, and all we fear,
Blest with Thy Presence, I can bear.
Thro' Waters, and thro' Flames I'll go,
Suff'rer and Solace of Thy Woe:
Trace Me some yet unheard-of Way,
That I Thy Ardour may repay;
And make My constant Passion known,
By more than Woman yet has done.

Had I a Wish that did not bear
The Stamp and Image of my Dear;
I'd pierce my Heart thro' ev'ry Vein,
And Die to let it out again.
No: VENUS shall my Witness be,
(If VENUS ever lov'd like Me)
That for one Hour I wou'd not quit
My Shepherd's Arms, and this Retreat,
To be the PERSIAN Monarch's Bride,
Part'ner of all his Pow'r and Pride;
Or Rule in Regal State above,
Mother of Gods, and Wife of JOVE.

O happy these of Human Race!
But soon, alas! our Pleasures pass.
He thank'd her on his bended Knee;
Then drank a Quart of Milk and Tea;
And leaving her ador'd Embrace,
Hasten'd to Court, to beg a Place.
While She, his Absence to bemoan,
The very Moment He was gone,
Call'd THYRSIS from beneath the Bed;
Where all this time He had been hid.

MORAL.

WHILE Men have these Ambitious Fancies ;
    And wanton Wenches read Romances ;
Our Sex will——What ? Out with it. Lye ;
And Their's in equal Strains reply.
The Moral of the Tale I sing
(A Posy for a Wedding Ring)
In this short Verse will be confin'd :
Love is a Jest ; and Vows are Wind.

AN

ENGLISH PADLOCK.

MISS DANAE, when Fair and Young
    (As HORACE has divinely sung)
Could not be kept from JOVE's Embrace
By Doors of Steel, and Walls of Brass.
The Reason of the Thing is clear ;
Would JOVE the naked Truth aver :
CUPID was with Him of the Party ;
And show'd himself sincere and hearty :
For, give That Whipster but his Errand ;
He takes my Lord Chief Justice' Warrant :
Dauntless as Death away He walks ;
Breaks the Doors open ; snaps the Locks ;
Searches the Parlour, Chamber, Study ;
Nor stops, 'till He has CULPRIT's Body.

Since This has been Authentick Truth,
By Age deliver'd down to Youth ;
Tell us, mistaken Husband, tell us,
Why so Mysterious, why so Jealous ?
Does the Restraint, the Bolt, the Bar
Make Us less Curious, Her less Fair ?

The Spy, which does this Treasure keep,
Does She ne'er say her Pray'rs, nor sleep?
Does She to no Excess incline?
Does She fly Musick, Mirth, and Wine?
Or have not Gold and Flatt'ry Pow'r,
To purchase One unguarded Hour?

Your Care does further yet extend:
That Spy is guarded by your Friend.——
But has This Friend nor Eye, nor Heart?
May He not feel the cruel Dart,
Which, soon or late, all Mortals feel?
May He not, with too tender Zeal,
Give the Fair Pris'ner Cause to see,
How much He wishes, She were free?
May He not craftily infer
The Rules of Friendship too severe,
Which chain Him to a hated Trust;
Which make Him Wretched, to be Just?
And may not She, this Darling She,
Youthful and healthy, Flesh and Blood,
Easie with Him, ill-us'd by Thee,
Allow this Logic to be good?

Sir, Will your Questions never end?
I trust to neither Spy nor Friend.
In short, I keep Her from the Sight
Of ev'ry Human Face.——She'll write.——
From Pen and Paper She's debarr'd.——
Has She a Bodkin and a Card?
She'll prick her Mind.——She will, You say:
But how shall She That Mind convey?
I keep Her in one Room: I lock it:
The Key (look here) is in this Pocket.
The Key-hole, is That left? Most certain.
She'll thrust her Letter thro'——Sir MARTIN.

Dear angry Friend, what must be done?
Is there no Way?——There is but One.
Send Her abroad; and let Her see,
That all this mingled Mass, which She

Being forbidden longs to know,
Is a dull Farce, an empty Show,
Powder, and Pocket-Glass, and Beau;
A Staple of Romance and Lies,
False Tears, and real Perjuries:
Where Sighs and Looks are bought and sold;
And Love is made but to be told:
Where the fat Bawd, and lavish Heir
The Spoils of ruin'd Beauty share:
And Youth seduc'd from Friends and Fame,
Must give up Age to Want and Shame.
Let Her behold the Frantick Scene,
The Women wretched, false the Men:
And when, these certain Ills to shun,
She would to Thy Embraces run;
Receive Her with extended Arms:
Seem more delighted with her Charms:
Wait on Her to the Park and Play:
Put on good Humour; make Her gay:
Be to her Virtues very kind:
Be to her Faults a little blind:
Let all her Ways be unconfin'd:
And clap your PADLOCK——on her Mind.

HANS CARVEL.

HANS CARVEL, Impotent and Old,
    Married a Lass of LONDON Mould:
Handsome? enough; extreamly Gay:
Lov'd Musick, Company, and Play:
High Flights She had, and Wit at Will:
And so her Tongue lay seldom still:
For in all Visits who but She,
To Argue, or to Repartée?

She made it plain, that Human Passion
Was order'd by Predestination;
That, if weak Women went astray,
Their Stars were more in Fault than They:

MATTHEW PRIOR

Whole Tragedies She had by Heart;
Enter'd into Roxana's Part:
To Triumph in her Rival's Blood,
The Action certainly was good.
How like a Vine young Ammon curl'd!
Oh that dear Conqu'ror of the World!
She pity'd Betterton in Age,
That ridicul'd the God-like Rage.

She, first of all the Town, was told,
Where newest India Things were sold:
So in a Morning, without Bodice,
Slipt sometimes out to Mrs. Thody's;
To cheapen Tea, to buy a Screen:
What else cou'd so much Virtue mean?
For to prevent the least Reproach,
Betty went with Her in the Coach.

But when no very great Affair
Excited her peculiar Care;
She without fail was wak'd at Ten;
Drank Chocolate, then slept again:
At Twelve She rose: with much ado
Her Cloaths were huddl'd on by Two:
Then; Does my Lady Dine at home?
Yes sure;——but is the Colonel come?
Next, how to spend the Afternoon,
And not come Home again too soon;
The Change, the City, or the Play,
As each was proper for the Day;
A Turn in Summer to Hyde-Park,
When it grew tolerably Dark.

Wife's Pleasure causes Husband's Pain:
Strange Fancies come in Hans's Brain:
He thought of what He did not name;
And wou'd reform; but durst not blame.
At first He therefore Preach'd his Wife
The Comforts of a Pious Life:
Told Her, how Transient Beauty was;
That All must die, and Flesh was Grass:

He bought Her Sermons, Psalms, and Graces;
And doubled down the useful Places.
But still the Weight of worldly Care
Allow'd Her little time for Pray'r:
And CLEOPATRA was read o'er,
While SCOT, and WAKE, and Twenty more,
That teach one to deny one's self,
Stood unmolested on the Shelf.
An untouch'd Bible grac'd her Toilet:
No fear that Thumb of Her's should spoil it.
In short, the Trade was still the same:
The Dame went out: the Colonel came.

What's to be done? poor CARVEL cry'd:
Another Batt'ry must be try'd:
What if to Spells I had Recourse?
'Tis but to hinder something Worse.
The End must justifie the Means:
He only Sins who Ill intends:
Since therefore 'tis to Combat Evil;
'Tis lawful to employ the Devil.

Forthwith the Devil did appear
(For name Him and He's always near)
Not in the Shape in which He plies
At Miss's Elbow when She lies;
Or stands before the Nurs'ry Doors,
To take the naughty Boy that roars:
But without Sawcer Eye or Claw,
Like a grave Barrister at Law.

HANS CARVEL, lay aside your Grief,
The Devil says: I bring Relief.
Relief, says HANS: pray let me crave
Your Name, Sir.——SATAN.——Sir, your Slave:
I did not look upon your Feet:
You'll pardon Me:——Ay, now I see't:
And pray, Sir, when came You from Hell?
Our Friends there, did You leave Them well?
All well: but pr'ythee, honest HANS,
(Says SATAN) leave your Complaisance:

85

MATTHEW PRIOR

The Truth is this : I cannot stay
Flaring in Sun-shine all the Day :
For, *entre Nous*, We Hellish Sprites,
Love more the Fresco of the Nights ;
And oft'ner our Receipts convey
In Dreams, than any other Way.
I tell You therefore as a Friend,
E'er Morning dawns, your Fears shall end :
Go then this Ev'ning, Master CARVEL,
Lay down your Fowls, and broach your Barrel ;
Let Friends and Wine dissolve your Care ;
Whilst I the great Receipt prepare :
To Night I'll bring it, by my Faith ;
Believe for once what SATAN saith.

Away went HANS : glad ? not a little ;
Obey'd the Devil to a Tittle ;
Invited Friends some half a Dozen,
The Colonel, and my Lady's Cousin.
The Meat was serv'd ; the Bowls were crown'd ;
Catches were sung ; and Healths went round :
Barbadoes Waters for the Close ;
'Till HANS had fairly got his Dose :
The Colonel toasted to the best :
The Dame mov'd off, to be undrest :
The Chimes went Twelve : the Guests withdrew :
But when, or how, HANS hardly knew.
Some Modern Anecdotes aver,
He nodded in his Elbow Chair ;
From thence was carry'd off to Bed :
JOHN held his Heels, and NAN his head.
My Lady was disturb'd : new Sorrow !
Which HANS must answer for to Morrow.

In Bed then view this happy Pair ;
And think how HYMEN Triumph'd there.
HANS, fast asleep, as soon as laid ;
The Duty of the Night unpaid :
The waking Dame, with Thoughts opprest,
That made Her Hate both Him and Rest :

By such a Husband, such a Wife!
'Twas ACME's and SEPTIMIUS' Life.
The Lady sigh'd: the Lover snor'd:
The punctual Devil kept his Word:
Appear'd to honest HANS again;
But not at all by Madam seen:
And giving Him a Magick Ring,
Fit for the Finger of a King;
Dear HANS, said He, this Jewel take,
And wear it long for SATAN's Sake:
'Twill do your Business to a Hair:
For long as You this Ring shall wear,
As sure as I look over LINCOLN,
That ne'er shall happen which You think on.

HANS took the Ring with Joy extream;
(All this was only in a Dream)
And thrusting it beyond his Joint,
'Tis done, He cry'd: I've gain'd my Point.——
What Point, said She, You ugly Beast?
You neither give Me Joy nor Rest:
'Tis done.——What's done, You drunken Bear?
You've thrust your Finger G——d knows where.

A Dutch *Proverb.*

FIRE, Water, Woman, are Man's Ruin;
  Says wise Professor VANDER BRÜIN.
By Flames a House I hir'd was lost
Last Year: and I must pay the Cost.
This Spring the Rains o'erflow'd my Ground:
And my best Flanders Mare was drown'd.
A Slave I am to CLARA's Eyes:
The Gipsey knows her Pow'r, and flies.
Fire, Water, Woman, are My Ruin:
And great Thy Wisdom, VANDER BRÜIN.

MATTHEW PRIOR

PAULO PURGANTI

AND

His WIFE:

An Honest, but a Simple Pair.

*Est enim quiddam, idque intelligitur in omni Virtute,
quod Deceat: quod Cogitatione magis à Virtute potest
quam Re separari.* Cic. de Officiis. Lib. 1.

BEYOND the fix'd and settl'd Rules
Of Vice and Virtue in the Schools,
Beyond the Letter of the Law,
Which keeps our Men and Maids in Awe,
The better Sort should set before 'em
A Grace, a Manner, a Decorum;
Something, that gives their Acts a Light;
Makes 'em not only just, but bright;
And sets 'em in that open Fame,
Which witty Malice cannot blame.

For 'tis in Life, as 'tis in Painting:
Much may be Right, yet much be Wanting:
From Lines drawn true, our Eye may trace
A Foot, a Knee, a Hand, a Face:
May justly own the Picture wrought
Exact to Rule, exempt from Fault:
Yet if the Colouring be not there,
The TITIAN Stroke, the GUIDO Air;
To nicest Judgment show the Piece;
At best 'twill only not displease:
It would not gain on JERSEY'S Eye:
BRADFORD would frown, and set it by.

Thus in the Picture of our Mind
The Action may be well design'd;
Guided by Law, and bound by Duty;
Yet want this *Je ne sçay quoy* of Beauty:
And tho' it's Error may be such,
As KNAGS and BURGESS cannot hit;
It yet may feel the nicer Touch
Of WICHERLEY's or CONGREVE's Wit.

What is this Talk? replies a Friend:
And where will this dry Moral end?
The Truth of what You here lay down
By some Example should be shown.——
With all my Heart,——for once;——read on.
An Honest, but a Simple Pair
(And Twenty other I forbear)
May serve to make this THESIS clear.

A Doctor of great Skill and Fame,
PAULO PURGANTI was his Name,
Had a good, comely, virtuous Wife:
No Woman led a better Life:
She to Intrigues was ev'n hard-hearted:
She chuckl'd when a Bawd was carted:
And thought the Nation ne'er wou'd thrive,
'Till all the Whores were burnt alive.

On marry'd Men, that dare be bad,
She thought no Mercy should be had;
They should be hang'd, or starv'd, or flead,
Or serv'd like ROMISH Priests in SWEDE.——
In short, all Lewdness She defy'd:
And stiff was her Parochial Pride.

Yet in an honest Way, the Dame
Was a great Lover of That same;
And could from Scripture take her Cue,
That Husbands should give Wives their Due.

Her Prudence did so justly steer
Between the Gay and the Severe,

That if in some Regards She chose
To curb poor PAULO in too close;
In others She relax'd again,
And govern'd with a looser Rein.

Thus tho' She strictly did confine
The Doctor from Excess of Wine;
With Oysters, Eggs, and Vermicelli
She let Him almost burst his Belly:
Thus drying Coffee was deny'd;
But Chocolate that Loss supply'd:
And for Tobacco (who could bear it?)
Filthy Concomitant of Claret!
(Blest Revolution!) one might see
Eringo Roots, and Bohé Tea.

She often set the Doctor's Band,
And strok'd his Beard, and squeez'd his Hand:
Kindly complain'd, that after Noon
He went to pore on Books too soon:
She held it wholesomer by much,
To rest a little on the Couch:——
About his Waste in Bed a-nights
She clung so close——for fear of Sprites.

The Doctor understood the Call;
But had not always wherewithal.

The Lion's Skin too short, you know,
(As PLUTARCH's Morals finely show)
Was lengthen'd by the Fox's Tail:
And Art supplies, where Strength may fail.

Unwilling then in Arms to meet
The Enemy, He could not beat;
He strove to lengthen the Campaign,
And save his Forces by Chicane.
FABIUS, the ROMAN Chief, who thus
By fair Retreat grew MAXIMUS,
Shows us, that all that Warrior can do
With Force inferior, is *Cunctando*.

One Day then, as the Foe drew near,
With Love, and Joy, and Life, and Dear;
Our Don, who knew this Tittle Tattle
Did, sure as Trumpet, call to Battel;
Thought it extreamly *à propos*,
To ward against the coming Blow:
To ward: but how? Ay, there's the Question:
Fierce the Assault, unarm'd the Bastion.

The Doctor feign'd a strange Surprise:
He felt her Pulse: he view'd her Eyes:
That beat too fast: These rowl'd too quick:
She was, He said, or would be Sick:
He judg'd it absolutely good,
That She should purge and cleanse her Blood.
SPAW Waters for that end were got:
If they past easily or not,
What matters it? the Lady's Feaver
Continu'd violent as ever.

For a Distemper of this Kind,
(BLACKMORE and HANS are of my Mind)
If once it youthful Blood infects,
And chiefly of the Female Sex;
Is scarce remov'd by Pill or Potion;
What-e'er might be our Doctor's Notion.

One luckless Night then, as in Bed
The Doctor and the Dame were laid;
Again this cruel Feaver came,
High Pulse, short Breath, and Blood in Flame.
What Measures shall poor PAULO keep
With Madam, in this piteous taking?
She, like MACBETH, has murder'd Sleep,
And won't allow Him Rest, tho' waking.
Sad State of Matters! when We dare
Nor ask for Peace, nor offer War:
Nor LIVY nor COMINES have shown,
What in this Juncture may be done.
GROTIUS might own, that PAULO's Case is
Harder, than any which He places
Amongst his BELLI and his PACIS.

MATTHEW PRIOR

He strove, alas! but strove in vain,
By dint of Logic to maintain,
That all the Sex was born to grieve,
Down to her Ladyship from EVE.
He rang'd his Tropes, and preach'd up Patience;
Back'd his Opinion with Quotations,
Divines and Moralists; and run ye on
Quite thro' from SENECA to BUNYAN.
As much in vain He bid Her try
To fold her Arms, to close her Eye;
Telling Her, Rest would do Her Good;
If any thing in Nature cou'd:
So held the GREEKS quite down from GALEN,
Masters and Princes of the Calling:
So all our Modern Friends maintain
(Tho' no great GREEKS) in WARWICK-LANE.

Reduce, my Muse, the wand'ring Song:
A Tale should never be too long.

The more He talk'd, the more She burn'd,
And sigh'd, and tost, and groan'd, and turn'd:
At last, I wish, said She, my Dear——
(And whisper'd something in his Ear.)
You wish! wish on, the Doctor cries:
Lord! when will Womankind be wise?
What, in your Waters? are You mad?
Why Poyson is not half so bad.
I'll do it——But I give You Warning:
You'll die before To-morrow Morning.——
'Tis kind, my Dear, what You advise;
The Lady with a Sigh replies:
But Life, You know, at best is Pain:
And Death is what We should disdain.
So do it therefore, and Adieu:
For I will die for Love of You:——
Let wanton Wives by Death be scar'd:
But, to my Comfort, I'm prepar'd.

THE

LADLE.

THE Sceptics think, 'twas long ago,
    Since Gods came down *Incognito*,
To see Who were Their Friends or Foes,
And how our Actions fell or rose :
That since They gave Things their Beginning ;
And set this Whirligig a Spinning ;
Supine They in their Heav'n remain,
Exempt from Passion, and from Pain :
And frankly leave us Human Elves,
To cut and shuffle for our selves :
To stand or walk, to rise or tumble,
As Matter, and as Motion jumble.

    The Poets now, and Painters hold
This *Thesis* both absurd and bold :
And your good-natur'd Gods, They say,
Descend some twice or thrice a-day :
Else all these Things We toil so hard in,
Would not avail one single Farthing :
For when the Hero We rehearse,
To grace His Actions, and Our Verse ;
'Tis not by dint of Human Thought,
That to his LATIUM He is brought :
IRIS descends by FATE's Commands,
To guide his Steps thro' Foreign Lands :
And AMPHITRITE clears his Way
From Rocks and Quick-sands in the Sea.

    And if You see Him in a Sketch ;
(Tho' drawn by PAULO or CARACHE)
He shows not half his Force and Strength,
Strutting in Armour, and at Length :

93

That He may make his proper Figure,
The Piece must yet be four Yards bigger:
The NYMPHS conduct Him to the Field:
One holds his Sword, and One his Shield:
MARS standing by asserts his Quarrel:
And FAME flies after with a Lawrel.

These Points, I say, of Speculation
(As 'twere to save or sink the Nation)
Men idly learned will dispute,
Assert, object, confirm, refute:
Each mighty angry, mighty right,
With equal Arms sustains the Fight;
'Till now no Umpire can agree 'em:
So both draw off, and sing *Te Deum*.

Is it in *Equilibrio*,
If Deities descend or no?
Then let th'Affirmative prevail,
As requisite to form my Tale:
For by all Parties 'tis confest,
That those Opinions are the best,
Which in their Nature most conduce
To present Ends, and private Use.

Two Gods came therefore from above,
One MERCURY, the t'other JOVE:
The Humour was (it seems) to know,
If all the Favours They bestow,
Could from our own Perverseness ease Us;
And if our Wish injoy'd would please Us.

Discoursing largely on this Theme,
O'er Hills and Dales Their Godships came;
'Till well nigh tir'd at almost Night,
They thought it proper to alight.

Note here, that it as true as odd is,
That in Disguise a God or Goddess
Exerts no supernat'ral Powers;
But acts on Maxims much like Ours.

They spy'd at last a Country Farm,
Where all was snug, and clean, and warm ;
For Woods before, and Hills behind
Secur'd it both from Rain and Wind :
Large Oxen in the Fields were lowing :
Good Grain was sow'd : good Fruit was growing :
Of last Year's Corn in Barns great Store ;
Fat Turkeys gobbling at the Door :
And Wealth (in short) with Peace consented,
That People here should live contented :
But did They in Effect do so ?
Have Patience, Friend ; and Thou shalt know.

The honest Farmer and his Wife,
To Years declin'd from Prime of Life,
Had struggl'd with the Marriage Noose ;
As almost ev'ry Couple does :
Sometimes, My Plague ! sometimes, My Darling !
Kissing to Day, to Morrow snarling ;
Jointly submitting to endure
That Evil, which admits no Cure.

Our Gods the outward Gate unbarr'd :
Our Farmer met 'em in the Yard ;
Thought They were Folks that lost their Way ;
And ask'd them civily to stay :
Told 'em, for Supper, or for Bed
They might go on, and be worse sped.——

So said, so done : the Gods consent :
All three into the Parlour went :
They complement : They sit : They chat ;
Fight o'er the Wars ; reform the State :
A thousand knotty Points They clear ;
Till Supper and my Wife appear.

Jove made his Leg, and kiss'd the Dame :
Obsequious Hermes did the same.
Jove kiss'd the Farmer's Wife, You say.
He did——but in an honest Way :
Oh ! not with half that Warmth and Life,
With which He kiss'd Amphitryon's Wife.——

95

MATTHEW PRIOR

Well then, Things handsomly were serv'd:
My Mistress for the Strangers carv'd.
How strong the Beer, how good the Meat,
How loud They laught, how much They eat,
In Epic sumptuous would appear;
Yet shall be pass'd in Silence here:
For I should grieve to have it said,
That by a fine Description led,
I made my Episode too long,
Or tir'd my Friend, to grace my Song.

The Grace-Cup serv'd, the Cloth away,
JOVE thought it time to show his Play:
Landlord and Landlady, He cry'd,
Folly and Jesting laid aside,
That Ye thus hospitably live,
And Strangers with good Chear receive,
Is mighty grateful to your Betters,
And makes ev'n Gods themselves your Debtors.
To give this *Thesis* plainer Proof,
You have to Night beneath your Roof
A Pair of Gods: (nay never wonder)
This Youth can Fly, and I can Thunder.
I'm JUPITER, and He MERCURIUS,
My Page, my Son indeed, but spurious.
Form then Three Wishes, You and Madam:
And sure, as You already had 'em,
The Things desir'd in half an Hour
Shall all be here, and in your Pow'r.

Thank Ye, great Gods, the Woman says:
Oh! may your Altars ever blaze.
A Ladle for our Silver Dish
Is what I want, is what I Wish.——
A Ladle! cries the Man, a Ladle!
'Odzooks, CORISCA, You have pray'd ill:
What should be Great, You turn to Farce:
I Wish the Ladle in your A——.

With equal Grief and Shame my Muse
The Sequel of the Tale pursues:
The Ladle fell into the Room,
And stuck in old CORISCA's Bum.
Our Couple weep Two Wishes past,
And kindly join to form the last,
To ease the Woman's aukward Pain,
And get the Ladle out again.

MORAL.

THIS Commoner has Worth and Parts,
   Is prais'd for Arms, or lov'd for Arts:
His Head achs for a Coronet:
And Who is Bless'd that is not Great?

Some Sense, and more Estate, kind Heav'n
To this well-lotted Peer has giv'n:
What then? He must have Rule and Sway:
And all is wrong, 'till He's in Play.

The Miser must make up his Plumb,
And dares not touch the hoarded Sum:
The sickly Dotard wants a Wife,
To draw off his last Dregs of Life.

Against our Peace We arm our Will:
Amidst our Plenty, *Something* still
For Horses, Houses, Pictures, Planting,
To Thee, to Me, to Him is wanting.
That cruel *Something* unpossess'd
Corrodes, and levens all the rest.
That *Something*, if We could obtain,
Would soon create a future Pain:
And to the Coffin, from the Cradle,
'Tis all a WISH, and all a LADLE.

MATTHEW PRIOR

Written at PARIS, 1700.
In the Beginning of
ROBE's GEOGRAPHY.

OF All that WILLIAM Rules, or ROBE
    Describes, Great RHEA, of Thy Globe;
When or on Post-Horse, or in Chaise,
With much Expence, and little Ease,
My destin'd Miles I shall have gone,
By THAMES or MAESE, by Po or RHONE,
And found no Foot of Earth my own;
GREAT MOTHER, let Me Once be able
To have a Garden, House, and Stable;
That I may Read, and Ride, and Plant,
Superior to Desire, or Want;
And as Health fails, and Years increase,
Sit down, and think, and die in Peace.
Oblige Thy Fav'rite Undertakers
To throw Me in but Twenty Acres:
This Number sure They may allow;
For Pasture Ten, and Ten for Plow:
'Tis all that I wou'd Wish, or Hope,
For ME, and JOHN, and NELL, and CROP.

Then, as Thou wil't, dispose the rest
(And let not FORTUNE spoil the Jest)
To Those, who at the Market-Rate
Can barter Honour for Estate.

Now if Thou grant'st Me my Request,
To make Thy Vot'ry truly blest,
Let curst Revenge, and sawcy Pride
To some bleak Rock far off be ty'd;
Nor e'er approach my Rural Seat,
To tempt Me to be Base, and Great.

98

And, GODDESS, This kind Office done,
Charge VENUS to command her Son,
(Where-ever else She lets Him rove)
To shun my House, and Field, and Grove:
Peace cannot dwell with Hate or Love.

Hear, gracious RHEA, what I say:
And Thy Petitioner shall Pray.

Written in the Beginning of

MEZERAY's

HISTORY of *FRANCE*.

I.

WHATE'ER thy Countrymen have done
By Law and Wit, by Sword and Gun,
In Thee is faithfully recited:
And all the Living World, that view
Thy Work, give Thee the Praises due,
At once Instructed and Delighted.

II.

Yet for the Fame of all these Deeds,
What Begger in the *Invalides*,
With Lameness broke, with Blindness smitten,
Wished ever decently to die,
To have been either MEZERAY,
Or any Monarch He has written?

III.

It strange, dear Author, yet it true is,
That down from PHARAMOND to LOÜIS,
All covet Life, yet call it Pain:
All feel the Ill, yet shun the Cure:
Can Sense this Paradox endure?
Resolve me, CAMBRAY, or FONTAINE.

G 2

IV.

The Man in graver Tragic known
(Tho' his best Part long since was done)
   Still on the Stage desires to tarry :
And He who play'd the *Harlequin*,
After the Jest still loads the Scene,
   Unwilling to retire, tho' Weary.

Written in the
Nouveaux Interests des Princes
*de l'*Europe.

B LEST be the Princes, who have fought
   For Pompous Names, or wide Dominion ;
Since by Their Error We are taught,
   That Happiness is but Opinion.

ADRIANI MORIENTIS
AD
Animam Suam.

A NIMULA, vagula, blandula,
   Hospes, Comesque Corporis,
Quæ nunc abibis in loca,
Pallidula, rigida, nudula?
Nec, ut soles, dabis joca.

By Monsieur Fontenelle.

M A petite Ame, ma Mignonne,
   Tu t'en vas donc, ma Fille, & Dieu sçaçhe où Tu vas :
Tu pars seulette, nuë, & tremblotante, Helas !
Que deviendra ton humeur folichonne?
Que deviendront tant de jolis ébats?

IMITATED.

POOR little, pretty, flutt'ring Thing,
  Must We no longer live together?
And dost Thou prune thy trembling Wing,
  To take thy Flight Thou know'st not whither?

Thy humorous Vein, thy pleasing Folly
  Lyes all neglected, all forgot:
And pensive, wav'ring, melancholy,
  Thou dread'st and hop'st Thou know'st not what.

A PASSAGE in the

MORIÆ ENCOMIUM

of ERASMUS Imitated.

IN awful Pomp, and Melancholy State,
  See settl'd REASON on the Judgment Seat:
Around Her croud DISTRUST, and DOUBT, and FEAR,
And thoughtful FORESIGHT, and tormenting CARE:
Far from the Throne, the trembling PLEASURES stand,
Chain'd up, or Exil'd by her stern Command.
Wretched her Subjects, gloomy sits the Queen;
'Till happy CHANCE reverts the cruel Scene:
And apish FOLLY with her wild Resort
Of Wit and Jest disturbs the solemn Court.

  See the fantastic Minstrelsy advance,
To breathe the Song, and animate the Dance.
Blest the Usurper! happy the Surprize!
Her Mimic Postures catch our eager Eyes:
Her Jingling Bells affect our captive Ear:
And in the Sights We see, and Sounds We hear.
Against our Judgment She our Sense employs:
The Laws of troubl'd REASON She destroys:
And in Their Place rejoyces to indite
Wild Schemes of Mirth, and Plans of loose Delight.

101

MATTHEW PRIOR

TO

Dr. *SHERLOCK*,

ON HIS

PRACTICAL DISCOURSE

Concerning DEATH.

FORGIVE the Muse, who in unhallow'd Strains
The Saint one Moment from his GOD detains:
For sure, whate'er You do, where-e'er You are,
'Tis all but one good Work, one constant Pray'r:
Forgive Her; and intreat That GOD, to Whom
Thy favour'd Vows with kind Acceptance come,
To raise her Notes to that sublime Degree,
Which suits a Song of Piety and Thee.

Wond'rous good Man! whose Labours may repel
The Force of Sin, may stop the Rage of Hell:
Thou, like the BAPTIST, from thy GOD wast sent
The crying Voice, to bid the World repent.

Thee YOUTH shall study; and no more engage
Their flatt'ring Wishes for uncertain AGE;
No more with fruitless Care, and cheated Strife
Chace fleeting Pleasure thro' this Maze of Life;
Finding the wretched All They here can have,
But present Food, and but a future Grave:
Each, great as PHILIP's Victor Son, shall view
This abject World, and weeping, ask a New.

Decrepit AGE shall read Thee, and confess,
Thy Labours can asswage, where Med'cines cease:
Shall bless thy Words, their wounded Souls Relief,
The Drops that sweeten their last Dregs of Life:
Shall look to Heav'n, and laugh at all beneath;
Own Riches gather'd, Trouble; Fame, a Breath;
And LIFE an Ill, whose only Cure is DEATH.

Thy even Thoughts with so much Plainness flow;
Their Sense untutor'd INFANCY may know:

Yet to such height is all That Plainness wrought;
WIT may admire, and letter'd PRIDE be taught:
Easie in Words thy Style, in Sense sublime:
  On it's blest Steps each Age and Sex may rise:
'Tis like the Ladder in the PATRIARCH's Dream,
  It's Foot on Earth, it's Height above the Skies.
Diffus'd it's Virtue, boundless is it's Pow'r:
'Tis Publick Health, and Universal Cure:
Of Heav'nly MANNA, 'tis a second Feast,
A Nation's Food, and All to ev'ry Taste.

  To it's last Height mad BRITAIN's Guilt was rear'd:
And various DEATH for various Crimes She fear'd:
With your kind Work her drooping Hopes revive:
You bid Her read, repent, adore, and live:
You wrest the Bolt from Heav'ns avenging Hand;
Stop ready DEATH, and save a sinking Land.

  O! save Us still; still bless Us with thy Stay:
O! want thy Heav'n, 'till We have learnt the Way:
Refuse to leave thy destin'd Charge too soon:
And for the Church's Good, defer thy own.
O! live; and let thy Works urge our Belief;
Live to explain thy Doctrine by thy Life;
'Till future INFANCY, baptiz'd by Thee,
Grow ripe in Years, and old in Piety;
'Till CHRISTIANS, yet unborn, be taught to die.

  Then in full Age, and hoary Holiness
Retire, great Teacher, to thy promis'd Bliss:
Untouch'd thy Tomb, uninjur'd be thy Dust,
As thy own Fame among the future Just;
'Till in last Sounds the dreadful Trumpet speaks:
'Till JUDGMENT calls; and quick'ned NATURE wakes:
'Till thro' the utmost Earth, and deepest Sea
Our scatter'd ATOMS find their destin'd Way,
In haste to cloath their Kindred Souls again;
Perfect our State, and build immortal Man:
Then fearless Thou, who well sustain'dst the Fight,
To Paths of Joy, and Tracts of endless Light
Lead up all those who heard Thee, and believ'd:
'Midst thy own Flock, great Shepherd, be receiv'd;
And glad all Heav'n with Millions Thou hast sav'd.

MATTHEW PRIOR

CARMEN SECULARE,

For the Year 1700.

TO THE

KING.

Aspice, venturo lætentur ut Omnia Sæc'lo :
O mihi tam longæ maneat pars ultima vitæ,
Spiritus & quantum sat erit tua dicere faƐta !

Virg. Eclog. 4.

I.

THY elder Look, Great JANUS, cast
  Into the long Records of Ages past :
Review the Years in fairest AƐion drest
With noted White, Superior to the rest ;
ÆRA's deriv'd, and Chronicles begun
From Empires founded, and from Battels won :
Show all the Spoils by valiant Kings achiev'd,
And groaning Nations by Their Arms reliev'd ;
The Wounds of Patriots in their Country's Cause,
And happy Pow'r sustain'd by wholesom Laws :
In comely Rank call ev'ry Merit forth :
Imprint on ev'ry AƐ it's Standard Worth :
The glorious Parallels then downward bring
To Modern Wonders, and to BRITAIN's King :
With equal Justice and Historic Care
Their Laws, Their Toils, Their Arms with His compare :
Confess the various Attributes of Fame
ColleƐed and compleat in WILLIAM's Name :
  To all the list'ning World relate
    (As Thou dost His Story read)
  That nothing went before so Great,
    And nothing Greater can succeed.

II.

Thy Native LATIUM was Thy darling Care,
Prudent in Peace, and terrible in War :
The boldest Virtues that have govern'd Earth
From LATIUM's fruitful Womb derive their Birth.
　　Then turn to Her fair-written Page :
From dawning Childhood to establish'd Age,
　　The Glories of Her Empire trace :
Confront the Heroes of Thy ROMAN Race :
And let the justest Palm the Victor's Temples grace.

III.

The Son of MARS reduc'd the trembling Swains,
And spread His Empire o'er the distant Plains :
But yet the SABINS violated Charms
Obscur'd the Glory of His rising Arms.
NUMA the Rights of strict Religion knew ;
On ev'ry Altar laid the Incense due ;
　　Unskill'd to dart the pointed Spear,
Or lead the forward Youth to noble War.
Stern BRUTUS was with too much Horror good,
Holding his *Fasces* stain'd with Filial Blood.
FABIUS was Wise, but with Excess of Care ;
He sav'd his Country ; but prolonged the War :
While DECIUS, PAULUS, CURIUS greatly fought ;
　　And by Their strict Examples taught,
　　How wild Desires should be controll'd ;
And how much brighter Virtue was, than Gold ;
They scarce Their swelling Thirst of Fame could hide ;
And boasted Poverty with too much Pride.
Excess in Youth made SCIPIO less rever'd :
And CATO dying seem'd to own, He fear'd.
JULIUS with Honor tam'd ROME's foreign Foes :
But Patriots fell, e'er the Dictator rose.
And while with Clemency AUGUSTUS reign'd ;
The Monarch was ador'd ; the City chain'd.

IV.

With justest Honour be Their Merits drest :
　　But be Their Failings too confest :

Their Virtue, like their TYBER's Flood
Rolling, it's Course design'd the Country's Good :
But oft the Torrent's too impetuous Speed
From the low Earth tore some polluting Weed :
And with the Blood of JOVE there always ran
Some viler Part, some Tincture of the Man.

V.

Few Virtues after These so far prevail,
But that Their Vices more than turn the Scale :
Valour grown wild by Pride, and Pow'r by Rage,
Did the true Charms of Majesty impair :
ROME by Degrees advancing more in Age,
Show'd sad Remains of what had once been fair;
'Till Heav'n a better Race of Men supplies;
And Glory shoots new Beams from Western Skies.

VI.

Turn then to PHARAMOND, and CHARLEMAIN,
And the long Heroes of the GALLIC Strain;
Experienc'd Chiefs, for hardy Prowess known,
And bloody Wreaths in vent'rous Battels won.
From the First WILLIAM, our great NORMAN King,
The bold PLANTAGENETS, and TUDORS bring;
Illustrious Virtues, who by turns have rose,
In foreign Fields to check BRITANNIA's Foes;
With happy Laws Her Empire to sustain,
And with full Pow'r assert Her ambient Main :
But sometimes too Industrious to be Great,
Nor Patient to expect the Turns of Fate,
They open'd Camps deform'd by Civil Fight,
And made proud Conquest trample over Right :
Disparted BRITAIN mourn'd Their doubtful Sway,
And dreaded Both, when Neither would obey.

VII.

From DIDIER, and Imperial ADOLPH trace
The Glorious Offspring of the NASSAW Race,
Devoted Lives to Publick Liberty;
The Chief still dying, or the Country free.

Then see the Kindred Blood of ORANGE flow,
From warlike CORNET, thro' the Loins of BEAU;
Thro' CHALON next; and there with NASSAW join,
From RHONE's fair Banks transplanted to the RHINE.
Bring next the Royal List of STUARTS forth,
Undaunted Minds, that rul'd the rugged North;
'Till Heav'n's Decrees by rip'ning Times are shown;
'Till SCOTLAND's Kings ascend the ENGLISH Throne;
And the fair Rivals live for ever One.

VIII.

   JANUS, mighty Deity,
  Be kind; and as Thy searching Eye
  Does our Modern Story trace,
  Finding some of STUART's Race
  Unhappy, pass Their Annals by:
No harsh Reflection let Remembrance raise:
Forbear to mention, what Thou canst not praise:
But as Thou dwell'st upon that Heav'nly *Name,
  To Grief for ever Sacred, as to Fame,
Oh! read it to Thy self; in Silence weep;
And Thy convulsive Sorrows inward keep;
Lest BRITAIN's Grief should waken at the Sound;
And Blood gush fresh from Her eternal Wound.

IX.

   Whither would'st Thou further look?
Read WILLIAM's Acts, and close the ample Book:
Peruse the Wonders of His dawning Life;
  How, like ALCIDES, He began;
With Infant Patience calm'd Seditious Strife,
And quell'd the Snakes which round his Cradle ran.

X.

   Describe His Youth, attentive to Alarms,
By Dangers form'd, and perfected in Arms:
When Conqu'ring, mild; when Conquer'd, not disgrac'd;
By Wrongs not lessen'd, nor by Triumphs rais'd:

      * *MARY.*

Superior to the blind Events
Of little Human Accidents;
And constant to His first Decree,
To curb the Proud, to set the Injur'd free;
To bow the haughty Neck, and raise the suppliant Knee.

XI.

His opening Years to riper Manhood bring;
And see the Hero perfect in the King:
Imperious Arms by Manly Reason sway'd,
And Power Supreme by free Consent obey'd:
With how much Haste His Mercy meets his Foes:
And how unbounded His Forgiveness flows:
With what Desire He makes His Subjects bless'd,
His Favours granted ere His Throne address'd:
What Trophies o'er our captiv'd Hearts He rears,
By Arts of Peace more potent, than by Wars:
How o'er Himself, as o'er the World, He Reigns,
His Morals strength'ning, what His Law ordains.

XII.

Thro' all His Thread of Life already spun,
Becoming Grace and proper Action run:
The Piece by VIRTUE's equal Hand is wrought,
Mix'd with no Crime, and shaded with no Fault:
    No Footsteps of the Victor's Rage
Left in the Camp, where WILLIAM did engage:
    No Tincture of the Monarch's Pride
    Upon the Royal Purple spy'd:
    His Fame, like Gold, the more 'tis try'd,
The more shall its intrinsic Worth proclaim;
Shall pass the Combat of the searching Flame,
    And triumph o'er the vanquish'd Heat,
        For ever coming out the same,
And losing nor it's Lustre, nor it's Weight.

XIII.

    JANUS be to WILLIAM just;
To faithful HISTORY His Actions trust:
    Command Her, with peculiar Care
To trace each Toil, and comment ev'ry War:

His saving Wonders bid Her write
In Characters distinctly bright;
That each revolving Age may read
The Patriot's Piety, the Hero's Deed:
And still the Sire inculcate to his Son
Transmissive Lessons of the King's Renown:
  That WILLIAM's Glory still may live;
  When all that present Art can give,
The Pillar'd Marble, and the Tablet Brass,
  Mould'ring, drop the Victor's Praise:
  When the great Monuments of His Pow'r
  Shall now be visible no more:
When SAMBRE shall have chang'd her winding Flood;
  And Children ask, where NAMUR stood.

XIV.

NAMUR, proud City, how her Towr's were arm'd!
  How She contemn'd th'approaching Foe!
'Till She by WILLIAM's Trumpets was allarm'd,
And shook, and sunk, and fell beneath His Blow.
    JOVE and PALLAS, mighty Pow'rs,
Guided the Hero to the hostile Tow'rs.
  PERSEUS seem'd less swift in War,
  When, wing'd with Speed, he flew thro' Air.
  Embattl'd Nations strive in vain
  The Hero's Glory to restrain:
Streams arm'd with Rocks, and Mountains red with Fire
  In vain against His Force conspire.
Behold Him from the dreadful Height appear!
And lo! BRITANNIA's Lions waving there.

XV.

  EUROPE freed, and FRANCE repell'd
  The Hero from the Height beheld:
He spake the Word, that War and Rage should cease:
He bid the MAESE and RHINE in Safety flow;
  And dictated a lasting Peace
  To the rejoicing World below:
To rescu'd States, and vindicated Crowns
His Equal Hand prescrib'd their ancient Bounds;

Ordain'd whom ev'ry Province should obey;
How far each Monarch should extend His Sway:
Taught 'em how Clemency made Pow'r rever'd;
And that the Prince Belov'd was truly Fear'd.
Firm by His Side unspotted HONOUR stood,
Pleas'd to confess Him not so Great as Good:
His Head with brighter Beams fair VIRTUE deck't,
Than Those which all His num'rous Crowns reflect:
Establish'd FREEDOM clap'd her joyful Wings;
Proclaim'd the First of Men, and Best of Kings.

XVI.

Whither would the Muse aspire
With PINDAR's Rage without his Fire?
Pardon me, JANUS, 'twas a Fault,
Created by too great a Thought:
Mindless of the God and Day,
I from thy Altars, JANUS, stray,
From Thee, and from My self born far away.
The fiery PEGASUS disdains
To mind the Rider's Voice, or hear the Reins:
When glorious Fields and opening Camps He views;
He runs with an unbounded Loose:
Hardly the Muse can sit the headstrong Horse:
Nor would She, if She could, check his impetuous Force:
With the glad Noise the Cliffs and Vallies ring;
While She thro' Earth and Air pursues the King.

XVII.

She now beholds Him on the BELGIC Shoar;
Whilst BRITAIN's Tears His ready Help implore,
Dissembling for Her sake his rising Cares,
And with wise Silence pond'ring vengeful Wars.
She thro' the raging Ocean now
Views Him advancing his auspicious Prow;
Combating adverse Winds and Winter Seas,
Sighing the Moments that defer Our Ease;
Daring to wield the Scepter's dang'rous Weight,
And taking the Command, to save the State:
Tho' e'er the doubtful Gift can be secur'd,
New Wars must be sustain'd, new Wounds endur'd.

XVIII.

Thro' rough IERNE's Camp She sounds Alarms,
And Kingdoms yet to be redeem'd by Arms;
In the dank Marshes finds her glorious Theme;
And plunges after Him thro' BOYN's fierce Stream.
She bids the NEREIDS run with trembling Haste,
To tell old OCEAN how the Hero past.
The God rebukes their Fear, and owns the Praise
Worthy that Arm, Whose Empire He obeys.

XIX.

Back to His ALBION She delights to bring
The humblest Victor, and the kindest King.
ALBION, with open Triumph would receive
    Her Hero, nor obtains His Leave:
Firm He rejects the Altars She would raise;
And thanks the Zeal, while He declines the Praise.
Again She follows Him thro' BELGIA's Land,
And Countries often sav'd by WILLIAM's Hand;
Hears joyful Nations bless those happy Toils,
Which freed the People, but return'd the Spoils.
In various Views She tries her constant Theme;
Finds Him in Councils, and in Arms the Same:
When certain to o'ercome, inclin'd to save,
Tardy to Vengeance, and with Mercy, Brave.

XX.

Sudden another Scene employs her Sight:
She sets her Hero in another Light:
Paints His great Mind Superior to Success,
Declining Conquest, to establish Peace:
She brings ASTREA down to Earth again,
And Quiet, brooding o'er His future Reign.

XXI.

Then with unweary'd Wing the Goddess soars
East, over DANUBE and PROPONTIS Shoars;
Where jarring Empires ready to engage,
Retard their Armies, and suspend their Rage;

'Till WILLIAM's Word, like That of Fate, declares,
If They shall study Peace, or lengthen Wars.
How sacred His Renown for equal Laws,
To whom the World defers it's Common Cause!
How fair His Friendships, and His Leagues how just,
Whom ev'ry Nation courts, Whom all Religions trust!

XXII.

From the MÆOTIS to the Northern Sea,
  The Goddess wings her desp'rate Way;
Sees the young MUSCOVITE, the mighty Head,
Whose Sov'reign Terror forty Nations dread,
Inamour'd with a greater Monarch's Praise,
And passing half the Earth to His Embrace:
She in His Rule beholds His VOLGA's Force,
O'er Precipices, with impetuous Sway
Breaking, and as He rowls his rapid Course,
Drowning, or bearing down, whatever meets his Way.
But her own King She likens to His THAMES,
With gentle Course devolving fruitful Streams:
Serene yet Strong, Majestic yet Sedate,
Swift without Violence, without Terror Great.
Each ardent Nymph the rising Current craves:
Each Shepherd's Pray'r retards the parting Waves:
The Vales along the Bank their Sweets disclose:
Fresh Flow'rs for ever rise: and fruitful Harvest grows.

XXIII.

Yet whither would th'advent'rous Goddess go?
Sees She not Clouds, and Earth, and Main below?
Minds She the Dangers of the LYCIAN Coast,
And Fields, where mad BELEROPHON was lost?
  Or is Her tow'ring Flight reclaim'd
By Seas from ICARUS's Downfall nam'd?
Vain is the Call, and useless the Advice:
To wise Perswasion Deaf, and human Cries,
  Yet upward She incessant flies;
Resolv'd to reach the high Empyrean Sphere,
And tell Great JOVE, She sings His Image here;

To ask for WILLIAM an Olympic Crown,
To CHROMIUS' Strength, and THERON'S Speed unknown :
Till lost in trackless Fields of shining Day,
   Unable to discern the Way
Which NASSAW's Virtue only could explore,
Untouch'd, unknown, to any Muse before,
She, from the noble Precipices thrown,
Comes rushing with uncommon Ruin down.
   Glorious Attempt ! Unhappy Fate !
The Song too daring, and the Theme too great !
   Yet rather thus She wills to die,
Than in continu'd Annals live, to sing
A second Heroe, or a vulgar King ;
   And with ignoble Safety fly
In sight of Earth, along a middle Sky.

XXIV.

To JANUS' Altars, and the numerous Throng,
   That round his mystic Temple press,
   For WILLIAM's Life, and ALBION'S Peace,
Ambitious Muse reduce the roving Song.
   JANUS, cast Thy forward Eye
Future, into great RHEA's pregnant Womb ;
   Where young Ideas brooding lye,
And tender Images of Things to come :
   'Till by Thy high Commands releas'd ;
'Till by Thy Hand in proper Atoms dress'd,
In decent Order They advance to Light ;
Yet then too swiftly fleet by human Sight ;
And meditate too soon their everlasting Flight.

XXV.

Nor Beaks of Ships in Naval Triumph born,
Nor Standards from the hostile Ramparts torn,
   Nor Trophies brought from Battles won,
Nor Oaken Wreath, nor Mural Crown
   Can any future Honours give
   To the Victorious Monarch's Name :
   The Plenitude of WILLIAM's Fame
Can no accumulated Stores receive.

MATTHEW PRIOR

Shut then, auspicious God, Thy Sacred Gate,
And make Us Happy, as our King is Great.
  Be kind, and with a milder Hand,
Closing the Volume of the finish'd Age,
   (Tho' Noble, 'twas an Iron Page)
  A more delightful Leaf expand,
Free from Alarms, and fierce BELLONA's Rage:
Bid the great Months begin their joyful Round,
By FLORA some, and some by CERES Crown'd:
Teach the glad Hours to scatter, as they fly,
Soft Quiet, gentle Love, and endless Joy:
Lead forth the Years for Peace and Plenty fam'd,
From SATURN's Rule, and better Metal nam'd.

XXVI.

Secure by WILLIAM's Care let BRITAIN stand;
  Nor dread the bold Invader's Hand:
From adverse Shoars in Safety let Her hear
Foreign Calamity, and distant War;
Of which let Her, great Heav'n, no Portion bear.
Betwixt the Nations let Her hold the Scale;
And as She wills, let either Part prevail:
Let her glad Vallies smile with wavy Corn:
Let fleecy Flocks her rising Hills adorn:
Around her Coast let strong Defence be spread:
Let fair Abundance on her Breast be shed:
And Heav'nly Sweets bloom round the Goddess' Head.

XXVII.

Where the white Towers and ancient Roofs did stand,
Remains of WOLSEY's or great HENRY's Hand,
To Age now yielding, or devour'd by Flame;
Let a young PHENIX raise her tow'ring Head:
Her Wings with lengthen'd Honour let Her spread;
And by her Greatness show her Builder's Fame.
August and Open, as the Hero's Mind,
  Be her capacious Courts design'd:
  Let ev'ry Sacred Pillar bear
Trophies of Arms, and Monuments of War.

The King shall there in PARIAN Marble breath,
His Shoulder bleeding fresh : and at His Feet
   Disarm'd shall lye the threat'ning DEATH :
(For so was saving JOVE's Decree compleat.)
Behind, That Angel shall be plac'd, whose Shield
   Sav'd EUROPE, in the Blow repell'd :
On the firm Basis, from his Oozy Bed
   BOYN shall raise his Laurell'd Head ;
   And his Immortal Stream be known,
Artfully waving thro' the wounded Stone.

XXVIII.

And Thou, Imperial WINDSOR, stand inlarg'd,
   With all the Monarch's Trophies charg'd :
Thou, the fair Heav'n, that dost the Stars inclose,
Which WILLIAM's Bosom wears, or Hand bestows
On the great Champions who support his Throne,
   And Virtues nearest to His own.

XXIX.

Round ORMOND's Knee Thou ty'st the Mystic String,
That makes the Knight Companion to the King.
From glorious Camps return'd, and foreign Feilds,
Bowing before thy sainted Warrior's Shrine,
Fast by his great Forefather's Coats, and Shields
Blazon'd from BOHUN's, or from BUTLER's Line,
He hangs His Arms ; nor fears those Arms should shine
With an unequal Ray ; or that His Deed
   With paler Glory should recede,
Eclips'd by Theirs ; or lessen'd by the Fame
Ev'n of His own Maternal NASSAW's Name.

XXX.

Thou smiling see'st great DORSET's Worth confest,
The Ray distinguishing the Patriot's Breast :
Born to protect and love, to help and please ;
Sov'reign of Wit, and Ornament of Peace.
O ! long as Breath informs this fleeting Frame,
Ne'er let me pass in Silence DORSET's Name ;
Ne'er cease to mention the continu'd Debt,
Which the great Patron only would forget,
And Duty, long as Life, must study to acquit.

XXXI.

Renown'd in Thy Records shall CA'NDISH stand,
Asserting Legal Pow'r, and just Command:
To the great House thy Favour shall be shown,
The Father's Star transmissive to the Son.
From Thee the TALBOT's and the SEYMOUR's Race
Inform'd, Their Sire's immortal Steps shall trace:
Happy may their Sons receive
The bright Reward, which Thou alone canst give.

XXXII.

And if a God these lucky Numbers guide;
If sure APOLLO o'er the Verse preside;
JERSEY, belov'd by all (For all must feel
    The Influence of a Form and Mind,
Where comely Grace and constant Virtue dwell,
Like mingl'd Streams, more forcible when join'd.)
    JERSEY shall at Thy Altars stand;
    Shall there receive the Azure Band,
That fairest Mark of Favour and of Fame,
    Familiar to the VILIER's Name.

XXXIII.

Science to raise, and Knowledge to enlarge,
    Be our great Master's future Charge;
To write His own Memoirs, and leave His Heirs
High Schemes of Government, and Plans of Wars;
By fair Rewards our Noble Youth to raise
To emulous Merit, and to Thirst of Praise;
To lead Them out from Ease e'er opening Dawn,
Through the thick Forest and the distant Lawn,
Where the fleet Stag employs their ardent Care;
And Chases give Them Images of War.
To teach Them Vigilance by false Alarms;
Inure Them in feign'd Camps to real Arms;
Practise Them now to curb the turning Steed,
Mocking the Foe; now to his rapid Speed
To give the Rein; and in the full Career,
To draw the certain Sword, or send the pointed Spear.

XXXIV.

Let Him unite His Subjects Hearts,
Planting Societies for peaceful Arts;
Some that in Nature shall true Knowledge found,
And by Experiment make Precept sound;
Some that to Morals shall recal the Age,
And purge from vitious Dross the sinking Stage;
Some that with Care true Eloquence shall teach,
And to just Idioms fix our doubtful Speech:
That from our Writers distant Realms may know,
   The Thanks We to our Monarch owe;
And Schools profess our Tongue through ev'ry Land,
That has invok'd His Aid, or blest His Hand.

XXXV.

Let His high Pow'r the drooping MUSES rear.
The MUSES only can reward His Care:
'Tis They that guard the great ATRIDES' Spoils:
'Tis They that still renew ULYSSES' Toils:
To Them by smiling JOVE 'twas giv'n, to save
Distinguish'd Patriots from the Common Grave;
To them, Great WILLIAM's Glory to recal,
When Statues moulder, and when Arches fall.
Nor let the MUSES, with ungrateful Pride,
   The Sources of their Treasure hide:
The Heroe's Virtue does the String inspire,
When with big Joy They strike the living Lyre:
   On WILLIAM's Fame their Fate depends:
With Him the Song begins: with Him it ends.
   From the bright Effluence of His Deed
   They borrow that reflected Light,
   With which the lasting Lamp They feed,
Whose Beams dispel the Damps of envious Night.

XXXVI.

Through various Climes, and to each distant Pole
In happy Tides let active Commerce rowl:
Let BRITAIN's Ships export an Annual Fleece,
Richer than ARGOS brought to ancient GREECE;

117

Returning loaden with the shining Stores,
Which lye profuse on either INDIA's Shores.
As our high Vessels pass their wat'ry Way,
Let all the Naval World due Homage pay;
With hasty Reverence their Top-Honours lower,
　　Confessing the asserted Power,
To Whom by Fate 'twas given, with happy Sway
To calm the Earth, and vindicate the Sea.

XXXVII.

Our Pray'rs are heard, our Master's Fleets shall go,
As far as Winds can bear, or Waters flow,
New Lands to make, new INDIES to explore,
In Worlds unknown to plant BRITANNIA's Power;
Nations yet wild by Precept to reclaim,
And teach 'em Arms, and Arts, in WILLIAM's Name.

XXXVIII.

With humble Joy, and with respectful Fear
The list'ning People shall His Story hear,
The Wounds He bore, the Dangers He sustain'd,
How far he Conquer'd, and how well he Reign'd;
Shall own his Mercy equal to His Fame;
And form their Children's Accents to His Name,
Enquiring how, and when from Heav'n He came.
Their Regal Tyrants shall with Blushes hide
Their little Lusts of Arbitrary Pride,
　　Nor bear to see their Vassals ty'd:
When WILLIAM's Virtues raise their opening Thought,
His forty Years for Publick Freedom fought,
　　EUROPE by His Hand sustain'd,
　　His Conquest by His Piety restrain'd,
And o'er Himself the last great Triumph gain'd.

XXXIX.

No longer shall their wretched Zeal adore
　　Ideas of destructive Power,
Spirits that hurt, and Godheads that devour:
New Incense They shall bring, new Altars raise,
And fill their Temples with a Stranger's Praise;

When the Great Father's Character They find
Visibly stampt upon the Hero's Mind;
And own a present Deity confest,
In Valour that preserv'd, and Power that bless'd.

XL.

Through the large Convex of the Azure Sky
(For thither Nature casts our common Eye)
Fierce Meteors shoot their arbitrary Light;
And Comets march with lawless Horror bright:
These hear no Rule, no righteous Order own;
Their Influence dreaded, as their Ways unknown:
Thro' threaten'd Lands They wild Destruction throw;
'Till ardent Prayer averts the Public Woe:
But the bright Orb that blesses all above,
The sacred Fire, the real Son of JOVE,
Rules not His Actions by Capricious Will;
Nor by ungovern'd Power declines to Ill:
Fix'd by just Laws He goes for ever right:
Man knows His Course, and thence adores His Light.

XLI.

O JANUS! would intreated Fate conspire
To grant what BRITAIN's Wishes could require;
Above, That Sun should cease his Way to go,
E'er WILLIAM cease to rule, and bless below:
　　But a relentless Destiny
　　Urges all that e'er was born:
Snatch'd from her Arms, BRITANNIA once must mourn
The Demi-God: The Earthly Half must die.
Yet if our Incense can Your Wrath remove;
If human Prayers avail on Minds above;
Exert, great God, Thy Int'rest in the Sky;
Gain each kind Pow'r, each Guardian Deity,
　　That conquer'd by the publick Vow,
They bear the dismal Mischief far away:
O! long as utmost Nature may allow,
　　Let Them retard the threaten'd Day:
Still be our Master's Life Thy happy Care:
Still let His Blessings with His Years increase:

MATTHEW PRIOR

To His laborious Youth consum'd in War,
Add lasting Age, adorn'd and crown'd with Peace:
Let twisted Olive bind those Laurels fast,
   Whose Verdure must for ever last.

XLII.

Long let this growing ÆRA bless His Sway:
And let our Sons His present Rule obey:
On His sure Virtue long let Earth rely:
And late let the Imperial Eagle fly,
To bear the Hero thro' His Father's Sky,
To LEDA's Twins, or He whose glorious Speed
On Foot prevail'd, or He who tam'd the Steed;
To HERCULES, at length absolv'd by Fate
From Earthly Toil, and above Envy great;
To VIRGIL's Theme, bright CYTHEREA's Son,
Sire of the LATIAN, and the BRITISH Throne;
   To all the radiant Names above,
   Rever'd by Men, and dear to JOVE.
   Late, JANUS, let the NASSAW-Star
New born, in rising Majesty appear,
   To triumph over vanquish'd Night,
   And guide the prosp'rous Mariner
With everlasting Beams of friendly Light.

An ODE.

Inscribed to the Memory of the

Honble Col. *George Villiers,*

Drowned in the River *Piava,* in the Country of *Friuli.* 1703.

In Imitation of *Horace,* Ode 28. Lib. 1.

Te Maris & Terræ numeroque carentis arenæ
Mensorem cohibent, Archyta, &c.

SAY, dearest VILLIERS, poor departed Friend
  (Since fleeting Life thus suddenly must end)
Say, what did all thy busie Hopes avail,
That anxious Thou from Pole to Pole didst sail;
E'er on thy Chin the springing Beard began
To spread a doubtful Down, and promise Man?
What profited thy Thoughts, and Toils, and Cares,
In Vigour more confirm'd, and riper Years?
To wake e'er Morning-dawn to loud Alarms,
And march 'till close of Night in heavy Arms?
To scorn the Summer Suns and Winter Snows,
And search thro' ev'ry Clime thy Country's Foes?
That Thou might'st Fortune to thy Side ingage;
That gentle Peace might quell BELLONA's Rage;
And ANNA's Bounty crown Her Soldier's hoary Age?

  In vain We think, that free-will'd Man has Pow'r
To hasten or protract th' appointed Hour.
Our Term of Life depends not on our Deed:
Before our Birth our Funeral was decreed.
Nor aw'd by Foresight, nor mis-led by Chance,
Imperious Death directs His Ebon Lance;
Peoples great HENRY's Tombs, and leads up HOLBEN's Dance.

MATTHEW PRIOR

Alike must ev'ry State, and ev'ry Age
Sustain the universal Tyrant's Rage :
For neither WILLIAM's Pow'r, nor MARY's Charms
Could or repel, or pacifie his Arms :
Young CHURCHILL fell, as Life began to bloom :
And BRADFORD's trembling Age expects the Tomb.
Wisdom and Eloquence in vain would plead
One Moment's Respite for the learned Head :
Judges of Writings and of Men have dy'd ;
MECÆNAS, SACKVILLE, SOCRATES, and HYDE :
And in their various Turns the Sons must tread
Those gloomy Journeys, which their Sires have led.

The ancient Sage, who did so long maintain,
That Bodies die, but Souls return again,
With all the Births and Deaths He had in Store,
Went out PYTHAGORAS, and came no more.
And modern As——L, whose capricious Thought
Is yet with Stores of wilder Notion fraught,
Too soon convinc'd, shall yield that fleeting Breath,
Which play'd so idly with the Darts of Death.

Some from the stranded Vessel force their Way :
Fearful of Fate, they meet it in the Sea :
Some who escape the Fury of the Wave,
Sicken on Earth, and sink into a Grave :
In Journeys or at home, in War or Peace,
By Hardships Many, Many fall by Ease.
Each changing Season does it's Poison bring :
Rheums chill the Winter ; Agues blast the Spring :
Wet, Dry, Cold, Hot, at the appointed Hour,
All act subservient to the Tyrant's Pow'r :
And when obedient Nature knows His Will,
A Fly, a Grape-stone, or a Hair can kill.

For restless PROSERPINE for ever treads
In Paths unseen, o'er our devoted Heads ;
And on the spacious Land, and liquid Main
Spreads slow Disease, or darts afflictive Pain :
Variety of Deaths confirms her endless Reign.

On curst PIAVA's Banks the Goddess stood;
Show'd her dire Warrant to the rising Flood;
When What I long must love, and long must mourn,
With fatal Speed was urging his Return;
In his dear Country to disperse his Care,
And arm himself by Rest for future War;
To chide his anxious Friend's officious Fears,
And promise to their Joys his elder Years.

Oh! destin'd Head; and oh! severe Decree:
Nor native Country Thou, nor Friend shalt see;
Nor War hast thou to wage, nor Year to come:
Impending Death is thine, and instant Doom.

Hark! the imperious Goddess is obey'd:
Winds murmur; Snows descend; and Waters spread:
Oh! Kinsman, Friend,——O! vain are all the Cries
Of human Voice; strong Destiny replies:
Weep You on Earth; for He shall sleep below:
Thence None return; and thither All must go.

Whoe'er Thou art, whom Choice or Business leads
To this sad River, or the neighb'ring Meads;
If Thou may'st happen on the dreary Shoars
To find the Object which This Verse deplores;
Cleanse the pale Corps with a religious Hand
From the polluting Weed and common Sand;
Lay the dead Hero graceful in a Grave;
(The only Honor He can now receive)
And fragrant Mould upon his Body throw;
And plant the Warrior Lawrel o'er his Brow:
Light lye the Earth; and flourish green the Bough.

So may just Heav'n secure thy future Life
From foreign Dangers, and domestic Strife:
And when th' Infernal Judges dismal Pow'r
From the dark Urn shall throw Thy destin'd Hour;
When yielding to the Sentence, breathless Thou
And pale shalt lye, as what Thou buriest now;
May some kind Friend the piteous Object see,
And equal Rites perform to That which once was Thee.

MATTHEW PRIOR

PROLOGUE,

SPOKEN AT

COURT before the QUEEN,

On Her Majesty's Birth-Day, 1704.

SHINE forth, Ye Planets, with distinguish'd Light,
   As when Ye hallow'd first this Happy Night:
Again transmit your Friendly Beams to Earth,
As when BRITANNIA joy'd for ANNA's Birth:
And Thou, propitious Star, whose sacred Pow'r
Presided o'er the Monarch's Natal Hour,
Thy Radiant Voyages for ever run,
Yielding to none but CYNTHIA, and the Sun:
With Thy fair Aspect still illustrate Heav'n:
Kindly preserve what Thou hast greatly giv'n:
Thy Influence for thy ANNA We implore:
Prolong One Life; and BRITAIN asks no more.
For Virtue can no ampler Power express,
Than to be Great in War, and Good in Peace:
For Thought no higher Wish of Bliss can frame,
Than to enjoy that Virtue STILL THE SAME.
Entire and sure the Monarch's Rule must prove,
Who founds Her Greatness on Her Subjects Love;
Who does our Homage for our Good require;
And Orders that which We should first Desire:
Our vanquish'd Wills that pleasing Force obey:
Her Goodness takes our Liberty away:
And haughty BRITAIN yields to Arbitrary Sway.

   Let the young AUSTRIAN then Her Terrors bear,
Great as He is, Her Delegate in War:
Let Him in Thunder speak to both his SPAINS,
That in these Dreadful Isles a Woman Reigns.
While the Bright Queen does on Her Subjects show'r
The gentle Blessings of Her softer Pow'r;

Gives sacred Morals to a vicious Age,
To Temples Zeal, and Manners to the Stage;
Bids the chaste Muse without a Blush appear,
And Wit be that which Heav'n and She may hear.

    MINERVA thus to PERSEUS lent Her Shield;
Secure of Conquest, sent Him to the Field:
The Hero acted what the Queen ordain'd:
So was His Fame compleat, and ANDROMEDE unchain'd.

    Mean time amidst Her Native Temples sate
The Goddess, studious of Her GRECIAN'S Fate;
Taught 'em in Laws and Letters to excell,
In Acting justly, and in Writing well.
Thus whilst She did Her various Pow'r dispose,
The World was freed from Tyrants, Wars, and Woes:
Virtue was taught in Verse, and ATHENS' Glory rose.

A
LETTER
TO
Monsieur *Boileau Despreaux*;
Occasion'd by the
VICTORY at *BLENHEIM*,
1704.

——*Cupidum, Pater optime, vires*
Deficiunt: neque enim Quivis horrentia Pilis
Agmina, nec Fractâ pereuntes cuspide Gallos——
                    Hor. Sat. 1. L. 2.

SINCE hir'd for Life, thy Servile Muse must sing
  Successive Conquests, and a glorious King;
Must of a Man Immortal vainly boast;
And bring him Lawrels, whatsoe'er they cost:

125

MATTHEW PRIOR

What Turn wilt Thou employ, what Colours lay
On the Event of that Superior Day,
In which one ENGLISH Subject's prosp'rous Hand
(So JOVE did will; so ANNA did command:)
Broke the proud Column of thy Master's Praise,
Which sixty Winters had conspir'd to raise?

From the lost Field a hundred Standards brought
Must be the Work of Chance, and Fortune's Fault:
BAVARIA's Stars must be accus'd, which shone,
That fatal Day the mighty Work was done,
With Rays oblique upon the GALLIC Sun.
Some DÆMON envying FRANCE mis-led the Fight:
And MARS mistook, tho' LOUIS order'd right.

When thy * young Muse invok'd the tuneful Nine,
To say how LOUIS did not pass the RHINE,
What Work had We with WAGENINGHEN, ARNHEIM,
Places that could not be reduc'd to Rhime?
And tho' the Poet made his last Efforts,
WURTS——who could mention in Heroic——WURTS?
But, tell me, hast thou reason to complain
Of the rough Triumphs of the last Campaign?
The DANUBE rescu'd, and the Empire sav'd,
Say, is the Majesty of Verse retriev'd?
And would it prejudice thy softer vein,
To sing the Princes, LOUIS and EUGENE?
Is it too hard in happy Verse to place
The VANS and VANDERS of the RHINE and MAES?
Her Warriors ANNA sends from TWEED and THAMES,
That FRANCE may fall by more harmonious Names.
Can'st thou not HAMILTON or LUMLY bear?
Would INGOLDSBY or PALMES offend thy Ear?
And is there not a Sound in MARLBRÔ's Name,
Which Thou and all thy Brethren ought to claim,
Sacred to Verse, and sure of endless Fame?

CUTTS is in Meeter something harsh to read:
Place me the Valiant GOURAM in his stead:

* Epistre 4. du Sr. Boileau Dépreaux au Roy.
En vain, pour Te Loüer, &c.

126

Let the Intention make the Number good:
Let generous SYLVIUS speak for honest WOOD.
And tho' rough CHURCHILL scarce in Verse will stand,
So as to have one Rhime at his Command;
With Ease the Bard reciting BLENHEIM's Plain,
May close the Verse, rememb'ring but the DANE.

I grant, old Friend, old Foe (for such We are
Alternate, as the Chance of Peace and War)
That we Poetic Folks, who must restrain
Our measur'd Sayings in an equal Chain,
Have Troubles utterly unknown to Those,
Who let their Fancy loose in rambling Prose.

For Instance now, how hard it is for Me
To make my Matter and my Verse agree?
In one great Day on HOCHSTET's fatal Plain
FRENCH and BAVARIANS twenty thousand slain;
Push'd thro' the DANUBE to the Shoars of STYX
Squadrons eighteen, Battalions twenty six;
Officers Captive made and private Men,
Of these twelve hundred, of those thousands ten;
Tents, Ammunition, Colours, Carriages,
Cannons, and Kettle-Drums——sweet Numbers these.
But is it thus You ENGLISH Bards compose?
With RUNICK Lays thus tag insipid Prose?
And when you should your Heroes Deeds rehearse,
Give us a Commissary's List in Verse?

Why Faith, DEPREAUX, there's Sense in what You say:
I told You where my Difficulty lay:
So vast, so numerous were great BLENHEIM's Spoils;
They scorn the Bounds of Verse, and mock the Muse's Toils.
To make the rough Recital aptly chime,
Or bring the Sum of GALLIA's Loss to Rhime,
'Tis mighty hard: What Poet would essay
To count the Streamers of my Lord Mayor's Day?
To number all the several Dishes drest
By honest LAMB, last Coronation Feast?
Or make Arithmetic and Epic meet;
And NEWTON's Thoughts in DRYDEN's Stile repeat?

MATTHEW PRIOR

O Poet, had it been APOLLO's Will,
That I had shar'd a Portion of thy Skill;
Had this poor Breast receiv'd the Heav'nly Beam;
Or could I hope my Verse might reach my Theam;
Yet, BOILEAU, yet the lab'ring Muse should strive,
Beneath the Shades of MARLBRÔ's Wreaths to live:
Should call aspiring Gods to bless her Choice;
And to their Fav'rite's Strain exalt her Voice,
Arms and a Queen to Sing; Who, Great and Good,
From peaceful THAMES to DANUBE's wond'ring Flood
Sent forth the Terror of her high Commands,
To save the Nations from invading Hands,
To prop fair Liberty's declining Cause,
And fix the jarring World with equal Laws.

The Queen should sit in WINDSOR's sacred Grove,
Attended by the Gods of War, and Love:
Both should with equal Zeal Her Smiles implore,
To fix Her Joys, or to extend Her Pow'r.

Sudden, the NYMPHS and TRITONS should appear;
And as great ANNA's Smiles dispel their Fear,
With active Dance should Her Observance claim;
With Vocal Shell should sound Her happy Name.
Their Master THAMES should leave the neighb'ring Shoar,
By his strong Anchor known, and Silver Oar;
Should lay his Ensigns at his Sov'raign's Feet,
And Audience mild with humble Grace intreat.

To Her, his dear Defence, He should complain,
That whilst He blesses Her indulgent Reign;
Whilst furthest Seas are by his Fleets survey'd,
And on his happy Banks each INDIA laid;
His Breth'ren MAES, and WAAL, and RHINE, and SAAR
Feel the hard Burthen of oppressive War;
That DANUBE scarce retains his rightful Course
Against two Rebel Armies neighb'ring Force;
And All must weep sad Captives to the SEIN,
Unless unchain'd and freed by BRITAIN's Queen.

The valiant Sov'reign calls Her Gen'ral forth ;
Neither recites Her Bounty, nor His Worth :
She tells Him, He must EUROPE's Fate redeem,
And by That Labour merit Her Esteem :
She bids Him wait Her to the Sacred Hall ;
Shows Him Prince EDWARD, and the conquer'd GAUL ;
Fixing the bloody Cross upon His Breast,
Says, He must Dye, or succour the Distress'd :
Placing the Saint an Emblem by His Side,
She tells Him, Virtue arm'd must conquer lawless Pride.

The Hero bows obedient, and retires :
The Queen's Commands exalt the Warrior's Fires.
His Steps are to the silent Woods inclin'd,
The great Design revolving in his Mind :
When to his Sight a Heav'nly Form appears :
Her Hand a Palm, her Head a Lawrel wears.

Me, She begins, the fairest Child of JOVE,
Below for ever sought, and bless'd above ;
Me, the bright Source of Wealth, and Power, and Fame ;
(Nor need I say, VICTORIA is my Name :)
Me the great Father down to Thee has sent :
He bids Me wait at Thy distinguish'd Tent,
To execute what ANNA's Wish would have :
Her Subject Thou, I only am Her Slave.

Dare then, Thou much belov'd by smiling Fate :
For ANNA's Sake, and in Her Name, be Great :
Go forth, and be to distant Nations known,
My future Fav'rite, and My darling Son.
At SCHELLENBERG I'll manifest sustain
Thy glorious Cause ; and spread my Wings again,
Conspicuous o'er Thy Helm, in BLENHEIM's Plain.

The Goddess said, nor would admit Reply ;
But cut the liquid Air, and gain'd the Sky.

His high Commission is thro' BRITAIN known ;
And thronging Armies to His Standard run.
He marches thoughtful ; and He speedy sails :
(Bless Him, ye Seas ! and prosper Him, ye Gales !)

MATTHEW PRIOR

BELGIA receives Him welcome to her Shores;
And WILLIAM's Death with lessen'd Grief deplores.
His Presence only must retrieve That LOSS:
MARLBRÔ to Her must be what WILLIAM was.
So when great ATLAS, from these low Aboads
Recall'd, was gather'd to his Kindred-Gods;
ALCIDES respited by prudent Fate,
Sustain'd the Ball, nor droop'd beneath the Weight.

Secret and Swift behold the Chief advance;
Sees half the Empire join'd, and Friend to FRANCE:
The BRITISH General dooms the Fight: His Sword
Dreadful He draws: The Captains wait the Word.
ANNE and St. GEORGE, the charging Hero cries:
Shrill Echo from the neighb'ring Wood replies
ANNE and St. GEORGE.——At That auspicious Sign
The Standards move; the adverse Armies join.
Of Eight great Hours, Time measures out the Sands;
And EUROPE's Fate in doubtful Balance stands:
The Ninth, VICTORIA comes:——o'er MARLBRÔ's Head ⎫
Confess'd She sits: the Hostile Troops recede:—— ⎬
Triumphs the GODDESS, from her Promise freed. ⎭

The Eagle, by the BRITISH Lion's Might
Unchain'd and Free, directs her upward Flight:
Nor did She e'er with stronger Pinions soar
From TYBER's Banks, than now from DANUBE's Shoar.

Fir'd with the Thoughts which these Ideas raise,
And great Ambition of my Country's Praise;
The ENGLISH Muse should like the MANTUAN rise; ⎫
Scornful of Earth and Clouds, should reach the Skies, ⎬
With Wonder (tho' with Envy still) pursu'd by human Eyes. ⎭

But We must change the Style.——Just now I said,
I ne'er was Master of the tuneful Trade.
Or the small Genius which my Youth could boast,
In Prose and Business lies extinct and lost:
Bless'd, if I may some younger Muse excite;
Point out the Game, and animate the Flight:
That from *Marseilles* to *Calais* FRANCE may know, ⎫
As We have Conqu'rors, We have Poets too; ⎬
And either Laurel does in BRITAIN grow: ⎭

That, tho' amongst our selves, with too much Heat,
We sometimes wrangle, when We should debate;
(A consequential Ill which Freedom draws;
A bad Effect, but from a Noble Cause :)
We can with universal Zeal advance,
To curb the faithless Arrogance of FRANCE.
Nor ever shall BRITANNIA's Sons refuse
To answer to thy Master, or thy Muse;
Nor want just Subject for victorious Strains,
While MARLBRÔ's Arm Eternal Laurel gains;
And where old SPENCER sung, a new ELISA reigns.

FOR

The PLAN of a FOUNTAIN,

On which is

The Effigies of the QUEEN on a Triumphal Arch,

The Figure of the DUKE of MARLBOROUGH, beneath,

and

The Chief Rivers of the World round the whole Work.

YE active Streams, where-e'er your Waters flow,
   Let distant Climes and furthest Nations know,
What Ye from THAMES and DANUBE have been taught,
How ANNE Commanded, and how MARLBRÔ Fought.

  Quacunque æterno properatis, Flumina, lapsu,
Divisis latè Terris, Populisque remotis
Dicite, nam vobis TAMISIS *narravit &* ISTER,
ANNA *quid Imperiis potuit, quid* MARLBURUS *Armis.*

MATTHEW PRIOR

THE

CHAMELEON.

AS the Chameleon, who is known
    To have no Colors of his own;
But borrows from his Neighbour's Hue
His White or Black, his Green or Blew;
And struts as much in ready Light,
Which Credit gives Him upon Sight;
As if the Rain-bow were in Tail
Settl'd on Him, and his Heirs Male:
So the young 'Squire, when first He comes
From Country School to WILL's or TOM's;
And equally, in Truth, is fit
To be a Statesman, or a Wit;
Without one Notion of his own,
He Santers wildly up and down;
'Till some Acquaintance, good or bad,
Takes notice of a staring Lad;
Admits Him in among the Gang:
They jest, reply, dispute, harangue:
He acts and talks, as They befriend Him,
Smear'd with the Colors, which They lend Him.

Thus merely, as his Fortune chances,
His Merit, or his Vice advances.

If happly He the Sect pursues,
That read and comment upon News;
He takes up Their mysterious Face:
He drinks his Coffee without Lace.
This Week his Mimic-Tongue runs o'er
What They have said the Week before.
His Wisdom sets all EUROPE right;
And teaches MARLBRÔ when to Fight.

Or if it be his Fate to meet
With Folks who have more Wealth than Wit;
He loves cheap *Port*, and double Bub;
And settles in the *Hum-Drum* Club.
He learns how Stocks will Fall or Rise;
Holds Poverty the greatest Vice;
Thinks Wit the Bane of Conversation;
And says, that Learning spoils a Nation.

But if, at first, He minds his Hits,
And drinks *Champaign* among the Wits;
Five deep, He toasts the tow'ring Lasses;
Repeats you Verses wrote on Glasses;
Is in the Chair; prescribes the Law;
And Lies with Those he never saw.

MERRY ANDREW.

SLY MERRY ANDREW, the last *Southwark* Fair
(At *Barthoi'mew* He did not much appear;
So peevish was the Edict of the May'r.)
At *Southwark*, therefore, as his Tricks He show'd,
To please our Masters, and his Friends, the Croud;
A huge Neats-Tongue He in his Right Hand held:
His Left was with a good Black-Pudding fill'd.
With a grave Look, in this odd Equipage,
The clownish Mimic traverses the Stage:
Why how now, ANDREW! cries his Brother Droll,
To-Day's Conceit, methinks, is something dull:
Come on, Sir, to our worthy Friends explain,
What does Your Emblematic Worship mean?
Quoth ANDREW; Honest English let Us speak:
Your Emble- (what d'ye call't?) is Heathen Greek.
To Tongue or Pudding Thou hast no Pretence:
Learning Thy Talent is; but Mine is Sense.
That busie Fool I was, which Thou art now;
Desirous to correct, not knowing how;

With very good Design, but little Wit,
Blaming or praising Things, as I thought fit.
I for this Conduct had what I deserv'd;
And dealing honestly, was almost starv'd.
But Thanks to my indulgent Stars, I Eat;
Since I have found the Secret to be Great.
O dearest ANDREW, says the humble Droll,
Henceforth may I Obey, and Thou Controll:
Provided Thou impart Thy useful Skill.
Bow then, says ANDREW; and, for once, I will.
Be of your Patron's Mind, whate'er He says;
Sleep very much; Think little; and Talk less:
Mind neither Good nor Bad, nor Right nor Wrong;
But Eat your Pudding, Slave; and Hold your Tongue.

A Rev'rend Prelate stopt his Coach and Six,
To laugh a little at our ANDREW's Tricks.
But when He heard him give this Golden Rule;
Drive on; (He cry'd) This Fellow is no Fool.

A

SIMILE.

DEAR THOMAS, didst Thou never pop
Thy Head into a Tin-man's Shop?
There, THOMAS, didst Thou never see
('Tis but by way of Simile)
A SQUIRREL spend his little Rage,
In jumping round a rowling Cage?
The Cage, as either Side turn'd up,
Striking a Ring of Bells a-top——?

Mov'd in the Orb, pleas'd with the Chimes,
The foolish Creature thinks he climbs:
But here or there, turn Wood or Wire,
He never gets two Inches higher.

So fares it with those merry Blades,
That frisk it under PINDUS' Shades.
In noble Songs, and lofty Odes,
They tread on Stars, and talk with Gods;
Still Dancing in an airy Round,
Still pleas'd with their own Verses Sound;
Brought back, how fast soe'er they go;
Always aspiring, always low.

The *FLIES*.

SAY, Sire of Insects, mighty SOL
  (A Fly upon the Chariot-Pole
Cries out) what Blew-Bottle alive
Did ever with such Fury drive?
Tell, BELZEBUB, Great Father, tell
(Says t'other, perch'd upon the Wheel)
Did ever any Mortal Fly
Raise such a Cloud of Dust, as I?

My Judgement turn'd the whole Debate:
My Valor sav'd the sinking State.
So talk two idle buzzing Things;
Toss up their Heads, and stretch their Wings.
But let the Truth to Light be brought:
This neither spoke, nor t'other fought:
No Merit in their own Behav'or:
Both rais'd, but by their Party's Favor.

From the Greek.

GREAT BACCHUS, born in Thunder and in Fire,
  By Native Heat asserts His dreadful Sire.
Nourish'd near shady Rills and cooling Streams,
He to the Nymphs avows his Am'rous Flames.
To all the Breth'ren at the *Bell* and *Vine*,
The Moral says; Mix Water with your Wine.

135

MATTHEW PRIOR

EPIGRAM.

FRANK Carves very ill, yet will palm all the Meats:
   He Eats more than Six; and Drinks more than he Eats.
Four Pipes after Dinner he constantly smokes;
And seasons his Whifs with impertinent Jokes.
Yet sighing, he says, We must certainly break;
And my cruel Unkindness compells him to speak:
For of late I invite Him——but Four Times a Week.

ANOTHER.

TO John I ow'd great Obligation;
   But John, unhappily, thought fit
To publish it to all the Nation:
   Sure John and I are more than Quit.

ANOTHER.

YES, every Poet is a Fool:
   By Demonstration Ned can show it:
Happy, cou'd Ned's inverted Rule
Prove every Fool to be a Poet.

ANOTHER.

THY Naggs (the leanest Things alive)
   So very hard Thou lov'st to drive;
I heard thy anxious Coach-man say,
It costs Thee more in Whips, than Hay.

136

To a Person who wrote Ill, and spake Worse against Me.

LYE, PHILO, untouch'd on my peaceable Shelf;
  Nor take it amiss, that so little I heed Thee;
I've no Envy to Thee, and some Love to my Self:
  Then why shou'd I answer; since first I must read Thee?

Drunk with HELICON's Waters and double-brew'd Bub,
  Be a Linguist, a Poet, a Critic, a Wag;
To the solid Delight of thy Well-judging Club,
  To the Damage alone of thy Bookseller BRAG.

Pursue me with Satyr: what Harm is there in't?
  But from all *vivâ voce* Reflection forbear:
There can be no Danger from what Thou shalt Print:
  There may be a little from what Thou may'st swear.

On the Same Person.

WHILE faster than his costive Brain indites,
  PHILO's quick Hand in flowing Letters writes;
His Case appears to Me like honest TEAGUE's,
When he was run away with, by his Legs.
PHOEBUS, give PHILO o'er Himself Command;
Quicken his Senses, or restrain His Hand.
Let Him be kept from Paper, Pen, and Ink:
So may He cease to Write, and learn to Think.

Quid sit futurum Cras fuge quærere.

FOR what To-morrow shall disclose,
  May spoil what You To-night propose:
ENGLAND may change; or CLOE stray:
Love and Life are for To-day.

MATTHEW PRIOR

HENRY and *EMMA*, *A* POEM,

Upon the Model of

The Nut-brown Maid.

To *CLOE*.

THOU, to whose Eyes I bend; at whose Command,
(Tho' low my Voice, tho' artless be my Hand)
I take the sprightly Reed, and sing, and play;
Careless of what the cens'ring World may say:
Bright CLOE, Object of my constant Vow,
Wilt thou awhile unbend thy serious Brow?
Wilt thou with Pleasure hear Thy Lover's Strains,
And with one Heav'nly Smile o'erpay His Pains?
No longer shall *the Nut-brown Maid* be old;
Tho' since her Youth three hundred Years have roll'd.
At Thy Desire, She shall again be rais'd;
And her reviving Charms in lasting Verse be prais'd.

No longer Man of Woman shall complain,
That He may Love, and not be Lov'd again:
That We in vain the fickle Sex pursue,
Who change the Constant Lover for the New.
Whatever has been writ, whatever said
Of Female Passion feign'd, or Faith decay'd;
Henceforth shall in my Verse refuted stand,
Be said to Winds, or writ upon the Sand.
And while my Notes to future Times proclaim
Unconquer'd Love, and ever-during Flame;
O fairest of the Sex! be Thou my Muse:
Deign on my Work thy Influence to diffuse.
Let me partake the Blessings I rehearse;
And grant me Love, the just Reward of Verse.

138

As Beauty's Potent Queen, with ev'ry Grace
That once was EMMA's, has adorn'd Thy Face;
And as Her Son has to My Bosom dealt
That constant Flame, which faithful HENRY felt:
O let the Story with Thy Life agree;
Let Men once more the bright Example see;
What EMMA was to Him, be Thou to Me.
Nor send Me by thy Frown from Her I love,
Distant and sad, a banish'd Man to rove.
But oh! with Pity long intreated Crown
My Pains and Hopes; and when thou say'st that One
Of all Mankind thou lov'st; Oh! think on Me alone.

WHERE beauteous Isis and her Husband TAME
With mingl'd Waves, for ever, flow the Same:
In Times of Yore, an antient Baron liv'd;
Great Gifts bestow'd, and great Respect receiv'd.

When dreadful EDWARD, with successful Care,
Led his free BRITONS to the GALLIC War;
This Lord had Headed his appointed Bands,
In firm Allegiance to his King's Commands.
And (all due Honors faithfully discharg'd)
Has brought back his Paternal Coat, inlarg'd
With a new Mark, the Witness of his Toil;
And no inglorious part of Foreign Spoil.

From the loud Camp retir'd, and noisy Court,
In Honorable Ease and Rural Sport,
The Remnant of his Days, He safely past;
Nor found they Lagg'd too slow, nor Flew too fast.
He made his Wish with his Estate comply;
Joyful to Live, yet not afraid to Dye.

One Child He had, a Daughter chast and fair;
His Age's Comfort, and his Fortune's Heir.
They call'd her EMMA; for the beauteous Dame
Who gave the Virgin Birth, had born the Name.
The Name th' indulgent Father doubly lov'd;
For in the Child the Mother's Charms improv'd.
Yet, as when little, round his Knees She plaid;
He call'd her oft, in Sport, His *Nut-brown Maid:*

MATTHEW PRIOR

The Friends and Tenants took the fondling Word;
(As still they please, who imitate their Lord)
Usage confirm'd what Fancy had begun:
The mutual Terms around the Lands were known;
And EMMA and *the Nut-Brown Maid* were One.

As with her Stature, still her Charms encreas'd;
Thro' all the Isle her Beauty was confess'd.
Oh! what Perfections must that Virgin share,
Who Fairest is esteem'd, where all are Fair?
From distant Shires repair the noble Youth,
And find, Report, for once, had lessen'd Truth.
By Wonder first, and then by Passion mov'd,
They came; they saw; they marvell'd; and they lov'd.
By public Praises, and by secret Sighs,
Each own'd the gen'ral Pow'r of EMMA's Eyes.
In Tilts and Turnaments the Valiant strove,
By glorious Deeds, to purchase EMMA's Love.
In gentle Verse, the Witty told their Flame,
And grac'd their choicest Songs with EMMA's Name.
In vain they Combated, in vain they Writ:
Useless their Strength, and impotent their Wit.
Great VENUS only must direct the Dart,
Which else will never reach the Fair one's Heart;
Spight of th' Attempts of Force, and soft Effects of Art.
Great VENUS must prefer the happy One:
In HENRY's Cause Her Favour must be shown:
And EMMA, of Mankind, must Love but Him alone.

While These, in Public, to the Castle came,
And by their Grandeur justify'd their Flame:
More secret Ways the careful HENRY takes;
His Squires, his Arms, and Equipage forsakes.
In borrow'd Name, and false Attire, array'd,
Oft He finds Means to see the beauteous Maid.

When EMMA hunts, in Huntsman's Habit drest,
HENRY on Foot pursues the bounding Beast.
In his right Hand his beachen Pole he bears:
And graceful at his Side his Horn he wears.
Still to the Glade, where She has bent her Way,
With knowing Skill he drives the future Prey.

Bids her decline the Hill, and shun the Brake;
And shews the Path her Steed may safest take.
Directs her Spear to fix the glorious Wound;
Pleas'd, in his Toils, to have her Triumph Crown'd:
And blows her Praises in no common Sound.

A Falc'ner HENRY is, when EMMA Hawks:
With her of Tarsels, and of Lures he talks.
Upon his Wrist the tow'ring Merlin stands;
Practis'd to rise, and stoop, at her Commands.
And when Superior now the Bird has flown,
And headlong brought the tumbling Quarry down:
With humble Rev'rence he accosts the Fair;
And with the honor'd Feather decks her Hair.
Yet still, as from the sportive Field She goes,
His down-cast Eye reveals his inward Woes.
And by his Look and Sorrow is exprest,
A nobler Game pursu'd, than Bird or Beast.

A Shepherd now along the Plain he roves;
And, with his jolly Pipe, delights the Groves.
The neighb'ring Swains around the Stranger throng,
Or to admire, or emulate his Song:
While, with soft Sorrow, he renews his Lays,
Nor heedful of their Envy, nor their Praise.
But soon as EMMA's Eyes adorn the Plain,
His Notes he raises to a nobler Strain;
With dutiful Respect, and studious Fear,
Lest any careless Sound offend her Ear.

A frantick Gipsey, now the House He haunts,
And in wild Phrases, speaks dissembled Wants.
With the fond Maids in Palmistry he deals:
They Tell the Secret first, which he Reveals:
Says who shall Wed, and who shall be Beguil'd;
What Groom shall Get, and Squire maintain the Child.
But when bright EMMA wou'd her Fortune know;
A softer Look unbends his op'ning Brow.
With trembling Awe, he gazes on her Eye;
And in soft Accents, forms the kind Reply;
That She shall prove as Fortunate as Fair,
And HYMEN's choicest Gifts are All reserv'd for Her.

MATTHEW PRIOR

Now oft had HENRY chang'd his sly Disguise;
Unmark'd by all, but beauteous EMMA's Eyes.
Oft had found Means alone to see the Dame,
And at her Feet to breath his am'rous Flame;
And oft, the Pangs of Absence to remove
By Letters, soft Interpreters of Love:
'Till Time and Industry (the mighty Two
That bring our Wishes nearer to our View)
Made him perceive, that the inclining Fair
Receiv'd his Vows with no reluctant Ear;
That VENUS had confirm'd her equal Reign,
And dealt to EMMA's Heart a share of HENRY's Pain.

While CUPID smil'd, by kind Occasion bless'd,
And, with the Secret kept, the Love increas'd;
The am'rous Youth frequents the silent Groves;
And much He meditates; for much He loves.
He loves: 'tis true; and is belov'd again:
Great are his Joys: but will they long remain?
EMMA with Smiles receives his present Flame;
But smiling, will She ever be the same?
Beautiful Looks are rul'd by fickle Minds;
And Summer Seas are turn'd by sudden Winds.
Another Love may gain her easie Youth:
Time changes Thought; and Flatt'ry conquers Truth.

O impotent Estate of human Life!
Where Hope and Fear maintain eternal Strife:
Where fleeting Joy does lasting Doubt inspire;
And most We Question, what We most Desire.
Amongst thy various Gifts, great Heav'n, bestow
Our Cup of Love unmix'd; forbear to throw
Bitter Ingredients in; nor pall the Draught
With nauseous Grief: for our ill-judging Thought
Hardly injoys the pleasurable Taste;
Or deems it not sincere; or fears it cannot last.

With Wishes rais'd, with Jealousies opprest
(Alternate Tyrants of the Human Breast)
By one great Tryal He resolves to prove
The Faith of Woman, and the Force of Love.

142

If scanning EMMA's Virtues, He may find
That beauteous Frame inclose a steady Mind;
He'll fix his Hope, of future Joy secure;
And live a Slave to HYMEN's happy Pow'r.
But if the Fair one, as he fears, is frail;
If pois'd aright in Reason's equal Scale,
Light fly her Merits, and her Faults prevail;
His Mind He vows to free from am'rous Care,
The latent Mischief from his Heart to tear,
Resume his Azure Arms, and shine again in War.

South of the Castle, in a verdant Glade,
A spreading Beach extends her friendly Shade:
Here oft the Nymph His breathing Vows had heard:
Here oft Her Silence had Her Heart declar'd.
As active Spring awak'd her Infant Buds;
And genial Life inform'd the verdant Woods;
HENRY, in Knots involving EMMA's Name,
Had half express'd, and half conceal'd his Flame
Upon This Tree: and as the tender Mark
Grew with the Year, and widen'd with the Bark:
VENUS had heard the Virgin's soft Address,
That, as the Wound, the Passion might increase.
As potent Nature shed her kindly Show'rs,
And deck'd the various Mead with op'ning Flow'rs;
Upon This Tree the Nymph's obliging Care
Had left a frequent Wreath for HENRY's Hair:
Which as with gay Delight the Lover found;
Pleas'd with his Conquest, with her Present crown'd,
Glorious thro' all the Plains He oft had gone,
And to each Swain the Mystic Honor shown;
The Gift still prais'd, the Giver still unknown.

His secret Note the troubled HENRY writes,
To the known Tree the Lovely Maid invites:
Imperfect Words and dubious Terms express,
That unforeseen Mischance disturb'd his Peace;
That He must something to Her Ear commend,
On which Her Conduct, and His Life depend.

Soon as the Fair one had the Note receiv'd;
The remnant of the Day alone She griev'd:
For diff'rent This from ev'ry former Note,
Which Venus dictated, and Henry wrote;
Which told her all his future Hopes were laid
On the dear Bosom of *his Nut-brown Maid*;
Which always bless'd her Eyes, and own'd her Pow'r;
And bid her oft Adieu, yet added more.

Now Night advanc'd. The House in Sleep were laid,
The Nurse experienc'd, and the prying Maid;
And last That Sprite, which does incessant haunt
The Lover's Steps, the ancient Maiden Aunt.
To her dear Henry Emma wings her Way,
With quicken'd Pace repairing forc'd Delay.
For Love, fantastic Pow'r, that is afraid
To stir abroad 'till Watchfulness be laid;
Undaunted then, o'er Cliffs and Valleys strays;
And leads his Vot'ries safe thro' pathless Ways.
Not Argus with his hundred Eyes shall find,
Where Cupid goes; tho' He poor Guide is blind.

The Maiden first arriving, sent her Eye,
To ask, if yet it's Chief Delight were nigh:
With Fear, and with Desire, with Joy, and Pain
She sees, and runs to meet Him on the Plain.
But oh! his Steps proclaim no Lover's Haste:
On the low Ground his fix'd Regards are cast:
His artful Bosom heaves dissembl'd Sighs;
And Tears suborn'd fall copious from his Eyes.

With Ease, alas! we Credit what we Love:
His painted Grief does real Sorrow move
In the afflicted Fair; Adown her Cheek
Trickling the genuine Tears their Current break.
Attentive stood the mournful Nymph: the Man
Broke Silence first: the Tale alternate ran.

HENRY.

SINCERE O tell me, hast thou felt a Pain,
Emma, beyond what Woman knows to feign?
Has Thy uncertain Bosom ever strove
With the first Tumults of a real Love?

Hast Thou now dreaded, and now blest his Sway;
By turns averse, and joyful to obey?
Thy Virgin Softness hast Thou e'er bewail'd,
As Reason yielded, and as Love prevail'd?
And wept the potent God's resistless Dart,
His killing Pleasure, his Ecstatic Smart,
And heav'nly Poison thrilling thro' thy Heart?
If so, with Pity view my wretched State;
At least deplore, and then forget my Fate:
To some more happy Knight reserve thy Charms,
By Fortune favor'd, and successful Arms:
And only, as the Sun's revolving Ray
Brings back each Year this melancholy Day;
Permit one Sigh, and set apart one Tear,
To an abandon'd Exile's endless Care.
For Me, alas! Out-cast of Human Race,
Love's Anger only waits, and dire Disgrace:
For lo! these Hands in Murther are imbru'd;
These trembling Feet by Justice are pursu'd:
Fate calls aloud, and hastens me away;
A shameful Death attends my longer Stay;
And I this Night must fly from Thee and Love,
Condemn'd in lonely Woods a banish'd Man to rove.

EMMA.

What is our Bliss, that changeth with the Moon;
And Day of Life, that darkens e'er 'tis Noon?
What is true Passion, if unblest it dies?
And where is EMMA's Joy, if HENRY flies?
If Love, alas! be Pain; the Pain I bear,
No Thought can figure, and no Tongue declare.
Ne'er faithful Woman felt, nor false one feign'd
The Flames, which long have in my Bosom reign'd:
The God of Love himself inhabits there,
With all his Rage, and Dread, and Grief, and Care,
His Complement of Stores, and total War.

O! cease then coldly to suspect my Love;
And let my Deed, at least, my Faith approve.
Alas! no Youth shall my Endearments share;
Nor Day nor Night shall interrupt my Care:

P.   K   145

No future Story shall with Truth upbraid
The cold Indiff'rence of *the Nut-brown Maid*:
Nor to hard Banishment shall HENRY run;
While careless EMMA sleeps on Beds of Down.
View Me resolv'd, where-e'er Thou lead'st, to go,
Friend to thy Pain, and Partner of thy Woe:
For I attest fair VENUS, and her Son,
That I, of all Mankind, will love but Thee alone.

HENRY.

Let Prudence yet obstruct Thy vent'rous Way;
And take good heed, what Men will think and say;
That Beauteous EMMA vagrant Courses took;
Her Father's House and civil Life forsook;
That full of youthful Blood, and fond of Man,
She to the Wood-land with an Exile ran.
Reflect, that lessen'd Fame is ne'er regain'd;
And Virgin Honor once, is always stain'd:
Timely advis'd, the coming Evil shun:
Better not do the Deed, than weep it done.
No Penance can absolve our guilty Fame;
Nor Tears, that wash out Sin, can wash out Shame.
Then fly the sad Effects of desp'rate Love;
And leave a banish'd Man thro' lonely Woods to rove.

EMMA.

Let EMMA's hapless Case be falsely told
By the rash Young, or the ill-natur'd Old:
Let ev'ry Tongue it's various Censures chuse,
Absolve with Coldness, or with Spight accuse:
Fair Truth, at last, her radiant Beams will raise;
And Malice vanquish'd heightens Virtue's Praise.
Let then thy Favour but indulge my Flight;
O! let my Presence make thy Travels light;
And potent VENUS shall exalt my Name
Above the Rumors of censorious Fame:
Nor from that busie Demon's restless Pow'r
Will ever EMMA other Grace implore,
Than that this Truth should to the World be known,
That I, of all Mankind, have lov'd but Thee alone.

HENRY.

But canst Thou wield the Sword, and bend the Bow?
With active Force repel the sturdy Foe?
When the loud Tumult speaks the Battel nigh,
And winged Deaths in whistling Arrows fly;
Wilt Thou, tho' wounded, yet undaunted stay,
Perform thy Part, and share the dangerous Day?
Then, as thy Strength decays, thy Heart will fail;
Thy Limbs all trembling, and thy Cheeks all pale:
With fruitless Sorrow Thou, inglorious Maid,
Wilt weep thy Safety by thy Love betray'd:
Then to thy Friend, by Foes o'er-charg'd, deny
Thy little useless Aid, and Coward fly:
Then wilt thou curse the Chance that made Thee love
A banish'd Man, condemn'd in lonely Woods to rove.

EMMA.

With fatal Certainty THALESTRIS knew
To send the Arrow from the twanging Yew:
And great in Arms, and foremost in the War,
BONDUCA brandished high the BRITISH Spear.
Could Thirst of Vengeance, and Desire of Fame
Excite the Female Breast with Martial Flame?
And shall not Love's diviner Pow'r inspire
More hardy Virtue, and more gen'rous Fire?

Near Thee, mistrust not, constant I'll abide,
And fall, or vanquish, fighting by thy Side.
Tho' my Inferior Strength may not allow,
That I should bear, or draw the Warrior Bow;
With ready Hand I will the Shaft supply,
And joy to see thy Victor Arrows fly.
Touch'd in the Battel by the Hostile Reed,
Should'st Thou (but Heav'n avert it!) should'st Thou bleed;
To stop the Wounds my finest Lawn I'd tear;
Wash them with Tears, and wipe them with my Hair:
Blest, when my Dangers and my Toils have shown,
That I, of all Mankind, could love but Thee alone.

HENRY.

But canst Thou, tender Maid, canst Thou sustain
Afflictive Want, or Hunger's pressing Pain?

K 2

147

Those Limbs, in Lawn and softest Silk array'd,
From Sun-beams guarded, and of Winds afraid;
Can they bear angry JOVE? Can they resist
The parching Dog-star, and the bleak North-East?
When chill'd by adverse Snows, and beating Rain,
We tread with weary Steps the longsome Plain;
When with hard Toil We seek our Ev'ning Food,
Berries and Acorns, from the neighb'ring Wood;
And find among the Cliffs no other House,
But the thin Covert of some gather'd Boughs;
Wilt Thou not then reluctant send thine Eye
Around the dreary Waste; and weeping try
(Tho' then, alas! that Tryal be too late)
To find thy Father's Hospitable Gate,
And Seats, where Ease and Plenty brooding sate?
Those Seats, whence long excluded Thou must mourn:
That Gate, for ever barr'd to thy Return:
Wilt Thou not then bewail ill-fated Love,
And hate a banish'd Man, condemn'd in Woods to rove?

EMMA.

Thy Rise of Fortune did I only wed,
From it's Decline determin'd to recede?
Did I but purpose to embark with Thee,
On the smooth Surface of a Summer's Sea;
While gentle ZEPHYRS play in prosp'rous Gales;
And Fortune's Favour fills the swelling Sails:
But would forsake the Ship, and make the Shoar,
When the Winds whistle, and the Tempests roar?
No, HENRY, no: One Sacred Oath has ty'd
Our Loves; One Destiny our Life shall guide;
Nor Wild, nor Deep our common Way divide.

When from the Cave Thou risest with the Day,
To beat the Woods, and rouse the bounding Prey;
The Cave with Moss and Branches I'll adorn,
And chearful sit, to wait my Lord's Return.
And when Thou frequent bring'st the smitten Deer;
(For seldom, Archers say, Thy Arrows err)
I'll fetch quick Fewel from the neighb'ring Wood,
And strike the sparkling Flint, and dress the Food:

With humble Duty and officious Haste,
I'll cull the furthest Mead for Thy Repast :
The choicest Herbs I to Thy Board will bring;
And draw Thy Water from the freshest Spring :
And when at Night with weary Toil opprest,
Soft Slumbers Thou injoy'st, and wholesome Rest ;
Watchful I'll guard Thee, and with Midnight Pray'r
Weary the Gods to keep Thee in their Care ;
And joyous ask, at Morn's returning Ray,
If Thou hast Health, and I may bless the Day.
My Thought shall fix, my latest Wish depend
On Thee, Guide, Guardian, Kinsman, Father, Friend :
By all these sacred Names be HENRY known
To EMMA's Heart : and grateful let Him own,
That She, of all Mankind, could love but Him alone.

HENRY.

Vainly thou tell'st Me, what the Woman's Care
Shall in the Wildness of the Wood prepare :
Thou, e'er thou goest, unhapp'yest of thy Kind,
Must leave the Habit, and the Sex behind.
No longer shall thy comely Tresses break
In flowing Ringlets on thy snowy Neck ;
Or sit behind thy Head, an ample Round,
In graceful Breeds with various Ribbon bound :
No longer shall the Boddice, aptly lac'd,
From thy full Bosome to thy slender Waste,
That Air and Harmony of Shape express,
Fine by Degrees, and beautifully less :
Nor shall thy lower Garments artful Pleat,
From thy fair Side dependent to thy Feet,
Arm their chaste Beauties with a modest Pride,
And double ev'ry Charm they seek to hide.
Th'Ambrosial Plenty of Thy shining Hair
Cropt off and lost, scarce lower than Thy Ear
Shall stand uncouth : a Horse-man's Coat shall hide
Thy taper Shape, and Comeliness of Side :
The short Trunk-Hose shall show Thy Foot and Knee
Licentious, aud to common Eye-sight free :
And with a bolder Stride, and looser Air,
Mingl'd with Men, a Man Thou must appear.

Nor Solitude, nor gentle Peace of Mind,
Mistaken Maid, shalt Thou in Forests find:
'Tis long, since CYNTHIA and her Train were there;
Or Guardian Gods made Innocence their Care.
Vagrants and Out-laws shall offend Thy View;
For such must be my Friends; a hideous Crew,
By adverse Fortune mix'd in Social Ill,
Train'd to assault, and disciplin'd to kill:
Their common Loves, a lewd abandon'd Pack,
The Beadle's Lash still flagrant on their Back;
By Sloth corrupted, by Disorder fed,
Made bold by Want, and prostitute for Bread:
With such must EMMA hunt the tedious Day,
Assist their Violence, and divide their Prey:
With such She must return at setting Light,
Tho' not Partaker, Witness of their Night.
Thy Ear, inur'd to charitable Sounds,
And pitying Love, must feel the hateful Wounds
Of Jest obscene, and vulgar Ribaldry,
The ill-bred Question, and the lewd Reply;
Brought by long Habitude from Bad to Worse,
Must hear the frequent Oath, the direful Curse,
That latest Weapon of the Wretches War,
And Blasphemy, sad Comrade of Despair.

Now, EMMA, now the last Reflection make,
What Thou would'st follow, what Thou must forsake:
By our ill-omen'd Stars, and adverse Heav'n,
No middle Object to thy Choice is given.
Or yield thy Virtue, to attain thy Love;
Or leave a banish'd Man, condemn'd in Woods to rove.

EMMA.

O Grief of Heart! that our unhappy Fates
Force Thee to suffer what thy Honor hates:
Mix Thee amongst the Bad; or make Thee run
Too near the Paths, which Virtue bids Thee shun.
Yet with her HENRY still let EMMA go;
With Him abhor the Vice, but share the Woe:
And sure My little Heart can never err
Amidst the worst; if HENRY still be there.

Our outward Act is prompted from within;
And from the Sinner's Mind proceeds the Sin:
By her own Choice free Virtue is approv'd;
Nor by the Force of outward Objects mov'd.
Who has assay'd no Danger, gains no Praise.
In a small Isle, amidst the widest Seas,
Triumphant Constancy has fix'd her Seat:
In vain the Syrens sing, the Tempests beat:
Their Flatt'ry She rejects, nor fears their Threat.

For Thee alone these little Charms I drest;
Condemn'd them, or absolv'd them by thy Test.
In comely Figure rang'd, my Jewels shone,
Or negligently plac'd, for Thee alone:
For Thee again they shall be laid aside:
The Woman, HENRY, shall put off her Pride
For Thee: my Cloaths, my Sex exchang'd for Thee,
I'll mingle with the People's wretched Lee;
O Line extream of human Infamy!
Wanting the Scissors, with these Hands I'll tear
(If that obstructs my Flight) this load of Hair.
Black Soot, or yellow Walnut shall disgrace
This little Red and White of EMMA's Face.
These Nails with Scratches shall deform my Breast,
Lest by my Look, or Color be express'd
The Mark of ought High-born, or ever better dress'd.
Yet in this Commerce, under this Disguise,
Let Me be grateful still to HENRY's Eyes.
Lost to the World, let Me to Him be known:
My Fate I can absolve; if He shall own,
That leaving all Mankind, I love but Him alone.

HENRY.

O wildest Thought of an abandon'd Mind!
Name, Habit, Parents, Woman left behind,
Ev'n Honor dubious, Thou preferr'st to go
Wild to the Woods with Me: Said EMMA so?
Or did I dream what EMMA never said?
O guilty Error! and O wretched Maid!

Whose roving Fancy would resolve the same
With Him, who next should tempt her easie Fame ;
And blow with empty Words the susceptible Flame.
Now why should doubtful Terms thy Mind perplex?
Confess thy Frailty, and avow the Sex :
No longer loose Desire for constant Love
Mistake ; but say, 'tis Man, with whom Thou long'st to rove.

EMMA.

Are there not Poisons, Racks, and Flames, and Swords;
That EMMA thus must die by HENRY's Words?
Yet what could Swords or Poison, Racks or Flame,
But mangle and disjoint this brittle Frame?
More fatal HENRY's Words ; they murder EMMA's Fame.

And fall these Sayings from that gentle Tongue,
Where civil Speech, and soft Persuasion hung ;
Whose artful Sweetness and harmonious Strain,
Courting my Grace, yet courting it in vain,
Call'd Sighs, and Tears, and Wishes to it's Aid ;
And, whilst it HENRY's glowing Flame convey'd,
Still blam'd the Coldness of *the Nut-brown Maid?*

Let envious Jealousie, and canker'd Spight
Produce my Action to severest Light,
And tax my open Day, or secret Night.
Did e'er my Tongue speak my unguarded Heart
The least inclin'd to play the Wanton's Part?
Did e'er my Eye One inward Thought reveal,
Which Angels might not hear, and Virgins tell?
And hast Thou, HENRY, in my Conduct known
One Fault, but That which I must ever own,
That I, of all Mankind, have lov'd but Thee alone?

HENRY.

Vainly thou talk'st of loving Me alone :
Each Man is Man ; and all Our Sex is One.
False are our Words ; and fickle is our Mind :
Nor in Love's Ritual can We ever find
Vows made to last, or Promises to bind.

By Nature prompted, and for Empire made,
Alike by Strength or Cunning We invade :
When arm'd with Rage We march against the Foe ;
We lift the Battel-Ax, and draw the Bow :
When fir'd with Passion We attack the Fair ;
Delusive Sighs and brittle Vows We bear :
Our Falshood and our Arms have equal Use ;
As they our Conquest, or Delight produce.

The foolish Heart Thou gav'st, again receive,
The only Boon departing Love can give.
To be less Wretched, be no longer True :
What strives to fly Thee, why should'st Thou pursue? }
Forget the Present Flame, indulge a New.
Single the loveliest of the am'rous Youth ;
Ask for his Vow ; but hope not for his Truth.
The next Man (and the next Thou shalt believe) }
Will pawn his Gods, intending to deceive ;   }
Will kneel, implore, persist, o'ercome, and leave. }
Hence let Thy CUPID aim his Arrows right ;   }
Be Wise and False, shun Trouble, seek Delight,   }
Change Thou the first, nor wait Thy Lover's Flight. }

Why should'st Thou weep? let Nature judge our Case :
I saw Thee Young, and Fair ; pursu'd the Chase
Of Youth, and Beauty : I another saw
Fairer, and Younger : yielding to the Law
Of our all-ruling Mother, I pursu'd
More Youth, more Beauty : Blest Vicissitude !
My active Heart still keeps it's pristine Flame ;
The Object alter'd, the Desire the same.

This Younger Fairer pleads her rightful Charms :
With present Power compels me to her Arms.
And much I fear, from my subjected Mind
(If Beauty's Force to constant Love can bind)
That Years may roll, e'er in Her turn the Maid
Shall weep the Fury of my Love decay'd ;
And weeping follow Me, as Thou dost now,
With idle Clamours of a broken Vow.

Nor can the wildness of thy Wishes err
So wide, to hope that Thou may'st live with Her.
Love, well Thou know'st, no Partnership allows:
CUPID averse rejects divided Vows.
Then from thy foolish Heart, vain Maid, remove
A useless Sorrow, and an ill-starr'd Love;
And leave me, with the Fair, at large in Woods to rove.

EMMA.

Are we in Life thro' one great Error led?
Is each Man perjur'd, and each Nymph betray'd?
Of the Superior Sex art Thou the worst?
Am I of Mine the most compleatly Curst?
Yet let me go with Thee; and going prove,
From what I will endure, how much I love.

This potent Beauty, this Triumphant Fair,
This happy Object of our diff'rent Care,
Her let me follow; Her let me attend,
A Servant: (She may scorn the Name of Friend.)
What She demands, incessant I'll prepare:
I'll weave Her Garlands; and I'll pleat Her Hair:
My busie Diligence shall deck Her Board;
(For there, at least, I may approach my Lord.)
And when Her HENRY's softer Hours advise
His Servant's Absence; with dejected Eyes
Far I'll recede, and Sighs forbid to rise.

Yet when encreasing Grief brings slow Disease;
And ebbing Life, on Terms severe as these,
Will have it's little Lamp no longer fed;
When HENRY's Mistress shows him EMMA dead;
Rescue my poor Remains from vile Neglect:
With Virgin Honors let my Herse be deckt,
And decent Emblem; and at least persuade
This happy Nymph, that EMMA may be laid,
Where Thou, dear Author of my Death, where She
With frequent Eye my Sepulchre may see.
The Nymph amidst her Joys may haply breath
One pious Sigh, reflecting on my Death,
And the sad Fate which She may one Day prove,
Who hopes from HENRY's Vows Eternal Love.

And Thou forsworn, Thou cruel, as Thou art,
If EMMA's Image ever touch'd thy Heart;
Thou sure must give one Thought, and drop one Tear
To Her, whom Love abandon'd to Despair;
To Her, who dying, on the wounded Stone
Bid it in lasting Characters be known,
That, of Mankind, She lov'd but Thee alone.

HENRY.

Hear, solemn JOVE; and, conscious VENUS, hear;
And Thou, bright Maid, believe Me, whilst I swear;
No Time, no Change, no future Flame shall move
The well-plac'd Basis of my lasting Love.
O Powerful Virtue! O Victorious Fair!
At least excuse a Tryal too severe:
Receive the Triumph, and forget the War.

No banish'd Man, condemn'd in Woods to rove,
Intreats thy Pardon, and implores thy Love:
No perjur'd Knight desires to quit thy Arms,
Fairest Collection of thy Sexe's Charms,
Crown of my Love, and Honor of my Youth:
HENRY, thy HENRY with Eternal Truth,
As Thou may'st wish, shall all his Life imploy,
And found his Glory in his EMMA's Joy.

In Me behold the Potent EDGAR's Heir,
Illustrious Earl: Him terrible in War
Let LOYRE confess; for She has felt His Sword,
And trembling fled before the BRITISH Lord.
Him great in Peace and Wealth fair DEVA knows;
For she amidst his spacious Meadows flows;
Inclines her Urn upon his fatten'd Lands;
And sees his num'rous Herd imprint her Sands.

And Thou, my Fair, my Dove, shalt raise thy Thought
To Greatness next to Empire; shalt be brought
With solemn Pomp to my Paternal Seat;
Where Peace and Plenty on Thy Word shall wait.
Music and Song shall wake the Marriage-Day:
And while the Priests accuse the Bride's Delay;
Myrtles and Roses shall obstruct Her Way.

Friendship shall still Thy Evening Feasts adorn;
And blooming Peace shall ever bless Thy Morn.
Succeeding Years their happy Race shall run;
And Age unheeded by Delight come on;
While yet Superior Love shall mock his Pow'r:
And when old Time shall turn the fated Hour,
Which only can our well-ty'd Knot unfold,
What rests of Both, One Sepulchre shall hold.

Hence then, for ever, from my EMMA's Breast
(That Heav'n of Softness, and that Seat of Rest)
Ye Doubts and Fears, and All that know to move
Tormenting Grief, and All that trouble Love,
Scatter'd by Winds recede, and wild in Forests rove.

EMMA.

O Day the fairest sure that ever rose!
Period and End of anxious EMMA's Woes!
Sire of her Joy, and Source of her Delight;
O! wing'd with Pleasure take thy happy Flight,
And give each future Morn a Tincture of thy White.
Yet tell thy Votary, potent Queen of Love,
HENRY, my HENRY, will He never rove?
Will He be ever Kind, and Just, and Good?
And is there yet no Mistress in the Wood?
None, none there is: The Thought was rash and vain;
A false Idea, and a fancy'd Pain.
Doubt shall for ever quit my strengthen'd Heart,
And anxious Jealousie's corroding Smart;
Nor other Inmate shall inhabit there,
But soft Belief, young Joy, and pleasing Care.

Hence let the Tides of Plenty ebb and flow,
And FORTUNE's various Gale unheeded blow.
If at my Feet the Suppliant Goddess stands,
And sheds her Treasure with unweary'd Hands;
Her present Favor cautious I'll embrace,
And not unthankful use the proffer'd Grace:
If She reclaims the Temporary Boon,
And tries her Pinions, flutt'ring to be gone;

Secure of Mind I'll obviate her Intent,
And unconcern'd return the Goods She lent.
Nor Happiness can I, nor Misery feel,
From any Turn of her Fantastic Wheel:
Friendship's great Laws, and Love's superior Pow'rs
Must mark the Colour of my future Hours.
From the Events which Thy Commands create
I must my Blessings or my Sorrows date;
And HENRY's Will must dictate EMMA's Fate.

Yet while with close Delight and inward Pride
(Which from the World my careful Soul shall hide)
I see Thee, Lord and End of my Desire,
Exalted high as Virtue can require;
With Pow'r invested, and with Pleasure chear'd;
Sought by the Good, by the Oppressor fear'd;
Loaded and blest with all the affluent Store,
Which human Vows at smoking Shrines implore;
Grateful and humble grant Me to employ
My Life, subservient only to thy Joy;
And at my Death to bless thy Kindness shown
To Her, who of Mankind could love but Thee alone.

WHILE thus the constant Pair alternate said,
Joyful above them and around them play'd
Angels and sportive LOVES, a numerous Crowd;
Smiling They clapt their Wings, and low They bow'd:
They tumbled all their little Quivers o'er,
To chuse propitious Shafts; a precious Store:
That when their God should take his future Darts,
To strike (however rarely) constant Hearts,
His happy Skill might proper Arms imploy,
All tipt with Pleasure, and all wing'd with Joy:
And Those, They vow'd, whose Lives should imitate
These Lovers Constancy, should share their Fate.

The Queen of Beauty stop'd her bridled Doves;
Approv'd the little Labour of the LOVES;
Was proud and pleas'd the mutual Vow to hear;
And to the Triumph call'd the God of War:
Soon as She calls, the God is always near.

MATTHEW PRIOR

Now Mars, she said, let Fame exalt her Voice;
Nor let thy Conquests only be her Choice:
But when She sings great Edward from the Field
Return'd, the Hostile Spear and Captive Shield
In Concord's Temple hung, and Gallia taught to yield.
And when, as prudent Saturn shall compleat
The Years design'd to perfect Britain's State,
The swift-wing'd Power shall take her Trump again,
To sing Her Fav'rite Anna's wond'rous Reign;
To recollect unweary'd Marlbrô's Toils,
Old Rufus' Hall unequal to his Spoils;
The British Soldier from his high Command
Glorious, and Gaul thrice Vanquish'd by his Hand:
Let Her at least perform what I desire;
With second Breath the Vocal Brass inspire:
And tell the Nations in no Vulgar Strain,
What Wars I manage, and what Wreaths I gain.

And when Thy Tumults and Thy Fights are past,
And when Thy Lawrels at my Feet are cast;
Faithful may'st Thou like *British* Henry prove,
And Emma-like let me return Thy Love.

Renown'd for Truth let all Thy Sons appear;
And constant Beauty shall reward their Care.

Mars smil'd, and bow'd; the Cyprian Deity
Turn'd to the glorious Ruler of the Sky:
And Thou, She smiling said, Great God of Days
And Verse, behold my Deed; and sing my Praise.
As on the *British* Earth, my Fav'rite Isle,
Thy gentle Rays and kindest Influence smile,
Thro' all her laughing Fields and verdant Groves,
Proclaim with Joy these memorable Loves.
From ev'ry annual Course let One great Day,
To celebrated Sports and Floral Play
Be set aside; and, in the softest Lays
Of Thy Poetic Sons, be solemn Praise,
And everlasting Marks of Honour paid,
To *the true Lover*, and *the Nut-brown Maid*.

AN
ODE,

Humbly Inscrib'd to the

QUEEN.

ON THE

Glorious Success

OF

Her MAJESTY's Arms,
1706.

Written in Imitation of SPENCER's Style.

Te non paventis funera Galliæ,
Duræque tellus audit Iberiæ:
Te cæde gaudentes Sicambri
Compositis venerantur Armis.   Hor.

MATTHEW PRIOR

THE
PREFACE.

WHEN I *first thought of Writing upon this Occasion, I found the* Ideas *so great and numerous, that I judg'd them more proper for the Warmth of an* Ode, *than for any other sort of Poetry : I therefore set* HORACE *before Me for a Pattern, and particularly his famous* Ode, *the Fourth of the Fourth Book,*

Qualem ministrum fulminis Alitem, *&c.*

which He wrote in Praise of DRUSUS *after his Expedition into* GERMANY, *and of* AUGUSTUS *upon his happy Choice of That* General. *And in the following Poem, tho' I have endeavor'd to imitate all the great Strokes of that* Ode, *I have taken the Liberty to go off from it, and to add variously, as the Subject and my own Imagination carry'd Me. As to the Style, the Choice I made of following the* Ode *in* Latin, *determin'd Me in* English *to the* Stanza; *and herein it was impossible not to have a Mind to follow our great Countryman* SPENCER; *which I have done (as well at least as I could) in the Manner of my Expression, and the Turn of my Number : Having only added one Verse to his Stanza, which I thought made the Number more Harmonious; and avoided such of his Words, as I found too obsolete. I have however retain'd some few of them, to make the Colouring look more like* SPENCER's: Behest, *Command;* Band, *Army;* Prowess, *Strength;* I weet, *I know;* I ween, *I think;* whilom, *heretofore; and* Two or Three *more of that Kind, which I hope the Ladies will pardon me, and not judge my* MUSE *less handsome, though for once she appears in a Farthingal. I have also, in* SPENCER's *Manner, used* Cæsar *for the Emperor,* Boya *for Bavaria,* Bavar *for that Prince,* Ister *for Danube,* Iberia *for Spain, &c.*

That noble Part of the Ode *which I just now mention'd,*

Gens, quæ cremato Fortis ab *Ilio*
Jactata *Tuscis* æquoribus, *&c.*

where HORACE *praises the* Romans, *as being descended from*
ÆNEAS, *I have turn'd to the Honor of the* BRITISH *Nation,
descended from* BRUTE, *likewise a* TROJAN. *That this* BRUTE,
Fourth or Fifth from ÆNEAS, *settled in* ENGLAND, *and built*
LONDON, *which he call'd* Troja Nova, *or* Troynovante, *is
a Story which* (*I think*) *owes it's Original, if not to* GEOFFRY *of*
Monmouth, *at least to the* Monkish *Writers; yet is not rejected
by Our great* CAMDEN, *and is told by* MILTON, *as if* (*at least*) *He
was pleas'd with it; though possibly He does not believe it:
However it carries a Poetical Authority, which is sufficient for
our Purpose. It is as certain that* BRUTE *came into* ENGLAND,
as that ÆNEAS *went into* ITALY; *and upon the Supposition of these
Facts,* VIRGIL *wrote the best Poem that the World ever read,
and* SPENCER *paid Queen* ELIZABETH *the greatest Compliment.*

I need not obviate one piece of Criticism, that I bring my Hero

From burning *Troy,* and *Xanthus* red with Blood:
whereas He was not born, when that City was destroy'd.
VIRGIL, *in the Case of His own* ÆNEAS *relating to* DIDO, *will
stand as a sufficient Proof, that a Man in his Poetical Capacity is
not accountable for a little Fault in Chronology.*

My Two Great Examples, HORACE *and* SPENSER, *in many
Things resemble each other: Both have a Height of Imagination,
and a Majesty of Expression in describing the* Sublime; *and Both
know to temper those Talents, and sweeten the Description, so as to
make it Lovely as well as Pompous: Both have equally That
agreeable Manner of mixing Morality with their Story, and That*
Curiosa Felicitas *in the Choice of their Diction, which every
Writer aims at, and so very few have reach'd: Both are particularly
Fine in their Images, and Knowing in their Numbers. Leaving
therefore our Two Masters to the Consideration and Study of Those,
who design to Excel in Poetry, I only beg Leave to add, That it is
long since I have* (*or at least ought to have*) *quitted* PARNASSUS, *and
all the flow'ry Roads on that Side the Country; tho' I thought my
self indispensably obliged, upon the present Occasion, to take a little
Journey into Those Parts.*

MATTHEW PRIOR

AN

ODE,

Humbly Inscrib'd to the

QUEEN.

I.

WHEN Great Augustus govern'd Antient Rome,
        And sent his Conqu'ring Bands to Foreign Wars;
Abroad when Dreaded, and Belov'd at Home,
He saw his Fame encreasing with his Years;
Horace, Great Bard (so Fate ordain'd) arose;
And Bold, as were his Countrymen in Fight,
Snatch'd their fair Actions from degrading Prose,
And set their Battels in Eternal Light:
High as their Trumpets Tune His Lyre he strung;
And with his Prince's Arms He moraliz'd his Song.

II.

When bright Eliza rul'd Britannia's State,
Widely distributing Her high Commands;
And boldly Wise, and fortunately Great,
Freed the glad Nations from Tyrannick Bands;
An equal Genius was in Spenser found:
To the high Theme He match'd his Noble Lays:
He travell'd England o'er on Fairy Ground,
In Mystic Notes to Sing his Monarch's Praise:
Reciting wond'rous Truths in pleasing Dreams,
He deck'd Eliza's Head with Gloriana's Beams.

III.

But, Greatest Anna! while Thy Arms pursue
Paths of Renown, and climb Ascents of Fame,
Which nor Augustus, nor Eliza knew;
What Poet shall be found to sing Thy Name?
What Numbers shall record, what Tongue shall say
Thy Wars on Land, Thy Triumphs on the Main?

O Fairest Model of Imperial Sway !
What Equal Pen shall write Thy wond'rous Reign ?
Who shall Attempts and Feats of Arms rehearse,
Not yet by Story told, nor parallel'd by Verse ?

IV.

Me all too mean for such a Task I weet :
Yet if the Sovereign Lady deigns to Smile,
I'll follow HORACE with impetuous Heat,
And cloath the Verse in SPENSER's Native Style.
By these Examples rightly taught to sing,
And Smit with Pleasure of my Country's Praise,
Stretching the Plumes of an uncommon Wing,
High as OLYMPUS I my Flight will raise :
And latest Times shall in my Numbers read
ANNA's Immortal Fame, and MARLBRÔ's hardy Deed.

V.

As the strong Eagle in the silent Wood,
Mindless of warlike Rage, and hostile Care,
Plays round the rocky Cliff, or crystal Flood ;
'Till by JOVE's high Behests call'd out to War,
And charg'd with Thunder of his angry King,
His Bosom with the vengeful Message glows :
Upward the Noble Bird directs his Wing ;
And tow'ring round his Master's Earth-born Foes,
Swift He collects his fatal Stock of Ire ;
Lifts his fierce Talon high, and darts the forked Fire.

VI.

Sedate and calm thus Victor MARLBRÔ sate,
Shaded with Laurels, in his Native Land ;
'Till ANNA calls Him from his soft Retreat,
And gives Her Second Thunder to his Hand.
Then leaving sweet Repose, and gentle Ease,
With ardent Speed He seeks the distant Foe :
Marching o'er Hills and Vales, o'er Rocks and Seas,
He meditates, and strikes the wond'rous Blow.
Our Thought flies slower than Our General's Fame :
Grasps He the Bolt ? (We ask) when He has hurl'd the Flame.

MATTHEW PRIOR

VII.

When fierce BAVAR on JUDOIGN's spacious Plain
Did from afar the BRITISH Chief behold;
Betwixt Despair, and Rage, and Hope, and Pain,
Something within his warring Bosom roll'd:
He views that Fav'rite of Indulgent Fame,
Whom whilom He had met on ISTER's Shoar:
Too well, alas! the Man He knows the same,
Whose Prowess there repell'd the BOYAN Pow'r;
And sent Them trembling thro' the frighted Lands,
Swift as the Whirlwind drives ARABIA's scatter'd Sands.

VIII.

His former Losses He forgets to grieve;
Absolves his Fate, if with a kinder Ray
It now would shine, and only give Him leave
To Balance the Account of BLENHEIM's Day.
So the fell Lion in the lonely Glade,
His Side still smarting with the Hunter's Spear,
Tho' deeply wounded, no way yet dismay'd,
Roars terrible, and meditates new War;
In sullen Fury traverses the Plain,
To find the vent'rous Foe, and Battel Him again.

IX.

Misguided Prince! no longer urge Thy Fate,
Nor tempt the Hero to unequal War;
Fam'd in Misfortune, and in Ruin Great,
Confess the Force of MARLBRÔ's stronger Star.
Those Laurel Groves (the Merits of thy Youth)
Which Thou from MAHOMET didst greatly gain,
While bold Assertor of resistless Truth,
Thy Sword did Godlike Liberty maintain,
Must from thy Brow their falling Honors shed;
And their transplanted Wreaths must deck a worthier Head.

X.

Yet cease the Ways of Providence to blame,
And Human Faults with Human Grief confess:
'Tis Thou art chang'd; while Heav'n is still the same:
From Thy ill Councils date Thy ill Success.

Impartial Justice holds Her equal Scales;
'Till stronger Virtue does the Weight incline:
If over Thee thy glorious Foe prevails;
He now Defends the Cause, that once was Thine.
Righteous the War, the Champion shall subdue;
For JOVE's great Handmaid POWER, must JOVE's Decrees pursue.

XI.

Hark! the dire Trumpets sound their shrill Alarms:
AUVERQUERQUE, branch'd from the renown'd NASSAWS,
Hoary in War, and bent beneath his Arms,
His Glorious Sword with Dauntless Courage draws.
When anxious BRITAIN mourn'd her parting Lord,
And all of WILLIAM that was Mortal Dy'd;
The faithful Hero had receiv'd This Sword
From His expiring Master's much-lov'd Side.
Oft from it's fatal Ire has LOUIS flown,
Where-e'er Great WILLIAM led, or MAESE and SAMBRE run.

XII.

But brandish'd high, in an ill-omen'd Hour
To Thee, proud GAUL, behold thy justest Fear,
The Master Sword, Disposer of thy Power:
'Tis That which CÆSAR gave the BRITISH Peer.
He took the Gift: Nor ever will I sheath
This Steel, (so ANNA's high Behests ordain)
The General said, unless by Glorious Death
Absolv'd, 'till Conquest has confirm'd Your Reign.
Returns like these Our Mistress bids us make,
When from a Foreign Prince a Gift Her BRITONS take.

XIII.

And now fierce GALLIA rushes on her Foes,
Her Force augmented by the BOYAN Bands:
So VOLGA's Stream, increas'd by Mountain Snows,
Rolls with new Fury down thro' RUSSIA's Lands.
Like two great Rocks against the raging Tide,
(If Virtue's Force with Nature's We compare)
Unmov'd the Two united Chiefs abide,
Sustain the Impulse, and receive the War.
Round their firm Sides in vain the Tempest beats;
And still the foaming Wave with lessen'd Pow'r retreats.

MATTHEW PRIOR

XIV.

The Rage dispers'd, the Glorious Pair advance,
With mingl'd Anger, and collected Might,
To turn the War, and tell aggressing FRANCE,
How BRITAIN's Sons and BRITAIN's Friends can fight.
On Conquest fix'd, and covetous of Fame,
Behold Them rushing thro' the GALLIC Host.
Thro' standing Corn so runs the sudden Flame,
Or Eastern Winds along SICILIA's Coast.
They deal their Terrors to the adverse Nation:
Pale Death attends their Arms, and ghastly Desolation.

XV.

But while with fiercest Ire BELLONA glows,
And EUROPE rather Hopes than Fears Her Fate;
While BRITAIN presses Her afflicted Foes;
What Horror damps the Strong, and quells the Great?
Whence look the Soldiers Cheeks dismay'd and pale?
Erst ever dreadful, know They now to dread?
The Hostile Troops, I ween, almost prevail;
And the Pursuers only not recede.
Alas! their lessen'd Rage proclaims their Grief!
For anxious, lo! They croud around their falling Chief!

XVI.

I thank Thee, Fate, exclaims the fierce BAVAR;
Let BOYA's Trumpet grateful Iö's sound:
I saw Him fall, their Thunderbolt of War:——
Ever to Vengeance sacred be the Ground——
Vain Wish! short Joy! the Hero mounts again
In greater Glory, and with fuller Light:
The Ev'ning Star so falls into the Main,
To rise at Morn more prevalently bright.
He rises safe: but near, too near his Side,
A good Man's grievous Loss, a faithful Servant dy'd.

XVII.

Propitious MARS! the Battel is regain'd:
The Foe with lessen'd Wrath disputes the Field:
The BRITON fights, by fav'ring Gods sustain'd:
Freedom must live; and lawless Power must yield.

Vain now the Tales which fab'ling Poets tell,
That wav'ring CONQUEST still desires to rove!
In MARLBRÔ's Camp the Goddess knows to dwell:
Long as the Hero's Life remains her Love.
Again FRANCE flies: again the Duke pursues:
And on RAMILLIA's Plains He BLENHEIM's Fame renews.

XVIII.

Great Thanks, O Captain great in Arms! receive
From thy Triumphant Country's public Voice:
Thy Country greater Thanks can only give
To ANNE, to Her who made those Arms Her Choice.
Recording SCHELLENBERG's, and BLENHEIM's Toils,
We dreaded lest Thou should'st those Toils repeat:
We view'd the Palace charg'd with GALLIC Spoils;
And in those Spoils We thought thy Praise compleat:
For never GREEK, We deem'd, nor ROMAN Knight,
In Characters like these did e'er his Acts indite.

XIX.

Yet mindless still of Ease, Thy Virtue flies
A Pitch to Old and Modern Times unknown:
Those goodly Deeds which We so highly prize,
Imperfect seem, great Chief, to Thee alone.
Those Heights, where WILLIAM's Virtue might have staid,
And on the Subject World look'd safely down,
By MARLBRÔ pass'd, the Props and Steps were made,
Sublimer yet to raise his Queen's Renown:
Still gaining more, still slighting what He gain'd,
Nought done the Hero deem'd, while ought undone remain'd.

XX.

When swift-wing'd RUMOR told the mighty GAUL,
How lessen'd from the Field BAVAR was fled;
He wept the Swiftness of the Champion's Fall;
And thus the Royal Treaty-Breaker said:
And lives He yet, the Great, the Lost BAVAR,
Ruin to GALLIA, in the Name of Friend?
Tell Me, how far has Fortune been severe?
Has the Foe's Glory, or our Grief an End?
Remains there, of the Fifty Thousand lost,
To save our threaten'd Realm, or guard our shatter'd Coast?

MATTHEW PRIOR

XXI.

To the close Rock the frighted Raven flies,
Soon as the rising Eagle cuts the Air:
The shaggy Wolf unseen and trembling lyes,
When the hoarse Roar proclaims the Lion near.
Ill-starr'd did We our Forts and Lines forsake,
To dare our BRITISH Foes to open Fight:
Our Conquest We by Stratagem should make:
Our Triumph had been founded in our Flight.
'Tis Our's, by Craft and by Surprize to gain:
'Tis Their's, to meet in Arms, and Battel in the Plain.

XXII.

The ancient Father of this Hostile Brood,
Their boasted BRUTE, undaunted snatch'd his Gods
From burning TROY, and XANTHUS red with Blood,
And fix'd on Silver THAMES his dire Abodes;
And this be TROYNOVANTE, He said, the Seat
By Heav'n ordain'd, My Sons, Your lasting Place:
Superior here to all the Bolts of Fate
Live, mindful of the Author of your Race,
Whom neither GREECE, nor War, nor Want, nor Flame,
Nor Great PELEIDES' Arm, nor JUNO's Rage could tame.

XXIII.

Their TUDOR's hence, and STUART's Off-spring flow:
Hence EDWARD, dreadful with his Sable Shield,
TALBOT, to GALLIA's Pow'r Eternal Foe,
And SEYMOUR, fam'd in Council, or in Field:
Hence NEVIL, Great to Settle or Dethrone,
And DRAKE, and CA'NDISH, Terrors of the Sea:
Hence BUTLER's Sons, o'er Land and Ocean known,
HERBERT's, and CHURCHILL's Warring Progeny:
Hence the long Roll which GALLIA should conceal:
For, oh! Who vanquish'd, loves the Victor's Fame to tell?

XXIV.

Envy'd BRITANNIA, sturdy as the Oak,
Which on her Mountain-Top She proudly bears,
Eludes the Ax, and sprouts against the Stroke;
Strong from her Wounds, and greater by her Wars.

And as Those Teeth, which CADMUS sow'd in Earth,
Produc'd new Youth, and furnish'd fresh Supplies:
So with young Vigor, and succeeding Birth,
Her Losses more than recompens'd arise;
And ev'ry Age She with a Race is Crown'd,
For Letters more Polite, in Battels more Renown'd.

XXV.

Obstinate Pow'r, whom Nothing can repel;
Not the fierce SAXON, nor the cruel DANE,
Nor deep Impression of the NORMAN Steel,
Nor EUROPE's Force amass'd by envious SPAIN,
Nor FRANCE on universal Sway intent,
Oft breaking Leagues, and oft renewing Wars,
Nor (frequent Bane of weaken'd Government)
Their own intestine Feuds, and mutual Jars;
Those Feuds and Jars, in which I trusted more,
Than in My Troops, and Fleets, and all the GALLIC Pow'r.

XXVI.

To fruitful RHEIMS, or fair LUTETIA's Gate
What Tidings shall the Messenger convey?
Shall the loud Herald our Success relate,
Or mitred Priest appoint the Solemn Day?
Alas! my Praises They no more must Sing;
They to my Statue now must Bow no more:
Broken, repuls'd is their Immortal King:
Fall'n, fall'n for ever is the GALLIC Pow'r——
The *Woman Chief* is Master of the War:
Earth She has freed by Arms, and vanquish'd Heav'n by Pray'r.

XXVII.

While thus the ruin'd Foe's Despair commends
Thy Council and Thy Deed, Victorious Queen,
What shall Thy Subjects say, and what Thy Friends?
How shall Thy Triumphs in Our Joy be seen?
Oh! daign to let the Eldest of the NINE
Recite BRITANNIA Great, and GALLIA Free:
Oh! with her Sister SCULPTURE let her join
To raise, Great ANNE, the Monument to Thee;
To Thee, of all our Good the Sacred Spring;
To Thee, our dearest Dread; to Thee, our softer KING.

XXVIII.

Let Europe sav'd the Column high erect,
Than Trajan's higher, or than Antonine's;
Where sembling Art may carve the fair Effect,
And full Atchievement of Thy great Designs.
In a calm Heav'n, and a serener Air,
Sublime the Queen shall on the Summit stand,
From Danger far, as far remov'd from Fear,
And pointing down to Earth Her dread Command.
All Winds, all Storms that threaten Human Woe,
Shall sink beneath Her Feet, and spread their Rage below.

XXIX.

There Fleets shall strive by Winds and Waters tost;
'Till the young Austrian on Iberia's Strand,
Great as Æneas on the Latian Coast,
Shall fix his Foot: and This, be This the Land,
Great Jove, where I for ever will remain
(The Empire's other Hope shall say) and here
Vanquish'd, Intomb'd I'll lye, or Crown'd I'll Reign——
O Virtue, to thy British Mother dear!
Like the fam'd Trojan suffer and abide;
For Anne is Thine, I ween, as Venus was His Guide.

XXX.

There, in Eternal Characters engrav'd,
Vigo, and Gibraltar, and Barcelone,
Their Force destroy'd, their Privileges sav'd,
Shall Anna's Terrors, and Her Mercies own:
Spain, from th'Usurper Bourbon's Arms retriev'd,
Shall with new Life and grateful Joy appear,
Numb'ring the Wonders which That Youth atchiev'd,
Whom Anna clad in Arms, and sent to War;
Whom Anna sent to claim Iberia's Throne;
And made Him more than King, in calling Him Her Son.

XXXI.

There Ister pleas'd, by Blenheim's glorious Field
Rolling, shall bid his Eastern Waves declare
Germania sav'd by Britain's ample Shield,
And bleeding Gaul afflicted by her Spear:

Shall bid Them mention MARLBRÔ, on that Shore
Leading his Islanders, renown'd in Arms,
Thro' Climes, where never BRITISH Chief before
Or pitch'd his Camp, or sounded his Alarms:
Shall bid Them bless the QUEEN, who made his Streams
Glorious as those of BOYN, and safe as those of THAMES.

XXXII.

BRABANTIA, clad with Fields, and crown'd with Tow'rs,
With decent Joy shall her Deliv'rer meet;
Shall own Thy Arms, Great QUEEN, and bless Thy Pow'rs,
Laying the Keys beneath Thy Subject's Feet.
FLANDRIA, by Plenty made the Home of War,
Shall weep her Crime, and bow to CHARLES restor'd;
With double Vows shall bless Thy happy Care,
In having drawn, and having sheath'd the Sword.
From these their Sister Provinces shall know
How ANNE supports a Friend, and how forgives a Foe.

XXXIII.

Bright Swords, and crested Helms, and pointed Spears
In artful Piles around the Work shall lye;
And Shields indented deep in ancient Wars,
Blazon'd with Signs of GALLIC Heraldry;
And Standards with distinguish'd Honors bright,
Marks of high Pow'r and National Command,
Which VALOIS' Sons, and BOURBON's bore in Fight,
Or gave to FOIX', or MONTMORANCY's Hand:
Great Spoils, which GALLIA must to BRITAIN yield,
From CRESSY's Battel sav'd, to grace RAMILLIA's Field.

XXXIV.

And as fine Art the Spaces may dispose,
The knowing Thought and curious Eye shall see
Thy Emblem, Gracious QUEEN, the BRITISH Rose,
Type of sweet Rule, and gentle Majesty:
The NORTHERN Thistle, whom no Hostile Hand
Unhurt too rudely may provoke, I ween;
HIBERNIA's Harp, Device of Her Command,
And Parent of Her Mirth, shall there be seen:
Thy vanquish'd Lillies, FRANCE, decay'd and torn,
Shall with disorder'd Pomp the lasting Work adorn.

XXXV.

Beneath, Great QUEEN, oh! very far beneath,
Near to the Ground, and on the humble Base,
To save Her self from Darkness, and from Death,
That MUSE desires the last, the lowest Place;
Who tho' unmeet, yet touch'd the trembling String;
For the fair Fame of ANNE and ALBION's Land,
Who durst of War and Martial Fury Sing:
And when Thy Will, and when Thy Subject's Hand
Had quell'd those Wars, and bid that Fury cease;
Hangs up her grateful Harp to Conquest, and to Peace.

CANTATA.

Set by Monsieur GALLIARD.

RECIT.

BENEATH a verdant Lawrel's ample Shade,
His Lyre to mournful Numbers strung,
HORACE, immortal Bard, supinely laid,
To VENUS thus address'd the Song:
Ten thousand little LOVES around
List'ning, dwelt on ev'ry Sound.

ARIET.

Potent VENUS, bid Thy Son
Sound no more His dire Alarms.
Youth on silent Wings is flown:
Graver Years come rolling on.
Spare my Age, unfit for Arms:
Safe and humble let Me rest,
From all am'rous Care releas'd.
Potent VENUS, bid Thy Son
Sound no more His dire Alarms.

RECIT.

Yet, VENUS, why do I each Morn prepare
The fragrant Wreath for CLOE's Hair?
Why, why do I all Day lament, and sigh,
Unless the beauteous Maid be nigh?
And why all Night pursue Her in my Dreams,
Thro' Flow'ry Meads, and Crystal Streams?

RECIT.

Thus sung the Bard; and thus the Goddess spoke:
Submissive bow to LOVE's imperious Yoke.
    Ev'ry State, and ev'ry Age
  Shall own My Rule, and fear My Rage:
  Compell'd by Me Thy Muse shall prove,
  That all the World was born to love.

ARIET.

Bid Thy destin'd Lyre discover
  Soft Desire, and gentle Pain:
Often praise, and always love Her:
  Thro' her Ear her Heart obtain.
Verse shall please, and Sighs shall move Her:
  CUPID does with PHOEBUS reign.

Her Right Name.

AS NANCY at Her Toylet sat,
   Admiring This, and blaming That;
Tell Me, She said; but tell Me true;
The Nymph who cou'd your Heart subdue,
What Sort of Charms does She possess?
Absolve Me Fair One: I'll confess;
With Pleasure I reply'd. Her Hair,
In Ringlets rather dark than fair,
Does down her Iv'ry Bosom roll,
And hiding Half, adorns the Whole.

In her high Forehead's fair half-round
Love sits in open Triumph crown'd:
He in the Dimple of her Chin,
In private State by Friends is seen.
Her Eyes are neither black, nor grey;
Nor fierce, nor feeble is their Ray:
Their dubious Lustre seems to show
Something that speaks nor Yes, nor No.
Her Lips no living Bard, I weet,
May say, how Red, how Round, how Sweet:
Old Homer only cou'd indite
Their vagrant Grace, and soft Delight:
They stand Recorded in his Book,
When Helen smil'd, and Hebe spoke——
The Gipsy turning to her Glass,
Too plainly show'd, She knew the Face:
And which am I most like, She said,
Your Cloe, or Your *Nut-brown Maid?*

Written in an OVID.

OVID is the surest Guide,
  You can name, to show the Way
To any Woman, Maid, or Bride,
  Who resolves to go astray.

A TRUE MAID.

NO, no; for my Virginity,
  When I lose that, says Rose, I'll dye:
Behind the Elmes, last Night, cry'd Dick,
Rose, were You not extreamly Sick?

ANOTHER.

TEN Months after FLORIMEL happen'd to wed,
  And was brought in a laudable Manner to Bed;
She warbl'd Her Groans with so charming a Voice,
That one half of the Parish was stun'd with the Noise.
But when FLORIMEL deign'd to lie privately in,
Ten Months before She and her Spouse were a-kin;
She chose with such Prudence her Pangs to conceal,
That her Nurse, nay her Midwife, scarce heard her once squeal.
Learn, Husbands, from hence, for the Peace of your Lives,
That Maids make not half such a Tumult, as Wives.

A REASONABLE AFFLICTION.

ON His Death-Bed poor LUBIN lies:
  His Spouse is in Despair:
With frequent Sobs, and mutual Cries,
  They Both express their Care.
A diff'rent Cause, says Parson SLY,
  The same Effect may give:
Poor LUBIN fears, that He shall Die;
  His Wife, that He may Live.

Another REASONABLE AFFLICTION.

FROM her own Native FRANCE as old ALISON past,
  She reproach'd *English* NELL with Neglect or with Malice,
That the Slattern had left, in the Hurry and Hast,
Her Lady's Complexion, and Eye-brows at CALAIS.

MATTHEW PRIOR

ANOTHER.

HER Eye-brow-Box one Morning lost,
  (The best of Folks are oft'nest crost)
Sad HELEN thus to JENNY said,
Her careless but afflicted Maid;
Put me to Bed then, wretched JANE:
Alas! when shall I rise again?
I can behold no Mortal now:
For what's an Eye without a Brow?

On the same Subject.

IN a dark Corner of the House,
  Poor HELEN sits, and sobs and cries:
She will not see her Loving Spouse,
  Nor her more dear *Picquet*-Allies:
  Unless She finds her Eye-brows,
  She'll e'en weep out her Eyes.

On the Same.

HELEN was just slipt into Bed:
  Her Eye-brows on the Toilet lay:
Away the Kitten with them fled,
As Fees belonging to her Prey.

For this Misfortune careless JANE,
Assure your self, was loudly rated:
  And Madam getting up again,
With her own Hand the Mouse-Trap baited.

On little Things, as Sages write,
Depends our Human Joy, or Sorrow:
  If We don't catch a Mouse To-night,
Alas! no Eye-brows for To-morrow.

PHYLLIS's AGE.

HOW old may PHYLLIS be, You ask,
     Whose Beauty thus all Hearts engages?
To Answer is no easie Task;
     For She has really two Ages.

Stiff in Brocard, and pinch'd in Stays,
     Her Patches, Paint, and Jewels on;
All Day let Envy view her Face;
     And PHYLLIS is but Twenty-one.

Paint, Patches, Jewels laid aside,
     At Night Astronomers agree,
The Evening has the Day bely'd;
     And PHYLLIS is some Forty-three.

Forma Bonum Fragile.

WHAT a frail Thing is Beauty, says Baron LE CRAS,
     Perceiving his Mistress had one Eye of Glass:
And scarcely had He spoke it;
When She more confus'd, as more angry She grew,
By a negligent Rage prov'd the Maxim too true:
     She dropt the Eye, and broke it.

A Critical Moment.

HOW capricious were Nature and Art to poor NELL?
     She was painting her Cheeks at the time her Nose fell.

MATTHEW PRIOR

An EPIGRAM.
Written to the Duke de NOAILLES.

VAIN the Concern which You express,
    That uncall'd ALARD will possess
Your House and Coach, both Day and Night;
And that MACKBETH was haunted less
    By BANQUO's restless Spright.

With Fifteen Thousand Pound a Year,
Do You complain, You cannot bear
    An Ill, You may so soon retrieve?
Good ALARD, faith, is modester
    By much, than You believe.

Lend Him but fifty *Louis d'or*;
And You shall never see Him more:
    Take the Advice; *Probatum est.*
Why do the Gods indulge our Store,
    But to secure our Rest?

EPILOGUE
TO
PHÆDRA.

Spoken by Mrs. OLDFIELD, *who acted* ISMENA.

LADIES, to Night your Pity I implore
    For One, who never troubled You before:
An OXFORD-Man, extreamly read in GREEK,
Who from EURIPIDES makes PHÆDRA speak;
And comes to Town, to let Us Moderns know,
How Women lov'd two thousand Years ago.

If that be all, said I, e'en burn your Play:
I' gad! We know all that, as well as They:
Show Us the youthful, handsome Charioteer,
Firm in his Seat, and running his Career;

Our Souls would kindle with as gen'rous Flames,
As e'er inspir'd the antient GRECIAN Dames:
Ev'ry ISMENA would resign her Breast;
And ev'ry dear HIPPOLYTUS be blest.

But, as it is, Six flouncing FLANDERS Mares
Are e'en as good, as any Two of Theirs;
And if HIPPOLYTUS can but contrive
To buy the gilded Chariot; JOHN can drive.

Now of the Bustle You have seen to Day,
And PHÆDRA's Morals in this Scholar's Play,
Something at least in Justice should be said:
But this HIPPOLYTUS so fills One's Head——
Well! PHÆDRA liv'd as chastly as She cou'd,
For she was Father JOVE's own Flesh and Blood.
Her aukward Love indeed was odly fated:
She and her POLY were too near related:
And yet that Scruple had been laid aside,
If honest THESEUS had but fairly dy'd:
But when He came, what needed He to know,
But that all Matters stood in *Statu quo?*
There was no harm, You see; or grant there were:
She might want Conduct; but He wanted Care.
'Twas in a Husband little less than rude,
Upon his Wife's Retirement to intrude——
He should have sent a Night or two before,
That He would come exact at such an Hour:
Then He had turn'd all Tragedy to Jest;
Found ev'ry Thing contribute to his Rest;
The *Picquet*-Friend dismiss'd, the Coast all clear,
And Spouse alone impatient for her Dear.

But if these gay Reflections come too late,
To keep the guilty PHÆDRA from her Fate;
If your more serious Judgment must condemn
The dire Effects of her unhappy Flame:
Yet, Ye chaste Matrons, and Ye tender Fair,
Let Love and Innocence engage your Care:
My spotless Flames to your Protection take;
And spare poor PHÆDRA, for ISMENA's sake.

MATTHEW PRIOR

EPILOGUE

TO

LUCIUS.

Spoken by Mrs. HORTON.

THE Female Author who recites to Day,
    Trusts to her Sex the Merit of her Play.
Like Father BAYES securely She sits down:
Pitt, Box and Gallery, Gad! All's our Own.
In antient GREECE, She says, when SAPPHO writ,
By their Applause the Critics show'd their Wit.
They tun'd their Voices to her LYRIC String;
Tho' they cou'd All do something more, than Sing.
But one Exception to this Fact we find;
That Booby PHAON only was unkind,
An ill-bred Boat-man, rough as Waves and Wind.
From SAPPHO down thro' all succeeding Ages,
And now on FRENCH, or on ITALIAN Stages,
Rough Satyrs, sly Remarks, ill-natur'd Speeches,
Are always aim'd at Poets, that wear Breeches.
Arm'd with LONGINUS, or with RAPIN, No Man
Drew a sharp Pen upon a Naked Woman.
The blust'ring Bully in our neighb'ring Streets,
Scorns to attack the Female that He meets:
Fearless the Petticoat contemns his Frowns:
The Hoop secures, whatever it surrounds.
The many-color'd Gentry there above,
By turns are rul'd by Tumult, and by Love:
And while their Sweet-hearts their Attention fix,
Suspend the Din of their damn'd clatt'ring Sticks.
Now Sirs——
To You our Author makes Her soft Request,
Who speak the kindest, and who write the best.
Your *Sympathetic* Hearts She hopes to move,
From tender Friendship, and endearing Love.

If PETRARCH's Muse did LAURA's Wit rehearse,
And COWLEY flatter'd dear ORINDA's Verse;
She hopes from You——Pox take her Hopes and Fears;
I plead her Sexe's Claim: what matters Hers?
By Our full Pow'r of Beauty We think fit,
To damn this *Salique* Law impos'd on Wit:
We'll try the Empire You so long have boasted;
And if We are not Prais'd, We'll not be Toasted.
Approve what One of us presents to Night;
Or ev'ry Mortal Woman here shall write:
Rural, Pathetic, Narrative, Sublime,
We'll write to You, and make You write in Rhime:
Female Remarks shall take up all Your Time.
Your Time, poor Souls! we'll take your very Money;
Female Third Days shall come so thick upon Ye.
As long as We have Eyes, or Hands, or Breath,
We'll Look, or Write, or Talk You All to Death.
Unless Ye yield for Better and for Worse:
Then the She-PEGASUS shall gain the Course;
And the Grey Mare will prove the better Horse.

The THIEF
AND THE
CORDELIER,
A BALLAD.
To the Tune of
King JOHN, *and the* ABBOT *of* CANTERBURY.

WHO has e'er been at PARIS, must needs know the *Greve*,
  The fatal Retreat of th'unfortunate Brave;
Where Honor and Justice most odly contribute,
To ease Hero's Pains by a Halter and Gibbet.
  Derry down, down, hey derry down.

There Death breaks the Shackles, which Force had put on;
And the Hangman compleats, what the Judge but begun:
There the 'Squire of the Pad, and the Knight of the Post,
Find their Pains no more balk'd, and their Hopes no more crost.
    Derry down, &c.

Great Claims are there made, and great Secrets are known;
And the King, and the Law, and the Thief has His own:
But my Hearers cry out; What a duce dost Thou ayl?
Cut off thy Reflections; and give Us thy Tale.
    Derry down, &c.

'Twas there, then, in civil Respect to harsh Laws,
And for want of false Witness, to back a bad Cause,
A NORMAN, tho' late, was oblig'd to appear:
And Who to assist, but a grave CORDELIER?
    Derry down, &c.

The 'Squire, whose good Grace was to open the Scene,
Seem'd not in great Haste, that the Show shou'd begin:
Now fitted the Halter, now travers'd the Cart;
And often took Leave; but was loath to Depart.
    Derry down, &c.

What frightens You thus, my good Son? says the Priest:
You Murther'd, are Sorry, and have been Confest.
O Father! My Sorrow will scarce save my Bacon:
For 'twas not that I Murther'd, but that I was Taken.
    Derry down, &c.

Pough! pr'ythee ne'er trouble thy Head with such Fancies:
Rely on the Aid You shall have from Saint FRANCIS:
If the Money You promis'd be brought to the Chest;
You have only to Dye: let the Church do the rest.
    Derry down, &c.

And what will Folks say, if they see You afraid?
It reflects upon Me; as I knew not my Trade:
Courage, Friend; To-day is your Period of Sorrow;
And Things will go better, believe Me, To-morrow.
    Derry down, &c.

To-morrow? our Hero reply'd in a Fright:
He that's hang'd before Noon, ought to think of To-night.
Tell your Beads, quoth the Priest, and be fairly truss'd up:
For You surely To-night shall in PARADISE Sup.
    Derry down, &c.

Alas! quoth the 'Squire, howe'er sumptuous the Treat,
Parblew, I shall have little Stomach to Eat:
I should therefore esteem it great Favor, and Grace;
Wou'd You be so kind, as to go in my Place.
    Derry down, &c.

That I wou'd, quoth the Father, and thank you to boot;
But our Actions, You know, with our Duty must suit.
The Feast, I propos'd to You, I cannot taste:
For this Night, by our Order, is mark'd for a Fast.
    Derry down, &c.

Then turning about to the Hangman, He said;
Dispatch me, I pr'ythee, this troublesome Blade:
For Thy Cord, and My Cord both equally tie;
And We Live by the Gold, for which other Men Dye.
    Derry down, &c.

An *EPITAPH*.

Stet quicunque volet potens
Aulæ culmine lubrico, &c.   Senec.

INTERR'D beneath this Marble Stone,
  Lie Saunt'ring JACK, and Idle JOAN.
While rolling Threescore Years and One
Did round this Globe their Courses run;
If Human Things went Ill or Well;
If changing Empires rose or fell;
The Morning past, the Evening came,
And found this Couple still the same.

MATTHEW PRIOR

They Walk'd and Eat, good Folks: What then?
Why then They Walk'd and Eat again:
They soundly slept the Night away:
They did just Nothing all the Day:
And having bury'd Children Four,
Wou'd not take Pains to try for more.
Nor Sister either had, nor Brother:
They seem'd just Tally'd for each other.

Their Moral and Oeconomy
Most perfectly They made agree:
Each Virtue kept it's proper Bound,
Nor Trespass'd on the other's Ground.
Nor Fame, nor Censure They regarded:
They neither Punish'd, nor Rewarded.
He car'd not what the Footmen did:
Her Maids She neither prais'd, nor chid:
So ev'ry Servant took his Course;
And bad at First, They all grew worse.
Slothful Disorder fill'd His Stable;
And sluttish Plenty deck'd Her Table.
Their Beer was strong; Their Wine was *Port*;
Their Meal was large; Their Grace was short.
They gave the Poor the Remnant-meat,
Just when it grew not fit to eat.

They paid the Church and Parish-Rate;
And took, but read not the Receit:
For which They claim'd their *Sunday*'s Due,
Of slumb'ring in an upper Pew.

No Man's Defects sought They to know;
So never made Themselves a Foe.
No Man's good Deeds did They commend;
So never rais'd Themselves a Friend.
Nor cherish'd They Relations poor:
That might decrease Their present Store:
Nor Barn nor House did they repair:
That might oblige Their future Heir.

They neither Added, nor Confounded:
They neither Wanted, nor Abounded.
Each *Christmas* They Accompts did clear;
And wound their Bottom round the Year.
Nor Tear, nor Smile did They imploy
At News of Public Grief, or Joy.
When Bells were Rung, and Bonfires made;
If ask'd, They ne'er deny'd their Aid:
Their Jugg was to the Ringers carry'd;
Who ever either Dy'd, or Marry'd.
Their Billet at the Fire was found;
Who ever was Depos'd, or Crown'd.

Nor Good, nor Bad, nor Fools, nor Wise;
They wou'd not learn, nor cou'd advise:
Without Love, Hatred, Joy, or Fear,
They led——a kind of——as it were:
Nor Wish'd, nor Car'd, nor Laugh'd, nor Cry'd:
And so They liv'd; and so They dy'd.

Horace Lib. I. Epist. IX.

*Septimius, Claudi, nimirum intelligit unus,
Quanti me facias:* &c.

Imitated.

To the RIGHT HONORABLE

Mr. *HARLEY.*

DEAR DICK, how e'er it comes into his Head,
Believes, as firmly as He does his Creed,
That You and I, SIR, are extremely great;
Tho' I plain MAT, You *Minister of State.*
One Word from Me, without all doubt, He says,
Wou'd fix his Fortune in some little Place.

Thus better than My self, it seems, He knows,
How far my Interest with my Patron goes;
And answering all Objections I can make,
Still plunges deeper in his dear Mistake.

From this wild Fancy, SIR, there may proceed
One wilder yet, which I foresee, and dread;
That I, in Fact, a real Interest have,
Which to my own Advantage I wou'd save,
And, with the usual Courtier's Trick, intend
To serve My self, forgetful of my Friend.

To shun this Censure, I all Shame lay by;
And make my Reason with his Will comply;
Hoping, for my Excuse, 'twill be confest,
That of two Evils I have chose the least.
So, SIR, with this Epistolary Scroll,
Receive the Partner of my inmost Soul:
Him you will find in Letters, and in Laws
Not unexpert, firm to his Country's Cause,
Warm in the Glorious Interest You pursue,
And, in one Word, a Good Man and a True.

To Mr. *HARLEY*.

Wounded by GUISCARD. 1711.

————*ab ipso*
Ducit opes animumque ferro. HOR.

I.

IN one great *Now*, Superior to an Age,
    The full Extremes of Nature's Force We find:
How Heav'nly Virtue can exalt; or Rage
    Infernal, how degrade the Human Mind.

II.

While the fierce Monk does at his Tryal stand;
  He chews Revenge, abjuring his Offence:
Guile in his Tongue, and Murther in his Hand,
  He stabs his Judge, to prove his Innocence.

III.

The guilty Stroke and Torture of the Steel
  Infix'd, our dauntless BRITON scarce perceives:
The Wounds His Countrey from His Death must feel,
  The PATRIOT views; for those alone He grieves.

IV.

The barb'rous Rage that durst attempt Thy Life,
  HARLEY, great Counsellor, extends Thy Fame:
And the sharp Point of cruel GUISCARD's Knife,
  In Brass and Marble carves Thy deathless Name.

V.

Faithful Assertor of Thy Country's Cause,
  BRITAIN with Tears shall bath Thy glorious Wound:
She for thy Safety shall enlarge Her Laws;
  And in Her Statutes shall Thy Worth be found.

VI.

Yet 'midst Her Sighs She Triumphs, on the Hand
  Reflecting, that diffus'd the Publick Woe;
A Stranger to her Altars, and her Land:
  No Son of Her's could meditate this Blow.

VII.

Mean Time Thy Pain is gracious ANNA's Care:
  Our Queen, our Saint, with sacrificing Breath
Softens Thy Anguish: In Her pow'rful Pray'r
  She pleads Thy Service, and forbids Thy Death.

VIII.

Great as Thou art, Thou canst demand no more,
  O Breast bewail'd by Earth, preserv'd by Heav'n!
No higher can aspiring Virtue soar:
  Enough to Thee of Grief, and Fame is giv'n.

187

MATTHEW PRIOR

An *Extempore* INVITATION
TO THE
EARL of *OXFORD*,
Lord High Treasurer. 1712.

My LORD,

OUR Weekly Friends To-morrow meet
  At MATTHEW's Palace, in *Duke-street*;
To try for once, if They can Dine
On Bacon-Ham, and Mutton-chine:
If weary'd with the great Affairs,
Which BRITAIN trusts to HARLEY's Cares,
Thou, humble Statesman, may'st descend,
Thy Mind one Moment to unbend;
To see Thy Servant from his Soul
Crown with Thy Health the sprightly Bowl:
Among the Guests, which e'er my House
Receiv'd, it never can produce
Of Honor a more glorious Proof——
Tho' DORSET us'd to bless the Roof.

Erle ROBERT's
MICE.
In CHAUCER's *Stile.*

TWAY Mice, full Blythe and Amicable,
  Batten beside Erle ROBERT's Table.
Lies there ne Trap their Necks to catch,
Ne old black Cat their Steps to watch.
Their Fill they eat of Fowl and Fish;
Feast-lyche as Heart of Mouse mote wish.

As Guests sat Jovial at the Board,
Forth leap'd our Mice: Eftsoons the Lord
Of Boling, whilome John the Saint,
Who maketh oft Propos full queint,
Laugh'd jocund, and aloud He cry'd,
To Matthew seated on t'oth' side;
To Thee, lean Bard, it doth partain
To understand these Creatures Tweine.
Come frame Us now some clean Device,
Or playsant Rhime on yonder Mice:
They seem, God shield Me, Mat. and Charles.

Bad as Sir Topaz, or 'Squire Quarles
(Matthew did for the nonce reply)
At Emblem, or Device am I:
But could I Chaunt, or Rhyme, pardie,
Clear as *Dan* Chaucer, or as Thee;
Ne Verse from Me (so God me shrive)
On Mouse, or other Beast alive.
Certes, I have these many Days
Sent myne Poetic Herd to graze.
Ne Armed Knight ydrad in War
With Lyon fierce will I compare:
Ne Judge unjust, with furred Fox,
Harming in Secret Guise the Flocks:
Ne Priest unworth of Goddess Coat,
To Swine ydrunk, or filthy Stoat.
Elk Similè farwell for aye,
From Elephant, I trow, to Flea.

Reply'd the friendlike Peer, I weene,
Matthew is angred on the Spleen.
Ne so, quoth Mat. ne shall be e'er,
With Wit that falleth all so fair:
Eftsoons, well weet Ye, mine Intent
Boweth to your Commaundement.
If by these Creatures Ye have seen,
Pourtrayed Charles and Matthew been;
Behoveth neet to wreck my Brain,
The rest in Order to explain.

189

That Cup-board, where the Mice disport,
I liken to St.* STEPHEN's Court:
Therein is Space enough, I trow,
For elke Comrade to come and goe:
And therein eke may Both be fed
With Shiver of the Wheaten Bread.
And when, as these mine Eyen survey,
They cease to skip, and squeak, and play;
Return they may to different Cells,
AUDITING One, whilst t'other TELLS.

Dear ROBERT, quoth the SAINT, whose Mind
In Bounteous Deed no Mean can bind;
Now as I hope to grow devout,
I deem this Matter well made out.
Laugh I, whilst thus I serious Pray?
Let that be wrought which MAT. doth say:
Yea, quoth the ERLE; but not to Day.

In the same Style.

FULL oft doth MAT. with TOPAZ dine,
    Eateth bak'd Meats, drinketh Greek Wine:
But TOPAZ his own Werke rehearseth;
And MAT. mote praise what TOPAZ verseth.
Now sure as Priest did e'er shrive Sinner,
Full hardly earneth MAT. his Dinner.

In the same Style.

FAIR SUSAN did her Wif-hede well menteine,
    Algates assaulted sore by Letchours tweine;
Now, and I read aright that Auncient Song,
Olde were the Paramours, the Dame full yong.

Had thilke same Tale in other Guise been tolde;
Had They been Yong (pardie) and She been Olde;
That, by St KIT, had wrought much sorer Tryal:
Full merveillous, I wote, were swilk Denyal.

* Exchequer.

A FLOWER,

Painted by

SIMON VARELST.

WHEN fam'd VARELST this little Wonder drew;
  FLORA vouchsaf'd the growing Work to view:
Finding the Painter's Science at a Stand,
The Goddess snatch'd the Pencil from his Hand;
And finishing the Piece, She smiling said;
Behold One Work of Mine, that ne'er shall fade.

TO THE

Lady ELIZABETH HARLEY,

Since Marchioness of CARMARTHEN,

On a Column of Her Drawing.

WHEN future Ages shall with Wonder view
  These glorious Lines, which HARLEY's Daughter drew;
They shall confess, that BRITAIN could not raise
A fairer Column to the Father's Praise.

PROTOGENES *and* APELLES.

WHEN Poets wrote, and Painters drew,
  As Nature pointed out the View:
E'er GOTHIC Forms were known in GREECE,
To spoil the well-proportion'd Piece:
And in our Verse e'er Monkish Rhimes
Had jangl'd their fantastic Chimes:

191

MATTHEW PRIOR

E'er on the flow'ry Lands of RHODES
Those Knights had fix'd their dull Abodes,
Who knew not much to paint or write,
Nor car'd to pray, nor dar'd to fight:
PROTOGENES, Historians note,
Liv'd there, a Burgess Scot and Lot;
And, as old PLINY's Writings show,
APELLES did the same at Co.
Agreed these Points of Time, and Place,
Proceed We in the present Case.

Picqu'd by PROTOGENES's Fame,
From Co to RHODES, APELLES came;
To see a Rival and a Friend,
Prepar'd to Censure, or Commend,
Here to absolve, and there object,
As Art with Candor might direct.
He sails, He lands, He comes, He rings:
His Servants follow with the Things:
Appears the Governante of th'House:
(For such in GREECE were much in use.)
If Young or Handsom, Yea or No,
Concerns not Me, or Thee to know.

Does 'Squire PROTOGENES live here?
Yes, Sir, says She with gracious Air,
And Curt'sey low; but just call'd out
By Lords peculiarly devout;
Who came on purpose, Sir, to borrow
Our VENUS, for the Feast To-morrow,
To grace the Church: 'tis VENUS' Day:
I hope, Sir, You intend to stay,
To see our VENUS: 'tis the Piece
The most renown'd throughout all GREECE,
So like th'Original, they say:
But I have no great Skill that Way.
But, Sir, at Six ('tis now past Three)
DROMO must make my Master's Tea:
At Six, Sir, if You please to come,
You'll find my Master, Sir, at Home.

Tea, says a Critic big with Laughter,
Was found some twenty Ages after:
Authors, before they write, shou'd read:
'Tis very true; but We'll proceed.

And, Sir, at present wou'd you please
To leave your Name——Fair Maiden, yes:
Reach me that Board. No sooner spoke
But done. With one judicious Stroke,
On the plain Ground APELLES drew
A Circle regularly true:
And will you please, Sweet-heart, said He,
To shew your Master this from Me?
By it He presently will know,
How Painters write their Names at Co.

He gave the Pannel to the Maid.
Smiling and Curt'sing, Sir, She said,
I shall not fail to tell my Master:
And, Sir, for fear of all Disaster,
I'll keep it my own self: Safe bind,
Says the old Proverb, and Safe find.
So, Sir, as sure as Key or Lock——
Your Servant Sir——at Six a Clock.

Again at Six APELLES came;
Found the same prating civil Dame.
Sir, that my Master has been here,
Will by the Board it self appear.
If from the perfect Line He found,
He has presum'd to swell the Round,
Or Colors on the Draught to lay;
'Tis thus (He order'd me to say)
Thus write the Painters of this Isle:
Let those of Co remark the Style.

She said; and to his Hand restor'd
The rival Pledge, the Missive Board.
Upon the happy Line were laid
Such obvious Light, and easie Shade;
That PARIS' Apple stood confest,
Or LEDA's Egg, or CLOE's Breast.

APELLES view'd the finish'd Piece;
And Live, said He, the Arts of GREECE!
Howe'er PROTOGENES and I
May in our Rival Talents vie;
Howe'er our Works may have express'd,
Who truest drew, or color'd best;
When He beheld my flowing Line;
He found at least I cou'd design:
And from his artful Round, I grant,
That He with perfect Skill can paint.

The dullest GENIUS cannot fail
To find the Moral of my Tale:
That the distinguish'd Part of Men,
With Compass, Pencil, Sword, or Pen,
Shou'd in Life's Visit leave their Name,
In Characters, which may proclaim
That They with Ardor strove to raise
At once their Arts, and Countrey's Praise:
And in their Working took great Care,
That all was Full, and Round, and Fair.

DEMOCRITUS *and* HERACLITUS.

DEMOCRITUS, dear Droll, revisit Earth,
And with our Follies glut Thy heighten'd Mirth·
Sad HERACLITUS, serious Wretch, return,
In louder Grief our greater Crimes to mourn.
Between You both I unconcern'd stand by:
Hurt, can I laugh? and Honest, need I cry?

For my own Tomb-stone.

TO Me 'twas giv'n to die: to Thee 'tis giv'n
To live: Alas! one Moment sets us ev'n.
Mark! how impartial is the Will of Heav'n?

GUALTERUS DANISTONUS.

Ad Amicos.

DUM Studeo fungi fallentis munere vitæ,
    Adfectoque viam sedibus Elysiis,
ARCTOA florens Sophiâ, SAMIISQUE superbus
    Discipulis, Animas morte carere cano.
Has ego corporibus profugas ad sidera mitto;
    Sideraque ingressis otia blanda dico:
Qualia conveniunt Divis, queis fata volebant
    Vitäi faciles mollitèr ire vias:
Vinaque Cœlicolis media inter gaudia libo;
    Et me quid majus suspicor esse viro.
Sed fuerint nulli forsan, quos spondeo, cœli;
    Nullaque sint DITIS Numina, nulla JOVIS:
Fabula sit terris agitur quæ vita relictis;
    Quique superstes, Homo; qui nihil, esto Deus.
Attamen esse hilares, & inanes mittere curas
    Proderit, ac vitæ commoditate frui,
Et festos agitâsse dies, ævique fugacis
    Tempora perpetuis detinuisse jocis.
His me parentem præceptis occupet Orcus,
    Et Mors; seu Divum, seu nihil esse velit:
Nam Sophia Ars illa est, quæ fallere suavitèr horas
    Admonet, atque Orci non timuisse minas.

IMITATED.

STUDIOUS the busie Moments to deceive,
    That fleet between the Cradle and the Grave,
I credit what the GREECIAN Dictates say,
And SAMIAN Sounds o'er SCOTIA's Hills convey.
When mortal Man resigns his transient Breath;
The Body only I give o'er to Death.
The Parts dissolv'd, and broken Frame I mourn:
What came from Earth, I see to Earth return.
The Immaterial Part, th'Æthereal Soul,
Nor can Change vanquish, nor can Death controul.
Glad I release it from it's Partner's Cares;
And bid good Angels waft it to the Stars.

Then in the flowing Bowl I drown those Sighs,
Which, Spight of Wisdom, from our Weakness rise.
The Draught to the Dead's Mem'ry I commend,
And offer to the now immortal Friend.
But if oppos'd to what my Thoughts approve,
Nor PLUTO's Rage there be, nor Pow'r of JOVE;
On it's dark Side if Thou the Prospect take;
Grant all forgot beyond black LETHE's Lake:
In total Death suppose the Mortal lye,
No new Hereafter, nor a future Sky:
Yet bear thy Lot content; yet cease to grieve:
Why, e'er Death comes, dost Thou forbear to live?
The little Time Thou hast, 'twixt Instant Now
And Fate's Approach, is All the Gods allow:
And of this little hast Thou ought to spare
To sad Reflection, and corroding Care?
The Moments past, if Thou art wise, retrieve
With pleasant Mem'ry of the Bliss they gave.
The present Hours in present Mirth imploy;
And bribe the Future with the Hopes of Joy.
The Future (few or more, how e'er they be)
Were destin'd e'rst; nor can by Fate's Decree
Be now cut off, betwixt the Grave and Thee.

THE FIRST
HYMN
OF
CALLIMACHUS.
TO
JUPITER.

WHILE we to JOVE select the holy Victim;
Whom apter shall we sing, than JOVE himself,
The God for ever Great, for ever King;
Who slew the Earth-born Race, and measures Right

POEMS ON SEVERAL OCCASIONS

To Heav'n's great Habitants? DICTÆAN hear'st Thou
More joyful, or LYCÆAN, long Dispute
And various Thought has trac'd. On IDA's Mount,
Or DICTE, studious of his Country's Praise,
The CRETAN boasts Thy Natal Place: but oft
He meets Reproof deserv'd: for He presumptuous
Has built a Tomb for Thee, who never know'st
To die, but liv'st the same To-day and Ever.
ARCADIAN therefore be Thy Birth: Great RHEA
Pregnant to high PARRHASIA's Cliffs retir'd,
And wild LYCÆUS, black with shading Pines:
Holy Retreat! Sithence no Female hither,
Conscious of Social Love and Nature's Rites,
Must dare approach, from the inferior Reptile
To Woman, Form Divine. There the blest Parent
Ungirt her spacious Bosom, and discharg'd
The pond'rous Birth: She sought a neighb'ring Spring,
To wash the recent Babe: In vain: ARCADIA,
(However streamy now) adust and dry,
Deny'd the Goddess Water: where deep MELAS,
And rocky CRATIS flow, the Chariot smoak'd,
Obscure with rising Dust: the thirsty Trav'ler
In vain requir'd the Current, then imprison'd
In subterranean Caverns: Forests grew
Upon the barren Hollows, high o'ershading
The Haunts of Savage Beasts, where now IAON,
And ERIMANTH incline their friendly Urns.

Thou too, O Earth, great RHEA said, bring forth;
And short shall be thy Pangs: She said; and high
She rear'd her Arm, and with her Scepter struck
The yawning Cliff: from it's disparted Height
Adown the Mount the gushing Torrent ran,
And chear'd the Vallies: There the Heav'nly Mother
Bath'd, mighty King, Thy tender Limbs: She wrapt them
In purple Bands: She gave the precious Pledge
To prudent NEDA, charging her to guard Thee,
Careful and secret: NEDA of the Nymphs
That tended the great Birth, next PHILYRE
And STYX, the eldest. Smiling She receiv'd Thee,

197

MATTHEW PRIOR

And conscious of the Grace, absolv'd her Trust:
Not unrewarded; since the River bore
The Fav'rite Virgin's Name: fair NEDA rowls
By LEPRION's ancient Walls, a fruitful Stream.
Fast by her flow'ry Bank the Sons of ARCAS,
Fav'rites of Heav'n, with happy Care protect
Their fleecy Charge; and joyous drink her Wave.

Thee, God, to CNOSSUS NEDA brought: the Nymphs
And CORYBANTES Thee their sacred Charge
Receiv'd; ADRASTE rock'd Thy golden Cradle:
The Goat, now bright amidst her fellow-Stars,
Kind AMALTHEA, reach'd her Tett distent
With Milk, Thy early Food: the sedulous Bee
Distill'd her Honey on Thy purple Lips.

Around, the fierce CURETES (Order solemn
To thy foreknowing Mother!) trod tumultuous
Their Mystic Dance, and clang'd their sounding Arms:
Industrious with the warlike Din to quell
Thy Infant-Cries, and mock the Ear of SATURN.

Swift Growth and wond'rous Grace, O heav'nly JOVE,
Waited Thy blooming Years: Inventive Wit,
And perfect Judgment crown'd Thy youthful Act.
That SATURN's Sons receiv'd the three-fold Empire
Of Heav'n, of Ocean, and deep Hell beneath,
As the dark Urn and Chance of Lot determin'd,
Old Poets mention, fabling. Things of Moment
Well nigh equivalent and neighb'ring Value
By Lot are parted: But high Heav'n, Thy Share,
In equal Balance laid 'gainst Sea or Hell,
Flings up the adverse Scale, and shuns Proportion.
Wherefore not Chance, but Pow'r, above Thy Brethren
Exalted Thee, their King. When Thy great Will
Commands Thy Chariot forth; impetuous Strength,
And fiery Swiftness wing the rapid Wheels,
Incessant; high the Eagle flies before Thee.
And oh! as I and mine consult Thy Augur,
Grant the glad Omen; let Thy Fav'rite rise
Propitious, ever soaring from the Right.

POEMS ON SEVERAL OCCASIONS

Thou to the lesser Gods hast well assign'd
Their proper Shares of Pow'r; Thy own, great JOVE,
Boundless and universal. Those who labor
The sweaty Forge, who edge the crooked Scythe,
Bend stubborn Steel, and harden gleening Armor,
Acknowledge VULCAN's Aid. The early Hunter
Blesses DIANA's Hand, who leads Him safe
O'er hanging Cliffs; who spreads his Net successful,
And guides the Arrow through the Panther's Heart.
The Soldier from successful Camps returning,
With Laurel wreath'd, and rich with hostile Spoil,
Severs the Bull to MARS. The skilful Bard,
Striking the THRACIAN Harp, invokes APOLLO,
To make his Hero and Himself Immortal.
Those, mighty JOVE, mean time, Thy glorious Care,
Who model Nations, publish Laws, announce
Or Life or Death, and found or change the Empire.
Man owns the Pow'r of Kings; and Kings of JOVE.

And as their Actions tend subordinate
To what Thy Will designs, Thou giv'st the Means
Proportion'd to the Work; Thou see'st impartial,
How They those Means imploy. Each Monarch rules
His different Realm, accountable to Thee,
Great Ruler of the World: These only have
To speak and be obey'd; to Those are giv'n
Assistant Days to ripen the Design;
To some whole Months; revolving Years to some:
Others, ill fated, are condemn'd to toil
Their tedious Life, and mourn their Purpose blasted
With fruitless Act, and Impotence of Council.

Hail! greatest Son of SATURN, wise Disposer
Of ev'ry Good: Thy Praise what Man yet born
Has sung? or who that may be born shall sing?
Again, and often hail! indulge our Prayer,
Great Father! grant us Virtue, grant us Wealth:
For without Virtue, Wealth to Man avails not;
And Virtue without Wealth exerts less Pow'r,
And less diffuses Good. Then grant us, Gracious,
Virtue, and Wealth; for both are of Thy Gift.

THE SECOND
HYMN
OF
CALLIMACHUS.
TO
APOLLO.

HAH! how the Laurel, great APOLLO's Tree,
 And all the Cavern shakes! far off, far off,
The Man that is unhallow'd: for the God,
The God approaches. Hark! He knocks: the Gates
Feel the glad Impulse: and the sever'd Bars
Submissive clink against their brazen Portals.
Why do the DELIAN Palms incline their Boughs,
Self-mov'd: and hov'ring Swans, their Throats releas'd
From native Silence, carol Sounds harmonious?

Begin, young Men, the Hymn: let all your Harps
Break their inglorious Silence; and the Dance,
In mystic Numbers trod, explain the Music.
But first by ardent Pray'r, and clear Lustration
Purge the contagious Spots of Human Weakness:
Impure no Mortal can behold APOLLO.
So may Ye flourish, favor'd by the God,
In Youth with happy Nuptials, and in Age
With silver Hairs, and fair Descent of Children;
So lay Foundations for aspiring Cities,
And bless your spreading Colonies Encrease.

Pay sacred Rev'rence to APOLLO's Song;
Lest wrathful the far-shooting God emitt
His fatal Arrows. Silent Nature stands;
And Seas subside, obedient to the Sound
Of Io, Io PEAN! nor dares THETIS
Longer bewail Her lov'd ACHILLES' Death:

For PHOEBUS was his Foe. Nor must sad NIOBE
In fruitless Sorrow persevere, or weep
Ev'n thro' the PHRYGIAN Marble. Hapless Mother!
Whose Fondness cou'd compare her Mortal Off-spring
To those which fair LATONA bore to JOVE.
Io! again repeat Ye, Io PEAN!

Against the Deity 'tis hard to strive.
He that resists the Power of PTOLEMY,
Resists the Pow'r of Heav'n: for Pow'r from Heav'n
Derives; and Monarchs rule by Gods appointed.

Recite APOLLO's Praise, 'till Night draws on,
The Ditty still unfinish'd; and the Day
Unequal to the Godhead's Attributes
Various, and Matter copious of your Songs.

Sublime at JOVE's right Hand APOLLO sits,
And thence distributes Honor, gracious King,
And Theme of Verse perpetual. From his Robe
Flows Light ineffable: his Harp, his Quiver,
And LICTIAN Bow are Gold: with golden Sandals
His Feet are shod; how rich! how beautiful!
Beneath his Steps the yellow Min'ral rises;
And Earth reveals her Treasures. Youth and Beauty
Eternal deck his Cheek: from his fair Head
Perfumes distill their Sweets; and chearful HEALTH,
His dutious Handmaid, thro' the Air improv'd,
With lavish Hand diffuses Scents Ambrosial.

The Spear-man's Arm by Thee, great God, directed,
Sends forth a certain Wound. The Laurel'd Bard,
Inspir'd by Thee, composes Verse Immortal.
Taught by thy Art Divine, the sage Physician
Eludes the Urn; and chains, or exiles Death.

Thee NOMIAN We adore; for that from Heav'n
Descending, Thou on fair AMPHRYSUS' Banks
Did'st guard ADMETUS' Herds. Sithence the Cow
Produc'd an ampler Store of Milk; the She-Goat
Not without Pain dragg'd her distended Udder;
And Ewes, that erst brought forth but single Lambs,
Now drop'd their Two-fold Burdens. Blest the Cattle,
On which APOLLO cast his fav'ring Eye!

MATTHEW PRIOR

But, PHOEBUS, Thou to Man beneficent,
Delight'st in building Cities. Bright DIANA,
Kind Sister to thy infant-Deity
New-wean'd, and just arising from the Cradle,
Brought hunted wild Goats-Heads, and branching Antlers
Of Stags, The Fruit and Honor of her Toil.
These with discerning Hand Thou knew'st to range,
(Young as Thou wast) and in the well-fram'd Models,
With Emblematic Skill, and mystic Order,
Thou shew'dst, where Towers, or Battlements should rise;
Where gates should open; or where Walls should compass:
While from thy childish Pastime Man receiv'd
The future Strength, and Ornament of Nations.

BATTUS, our great Progenitor, now touch'd
The LYBIAN Strand; when the fore-boding Crow
Flew on the Right before the People, marking
The Country destin'd the auspicious Seat
Of future Kings, and Favor of the God,
Whose Oath is sure, and Promise stands Eternal.

Or BOEDROMIAN hear'st Thou pleas'd, or CLARIAN,
PHOEBUS, great King? for diff'rent are Thy Names,
As Thy kind Hand has founded many Cities,
Or dealt benign Thy various Gifts to Man.
CARNEAN let Me call Thee; for my Country
Calls Thee CARNEAN: the fair Colony
Thrice by Thy gracious Guidance was transported,
E'er settl'd in CYRENE; there W'appointed
Thy annual Feasts, kind God, and bless thy Altars
Smoking with Hecatombs of slaughter'd Bulls;
As CARNUS, thy High-Priest, and favor'd Friend,
Had er'st ordain'd; and with mysterious Rites,
Our great Forefathers taught their Sons to worship.
Io CARNEAN PHOEBUS! Io PEAN!

The yellow *Crocus* there, and fair *Narcissus*
Reserve the Honors of their Winter-Store,
To deck Thy Temple; 'till returning Spring
Diffuses Nature's various Pride; and Flow'rs
Innumerable, by the soft South-west
Open'd, and gather'd by Religious Hands,

Rebound their Sweets from th'odorif'rous Pavement.
Perpetual Fires shine hallow'd on Thy Altars.
When Annual the CARNEAN Feast is held,
The warlike LIBYANS clad in Armor, lead
The Dance, with clanging Swords and Shields They beat
The dreadful Measure : in the Chorus join
Their Women, Brown but Beautiful : such Rites
To Thee well-pleasing. Nor had yet Thy Votaries,
From GREECE transplanted, touch'd CYRENE's Banks,
And Lands determin'd for their last Abodes;
But wander'd thro' AZILIS' horrid Forrest
Dispers'd; when from MYRTUSA's craggy Brow,
Fond of the Maid, auspicious to the City,
Which must hereafter bear her favor'd Name,
Thou Gracious deign'st to let the Fair One view
Her *Typic* People ; Thou with Pleasure taught'st Her
To draw the Bow, to slay the shaggy Lyon,
And stop the spreading Ruin of the Plains.
Happy the Nymph, who honor'd by Thy Passion,
Was aided by thy Pow'r ! The monstrous PYTHON
Durst tempt Thy Wrath in vain : for dead He fell,
To thy great Strength, and golden Arms unequal.

Io ! while Thy unerring Hand elanc'd
Another, and another Dart ; The People
Joyful repeated, Io ! Io PEAN !
Elance the Dart, APOLLO : for the Safety,
And Health of Man, gracious Thy Mother bore Thee.

ENVY Thy latest Foe suggested thus :
Like Thee I am a Pow'r Immortal ; therefore
To Thee dare speak. How can'st Thou favor partial
Those Poets who write little ? Vast and Great
Is what I Love : The far extended Ocean
To a small Riv'let I prefer. APOLLO
Spurn'd ENVY with His Foot ; and thus the God :
DÆMON, the head-long Current of EUPHRATES,
ASSYRIAN River, copious runs, but Muddy ;
And carries forward with his stupid Force
Polluting Dirt ; His Torrent still augmenting,
His Wave still more defil'd : mean while the Nymphs

203

MELISSAN, Sacred and Recluse to CERES,
Studious to have their Off'rings well receiv'd,
And fit for Heav'nly Use, from little Urns
Pour Streams select, and Purity of Waters.

Io! APOLLO, mighty King, let ENVY
Ill-judging and Verbose, from LETHE's Lake
Draw Tons unmeasurable; while Thy Favor
Administers to my ambitious Thirst
The wholesome Draught from AGANIPPE's Spring
Genuine, and with soft Murmurs gently rilling
Adown the Mountains, where Thy Daughters haunt.

CHARITY.

A

PARAPHRASE

On the Thirteenth CHAPTER *of the First* EPISTLE

TO THE

CORINTHIANS.

DID sweeter Sounds adorn my flowing Tongue,
    Than ever Man pronounc'd, or Angel sung:
Had I all Knowledge, Human and Divine,
That Thought can reach, or Science can define;
And had I Pow'r to give that Knowledge Birth,
In all the Speeches of the babling Earth:
Did SHADRACH's Zeal my glowing Breast inspire,
To weary Tortures, and rejoice in Fire:
Or had I Faith like That which ISRAEL saw,
When MOSES gave them Miracles, and Law:

Yet, gracious CHARITY, indulgent Guest,
Were not Thy Pow'r exerted in my Breast;
Those Speeches would send up unheeded Pray'r:
That Scorn of Life would be but wild Despair:
A Tymbal's Sound were better than my Voice:
My Faith were Form: my Eloquence were Noise.

CHARITY, decent, modest, easy, kind,
Softens the high, and rears the abject Mind;
Knows with just Reins, and gentle Hand to guide,
Betwixt vile Shame, and arbitrary Pride.
Not soon provok'd, She easily forgives;
And much She suffers, as She much believes.
Soft Peace She brings where-ever She arrives:
She builds our Quiet, as She forms our Lives;
Lays the rough Paths of peevish Nature ev'n;
And opens in each Heart a little HEAV'N.

Each other Gift, which GOD on Man bestows,
It's proper Bounds, and due Restriction knows;
To one fixt Purpose dedicates it's Pow'r;
And finishing it's Act, exists no more.
Thus, in Obedience to what HEAV'N decrees,
Knowledge shall fail, and Prophecy shall cease:
But lasting CHARITY's more ample Sway,
Nor bound by Time, nor subject to Decay,
In happy Triumph shall for ever live,
And endless Good diffuse, and endless Praise receive.

As thro' the Artist's intervening Glass,
Our Eye observes the distant Planets pass;
A little we discover; but allow,
That more remains unseen, than Art can show:
So whilst our Mind it's Knowledge wou'd improve;
(It's feeble Eye intent on Things above)
High as We may, We lift our Reason up,
By FAITH directed, and confirm'd by HOPE:
Yet are We able only to survey
Dawnings of Beams, and Promises of Day.
HEAV'N's fuller Effluence mocks our dazl'd Sight;
Too great it's Swiftness, and too strong it's Light.

But soon the mediate Clouds shall be dispell'd;
The Sun shall soon be Face to Face beheld,
In all His Robes, with all His Glory on,
Seated sublime on His Meridian Throne.

Then constant FAITH, and holy HOPE shall dye,
One lost in Certainty, and One in Joy:
Whilst Thou, more happy Pow'r, fair CHARITY,
Triumphant Sister, greatest of the Three,
Thy Office, and Thy Nature still the same,
Lasting thy Lamp, and unconsum'd thy Flame,
Shalt still survive——
Shalt stand before the Host of HEAV'N confest,
For ever blessing, and for ever blest.

Engraven on a COLUMN

In the Church of HALSTEAD *in* ESSEX,

The spire of which, burnt down by Lightning, was rebuilt at the Expense of Mr. SAMUEL FISKE, 1717.

VIEW not this Spire by Measure giv'n
     To Buildings rais'd by common Hands:
That Fabric rises high as Heav'n,
     Whose *Basis* on Devotion stands.

While yet We draw this vital Breath,
     We can our FAITH and HOPE declare:
But CHARITY beyond our Death,
     Will ever in our Works appear.

Best be He call'd among good Men,
     Who to his GOD this Column rais'd:
Tho' Lightning strike the Dome again;
     The Man, who built it, shall be prais'd.

Yet Spires and Towers in Dust shall lye,
     The weak Efforts of Human Pains:
And FAITH, and HOPE themselves shall dye;
     While Deathless CHARITY remains.

Written in MONTAIGNE'S *Essays,*

Given to the Duke of SHREWSBURY *in* FRANCE,
after the Peace, 1713.

DICTATE, O mighty Judge, what Thou hast seen
 Of Cities, and of Courts, of Books, and Men ;
And deign to let Thy Servant hold the Pen.

Thro' Ages thus I may presume to live ;
And from the Transcript of Thy Prose receive,
What my own short-liv'd Verse can never give.

Thus shall fair BRITAIN with a gracious Smile
Accept the Work ; and the instructed Isle,
For more than Treaties made, shall bless my Toil.

Nor longer hence the GALLIC Style preferr'd,
Wisdom in ENGLISH *Idiom* shall be heard ;
While TALBOT tells the World, where MONTAIGNE err'd.

An EPISTLE,

Desiring the QUEEN'S *Picture.*

Written at PARIS, 1714. *But left unfinish'd by the
sudden News of Her* MAJESTY'S *Death.*

THE Train of Equipage and Pomp of State,
 The shining Side-board, and the burnish'd Plate
Let other Ministers, Great ANNE, require ;
And partial fall Thy Gift to their Desire.
To the fair Portrait of my Sov'reign Dame,
To That alone, eternal be my Claim.

MATTHEW PRIOR

My bright Defender, and my dread Delight,
If ever I found Favor in Thy Sight;
If all the Pains that for Thy BRITAIN's Sake
My past has took, or future Life may take,
Be grateful to my QUEEN; permit my Pray'r,
And with This Gift reward my total Care.

Will Thy indulgent Hand, fair Saint, allow
The Boon? and will Thy Ear accept the Vow?
That in despight of Age, of impious Flame,
And eating Time, Thy Picture like Thy Fame
Entire may last; that as their Eyes survey
The semblant Shade, Men yet unborn may say;
Thus Great, thus Gracious look'd BRITANNIA's Queen;
Her Brow thus smooth, Her Look was thus serene;
When to a Low, but to a Loyal Hand
The mighty Empress gave Her high Command,
That He to Hostile Camps, and Kings shou'd haste,
To speak Her Vengeance as Their Danger past;
To say, She Wills detested Wars to cease;
She checks Her Conquest, for Her Subjects Ease;
And bids the World attend Her Terms of Peace.

Thee, Gracious ANNE, Thee present I adore,
Thee, QUEEN of PEACE——If Time and Fate have Pow'r
Higher to raise the Glories of thy Reign;
In Words sublimer, and a nobler Strain,
May future Bards the mighty Theme rehearse.
Here, STATOR JOVE, and PHOEBUS King of Verse,
The Votive Tablet I suspend * * * *

ALMA:

OR, THE

PROGRESS

OF THE

MIND.

In Three Cantos.

Πάντα γελως, καὶ πάντα κόνις, καὶ πάντα τὸ μηδὲν·
Πάντα γὰρ ἐξ ἀλόγων ἐστὶ τὰ γιγνόμενα.

Incert. ap. Stob[æ]um.

THE

FIRST CANTO.

MATTHEW met RICHARD; when or where
    From Story is not mighty clear:
Of many knotty Points They spoke;
And *Pro* and *Con* by turns They took.
Ratts half the Manuscript have eat:
Dire Hunger! which We still regret:
O! may they ne'er again digest
The Horrors of so sad a Feast.
Yet less our Grief, if what remains,
Dear JACOB, by thy Care and Pains
Shall be to future Times convey'd.
It thus begins:
   *   *   *   *   Here MATTHEW said:

   ALMA in Verse; in Prose, the MIND,
By ARISTOTLE'S Pen defin'd,
Throughout the Body squat or tall,
Is, *bonâ fide*, All in All.
And yet, slap dash, is All again
In every Sinew, Nerve, and Vein.
Runs here and there, like HAMLET's Ghost;
While every where She rules the roast.

   This *System*, RICHARD, We are told,
The Men of OXFORD firmly hold.
The CAMBRIDGE Wits, You know, deny
With *Ipse dixit* to comply.
They say (for in good truth They speak
With small Respect of that old GREEK)
That, putting all his Words together,
'Tis Three blew Beans in One blew Bladder.

ALMA, They strenuously maintain,
Sits Cock-horse on Her Throne, the Brain;
And from that Seat of Thought dispenses
Her Sov'reign Pleasure to the Senses.
Two *Optic* Nerves, They say, She tyes,
Like Spectacles, a-cross the Eyes;
By which the Spirits bring her Word,
Whene'er the Balls are fix'd, or stirr'd;
How quick at Park and Play they strike;
The Duke they court; the Toast they like;
And at Sᵀ JAMES's turn their Grace
From former Friends, now out of Place.

Without these Aids, to be more serious,
Her Pow'r, They hold, had been precarious:
The Eyes might have conspir'd her Ruin;
And She not known, what They were doing.
Foolish it had been, and unkind,
That They shou'd see, and She be blind.

Wise Nature likewise, They suppose,
Has drawn two Conduits down our Nose:
Cou'd ALMA else with Judgment tell,
When *Cabbage* stinks, or *Roses* smell?
Or who wou'd ask for her Opinion
Between an *Oyster*, and an *Onion*?
For from most Bodies, DICK, You know,
Some little Bits ask Leave to flow;
And, as thro' these Canals They roll,
Bring up a Sample of the Whole.
Like Footmen running before Coaches,
To tell the Inn, what Lord approaches.

By Nerves about our Palate plac'd,
She likewise judges of the Taste.
Else (dismal Thought!) our Warlike Men
Might drink thick *Port* for fine *Champagne*;
And our ill-judging Wives and Daughters
Mistake Small-beer for *Citron*-Waters.

Hence too, that She might better hear,
She sets a Drum at either Ear;
And Loud or Gentle, Harsh or Sweet,
Are but th'*Alarums* which They beat.

Last, to enjoy her Sense of Feeling
(A thing She much delights to deal in)
A thousand little Nerves She sends
Quite to our Toes, and Fingers Ends;
And These in Gratitude again
Return their Spirits to the Brain;
In which their Figure being printed
(As just before, I think, I hinted)
ALMA inform'd can try the Case,
As She had been upon the Place.

Thus, while the Judge gives diff'rent Journeys
To Country Counsel, and Attornies;
He on the Bench in quiet sits,
Deciding, as They bring the Writs.
The POPE thus prays and sleeps at ROME,
And very seldom stirs from Home:
Yet sending forth his Holy Spies,
And having heard what They advise,
He rules the Church's blest Dominions;
And sets Men's Faith by His Opinions.

The Scholars of the STAGYRITE,
Who for the Old Opinion fight,
Would make their Modern Friends confess,
The diff'rence but from More to Less.
The MIND, say They, while You sustain
To hold her Station in the Brain;
You grant, at least, She is extended:
Ergo the whole Dispute is ended.
For, 'till To-morrow shou'd You plead
From Form and Structure of the Head;
The MIND as visibly is seen
Extended thro' the whole *Machine*.
Why shou'd all Honor then be ta'en
From Lower Parts to load the Brain;
When other Limbs we plainly see,

Each in his way, as brisk as He?
For Music, grant the Head receives it;
It is the Artist's Hand that gives it.
And tho' the Scull may wear the Laurel;
The Soldier's Arm sustains the Quarrel.
Besides, the Nostrils, Ears, and Eyes
Are not his Parts, but his Allies.
Ev'n what You hear the Tongue proclaim,
Comes *ab Origine* from them.
What could the Head perform Alone,
If all Their friendly Aids were gone?
A foolish figure He must make;
Do nothing else, but sleep and ake.

Nor matters it, that You can show,
How to the Head that Spirits go.
Those Spirits started from some Goal,
Before they thro' the Veins cou'd roll.
Now We shou'd hold Them much to blame,
If They went back, before They came.

If therefore, as We must suppose,
They came from Fingers, and from Toes;
Or Toes, or Fingers, in this Case,
Of *Num-scull's* Self shou'd take the Place.
Disputing fair, You grant thus much,
That all Sensation is but Touch.
Dip but your Toes into cold Water;
Their Correspondent Teeth will chatter:
And strike the Bottom of your Feet;
You set your Head into a Heat.
The Bully beat, and happy Lover
Confess, that Feeling lies all over.

Note here, LUCRETIUS dares to teach
(As all our Youth may learn from CREECH)
That Eyes were made, but cou'd not view;
Nor Hands embrace, nor Feet pursue:
But heedless Nature did produce
The Members first, and then the Use.
What Each must act, was yet unknown,
'Till All is mov'd by Chance alone.

MATTHEW PRIOR

A Man first builds a Country Seat;
Then finds the Walls not good to eat.
Another plants, and wond'ring sees
Nor Books, nor Medals on his Trees.
Yet Poet and Philosopher
Was He, who durst such Whims aver.
Blest, for his Sake, be human Reason,
That came at all, tho' late, in Season.

But no Man sure e'er left his House,
And saddl'd *Ball*, with Thoughts so wild,
To bring a Midwife to his Spouse,
Before He knew She was with Child.
And no Man ever reapt his Corn,
Or from the Oven drew his Bread,
E'er Hinds and Bakers yet were born,
That taught him both to Sow, and Knead.
Before They're ask'd, can Maids refuse?
Can——Pray, says DICK, hold in your Muse.
While You *Pindaric* Truths rehearse;
She hobbles in *Alternate* Verse.
Verse? MAT. reply'd: is that my Care?
Go on, quoth RICHARD, soft and fair.

This looks, friend DICK, as Nature had
But exercis'd the *Salesman's* Trade:
As if She haply had sat down,
And cut out Cloaths for all the Town;
Then sent them out to *Monmouth*-Street,
To try, what Persons they wou'd fit.
But ev'ry Free and Licenc'd Taylor
Would in this *Thesis* find a Failure.
Should Whims like these his Head perplex,
How could he work for either Sex?
His Cloaths, as Atomes might prevail,
Might fit a Pismire, or a Whale.
No, no: He views with studious Pleasure
Your Shape, before He takes your Measure.
For real KATE He made the Boddice,
And not for an *Ideal* Goddess.

No Error near his Shop-board lurk'd:
He knew the Folks for whom He work'd.
Still to Their Size He aim'd his Skill:
Else, pr'ythee, who wou'd pay his Bill?

Next, DICK, if Chance her self shou'd vary;
Observe, how Matters would miscarry:
Across your Eyes, Friend, place your Shoes;
Your Spectacles upon your Toes:
Then You and MEMMIUS shall agree,
How nicely Men would walk, or see.

But Wisdom, peevish and cross-grain'd,
Must be oppos'd, to be sustain'd.
And still your Knowledge will increase,
As You make other People's less.
In Arms and Science 'tis the same:
Our Rival's Hurts create our Fame.
At FAUBERT's if Disputes arise
Among the Champions for the Prize;
To prove, who gave the fairer Butt,
JOHN shows the Chalk on ROBERT's Coat.
So, for the Honor of your Book,
It tells, where other Folks mistook:
And, as their Notions You confound,
Those You invent get farther Ground.

The Commentators on old ARI-
STOTLE ('tis urg'd) in Judgment vary:
They to their own Conceits have brought
The Image of his general Thought.
Just as the Melancholic Eye
Sees Fleets and Armies in the Sky;
And to the poor Apprentice Ear
The Bells sound *Whittington* Lord May'r.
The Conj'rer thus explains his *Scheme*
Thus Spirits walk, and Prophets dream:
NORTH BRITONS thus have *Second Sight*;
And GERMANS free from Gunshot fight.

THEODORET, and ORIGEN,
And fifty other Learned Men

Attest, that if their Comments find
The Traces of their Master's Mind;
ALMA can ne'er decay nor dye:
This flatly t'other Sect deny,
SIMPLICIUS, THEOPHRAST, DURAND;
Great Names, but hard in Verse to stand.
They wonder Men should have mistook
The *Tenets* of their Master's Book;
And hold, that ALMA yields her Breath,
O'ercome by Age, and seiz'd by Death.
Now which were Wise? and which were Fools?
Poor ALMA sits between two Stools:
The more She reads, the more perplext;
The Comment ruining the Text:
Now fears, now hopes her doubtful Fate:
But, RICHARD, let her look to That——
Whilst We our own Affairs pursue.

These diff'rent *Systems*, Old or New,
A Man with half an Eye may see,
Were only form'd to disagree.
Now to bring Things to fair Conclusion,
And save much Christian Ink's Effusion;
Let me propose an Healing *Scheme*,
And sail along the Middle Stream:
For, DICK, if We could reconcile
  Old ARISTOTLE with GASSENDUS;
How many would admire our Toil;
  And yet how few would comprehend us?

Here, RICHARD, let my *Scheme* commence.
Oh! may my Words be lost in Sense;
While pleas'd THALIA deigns to write
The Slips and Bounds of ALMA's Flight.

My simple *System* shall suppose,
That ALMA enters at the Toes;
That then She mounts by just Degrees
Up to the Ancles, Legs, and Knees:
Next, as the Sap of Life does rise,
She lends her Vigor to the Thighs:

And, all these under-Regions past,
She nestles somewhere near the Waste:
Gives Pain or Pleasure, Grief or Laughter;
As We shall show at large hereafter.
Mature, if not improv'd, by Time
Up to the Heart She loves to climb:
From thence, compell'd by Craft and Age,
She makes the Head her latest Stage.

From the Feet upward to the Head;
Pithy, and short, says DICK: proceed.

DICK, this is not an idle Notion:
Observe the Progress of the Motion.
First I demonstratively prove,
That Feet were only made to move;
And Legs desire to come and go:
For they have nothing else to do.

Hence, long before the Child can crawl,
He learns to kick, and wince, and sprawl:
To hinder which, your Midwife knows
To bind Those Parts extremely close;
Lest ALMA newly enter'd in,
And stunn'd at her own Christ'ning's Din,
Fearful of future Grief and Pain,
Should silently sneak out again.
Full piteous seems young ALMA's Case:
As in a luckless Gamester's Place,
She would not play, yet must not pass.

Again as She grows something stronger,
And Master's Feet are swath'd no longer,
If in the Night too oft He kicks,
Or shows his *Loco-motive* Tricks;
These first Assaults fat KATE repays Him,
When half asleep She overlays Him.

Now mark, Dear RICHARD, from the Age
That Children tread this Worldly Stage,
Broom-staff or Poaker they bestride,
And round the Parlor love to ride;

217

MATTHEW PRIOR

'Till thoughtful Father's pious Care
Provides his Brood, next *Smithfield* Fair,
With Supplemental Hobby-Horses :
And happy be their Infant Courses !

Hence for some Years they ne'er stand still :
Their Legs, You see, direct their Will.
From opening Morn 'till setting Sun,
A-round the Fields and Woods They run :
They frisk, and dance, and leap, and play ;
Nor heed, what FRIEND or SNAPE can say.

To Her next Stage as ALMA flies,
And likes, as I have said, the Thighs :
With *Sympathetic* Pow'r She warms,
Their good Allies and Friends, the Arms.
While BETTY dances on the Green ;
And SUSAN is at Stool-ball seen :
While JOHN for Nine-pins does declare ;
And ROGER loves to pitch the Bar ;
Both Legs and Arms spontaneous move :
Which was the Thing I meant to prove.

Another Motion now She makes :
O need I name the Seat She takes ?
His Thought quite chang'd the Stripling finds ;
The Sport and Race no more He minds :
Neglected *Tray* and *Pointer* lye ;
And Covies unmolested fly.
Sudden the jocund Plain He leaves ;
And for the Nymph in Secret grieves.
In dying Accents He complains
Of cruel Fires, and raging Pains.
The Nymph too longs to be alone ;
Leaves all the Swains ; and sighs for One.
The Nymph is warm'd with young Desire ;
And feels, and dies to quench His Fire.
They meet each Evening in the Grove :
Their Parley but augments their Love.
So to the Priest their Case They tell :
He ties the Knot ; and all goes well.

But, O my MUSE, just Distance keep:
Thou art a Maid, and must not peep.
In nine Months Time the Boddice loose,
And Petticoats too short, disclose,
That at This Age the active Mind
About the Waste lies most confin'd;
And that young Life, and quick'ning Sense
Spring from His Influence darted thence.
So from the Middle of the World
The SUN's prolifick Rays are hurl'd:
'Tis from That Seat He darts those Beams,
Which quicken Earth with genial Flames.

DICK, who thus long had passive sat,
Here stroak'd his Chin, and cock'd his Hat;
Then slapp'd his Hand upon the Board;
And thus the Youth put in his Word.
Love's Advocates, sweet Sir, would find Him
A higher Place, than You assign'd Him.
Love's Advocates, DICK, who are those?——
The Poets, You may well suppose.
I'm sorry, Sir, You have discarded
The Men, with whom 'till now You herded.
Prose-Men alone, for private Ends,
I thought, forsook their ancient Friends.
In cor stillavit, crys LUCRETIUS;
If He may be allow'd to teach Us.
The self-same Thing soft OVID says
(A proper Judge in such a Case.)
HORACE his Phrase is *torret Jecur*;
And happy was that curious Speaker.
Here VIRGIL too has plac'd this Passion:
What signifies too long Quotation?
In *Ode* and *Epic* plain the Case is,
That Love holds One of these Two Places.

DICK, without Passion or Reflection,
I'll strait demolish this Objection.

First Poets, all the World agrees,
Write half to profit, half to please.

MATTHEW PRIOR

Matter and Figure They produce;
For Garnish This, and That for Use;
And, in the Structure of their Feasts,
They seek to feed, and please their Guests:
But One may balk this good Intent,
And take Things otherwise than meant.
Thus, if You Dine with my Lord May'r,
Roast-Beef, and Ven'son is your Fare;
Thence You proceed to Swan, and Bustard,
And persevere in Tart, and Custard:
But *Tulip-leaves*, and *Limon-peel*
Help only to adorn the Meal;
And painted Flags, superb and neat,
Proclaim You welcome to the Treat.
The Man of Sense his Meat devours;
But only smells the Peel, and Flow'rs:
And He must be an idle Dreamer,
Who leaves the Pie, and gnaws the Streamer.

That CUPID goes with Bow and Arrows,
And VENUS keeps her Coach and Sparrows,
Is all but Emblem, to acquaint One,
The Son is sharp, the Mother wanton.
Such Images have sometimes shown
A *Mystic* Sense, but oft'ner None.
For who conceives, what Bards devise,
That Heav'n is plac'd in CELIA's Eyes?
Or where's the Sense, direct or moral,
That Teeth are Pearl, or Lips are Coral?

Your HORACE owns, He various writ,
As wild, or sober Maggots bit:
And, where too much the Poet ranted,
The Sage Philosopher recanted.
His grave *Epistles* may disprove
The wanton *Odes* He made to LOVE.

LUCRETIUS keeps a mighty Pother
With CUPID, and his fancy'd Mother:
Calls her great Queen of Earth and Air;
Declares, that Winds and Seas obey Her;

220

And, while Her Honor he rehearses,
Implores Her to inspire his Verses.

Yet, free from this Poetic Madness;
Next Page, He says in sober Sadness,
That She and all her fellow-Gods
Sit idling in their high Abodes,
Regardless of this World below,
Our Health or Hanging, Weal or Woe;
Nor once disturb their Heav'nly Spirits
With SCAPIN's Cheats, or CÆSAR's Merits.

Nor e'er can LATIN Poets prove,
Where lies the real Seat of Love.
Jecur they burn, and *Cor* they pierce,
As either best supplies their Verse:
And, if Folks ask the Reason for't,
Say, one was long, and t'other short.
Thus, I presume, the BRITISH Muse,
May take the Freedom Strangers use.
In Prose our Property is greater:
Why should it then be less in Metre?
If CUPID throws a single Dart;
We make him wound the Lover's *Heart*:
But if He takes his Bow, and Quiver;
'Tis sure, He must transfix the *Liver*:
For Rhime with Reason may dispense;
And Sound has Right to govern Sense.

But let your Friends in Verse suppose,
What ne'er shall be allow'd in Prose:
Anatomists can make it clear,
The *Liver* minds his own Affair:
Kindly supplies our publick Uses;
And parts, and strains the Vital Juices:
Still lays some useful Bile aside,
To tinge the Chyle's insipid Tide:
Else We should want both Gibe and Satyr;
And all be burst with pure Good-nature.
Now Gall is bitter with a Witness;
And Love is all Delight and Sweetness.

221

MATTHEW PRIOR

My *Logic* then has lost it's Aim,
If Sweet and Bitter be the same :
And He, methinks, is no great Scholar,
Who can mistake Desire for Choler.

The like may of the *Heart* be said :
Courage and Terror there are bred.
All those, whose *Hearts* are loose and low,
Start, if they hear but the *Tattoo* :
And mighty Physical their Fear is :
For, soon as Noise of Combat near is,
Their Heart, descending to their Breeches,
Must give their Stomach cruel twitches.
But Heroes who o'ercome or dye,
Have their Hearts hung extremely high ;
The Strings of which, in Battel's Heat,
Against their very *Corslets* beat ;
Keep Time with their own Trumpet's Measure ;
And yield 'em most excessive Pleasure.

Now if 'tis chiefly in the Heart,
That Courage does it self exert ;
'Twill be prodigious hard to prove,
That This is eke the Throne of Love.
Would Nature make One Place the Seat
Of fond Desire, and fell Debate ?
Must People only take Delight in
Those Hours, when They are tir'd with Fighting ?
And has no Man, but who has kill'd
A Father, right to get a Child ?
These Notions then I think but idle :
And Love shall still possess the Middle.

This Truth more plainly to discover,
Suppose your Hero were a Lover.
Tho' He before had Gall and Rage,
Which Death, or Conquest must asswage ;
He grows dispirited and low :
He hates the Fight, and shuns the Foe.

In scornful Sloth ACHILLES slept ;
And for his Wench, like TALL-BOY, wept :

Nor would return to War and Slaughter;
'Till They brought back the Parson's Daughter.

ANTONIUS fled from ACTIUM's Coast,
AUGUSTUS pressing, ASIA lost:
His Sails by CUPID's Hand unfurl'd,
To keep the Fair, he gave the World.

EDWARD our Fourth, rever'd and crown'd,
Vig'rous in Youth, in Arms renown'd;
While ENGLAND's Voice, and WARWICK's Care
Design'd him GALLIA's beauteous Heir;
Chang'd Peace and Pow'r for Rage and Wars,
Only to dry One Widow's Tears.

FRANCE's fourth HENRY we may see,
A Servant to the fair D'ESTREE;
When quitting COUTRAS prosp'rous Field,
And Fortune taught at length to yield,
He from his Guards and Mid-night Tent,
Disguis'd o'er Hills and Vallies went,
To wanton with the sprightly Dame;
And in his Pleasure lost his Fame.

Bold is the Critic, who dares prove,
These Heroes were no Friends to Love;
And bolder He, who dares aver,
That they were Enemies to War.
Yet, when their Thought should, now or never,
Have rais'd their *Heart*, or fir'd their *Liver*;
Fond ALMA to those Parts was gone,
Which LOVE more justly calls his own.

Examples I could cite You more;
But be contented with these Four:
For when One's Proofs are aptly chosen;
Four are as valid as four Dozen.
One came from GREECE, and one from ROME;
The other Two grew nearer Home.
For some in Antient Books delight:
Others prefer what Moderns write:
Now I should be extremely loath,
Not to be thought expert in Both.

THE
SECOND CANTO.

BUT shall we take the Muse abroad,
  To drop her idly on the Road?
And leave our Subject in the middle;
As Butler did his Bear and Fiddle?
Yet He, consummate Master, knew
When to recede, and where pursue:
His noble Negligences teach,
What Others Toils despair to reach.
He, perfect Dancer, climbs the Rope,
And balances your Fear and Hope:
If after some distinguish'd Leap,
He drops his Pole, and seems to slip;
Straight gath'ring all his active Strength,
He rises higher half his Length.
With Wonder You approve his Slight;
And owe your Pleasure to your Fright.
But, like poor Andrew, I advance,
False *Mimic* of my Master's Dance:
A-round the Cord a while I sprawl;
And thence, tho' low, in earnest fall.

My Preface tells You, I digress'd:
He's half absolv'd who has confess'd.

I like, quoth Dick, your *Simile*:
And in Return, take Two from Me.
As Masters in the *Clare-obscure*,
With various Light your Eyes allure:
A flaming Yellow here They spread;
Draw off in Blew, or charge in Red:
Yet from these Colors odly mix'd,
Your Sight upon the Whole is fix'd.

Or as, again, your Courtly Dames,
(Whose Cloaths returning Birth-Day claims,)
By Arts improve the Stuffs they vary;
And Things are best, as most contrary.
The Gown with stiff Embroid'ry shining,
Looks charming with a slighter Lining:
The Out-, if INDIAN Figures stain;
The In-side must be rich and plain.
So You, great Authors, have thought fit,
To make Digression temper Wit:
When Arguments too fiercely glare;
You calm 'em with a milder Air:
To break their Points, You turn their Force;
And *Furbelow* the plain Discourse.

RICHARD, quoth MAT, these Words of Thine,
Speak something sly, and something fine:
But I shall e'en resume my *Theme*;
However Thou may'st praise, or blame.

As People marry now, and settle;
Fierce Love abates his usual Mettle:
Worldly Desires, and Household Cares
Disturb the Godhead's soft Affairs:
So now, as Health or Temper changes,
In larger Compass ALMA ranges,
This Day below, the next above;
As light, or solid Whimsies move.
So Merchant has his House in Town,
And Country-Seat near BANSTED Down:
From One he dates his Foreign Letters,
Sends out his Goods, and duns his Debtors:
In t'other, at his Hours of Leisure,
He smokes his Pipe, and takes his Pleasure.

And now your Matrimonial CUPID,
Lash'd on by Time, grows tir'd and stupid.
For Story and Experience tell Us,
That Man grows cold, and Woman jealous.
Both would their little Ends secure:
He sighs for Freedom, She for Pow'r.

His Wishes tend abroad to roam;
And Her's, to domineer at Home.
Thus Passion flags by slow Degrees;
And ruffl'd more, delighted less,
The busy Mind does seldom go
To those once charming Seats below:
But, in the Breast incamp'd, prepares
For well-bred Feints, and future Wars.
The Man suspects his Lady's crying
(When he last Autumn lay a-dying)
Was but to gain him to appoint Her
By Codicil a larger Jointure.
The Woman finds it all a Trick,
That He could swoon, when She was sick;
And knows, that in That Grief he reckon'd
On black-ey'd SUSAN for his Second.

Thus having strove some tedious Years
With feign'd Desires, and real Fears;
And tir'd with Answers, and Replies,
Of JOHN affirms, and MARTHA lies;
Leaving this endless Altercation,
The Mind affects a higher Station.

POLTIS, that gen'rous King of THRACE,
I think, was in this very Case.
All ASIA now was by the Ears:
And Gods beat up for Voluntiers
To GREECE, and TROY; while POLTIS sat
In Quiet, governing his State.
And whence, said the Pacific King,
Does all this Noise, and Discord spring?
Why, PARIS took ATRIDES' Wife——
With Ease I could compose this Strife:
The injur'd Hero should not lose,
Nor the young Lover want a Spouse:
But HELEN chang'd her first Condition,
Without her Husband's just Permission.
What from the Dame can PARIS hope?
She may as well from Him elope.
Again, how can her old Good-man

With Honor take Her back again?
From hence I logically gather,
The Woman cannot live with Either.
Now I have Two right honest Wives,
For whose Possession No Man strives:
One to ATRIDES I will send;
And t'other to my TROJAN Friend.
Each Prince shall thus with Honor have,
What Both so warmly seem to crave:
The Wrath of Gods and Man shall cease;
And POLTIS live and die in Peace.

DICK, if this Story pleaseth Thee,
Pray thank DAN POPE, who told it Me.

Howe'er swift ALMA's Flight may vary;
(Take this by way of *Corollary* :)
Some Limbs She finds the very same,
In Place, and Dignity, and Name:
These dwell at such convenient Distance,
That each may give his Friend Assistance.
Thus He who runs or dances, begs
The equal Vigor of Two Legs:
So much to both does ALMA trust,
She ne'er regards, which goes the first.
TEAGUE could make neither of them stay,
When with Himself he ran away.
The Man who struggles in the Fight,
Fatigues left Arm, as well as right:
For whilst one Hand exalts the Blow,
And on the Earth extends the Foe;
T'other would take it wond'rous ill,
If in your Pocket He lay still.
And when you shoot, and shut one Eye,
You cannot think, He would deny
To lend the t'other friendly Aid,
Or wink, as Coward, and affraid.
No, Sir; whilst He withdraws his Flame,
His Comrade takes the surer Aim.
One Moment if his Beams recede;
As soon as e'er the Bird is dead,

Opening again, He lays his Claim,
To half the Profit, half the Fame,
And helps to Pocket up the Game.
'Tis thus, One Tradesman slips away,
To give his Part'ner fairer Play.

Some Limbs again in Bulk or Stature
Unlike, and not a-kin by Nature,
In Concert act, like modern Friends;
Because one serves the t'other's Ends.
The Arm thus waits upon the Heart,
So quick to take the Bully's Part,
That one, tho' warm, decides more slow,
Than t'other executes the Blow.
A Stander-by may chance to have it,
E'er HACK himself perceives, He gave it.

The am'rous Eyes thus always go
A-stroling for their Friends below:
For long before the 'Squire and Dame
Have *tête à tête* reliev'd their Flame;
E'er Visits yet are brought about,
The Eye by Sympathy looks out;
Knows FLORIMEL, and longs to meet Her;
And, if He sees, is sure to greet Her,
Tho' at Sash-Window, on the Stairs,
At Court, nay (Authors say) at Pray'rs.———

The Funeral of some valiant Knight
May give this Thing it's proper Light.
View his Two Gantlets: these declare,
That Both his Hands were us'd to War.
And from his Two gilt Spurs 'tis learn'd,
His Feet were equally concern'd.
But have You not with Thought beheld
The Sword hang dangling o'er the Shield?
Which shows the Breast, That Plate was us'd to,
Had an Ally right Arm to trust to.
And by the Peep-holes in his Crest,
Is it not virtually confest,
That there his Eye took distant Aim,

And glanc'd Respect to that bright Dame,
In whose Delight his Hope was center'd,
And for whose Glove his Life he ventur'd?

Objections to my general *System*
May 'rise, perhaps, and I have mist them:
But I can call to my Assistance
Proximity (mark that!) and Distance:
Can prove, that all Things, on Occasion,
Love Union, and desire Adhesion;
That ALMA merely is a Scale;
And Motives, like the Weights, prevail.
If neither Side turn down or up,
With Loss or Gain, with Fear or Hope;
The Balance always would hang ev'n,
Like MAH'MET's Tomb, 'twixt Earth and Heav'n.

This, RICHARD, is a curious Case:
Suppose your Eyes sent equal Rays
Upon two distant Pots of Ale,
Not knowing, which was Mild or Stale:
In this sad State your doubtful Choice
Would never have the casting Voice:
Which Best, or Worst, You could not think;
And die You must, for want of Drink:
Unless some Chance inclines your Sight,
Setting one Pot in fairer Light;
Then You prefer or A, or B,
As Lines and Angles best agree:
Your Sense resolv'd impells your Will;
She guides your Hand,——So drink your Fill.

Have you not seen a Baker's Maid
Between two equal Panniers sway'd?
Her Tallies useless lie, and idle,
If plac'd exactly in the Middle:
But forc'd from this unactive State,
By virtue of some casual Weight;
On either Side You hear 'em clatter,
And judge of right and left-hand Matter.

229

MATTHEW PRIOR

Now, RICHARD, this coercive Force,
Without your Choice, must take it's Course.
Great Kings to Wars are pointed forth,
Like loaded Needles to the North.
And Thou and I, by Pow'r unseen,
Are barely Passive, and suck'd in
To HENAULT's Vaults, or CELIA's Chamber,
As Straw and Paper are by Amber.
If we sit down to play or set
(Suppose at *Ombre* or *Basset*)
Let People call us Cheats, or Fools;
Our Cards and We are equal Tools.
We sure in vain the Cards condemn:
Our selves both cut and shuffl'd them.
In vain on Fortune's Aid rely:
She only is a Stander-by.
Poor Men! poor Papers! We and They
Do some impulsive Force obey;
And are but play'd with :——Do not play.
But Space and Matter we should blame:
They palm'd the Trick that lost the Game.

Thus to save further Contradiction,
Against what You may think but Fiction;
I for Attraction, DICK, declare:
Deny it those bold Men that dare.
As well your Motion, as your Thought
Is all by hidden Impulse wrought:
Ev'n saying, that You Think or Walk,
How like a Country 'Squire you talk?

Mark then;——Where Fancy or Desire
Collects the Beams of Vital Fire;
Into that Limb fair ALMA slides,
And there, *pro tempore*, resides.
She dwells in NICHOLINI's Tongue,
When PYRRHUS chants the Heav'nly Song.
When PEDRO does the Lute command,
She guides the cunning Artist's Hand.
Thro' MACER's Gullet she runs down,
When the vile Glutton dines alone.

And void of Modesty and Thought,
She follows BIBO's endless Draught.
Thro' the soft Sex again She ranges;
As Youth, Caprice, or Fashion changes.
Fair ALMA careless and serene,
In FANNY's sprightly Eyes is seen;
While they diffuse their Infant Beams,
Themselves not conscious of their Flames.
Again fair ALMA sits confest,
On FLORIMEL's experter Breast;
When She the rising Sigh constrains,
And by concealing speaks her Pains.
In CYNTHIA's Neck fair ALMA glows;
When the vain Thing her Jewels shows:
When JENNY's Stays are newly lac'd,
Fair ALMA plays about her Waste;
And when the swelling Hoop sustains
The rich Brocard, fair ALMA deigns
Into that lower Space to enter,
Of the large Round, Her self the Center.

Again: That Single Limb or Feature
(Such is the cogent Force of Nature)
Which most did ALMA's Passion move,
In the first Object of her Love,
For ever will be found confest,
And printed on the am'rous Breast.

O ABELARD, ill-fated Youth,
Thy Tale will justify this Truth:
But well I weet, thy cruel Wrong
Adorns a nobler Poet's Song.
Dan POPE for thy Misfortune griev'd,
With kind Concern, and Skill has weav'd
A silken Web; and ne'er shall fade
It's Colors: gently has He laid
The Mantle o'er thy sad Distress:
And VENUS shall the Texture bless.
He o'er the weeping Nun has drawn,
Such artful Folds of Sacred Lawn,

231

That Love with equal Grief and Pride,
Shall see the Crime, He strives to hide:
And softly drawing back the Veil,
The God shall to his Vot'ries tell
Each conscious Tear, each blushing Grace,
That deck'd Dear Eloisa's Face.

Happy the Poet, blest the Lays,
Which Buckingham has deign'd to praise.

Next, Dick, as Youth and Habit sways,
A hundred Gambols Alma plays.
If, whilst a Boy, Jack run from Schole,
Fond of his Hunting-horn, and Pole;
Tho' Gout and Age his Speed detain,
Old John halloo's his Hounds again.
By his Fire-side he starts the Hare;
And turns Her in his Wicker-Chair:
His Feet, however lame, You find,
Have got the better of his Mind.

If while the Mind was in her Leg,
The Dance affected nimble Peg;
Old Madge, bewitch'd at Sixty one,
Calls for *Green Sleeves*, and *Jumping Joan*.
In public Mask, or private Ball,
From *Lincoln's Inn*, to *Goldsmith's Hall*,
All Christmas long away She trudges;
Trips it with Prentices and Judges:
In vain her Children urge her Stay;
And Age or Palsey bar the Way.
But if those Images prevail,
Which whilom did affect the Tail;
She still reviews the ancient Scene;
Forgets the forty Years between:
Awkwardly gay, and odly merry,
Her Scarf pale Pink, her Head-Knot Cherry;
O'er heated with *Ideal* Rage,
She cheats her Son, to wed her Page.

If Alma, whilst the Man was young,
Slip'd up too soon into his Tongue:

Pleas'd with his own fantastic Skill,
He lets that Weapon ne'er lie still.
On any Point if You dispute ;
Depend upon it, He'll confute :
Change Sides ; and You increase your Pain :
For He'll confute You back again.
For One may speak with TULLY's Tongue ;
Yet all the while be in the wrong.
And 'tis remarkable, that They
Talk most, who have the least to say.
Your dainty Speakers have the Curse,
To plead bad Causes down to worse :
As Dames, who Native Beauty want,
Still uglier look, the more They paint.

Again : If in the Female Sex
ALMA should on this Member fix ;
(A cruel and a desp'rate Case,
From which Heav'n shield my lovely Lass !)
For evermore all Care is vain,
That would bring ALMA down again.
As in habitual Gout, or Stone,
The only Thing that can be done,
Is to correct your Drink and Diet,
And keep the inward Foe in Quiet :
So, if for any Sins of Our's,
Or our Forefathers, Higher Pow'rs,
Severe tho' just, afflict our Life
With that Prime Ill, a talking Wife ;
'Till Death shall bring the kind Relief,
We must be Patient, or be Deaf.

You know, a certain Lady, DICK,
Who saw Me, when I last was sick :
She kindly talk'd, at least three Hours,
Of *Plastic* Forms, and *Mental* Pow'rs :
Describ'd our pre-existing Station,
Before this vile Terrene Creation :
And lest I should be weary'd, Madam,
To cut Things short, came down to ADAM ;

MATTHEW PRIOR

From whence, as fast as She was able,
She drowns the World, and builds up BABEL;
Thro' SYRIA, PERSIA, GREECE She goes;
And takes the ROMANS in the Close.

But We'll descant on gen'ral Nature:
This is a *System*, not a Satyr.

Turn We this Globe; and let Us see,
How diff'rent Nations disagree,
In what We wear, or eat and drink;
Nay, DICK, perhaps in what We think.
In Water as You smell and tast
The Soyls, thro' which it rose and past:
In ALMA's Manners You may read
The Place, where She was born and bred.

One People from their swadling Bands
Releas'd their Infants Feet and Hands:
Here ALMA to these Limbs was brought;
And SPARTA's Offspring kick'd and fought.

Another taught their Babes to talk,
E'er they could yet in Goe-carts walk:
There ALMA settl'd in the Tongue;
And Orators from ATHENS sprung.

Observe but in these Neighb'ring Lands,
The diff'rent Use of Mouths and Hands:
As Men repos'd their various Hopes,
In Battles These, and Those in Tropes.

In BRITAIN's Isles, as HEYLYN notes,
The Ladies trip in Petticoats;
Which, for the Honor of their Nation,
They quit but on some great Occasion.
Men there in Breeches clad You view:
They claim that Garment, as their due.
In TURKEY the Reverse appears;
Long Coats the haughty Husband wears,
And greets His Wife with angry Speeches;
If She be seen without her Breeches.

In our Fantastic *Climes* the Fair
With cleanly Powder dry their Hair:
And round their lovely Breast and Head
Fresh Flow'rs their mingl'd Odors shed.
Your nicer HOTTENTOTES think meet
With Guts and Tripe to deck their Feet:
With down-cast Looks on TOTTA's Legs,
The ogling Youth most humbly begs,
She would not from his Hopes remove
At once his Breakfast, and his Love:
And if the skittish Nymph should fly;
He in a double Sense must die.

We simple *Toasters* take Delight
To see our Women's Teeth look white.
And ev'ry saucy ill-bred Fellow
Sneers at a Mouth profoundly yellow.
In CHINA none hold Women sweet,
Except their Snags are black as Jett.
King CHIHU put Nine Queens to Death,
Convict on Statute, *Iv'ry Teeth*.

At TONQUIN if a Prince should die;
(As Jesuits write, who never lye)
The Wife, and Counsellor, and Priest,
Who serv'd Him most, and lov'd Him best;
Prepare, and light his Fun'ral Fire,
And chearful on the Pile expire.
In EUROPE 'twould be hard to find
In each Degree One half so kind.

Now turn We to the farthest East,
And there observe the Gentry Drest.
Prince GIOLO, and his Royal Sisters,
Scarr'd with ten thousand comely Blisters;
The Marks remaining on the Skin,
To tell the Quality within.
Distinguish'd Slashes deck the Great:
As each excells in Birth, or State;
His Oylet-holes are more, and ampler:
The King's own Body was a Samplar.

MATTHEW PRIOR

Happy the Climate, where the *Beau*
Wears the same Suit for Use, and Show:
And at a small Expence your Wife,
If once well pink'd, is cloth'd for Life.

Westward again the INDIAN Fair,
Is nicely smear'd with Fat of Bear.
Before You see, You smell your Toast,
And sweetest She, who stinks the most.
The finest Sparks, and cleanest *Beaux*
Drip from the Shoulders to the Toes.
How sleek their Skins! their Joints how easy!
There Slovens only are not greasy.

I mention'd diff'rent Ways of Breeding:
Begin We in our Children's Reading.
To Master JOHN the ENGLISH Maid
A Horn-book gives of Ginger-bread:
And that the Child may learn the better,
As He can name, He eats the Letter:
Proceeding thus with vast Delight,
He spells, and gnaws, from Left to Right.
But shew a HEBREW's hopeful Son,
Where We suppose the Book begun;
The Child would thank You for your Kindness,
And read quite backward from our *Finis*:
Devour He Learning ne'er so fast;
Great A would be reserv'd the last.

An equal Instance of this Matter,
Is in the Manners of a Daughter.
In EUROPE, if a harmless Maid,
By Nature and by Love betray'd,
Should e'er a Wife become a Nurse;
Her Friends would look on Her the Worse.
In CHINA, DAMPIER's Travels tell Ye;
(Look in his Index for PAGELLI:)
Soon as the BRITISH Ships unmoore,
And jolly Long-boat rows to Shore;
Down come the Nobles of the Land:
Each brings his Daughter in his Hand,

Beseeching the Imperious Tar
To make Her but One Hour his Care.
The tender Mother stands affrighted,
Lest her dear Daughter should be slighted:
And poor Miss YAYA dreads the Shame
Of going back the Maid She came.

Observe how Custom, DICK, compells
The Lady that in EUROPE dwells :
After her Tea She slips away ;
And what to do, One need not say.
Now see how great POMONQUE's Queen
Behav'd Herself amongst the Men :
Pleas'd with her Punch, the Gallant Soul
First drank, then water'd in the Bowl ;
And sprinkl'd in the Captain's Face
The Marks of Her Peculiar Grace——

To close this Point, We need not roam
For Instances so far from Home.
What parts gay FRANCE from sober SPAIN ?
A little rising Rocky Chain.
Of Men born South or North o'th' Hill,
Those seldom move ; These ne'er stand still.
DICK, You love Maps, and may perceive
ROME not far distant from GENEVE.
If the good POPE remains at Home,
He's the First Prince in CHRISTENDOME.
Choose then, good POPE, at Home to stay ;
Nor Westward curious take Thy Way.
Thy Way unhappy should'st Thou take
From TIBER's Bank to LEMAN-Lake ;
Thou art an Aged Priest no more,
But a Young flaring Painted Whore :
Thy Sex is lost : Thy Town is gone,
No longer ROME, but BABYLON.
That some few Leagues should make this Change,
To Men unlearn'd seems mighty strange.

But need We, Friend, insist on This ?
Since in the very CANTONS SWISS,

All Your Philosophers agree,
And prove it plain, that One may be
A Heretic, or True Believer,
On this, or t'other Side a River.

Here with an artful Smile, quoth DICK,
Your Proofs come mighty full, and thick——

The Bard on this extensive Chapter,
Wound up into Poetic Rapture,
Continu'd: RICHARD, cast your Eye
By Night upon a Winter-Sky:
Cast it by Day-light on the Strand,
Which compasses fair ALBION's Land:
If You can count the Stars that glow
Above, or Sands that lie below;
Into those Common-places look,
Which from great Authors I have took;
And count the Proofs I have collected,
To have my Writings well protected.
These I lay by for Time of Need;
And Thou may'st at thy Leisure read.
For standing every Critic's Rage,
I safely will to future Age
My *System*, as a Gift, bequeath,
Victorious over Spight, and Death.

THE

THIRD CANTO.

RICHARD, who now was half a-sleep,
    Rous'd; nor would longer Silence keep:
And Sense like this, in vocal Breath
Broke from his twofold Hedge of Teeth.
Now if this Phrase too harsh be thought;
POPE, tell the World, 'tis not my Fault.
Old HOMER taught us thus to speak:
If 'tis not Sense; at least 'tis GREEK.

As Folks, quoth RICHARD, prone to Leasing,
Say Things at first because they're pleasing;
Then prove what they have once asserted,
Nor care to have their Lie deserted;
'Till their own Dreams at length deceive 'em;
And oft repeating, they believe 'em.
Or as again those am'rous Blades,
Who trifle with their Mother's Maids;
Tho' at the first their wild Desire,
Was but to quench a present Fire;
Yet if the object of their Love
Chance by LUCINA's Aid to prove;
They seldom let the Bantling roar
In Basket, at a Neighbour's Door:
But by the flatt'ring Glass of Nature,
Viewing themselves in *Cake-bread's* Feature;
With serious Thought and Care support,
What only was begun in Sport.

Just so with You, my Friend, it fares,
Who deal in Philosophic Wares:
Atoms You cut; and Forms You measure,
To gratifie your private Pleasure;
'Till airy Seeds of casual Wit
Do some fantastic Birth beget:
And pleas'd to find your *System* mended,
Beyond what You at first intended,
The happy Whimsey You pursue;
'Till You at length believe it true.
Caught by your own delusive Art,
You fancy first, and then assert.

Quoth MATTHEW: Friend, as far as I
Thro' Art or Nature cast my Eye,
This *Axiom* clearly I discern,
That One must Teach, and t'Other Learn.
No Fool PYTHAGORAS was thought:
Whilst He his weighty Doctrines taught;
He made his list'ning Scholars stand,
Their Mouth still cover'd with their Hand:
Else, may be, some odd-thinking Youth,

Less Friend to Doctrine than to Truth,
Might have refus'd to let his Ears
Attend the Musick of the Spheres;
Deny'd all *transmigrating* Scenes,
And introduc'd the Use of Beans.
From great LUCRETIUS take His Void;
And all the World is quite destroy'd.
Deny DES-CART His subtil Matter;
You leave Him neither Fire, nor Water.
How odly would Sir ISAAC look,
If You, in Answer to his Book,
Say in the Front of your Discourse,
That Things have no *Elastic* Force?
How could our *Chymic* Friends go on,
To find the *Philosophic* Stone;
If You more pow'rful Reasons bring,
To prove, that there is no such Thing?

Your Chiefs in Sciences and Arts,
Have great Contempt of ALMA's Parts.
They find, She giddy is, or dull;
She doubts, if Things are void, or full:
And who should be presum'd to tell,
What She Her self should see, or feel?
She doubts, if two and two make four;
Tho' She has told them ten times o'er.
It can't——it may be——and it must:
To which of these must ALMA trust?
Nay, further yet They make Her go,
In doubting, if She doubts, or no.
Can *Syllogysm* set Things right?
No: *Majors* soon with *Minors* fight:
Or, Both in friendly Consort join'd;
The *Consequence* limps false behind.
So to some Cunning-Man She goes,
And asks of Him, how much She knows.
With Patience grave He hears Her speak;
And from his short Notes, gives Her back
What from her Tale He comprehended:
Thus the Dispute is wisely ended.

From the Account the Loser brings,
The Conj'ror knows, who stole the Things.

'Squire (interrupted DICK) since when
Were You amongst these Cunning-Men?

Dear DICK, quoth MAT, let not Thy Force
Of Eloquence spoil my Discourse.
I tell Thee, this is ALMA's Case,
Still asking, what some Wise-man says,
Who does his Mind in Words reveal,
Which All must grant; tho' Few can spell.
You tell Your Doctor, that Y'are ill:
And what does He, but write a Bill,
Of which You need not read one Letter?
The worse the Scrawl, the Dose the better.
For if You knew but what You take;
Tho' You recover, He must break.

Ideas, Forms, and *Intellects,*
Have furnish'd out three diff'rent Sects.
Substance, or *Accident* divides
All EUROPE into adverse Sides.

Now, as engag'd in Arms or Laws,
You must have Friends to back your Cause:
In *Philosophic* Matters so
Your Judgment must with others go.
For as in Senates, so in Scholes,
Majority of Voices rules.

Poor ALMA, like a lonely Deer,
O'er Hills and Dales does doubtful err:
With panting Haste, and quick Surprise,
From ev'ry Leaf that stirs, She flies;
'Till mingl'd with the neighb'ring Herd,
She slights what erst She singly fear'd:
And now, exempt from Doubt and Dread,
She dares pursue; if They dare lead:
As Their Example still prevails;
She tempts the Stream, or leaps the Pales.

He then, quoth DICK, who by Your Rule
Thinks for Himself, becomes a Fool.
As Party-Man who leaves the rest,
Is call'd but *Whimsical* at Best.
Now, by Your Favour, Master MAT,
Like RALPHO, here I smell a Rat.
I must be listed in Your Sect;
Who, tho' They teach not, can protect.
Right, RICHARD, MAT. in Triumph cri'd;
So put off all Mistrust and Pride.
And while My Principles I beg;
Pray answer only with Your Leg.
Believe what friendly I advise:
Be first secure; and then be wise.
The Man within the Coach that sits,
And to another's Skill submits,
Is safer much (whate'er arrives)
And warmer too, than He that drives.

So, DICK *Adept*, tuck back Thy Hair;
And I will pour into Thy Ear
Remarks, which None did e'er disclose,
In smooth-pac'd Verse, or hobling Prose.
Attend, Dear DICK; but don't reply:
And Thou may'st prove as Wise as I.

When ALMA now in diff'rent Ages,
Has finish'd Her ascending Stages;
Into the Head at length She gets,
And There in Public Grandeur sits,
To judge of Things, and censure Wits.

Here, RICHARD, how could I explain,
The various Lab'rinths of the Brain?
Surprise My Readers, whilst I tell 'em
Of *Cerebrum*, and *Cerebellum*?
How could I play the Commentator
On *Dura*, and on *Pia Mater*?
Where Hot and Cold, and Dry and Wet,
Strive each the t'other's Place to get;

And with incessant Toil and Strife,
Would keep Possession during Life.
I could demonstrate every Pore,
Where Mem'ry lays up all her Store;
And to an Inch compute the Station,
'Twixt Judgment, and Imagination.
O Friend! I could display much Learning,
At least to Men of small Discerning.
The Brain contains ten thousand Cells:
In each some active Fancy dwells;
Which always is at Work, and framing
The several Follies I was naming.
As in a Hive's vimineous Dome,
Ten thousand Bees enjoy their Home;
Each does her studious Action vary,
To go and come, to fetch and carry:
Each still renews her little Labor;
Nor justles her assiduous Neighbour:
Each——whilst this *Thesis* I maintain;
I fancy, DICK, I know thy Brain.
O with the mighty *Theme* affected,
Could I but see thy Head dissected!

My Head, quoth DICK, to serve your Whim?
Spare That, and take some other Limb.
Sir, in your nice Affairs of *System*,
Wise Men propose; but Fools assist 'em.

Says MATTHEW: RICHARD, keep thy Head,
And hold thy Peace; and I'll proceed.

Proceed? quoth DICK: Sir, I aver,
You have already gone too far.
When People once are in the Wrong;
Each Line they add, is much too long.
Who fastest walks, but walks astray,
Is only furthest from his Way.
Bless your Conceits! must I believe,
Howe'er absurd, what You conceive;
And, for your Friendship, live and dye
A Papist in Philosophy?

MATTHEW PRIOR

I say, whatever You maintain
Of ALMA in the Heart, or Brain;
The plainest Man alive may tell Ye,
Her Seat of Empire is the Belly:
From hence She sends out those Supplies,
Which make Us either stout, or wise:
The Strength of ev'ry other Member,
Is founded on your Belly-Timber:
The Qualms or Raptures of your Blood
Rise in Proportion to your Food:
And if you would improve your Thought;
You must be fed, as well as taught.
Your Stomach makes your Fabric roll;
Just as the Biass rules the Bowl.
That great ACHILLES might imploy
The Strength, design'd to ruin TROY;
He Din'd on Lion's Marrow, spread
On Toasts of Ammunition-Bread:
But by His Mother sent away,
Amongst the THRACIAN Girls to play,
Effeminate He sat, and quiet:
Strange Product of a Cheese-cake Diet!
Now give my Argument fair Play;
And take the Thing the t'other Way:
The Youngster, who at Nine and Three
Drinks with his Sisters Milk and Tea,
From Break-fast reads, 'till twelve a Clock,
BURNET and HEYLYN, HOBBES and LOCK:
He pays due Visits after Noon
To Cousin ALICE, and Uncle JOHN:
At Ten from Coffee-House or Play
Returning, finishes the Day.
But give him Port, and potent Sack;
From *Milk-sop* He starts up *Mohack*:
Holds that the Happy know no Hours;
So thro' the Street at Midnight scow'rs:
Breaks Watch-men's Heads, and Chair-men's Glasses;
And thence proceeds to nicking Sashes:
Till by some tougher Hand o'ercome,
And first knock'd down, and then led Home;

He damns the Foot-man, strikes the Maid,
And decently reels up to Bed.

Observe the various Operations
Of Food, and Drink in several Nations.
Was ever TARTAR fierce or cruel,
Upon the Strength of Water-Gruel?
But who shall stand His Rage and Force;
If first he rides, then eats his Horse?
Sallads, and Eggs, and lighter Fare
Tune the ITALIAN Spark's Guitar.
And, if I take *Dan* CONGREVE right;
Pudding and Beef make BRITONS fight.
TOKAY and COFFEE cause this Work,
Between the GERMAN and the TURK:
And Both, as They Provisions want,
Chicane, avoid, retire, and faint.

Hunger and Thirst, or Guns and Swords,
Give the same Death in diff'rent Words.
To push this Argument no further;
To starve a Man, in Law, is Murther.

As in a WATCHE's fine Machine,
Tho' many artful Springs are seen;
The added Movements, which declare,
How full the Moon, how old the Year,
Derive their secondary Pow'r
From that, which simply points the Hour.
For, tho' these Gim-cracks were away;
(QUARE would not swear; but QUARE would say)
However more reduc'd and plain,
The Watch would still a Watch remain:
But if the *Horal* Orbite ceases;
The whole stands still, or breaks to pieces;
Is now no longer what it was;
And You may e'en go sell the Case.
So if unprejudic'd you scan
The Goings of this Clock-work, Man;
You find a hundred Movements made
By fine Devices in his Head:

MATTHEW PRIOR

But 'tis the Stomach's solid Stroke,
That tells his Being, what's a Clock.
If You take off his *Rhet'ric*-Trigger;
He talks no more in Mood and Figure:
Or clog his *Mathematic*-Wheel;
His Buildings fall; his Ship stands still.
Or lastly, break his *Politic*-Weight;
His Voice no longer rules the State.
Yet if these finer Whims were gone;
Your Clock, tho' plain, would still go on:
But spoil the Engine of Digestion;
And You entirely change the Question.
ALMA's Affairs no Pow'r can mend;
The Jest, alas! is at an End:
Soon ceases all this worldly Bustle;
And you consign the Corps to RUSSEL.

Now make your ALMA come or go,
From Leg to Hand, from Top to Toe;
Your *System*, without My Addition,
Is in a very sad Condition.
So HARLEQUIN extoll'd his Horse,
Fit for the War, or Road, or Course;
His Mouth was soft; his Eye was good;
His Foot was sure as ever trod:
One Fault he had, a Fault indeed;
And what was that? The Horse was Dead.

DICK, from these Instances and Fetches,
Thou mak'st of Horses, Clocks, and Watches,
Quoth MAT, to Me thou seem'st to mean,
That ALMA is a mere *Machine*;
That telling others what's a Clock,
She knows not what Her self has struck;
But leaves to Standers-by the Tryal,
Of what is mark'd upon her Dial.

Here hold a Blow, good Friend, quoth DICK,
And rais'd his Voice exceeding quick:
Fight fair, Sir: what I never meant
Don't You infer. In Argument,

Similies are like Songs in Love:
They much describe; they nothing prove.

MAT, who was here a little gravel'd,
Tost up his Nose, and would have cavil'd:
But calling HERMES to his Aid,
Half pleas'd, half angry, thus He said:

Where mind ('tis for the Author's Fame)
That MATTHEW call'd, and HERMES came.
In Danger Heroes, and in Doubt
Poets find Gods to help 'em out.

Friend RICHARD, I begin to see,
That You and I shall scarce agree.
Observe how odly you behave:
The more I grant, the more You crave.
But, Comrade, as I said just now,
I should affirm, and You allow.
We *System*-makers can sustain
The *Thesis*, which, You grant, was plain;
And with Remarks and Comments teaze Ye;
In case the Thing before was easy.
But in a Point obscure and dark,
We fight as LEIBNITS did with CLARK;
And when no Reason we can show,
Why Matters This or That Way go;
The shortest Way the Thing We try,
And what We know not, We deny:
True to our own o'erbearing Pride,
And false to all the World beside.

That old Philosopher grew cross,
Who could not tell what Motion was:
Because He walk'd against his Will;
He fac'd Men down, that He stood still.
And He who reading on the Heart,
(When all his *Quodlibets* of Art
Could not expound it's Pulse and Heat)
Swore, He had never felt it beat.
CHRYSIPPUS, foil'd by EPICURUS,
Makes bold (JOVE bless Him!) to assure Us,

MATTHEW PRIOR

That all things, which our Mind can view,
May be at once both false, and true.
And MALBRANCH has an odd Conceit,
As ever enter'd FRENCHMAN's Pate:
Says He, so little can our Mind
Of Matter, or of Spirit find,
That We by Guess, at least, may gather
Something, which may be Both, or Neither.
Faith, DICK, I must confess, 'tis true
(But this is only *Entre Nous*)
That many knotty Points there are,
Which All discuss, but Few can clear:
As Nature slily had thought fit,
For some by-Ends, to cross-bite Wit.
Circles to square, and Cubes to double,
Would give a Man excessive Trouble:
The Longitude uncertain roams,
In spight of WH——N and his Bombs.
What *System*, DICK, has right averr'd
The Cause, why Woman has no Beard;
Or why, as Years our Frame attack,
Our Hair grows white, our Teeth grow black?
In Points like These We must agree,
Our Barber knows as much as We.
Yet still unable to explain,
We must persist the best We can;
With Care our *Systems* still renew,
And prove Things likely, tho' not true.

I could, Thou see'st, in quaint Dispute,
By dint of *Logic* strike Thee mute;
With learned Skill, now push, now parry,
From *Darii* to *Bocardo* vary,
And never yield, or what is worst,
Never conclude the Point discours'd.
Yet, that You *hic & nunc* may know,
How much You to my Candor owe;
I'll from the Disputant descend,
To show Thee, I assume the Friend:
I'll take Thy Notion for my own——
(So most Philosophers have done)

It makes my *System* more complete:
DICK, can it have a Nobler Fate?
Take what Thou wilt, said DICK, Dear Friend;
But bring thy Matters to an End.

I find, quoth MAT, Reproof is vain:
Who first offend will first complain.
Thou wishest, I should make to Shoar;
Yet still put'st in Thy thwarting Oar.
What I have told Thee fifty times
In Prose, receive for once in Rhimes:
A huge fat Man in Countrey-Fair,
Or City-Church, (no matter where)
Labor'd and push'd amidst the Croud,
Still bauling out extremely loud;
Lord save Us! why do People press?
Another marking his Distress,
Friendly reply'd; Plump Gentleman,
Get out as fast as e'er You can:
Or cease to push, or to exclaim:
You make the very Croud You blame.

Says DICK, your Moral does not need
The least Return; So e'en proceed:
Your Tale, howe'er apply'd, was short:
So far, at least, I thank You for't.

MAT. took his Thanks, and in a Tone
More Magisterial, thus went on.

Now ALMA settles in the Head;
As has before been sung, or said:
And here begins this Farce of Life;
Enter Revenge, Ambition, Strife:
Behold on both Sides Men advance,
To form in Earnest BAYS's Dance.
L'AVARE not using Half his Store,
Still grumbles, that He has no more;
Strikes not the present Tun, for fear
The Vintage should be bad next Year:
And eats To-day with inward Sorrow,
And Dread of fancy'd Want To-morrow.

MATTHEW PRIOR

Abroad if the *Sour-tout* You wear,
Repells the Rigor of the Air;
Would You be warmer, if at Home
You had the Fabric, and the Loom?
And if two Boots keep out the Weather;
What need You have two Hides of Leather?
Could PEDRO, think You, make no Tryal
Of a *Sonata* on his Viol,
Unless he had the total Gut,
Whence every String at first was cut?

When RARUS shows You his Carton;
He always tells You, with a Groan,
Where two of that same Hand were torn,
Long before You, or He were born.

Poor VENTO's Mind so much is crost,
For Part of His PETRONIUS lost;
That He can never take the Pains
To understand what yet remains.

What Toil did honest CURIO take?
What strict Enquiries did He make,
To get one Medal wanting yet,
And perfect all his ROMAN Sett?
'Tis found: and O his happy Lot!
'Tis bought, lock'd up, and lies forgot:
Of These no more You hear Him speak:
He now begins upon the GREEK.
These rang'd and show'd, shall in their Turns
Remain obscure, as in their Urns.
My Copper-Lamps at any Rate,
For being True Antique, I bought;
Yet wisely melted down my Plate,
On Modern Models to be wrought:
And Trifles I alike pursue;
Because They're Old; because They're New.

DICK, I have seen You with Delight,
For GEORGY make a Paper-Kite.
And simple Odes too many show Ye,
My servile Complaisance to CLOE.

Parents and Lovers are decreed
By Nature Fools——That's brave indeed!
Quoth DICK: such Truths are worth receiving:
Yet still DICK look'd, as not believing.

Now, ALMA, to Divines and Prose
I leave Thy Frauds, and Crimes, and Woes:
Nor think To-night of Thy Ill-Nature,
But of Thy Follies, Idle Creature,
The turns of Thy uncertain Wing,
And not the Malice of Thy Sting:
Thy Pride of being great and wise,
I do but mention, to despise.
I view with Anger and Disdain,
How little gives Thee Joy, or Pain:
A Print, a *Bronze*, a Flow'r, a Root,
A Shell, a Butter-fly can do't.
Ev'n a Romance, a Tune, a Rhime
Help Thee to pass the tedious Time,
Which else would on thy Hand remain:
Tho' flown, it ne'er looks back again.
And Cards are dealt, and Chess-boards brought,
To ease the Pain of Coward-Thought.
Happy Result of Human Wit!
That ALMA may Her self forget.

DICK, thus We act; and thus We are,
Or toss'd by Hope, or sunk by Care.
With endless Pain This Man pursues
What, if he gain'd, He could not use:
And T'other fondly Hopes to see
What never was, nor e'er shall be.
We err by Use, go wrong by Rules;
In Gesture grave, in Action Fools:
We join Hypocrisie to Pride,
Doubling the Faults, We strive to hide.
Or grant, that with extreme Surprize,
We find our selves at Sixty wise;
And twenty pretty Things are known,
Of which we can't accomplish One;

MATTHEW PRIOR

Whilst, as my *System* says, the Mind
Is to these upper Rooms confin'd :
Should I, my Friend, at large repeat
Her borrow'd Sense, her fond Conceit ;
The Bede-roll of her vicious Tricks ;
My Poem would be too prolix.
For could I my Remarks sustain,
Like SOCRATES, or MILES MONTAIGNE ;
Who in these Times would read my Books,
But TOM o' STILES, or JOHN o' NOKES ?

As BRENTFORD Kings discrete and wise,
After long Thought and grave Advice,
Into LARDELLA's Coffin peeping,
Saw nought to cause their Mirth or Weeping :
So ALMA now to Joy or Grief
Superior, finds her late Relief :
Weary'd of being High, or Great,
And nodding in her Chair of State ;
Stun'd and worn out with endless Chat,
Of WILL did this, and NAN said that ;
She finds, poor Thing, some little Crack,
Which Nature, forc'd by Time, must make ;
Thro' which She wings her destin'd Way :
Upward She soars ; and down drops Clay :
While some surviving Friend supplies
Hic jacet, and a hundred Lies.

O RICHARD, 'till that Day appears,
Which must decide our Hopes and Fears :
Would FORTUNE calm her present Rage,
And give us Play-things for our Age :
Would CLOTHO wash her Hands in Milk,
And twist our Thread with Gold and Silk :
Would She in Friendship, Peace, and Plenty,
Spin out our Years to four times Twenty :
And should We both in this Condition,
Have conquer'd Love, and worse Ambition ;
(Else those two Passions, by the way,
May chance to show us scurvy Play :)

Then RICHARD, then should We sit down,
Far from the Tumult of this Town:
I fond of my well-chosen Seat,
My Pictures, Medals, Books compleat:
Or should We mix our friendly Talk,
O'er-shaded in that Fav'rite Walk,
Which Thy own Hand had whilom planted,
Both pleas'd with all we thought We wanted:
Yet then, ev'n then one cross Reflection
Would spoil Thy Grove, and My Collection:
Thy Son and his, e'er that, may die;
And Time some uncouth Heir supply;
Who shall for nothing else be known,
But spoiling All, that Thou hast done.
Who set the Twigs, shall He remember,
That is in Hast to sell the Timber?
And what shall of thy Woods remain,
Except the Box that threw the Main?

Nay may not Time and Death remove
The near Relations, whom I love?
And my Coz TOM, or his Coz MARY
(Who hold the Plough, or skim the Dairy)
My Fav'rite Books and Pictures sell
To SMART, or DOILEY by the Ell?
Kindly throw in a little Figure,
And set their Price upon the bigger?
Those who could never read their Grammar;
When my dear Volumes touch the Hammer;
May think Books best, as richest bound.
My Copper Medals by the Pound
May be with learned Justice weigh'd:
To turn the Ballance, OTHO's Head
May be thrown in; And for the Mettle,
The Coin may mend a Tinker's Kettle——

Tir'd with these Thoughts——Less tir'd than I,
Quoth DICK, with Your Philosophy——
That People live and dye, I knew
An hour ago, as well as You.

253

And if Fate spins Us longer Years,
Or is in haste to take the Shears;
I know, We must Both Fortunes try,
And bear our Evils, wet or dry.
Yet let the Goddess smile, or frown;
Bread We shall eat, or white, or brown:
And in a Cottage, or a Court,
Drink fine *Champaigne*, or muddl'd *Port*.
What need of Books these Truths to tell,
Which Folks perceive, who cannot spell?
And must We Spectacles apply,
To view, what hurts our naked Eye?

Sir, if it be Your Wisdom's Aim,
To make Me merrier than I am;
I'll be all Night at Your Devotion——
Come on, Friend; broach the pleasing Notion:
But if You would depress my Thought;
Your *System* is not worth a Groat——

For PLATO's Fancies what care I?
I hope You would not have me die,
Like simple CATO in the Play,
For any Thing that He can say?
E'en let Him of *Ideas* speak
To Heathens in his Native GREEK.
If to be sad is to be wise;
I do most heartily despise
Whatever SOCRATES has said,
Or TULLY writ, or WANLEY read.

Dear DRIFT, to set our Matters right,
Remove these Papers from my Sight;
Burn MAT's DES-CART', and ARISTOTLE:
Here, JONATHAN, Your Master's Bottle.

SOLOMON

ON THE

VANITY

OF THE

WORLD.

A

POEM

In THREE BOOKS.

'Ο Βίος γὰρ ὄνομ' ἔχει, πόνος δ' ἔργῳ πέλει.

Eurip.

Siquis Deus mihi largiatur, ut ex hac ætate repuerascam,
& in cunis vagiam, valdè recusem.

Cicero de Senect.

The *bewailing of Man's Miseries* hath been elegantly
and copiously set forth by Many, in the Writings as
well of Philosophers, as Divines.   And it is both a
pleasant and a profitable Contemplation.

Lord Bacon's *Advancement of Learning.*

MATTHEW PRIOR

THE

PREFACE.

IT is hard for a Man to speak of himself with any tolerable Satisfaction or Success: He can be no more pleased in blaming himself, than in reading a Satyr made on him by another: and though He may justly desire, that a Friend should praise him; yet if He makes his own Panegyric, He will get very Few to read it. It is harder for him to speak of his own Writings. An Author is in the Condition of a Culprit: the Public are his Judges: by allowing too much, and condescending too far, He may injure his own Cause, and become a kind of Felo de se; and by Pleading and Asserting too boldly, He may displease the Court that sits upon him: His Apology may only heighten his Accusation. I would avoid these Extremes: and though, I grant, it would not be very civil to trouble the Reader with a long Preface, before he enters upon an indifferent Poem; I would say something to per-swade him to take it as it is, or to excuse it for not being better.

The Noble Images and Reflections, the profound Reasonings upon Human Actions, and excellent Precepts for the Government of Life, which are found in the PROVERBS, ECCLESIASTES, and other Books commonly attributed to SOLOMON, afford Subjects for finer Poems in every Kind, than have, I think, as yet appeared in the GREEK, LATIN, or any Modern Language: How far They were Verse in their Original, is a Dissertation not to be entred into at present.

Out of this great Treasure, which lies heaped up together, in a confused Magnificence, above all Order, I had a Mind to collect and digest such Observations, and Apophthegms, as most particularly tend to the Proof of that great Assertion, laid down in the beginning of the ECCLESIASTES, ALL IS VANITY.

Upon the Subject thus chosen, such various Images present themselves to a Writer's Mind, that He must find it easier to

*judge, what should be rejected, than what ought to be received.
The Difficulty lies in drawing, and disposing; or (as the Painters
term it) in grouping such a Multitude of different Objects, pre-
serving still the Justice and Conformity of Style and Coloring, the
Simplex duntaxat & unum, which* HORACE *prescribes, as requisite to make the whole Picture beautiful and perfect.*

*As Precept, however true in Theory, or useful in Practice,
would be but dry and tedious in Verse, especially if the Recital
be long; I found it necessary to form some Story, and give a kind of
Body to the Poem. Under what Species it may be comprehended,
whether* Didascalic, *or* Heroic, *I leave to the Judgment of the
Critics; desiring them to be favourable in their Censure; and not
sollicitous what the Poem is called, provided it may be accepted.*

The chief Personage or Character in the Epic, *is always
proportioned to the Design of the Work, to carry on the Narration,
and the Moral.* HOMER *intended to shew us in his* Iliad, *that
Dissentions amongst great Men obstruct the Execution of the
noblest Enterprizes, and tend to the Ruin of a State or Kingdom.
His* ACHILLES *therefore is haughty, and passionate, impatient of any
Restraint by Laws, and arrogant in Arms. In His* Odysses *the
same Poet endeavours to explain, that the hardest Difficulties may
be overcome by Labor, and our Fortune restored after the severest
Afflictions.* ULYSSES *therefore is valiant, virtuous and patient.*
VIRGIL's *Design was to tell us, how from a small Colony esta-
blished by the* TROJANS *in* ITALY, *the* ROMAN *Empire rose, and
from what antient Families* AUGUSTUS *(who was His Prince and
Patron) descended. His Hero therefore was to fight his Way to
the Throne, still distinguish'd and protected by the Favor of the
Gods. The Poet to this End takes off from the Vices of* ACHILLES,
and adds to the Virtues of ULYSSES; *from both perfecting a Character proper for his Work in the Person of* ÆNEAS.

As VIRGIL *copy'd after* HOMER, *other Epic Poets have copied
after them both.* TASSO's Gierusalemme Liberata *is directly*
Troy Town Sacked; *with this Difference only, that the two chief
Characters in* HOMER, *which the* LATIN *Poet had joined in One,
the* ITALIAN *has separated in his* GODFREY *and* RINALDO: *but
He makes them both carry on his Work with very great Success.*
RONSARD's FRANCIADE, *(incomparably good as far as it goes)
is again* VIRGIL's Æneis. *His Hero comes from a Foreign
Country, settles a Colony, and lays the Foundation of a future*

MATTHEW PRIOR

Empire. I instance in these, as the greatest ITALIAN *and* FRENCH *Poets in the* Epic. *In our Language* SPENSER *has not contented himself with this submissive Manner of Imitation: He lanches out into very flowery Paths, which still seem to conduct him into one great Road. His* Fairy Queen *(had it been finished) must have ended in the Account, which every Knight was to give of his Adventures, and in the accumulated Praises of his Heroine* GLORIANA. *The Whole would have been an Heroic Poem, but in another Cast and Figure, than any that had ever been written before. Yet it is observable, that every Hero (as far as We can judge by the Books still remaining) bears his distinguished Character, and represents some particular Virtue conducive to the whole Design.*

To bring this to our present Subject: The Pleasures of Life do not compensate the Miseries: Age steals upon Us unawares; and Death, as the only Cure of our Ills, ought to be expected, but not feared. This Instruction is to be illustrated by the Action of some great Person. Who therefore more proper for the Business than SOLOMON *himself? And why may He not be supposed now to repeat what, We take it for granted, He acted almost three thousand Years since? If in the fair Situation where this Prince was placed, He was acquainted with Sorrow; If endowed with the greatest Perfections of Nature, and possess'd of all the Advantages of external Condition, He could not find Happiness; the rest of Mankind may safely take the Monarch's Word for the Truth of what He asserts. And the Author who would perswade, that We should bear the Ills of Life patiently, meerly because* SOLOMON *felt the same, has a better Argument, than* LUCRETIUS *had, when in his imperious way, He at once convinces and commands, that We ought to submit to Death without repining, because* EPICURUS *died.*

The whole Poem is a Soliloquy: SOLOMON *is the Person that speaks: He is at once the Hero and the Author; but He tells Us very often what others say to Him. Those chiefly introduced are His Rabbies and Philosophers in the First Book, and His Women and their Attendants in the Second: With These the Sacred History mention Him to have conversed; as likewise with the Angel brought down in the Third Book, to help Him out of His Difficulties, or at least to teach Him how to overcome them.*

Nec Deus intersit nisi dignus vindice nodus.

POEMS ON SEVERAL OCCASIONS

I presume this Poetical Liberty may be very justly allowed Me on so solemn an Occasion.

In my Description I have endeavoured to keep to the Notions and Manners of the JEWISH *Nation, at the time when* SOLOMON *lived: And where I allude to the Customs of the* GREEKS, *I believe I may be justified by the strictest Chronology; though a Poet is not obliged to the Rules, that confine an Historian.* VIRGIL *has anticipated Two hundred Years; or the* TROJAN *Hero and* CARTHAGINIAN *Queen could not have been brought together: And without the same Anachronism several of the finest Parts of his Æneis must have been omitted. Our Country-man* MILTON *goes yet further. He takes up many of his Material Images some Thousands of Years after the Fall of Man: Nor could He otherwise have written, or We read one of the sublimest Pieces of Invention that was ever yet produced. This likewise takes off the Objection, that some Names of Countries, Terms of Art, and Notions in Natural Philosophy are otherwise expressed, than can be warranted by the* Geography *or Astronomy of* SOLOMON'S *Time. Poets are allowed the same Liberty in their Descriptions and Comparisons, as Painters in their Draperies and Ornaments: Their Personages may be dress'd, not exactly in the same Habits which they wore, but in such as make them appear most graceful. In this case Probability must attone for the want of Truth. This Liberty has indeed been abused by Eminent Masters in either Science.* RAPHAEL *and* TASSO *have shewed their Discretion, where* PAUL VERONESE *and* ARIOSTO *are to answer for their Extravagancies. It is the Excess, not the Thing it self, that is blameable.*

I would say one Word of the Measure, in which This, and most Poems of the Age are written. Heroic *with continued Rhime, as* DONNE *and his Contemporaries used it, carrying the Sense of one Verse most commonly into another, was found too dissolute and wild, and came very often too near Prose. As* DAVENANT *and* WALLER *corrected, and* DRYDEN *perfected it; It is too Confined: It cuts off the Sense at the end of every first Line, which must always rhime to the next following; and consequently produces too frequent an Identity in the Sound, and brings every Couplet to the Point of an Epigram. It is indeed too broken and weak, to convey the Sentiments and represent the Images proper for* Epic. *And as it tires the Writer while he composes, it must do the same to the Reader while he repeats; especially in a Poem of any considerable length.*

If striking out into Blank Verse, *as* MILTON *did (and in this kind Mr.* PHILIPPS, *had He lived, would have excelled) or running the Thought into* Alternate *and* Stanza, *which allows a greater Variety, and still preserves the Dignity of the Verse; as* SPENSER *and* FAIRFAX *have done; If either of these, I say, be a proper Remedy for my Poetical Complaint, or if any other may be found, I dare not determine: I am only enquiring, in order to be better informed; without presuming to direct the Judgment of Others. And while I am speaking of the Verse it self, I give all just Praise to many of my Friends now living; who have in* Epic *carried the Harmony of their Numbers as far, as the Nature of this Measure will permit. But once more; He that writes in Rhimes, dances in Fetters: And as his Chain is more extended, he may certainly take larger Steps.*

I need make no Apology for the short Digressive Panegyric *upon* GREAT BRITAIN, *in the First Book: I am glad to have it observed, that there appears throughout all my Verses a Zeal for the Honor of my Country: and I had rather be thought a good* English-man, *than the best Poet, or greatest Scholar that ever wrote.*

And now, as to the publishing of this Piece, though I have in a literal Sense observed HORACE's Nonum premattur in Annum; *yet have I by no means obeyed our Poetical Lawgiver, according to the Spirit of the Precept. The Poem has indeed been written and laid aside much longer than the Term prescribed; but in the mean time I had little Leisure, and less Inclination to revise or print it. The frequent Interruptions I have met with in my private Studies, and great Variety of Public Life, in which I have been imployed; my Thoughts (such as they are) having generally been expressed in Foreign Language, and even formed by a Habitude very different from what the Beauty and Elegance of* English Poetry *requires: All These, and some other Circumstances, which we had as good pass by at present, do justly contribute to make my Excuse in this Behalf very plausible. Far indeed from designing to print, I had locked up these Papers in my* Scritoire, *there to lie in Peace, 'till my Executors might have taken Them out. What altered this Design; or how my* Scritoire *came to be unlocked before my Coffin was nailed; is the Question. The true Reason*

I take to be the best: Many of my Friends of the first Quality, finest Learning, and greatest Understanding, have wrested the Key from my Hands by a very kind and irresistible Violence: And the Poem is published, not without my Consent indeed, but a little against my Opinion; and with an implicite Submission to the Partiality of Their Judgment. As I give up here the Fruits of many of my vacant Hours to Their Amusement and Pleasure; I shall always think my self happy, if I may dedicate my most serious Endeavours to Their Interest and Service. And I am proud to finish this Preface by saying, that the Violence of many Enemies, whom I never justly offended, is abundantly recompensed, by the Goodness of more Friends, whom I can never sufficiently oblige. And if I here assume the Liberty of mentioning My Lord HARLEY and Lord BATHURST as the Authors of this Amicable Confederacy, among All Those, whose Names do me great Honor in the beginning of my Book: These Two only ought to be angry with me; for I disobey their positive Order, whilst I make even this small Acknowledgment of their particular Kindness.

MATTHEW PRIOR

KNOWLEDGE;

THE

FIRST BOOK.

The ARGUMENT.

SOLOMON *seeking Happiness from* Knowledge, *convenes
the Learned Men of His Kingdom*; *requires them to explain
to Him the various Operations and Effects of Nature*; *discourses
of Vegetables, Animals, and Man*; *proposes some Questions con-
cerning the Origin, and Situation of the habitable Earth*; *proceeds
to examine the* System *of the visible Heaven*; *doubts if there may
not be a Plurality of Worlds*; *enquires into the Nature of Spirits
and Angels*; *and wishes to be more fully informed, as to the
Attributes of the Supreme* Being. *He is imperfectly answered by
the* Rabbins, *and Doctors*; *blames His own Curiosity*; *and concludes, that as to Human Science,* ALL IS VANITY.

TEXTS *chiefly alluded to in this Book.*

The Words of the Preacher, the Son of DAVID, King of JERUSALEM. ECCLESIASTES, Chap. I. Vers. 1.

Vanity of Vanities, saith the Preacher, Vanity of Vanities, all is Vanity. Vers. 2

I communed with mine own Heart, saying, lo, I am come to great Estate, and have gotten more Wisdom, than all they that have been before me in JERUSALEM: Yea my Heart had great Experience of Wisdom and Knowledge. Vers. 16.

He spake of Trees, from the *Cedar*-tree that is in LEBANON, even unto the *Hyssop* that springeth out of the Wall: he spake also of Beasts, and of Fowl, and of creeping Things, and of Fishes. 1 KINGS, Chap. IV. Vers. 33.

I know, that whatsoever God doeth, it shall be for ever: nothing can be put to it, nor any thing taken from it: and God doeth it, that Men should fear before him. ECCLESIASTES, Chap. III. Vers. 14.

He hath made every *thing* beautiful in his time: Also he hath set the World in their Heart, so that no Man can find out the Work that God maketh from the beginning to the end. Vers. 11.

For in much Wisdom is much Grief: and He that increaseth Knowledge, increaseth Sorrow. Chap. I. Vers. 18.

And further, by these, my Son, be admonished: of making many Books there is no End; and much Study is a weariness of the Flesh. Chap. 12. Vers. 12.

MATTHEW PRIOR

KNOWLEDGE:

THE

FIRST BOOK.

YE Sons of Men, with just Regard attend,
 Observe the Preacher, and believe the Friend,
Whose serious MUSE inspires Him to explain,
That all we Act, and all we Think is Vain.
That in this Pilgrimage of Seventy Years,
O'er Rocks of Perils, and thro' Vales of Tears
Destin'd to march, our doubtful Steps we tend,
Tir'd with the Toil, yet fearful of it's End.
That from the Womb We take our fatal Shares
Of Follies, Passions, Labors, Tumults, Cares ;
And at Approach of Death shall only know
The Truths, which from these pensive Numbers flow,
That We pursue false Joy, and suffer real Woe.

Happiness, Object of that waking Dream,
Which we call Life, mistaking ; Fugitive Theme
Of my pursuing Verse, Ideal Shade,
Notional Good, by Fancy only made,
And by Tradition nurs'd, fallacious Fire,
Whose dancing Beams mis-lead our fond Desire,
Cause of our Care, and Error of our Mind :
O ! had'st Thou ever been by Heav'n design'd
To ADAM, and his Mortal Race ; the Boon
Entire, had been reserv'd for SOLOMON :
On Me the partial Lot had been bestow'd ;
And in my Cup the golden Draught had flow'd.

But O ! e'er yet Original Man was made ;
E'er the Foundations of this Earth were laid ;
It was, opponent to our Search, ordain'd,
That Joy, still sought, should never be attain'd.

This, sad Experience cites me to reveal;
And what I dictate, is from what I feel.

Born as I was, great DAVID's fav'rite Son,
Dear to my People, on the HEBREW Throne
Sublime, my Court with OPHIR's Treasures blest,
My Name extended to the farthest East,
My Body cloth'd with ev'ry outward Grace,
Strength in my Limbs, and Beauty in my Face,
My shining Thought with fruitful Notions crown'd,
Quick my Invention, and my Judgment sound.
Arise (I commun'd with my self) arise;
Think, to be Happy; to be Great, be Wise:
Content of Spirit must from Science flow;
For 'tis a Godlike Attribute, to Know.

I said; and sent my Edict thro' the Land:
Around my Throne the Letter'd *Rabbins* stand,
Historic Leaves revolve, long Volumes spread,
The Old discoursing, as the Younger read:
Attent I heard, propos'd my Doubts, and said;

The *Vegetable* World, each Plant, and Tree,
It's Seed, it's Name, it's Nature, it's Degree
I am allow'd, as FAME reports, to know,
From the fair *Cedar*, on the craggy Brow
Of LEBANON nodding supremely tall,
To creeping *Moss*, and *Hyssop* on the Wall:
Yet just and conscious to my self, I find
A thousand Doubts oppose the searching Mind.

I know not why the *Beach* delights the Glade
With Boughs extended, and a rounder Shade;
Whilst tow'ring *Firrs* in *Conic* forms arise,
And with a pointed Spear divide the Skies:
Nor why again the changing *Oak* should shed
The Yearly Honour of his stately Head;
Whilst the distinguish'd *Yew* is ever seen,
Unchang'd his Branch, and permanent his Green.
Wanting the Sun why does the *Caltha* fade?
Why does the *Cypress* flourish in the Shade?

MATTHEW PRIOR

The *Fig* and *Date* why love they to remain
In middle Station, and an even Plain ;
While in the lower Marsh the *Gourd* is found ;
And while the Hill with *Olive*-shade is crown'd ?
Why does one Climate, and one Soil endue
The blushing *Poppy* with a crimson Hue ;
Yet leave the *Lilly* pale, and tinge the *Violet* blue ?
Why does the fond *Carnation* love to shoot
A various Colour from one Parent Root ;
While the fantastic *Tulip* strives to break
In two-fold Beauty, and a parted Streak ?
The twining *Jasmine*, and the blushing *Rose*,
With lavish Grace their Morning Scents disclose :
The smelling *Tub'rose* and *Junquele* declare,
The stronger Impulse of an Evening Air.
Whence has the Tree (resolve me) or the Flow'r
A various Instinct, or a diff'rent Pow'r ?
Why should one Earth, one Clime, one Stream, one Breath
Raise This to Strength, and sicken That to Death ?

Whence does it happen, that the Plant which well
We name the *Sensitive*, should move and feel ?
Whence know her Leaves to answer her Command,
And with quick Horror fly the neighb'ring Hand ?

Along the Sunny Bank, or wat'ry Mead,
Ten thousand Stalks their various Blossoms spread :
Peaceful and lowly in their native Soil,
They neither know to spin, nor care to toil ;
Yet with confess'd Magnificence deride
Our vile Attire, and Impotence of Pride.
The *Cowslip* smiles, in brighter yellow dress'd,
Than That which veils the nubile Virgin's Breast.
A fairer Red stands blushing in the *Rose*,
Than That which on the Bridegroom's Vestment flows.
Take but the humblest *Lilly* of the Field ;
And if our Pride will to our Reason yield,
It must by sure Comparison be shown,
That on the Regal Seat great DAVID's Son,
Aray'd in all his Robes, and Types of Pow'r,
Shines with less Glory, than that simple Flow'r.

266

Of Fishes next, my Friends, I would enquire,
How the mute Race engender, or respire;
From the small Fry that glide on JORDAN's Stream
Unmark'd, a Multitude without a Name,
To that *Leviathan*, who o'er the Seas
Immense rolls onward his impetuous Ways,
And mocks the Wind, and in the Tempest plays.
How They in Warlike Bands march greatly forth
From freezing Waters, and the colder North,
To Southern Climes directing their Career,
Their Station changing with th'inverted Year.
How all with careful Knowledge are indu'd,
To chuse their proper Bed, and Wave, and Food:
To guard their Spawn, and educate their Brood.

Of Birds, how each according to her Kind
Proper Materials for her Nest can find;
And build a Frame, which deepest Thought in Man
Would or amend, or imitate in vain.
How in small Flights They know to try their Young,
And teach the callow Child her Parent's Song.
Why these frequent the Plain, and those the Wood.
Why ev'ry Land has her specific Brood.
Where the tall *Crane*, or winding *Swallow* goes,
Fearful of gathering Winds, and falling Snows:
If into Rocks, or hollow Trees they creep,
In temporary Death confin'd to Sleep;
Or conscious of the coming Evil, fly
To milder Regions, and a Southern Sky.

Of Beasts and creeping Insects shall we trace
The wond'rous Nature, and the various Race;
Or wild or tame, or Friend to Man or Foe,
Of Us, what They, or what of Them We know?

Tell me, Ye studious, who pretend to see
Far into Nature's Bosom, whence the *Bee*
Was first inform'd her vent'rous Flight to steer
Thro' tractless Paths, and an Abyss of Air.
Whence she avoids the slimy Marsh, and knows
The fertile Hills where sweeter Herbage grows,
And Hony-making Flow'rs their opening Buds disclose.

MATTHEW PRIOR

How from the thicken'd Mist, and setting Sun
Finds She the Labor of her Day is done?
Who taught Her against Winds and Rains to strive,
To bring her Burden to the certain Hive,
And thro' the liquid Fields again to pass
Dutious, and hark'ning to the sounding Brass?

And, O Thou Sluggard, tell me why the *Ant*
'Midst Summer's Plenty thinks of Winter's Want:
By constant Journeys careful to prepare
Her Stores; and bringing home the Corny Ear,
By what Instruction does She bite the Grain,
Lest hid in Earth, and taking Root again,
It might elude the Foresight of her Care?
Distinct in either Insect's Deed appear
The marks of Thought, Contrivance, Hope, and Fear.

Fix thy corporeal, and internal Eye
On the Young *Gnat*, or new-engender'd *Fly*;
On the vile *Worm*, that Yesterday began
To crawl; Thy Fellow-Creatures, abject Man!
Like Thee they breath, they move, they tast, they see,
They show their Passions by their Acts like Thee:
Darting their Stings, they previously declare
Design'd Revenge, and fierce intent of War:
Laying their Eggs, they evidently prove
The Genial Pow'r, and full Effect of Love.
Each then has Organs to digest his Food,
One to beget, and one receive the Brood:
Has Limbs and Sinews, Blood and Heart, and Brain,
Life, and her proper Functions to sustain;
Tho' the whole Fabric smaller than a Grain.
What more can our penurious Reason grant
To the large *Whale*, or Castled *Elephant*,
To those enormous Terrors of the NILE,
The crested *Snake*, and long-tail'd *Crocodile*,
Than that all differ but in Shape and Name,
Each destin'd to a less, or larger Frame?

For potent Nature loves a various Act,
Prone to enlarge, or studious to contract:

Now forms her Work too small, now too immense,
And scorns the Measures of our feeble Sense.
The Object spread too far, or rais'd too high,
Denies it's real Image to the Eye:
Too little, it eludes the dazl'd Sight;
Becomes mixt Blackness, or unparted Light.
Water and Air the varied Form confound;
The Strait looks crooked, and the Square grows round.

Thus while with fruitless Hope, and weary Pain,
We seek great Nature's Pow'r, but seek in vain;
Safe sits the Goddess in her dark Retreat;
Around Her, Myriads of *Ideas* wait,
And endless Shapes, which the Mysterious Queen
Can take or quit, can alter or retain:
As from our lost Pursuit She wills to hide
Her close Decrees, and chasten human Pride.

Untam'd and fierce the *Tiger* still remains:
He tires his Life in biting on his Chains:
For the kind Gifts of Water, and of Food,
Ungrateful, and returning Ill for Good,
He seeks his Keeper's Flesh, and thirsts his Blood:
While the strong *Camel*, and the gen'rous *Horse*,
Restrain'd and aw'd by Man's inferior Force,
Do to the Rider's Will their Rage submit,
And answer to the Spur, and own the Bit;
Stretch their glad Mouths to meet the Feeder's Hand,
Pleas'd with his Weight, and proud of his Command.

Again: the lonely *Fox* roams far abroad,
On secret Rapin bent, and Midnight Fraud;
Now haunts the Cliff, now traverses the Lawn;
And flies the hated Neighborhood of Man:
While the kind *Spaniel*, and the faithful *Hound*,
Likest that *Fox* in Shape and Species found,
Refuses thro' these Cliffs and Lawns to roam;
Pursues the noted Path, and covets home;
Does with kind Joy Domestic Faces meet;
Takes what the glutted Child denies to eat;
And dying, licks his long-lov'd Master's Feet.

MATTHEW PRIOR

By what immediate Cause They are inclin'd,
In many Acts, 'tis hard, I own, to find.
I see in others, or I think I see,
That strict their Principles, and our's agree.
Evil like Us they shun, and covet Good;
Abhor the Poison, and receive the Food.
Like Us they love or hate: like Us they know,
To joy the Friend, or grapple with the Foe.
With seeming Thought their Action they intend,
And use the Means proportion'd to the End.
Then vainly the Philosopher avers,
That Reason guides our Deed, and Instinct their's.
How can We justly diff'rent Causes frame,
When the Effects entirely are the same?
Instinct and Reason how can we divide?
'Tis the Fool's Ign'rance, and the Pedant's Pride.

With the same Folly sure, Man vaunts his Sway:
If the brute Beast refuses to Obey.
For tell me, when the empty Boaster's Word
Proclaims himself the Universal Lord;
Does He not tremble, lest the *Lion's* Paw
Should join his Plea against the fancy'd Law?
Would not the Learned Coward leave the Chair;
If in the Schools or Porches should appear
The fierce *Hyæna*, or the foaming *Bear*?

The Combatant too late the Field declines;
When now the Sword is girded to his Loins.
When the swift Vessel flies before the Wind;
Too late the Sailor views the Land behind.
And 'tis too late now back again to bring
Enquiry, rais'd and tow'ring on the Wing;
Forward She strives, averse to be with-held
From nobler Objects, and a larger Field.

Consider with me this Ætherial Space,
Yielding to Earth and Sea the middle Place.
Anxious I ask Ye, how the Pensile Ball
Should never strive to rise, nor fear to fall.
When I reflect, how the revolving Sun
Does round our Globe his crooked Journies run;

I doubt of many Lands, if they contain
Or Herd of Beast, or Colony of Man :
If any Nations pass their destin'd Days
Beneath the neighb'ring Sun's directer Rays:
If any suffer on the Polar Coast,
The Rage of ARCTOS, and eternal Frost.

May not the Pleasure of Omnipotence
To each of These some secret Good dispense?
Those who amidst the Torrid Regions live,
May they not Gales unknown to us receive;
See daily Show'rs rejoice the thirsty Earth,
And bless the flow'ry Buds succeeding Birth?
May they not pity Us, condemn'd to bear
The various Heav'n of an obliquer Sphere;
While by fix'd Laws, and with a just Return,
They feel twelve Hours that shade, for twelve that burn;
And praise the neighb'ring Sun, whose constant Flame
Enlightens them with Seasons still the same?
And may not Those, whose distant Lot is cast
North beyond TARTARY's extended Waste,
Where thro' the Plains of one continual Day,
Six shining Months pursue their even Way;
And Six succeeding urge their dusky Flight,
Obscur'd with Vapors and o'erwhelm'd in Night;
May not, I ask, the Natives of these Climes
(As Annals may inform succeeding Times)
To our Quotidian Change of Heav'n prefer
Their one Vicissitude, and equal Share
Of Day and Night, disparted thro' the Year?
May they not scorn our Sun's repeated Race,
To narrow bounds prescrib'd, and little space,
Hast'ning from Morn, and headlong driv'n from Noon,
Half of our Daily Toil yet scarcely done?
May they not justly to our Climes upbraid
Shortness of Night, and Penury of Shade;
That e'er our weary'd Limbs are justly blest
With wholesom Sleep, and necessary Rest;
Another Sun demands return of Care,
The remnant Toil of Yesterday to bear?

Whilst, when the Solar Beams salute their Sight,
Bold and secure in half a Year of Light,
Uninterrupted Voyages they take
To the remotest Wood, and farthest Lake;
Manage the Fishing, and pursue the Course
With more extended Nerves, and more continu'd Force.
And when declining Day forsakes their Sky;
When gath'ring Clouds speak gloomy Winter nigh;
With Plenty for the coming Season blest,
Six solid Months (an Age) they live, releas'd
From all the Labor, Process, Clamor, Woe,
Which our sad Scenes of daily Action know:
They light the shining Lamp, prepare the Feast,
And with full Mirth receive the welcome Guest;
Or tell their tender Loves (the only Care
Which now they suffer) to the list'ning Fair;
And rais'd in Pleasure, or repos'd in Ease
(Grateful Alternates of substantial Peace)
They bless the long Nocturnal Influence shed
On the crown'd Goblet, and the Genial Bed.

In foreign Isles which our Discov'rers find,
Far from this length of Continent disjoin'd,
The rugged *Bears*, or spotted *Lynx*'s brood;
Frighten the Vallies, and infest the Wood:
The hungry *Crocodile*, and hissing *Snake*
Lurk in the troubl'd Stream and fenny Brake:
And Man untaught, and rav'nous as the Beast,
Does Valley, Wood, and Brake, and Stream infest.
Deriv'd these Men and Animals their Birth
From Trunk of Oak, or pregnant Womb of Earth?
Whence then the Old Belief, that All began
In EDEN's Shade, and one created Man?
Or grant, this Progeny was wafted o'er
By coasting Boats from next adjacent Shoar:
Would Those, from whom We will suppose they spring,
Slaughter to harmless Lands, and Poyson bring?
Would they on Board or *Bears*, or *Lynxes* take,
Feed the She-*Adder*, and the brooding *Snake*?
Or could they think the new Discover'd Isle
Pleas'd to receive a pregnant *Crocodile*?

And since the Savage Lineage we must trace
From NOAH sav'd, and his distinguish'd Race;
How should their Fathers happen to forget
The Arts which NOAH taught, the Rules He set,
To sow the Glebe, to plant the gen'rous Vine,
And load with grateful Flames the Holy Shrine?
While the great Sire's unhappy Sons are found,
Unpress'd their Vintage, and untill'd their Ground,
Stragling o'er Dale and Hill in quest of Food,
And rude of Arts, of Virtue, and of God.

How shall We next o'er Earth and Seas pursue
The vary'd Forms of ev'ry thing we view;
That all is chang'd, tho' all is still the same,
Fluid the Parts, yet durable the Frame?
Of those Materials, which have been confess'd
The pristine Springs, and Parents of the rest,
Each becomes other. Water stop'd gives Birth
To Grass and Plants, and thickens into Earth:
Diffus'd it rises in a higher Sphere;
Dilates it's Drops, and softens into Air:
Those finer Parts of Air again aspire;
Move into Warmth, and brighten into Fire:
That Fire once more by thicker Air o'ercome,
And downward forc'd, in Earth's capacious Womb
Alters it's Particles; is Fire no more;
But lies resplendent Dust, and Shining Oar:
Or running thro' the mighty Mother's Veins,
Changes it's Shape; puts off it's old Remains;
With wat'ry Parts it's lessen'd Force divides;
Flows into Waves, and rises into Tides.

Disparted Streams shall from their Chanels fly,
And deep surcharg'd by sandy Mountains lye,
Obscurely sepulcher'd. By eating Rain,
And furious Wind, down to the distant Plain
The Hill, that hides his Head above the Skies,
Shall fall: The Plain by slow Degrees shall rise
Higher than er'st had stood the Summit-Hill:
For Time must Nature's great Behests fulfill.

P.   S   273

MATTHEW PRIOR

Thus by a length of Years, and Change of Fate,
All Things are light or heavy, small or great:
Thus JORDAN's Waves shall future Clouds appear;
And EGYPT's *Pyramids* refine to Air.
Thus later Age shall ask for PISON's Flood;
And Travellers enquire, where BABEL stood.

Now where we see these Changes often fall,
Sedate we pass them by, as Natural:
Where to our Eye more rarely they appear,
The Pompous Name of Prodigy they bear:
Let active Thought these close *Mæanders* trace:
Let Human Wit their dubious Bound'ries place.
Are all Things Miracle; or nothing such?
And prove We not too little, or too much?

For that a Branch cut off, a wither'd Rod
Should at a Word pronounc'd revive and bud:
Is this more strange, than that the Mountain's Brow,
Strip'd by *December*'s Frost, and white with Snow,
Should push, in Spring, ten thousand thousand Buds;
And boast returning Leaves, and blooming Woods?
That each successive Night from opening Heav'n
The Food of Angels should to Man be giv'n;
Is this more strange, than that with common Bread
Our fainting Bodies every Day are fed;
Than that each Grain and Seed consum'd in Earth,
Raises it's Store, and multiplies it's Birth;
And from the handful, which the Tiller sows,
The labour'd Fields rejoice, and future Harvest flows?

Then from whate'er We can to Sense produce
Common and plain, or wond'rous and abstruse,
From Nature's constant or Eccentric Laws,
The thoughtful Soul this gen'ral Influence draws,
That an Effect must presuppose a Cause.
And while She does her upward Flight sustain,
Touching each Link of the continu'd Chain,
At length she is oblig'd and forc'd to see
A First, a Source, a Life, a Deity;
What has for ever been, and must for ever be.

This great Existence thus by Reason found,
Blest by all Pow'r, with all Perfection crown'd;
How can we bind or limit His Decree,
By what our Ear has heard, or Eye may see?
Say then: Is all in Heaps of Water lost,
Beyond the Islands, and the Mid-land Coast?
Or has that God, who gave our World it's Birth,
Sever'd those Waters by some other Earth,
Countries by future Plow-shares to be torn,
And Cities rais'd by Nations yet unborn?
E'er the progressive Course of restless Age
Performs Three thousand times it's Annual Stage;
May not our Pow'r and Learning be supprest;
And Arts and Empire learn to travel West?

Where, by the Strength of this *Idea* charm'd,
Lighten'd with Glory, and with Rapture warm'd,
Ascends my Soul? what sees She White and Great
Amidst subjected Seas? An ISLE, the Seat
Of Pow'r and Plenty; Her Imperial Throne,
For Justice and for Mercy sought and known;
Virtues Sublime, great Attributes of Heav'n,
From thence to this distinguish'd Nation given.
Yet farther West the Western ISLE extends
Her happy Fame; her Armed Fleets She sends
To Climates folded yet from human Eye;
And Lands, which We imagine Wave and Sky.
From Pole to Pole She hears her Acts resound,
And rules an Empire by no Ocean bound;
Knows her Ships anchor'd, and her Sails unfurl'd
In other INDIES, and a second World.

Long shall BRITANNIA (That must be her Name)
Be first in Conquest, and preside in Fame:
Long shall her favor'd Monarchy engage
The Teeth of Envy, and the Force of Age:
Rever'd and Happy She shall long remain,
Of human Things least changeable, least vain.
Yet All must with the gen'ral Doom comply;
And this Great Glorious Pow'r, tho' last, must dye.

s 2

MATTHEW PRIOR

Now let us leave this Earth, and lift our Eye
To the large Convex of yon' Azure Sky:
Behold it like an ample Curtain spread,
Now streak'd and glowing with the Morning Red;
Anon at Noon in flaming Yellow bright,
And chusing Sable for the peaceful Night.
Ask Reason now, whence Light and Shade were giv'n,
And whence this great Variety of Heav'n:
Reason our Guide, what can She more reply,
Than that the Sun illuminates the Sky;
Than that Night rises from his absent Ray,
And his returning Lustre kindles Day?

But we expect the Morning Red in vain:
'Tis hid in Vapors, or obscur'd by Rain.
The Noontyde Yellow we in vain require:
'Tis black in Storm, or red in Light'ning Fire.
Pitchy and dark the Night sometimes appears,
Friend to our Woe, and Parent of our Fears:
Our Joy and Wonder sometimes She excites,
With Stars unnumber'd, and eternal Lights.
Send forth, Ye Wise, send forth your lab'ring Thought:
Let it return with empty Notions fraught,
Of airy Columns every Moment broke,
Of circling Whirlpools, and of Spheres of Smoke:
Yet this Solution but once more affords
New Change of Terms, and scaffolding of Words:
In other Garb my Question I receive;
And take the Doubt the very same I gave.

Lo! as a Giant strong the lusty Sun
Multiply'd Rounds in one great Round does run,
Twofold his Course, yet constant his Career,
Changing the Day, and finishing the Year.
Again when his descending Orb retires,
And Earth perceives the Absence of his Fires;
The Moon affords us Her alternate Ray,
And with kind Beams distributes fainter Day:
Yet keeps the Stages of her Monthly Race,
Various her Beams, and changeable her Face.

Each Planet shining in his proper Sphere,
Does with just Speed his radiant Voyage steer:
Each sees his Lamp with diff'rent Lustre crown'd:
Each knows his Course with diff'rent Periods bound;
And in his Passage thro' the liquid Space,
Nor hastens, nor retards his Neighbor's Race.
Now shine these Planets with substantial Rays?
Does innate Lustre gild their measur'd Days?
Or do they (as your Schemes, I think, have shown)
Dart furtive Beams, and Glory not their own,
All Servants to that Source of Light, the Sun?

Again I see ten thousand thousand Stars,
Nor cast in Lines, in Circles, nor in Squares:
(Poor Rules, with which our bounded Mind is fill'd,
When We would plant, or cultivate, or build)
But shining with such vast, such various Light,
As speaks the Hand, that form'd them, Infinite:
How mean the Order and Perfection sought
In the best Product of the human Thought,
Compar'd to the great Harmony that reigns
In what the Spirit of the World ordains!

Now if the Sun to Earth transmits his Ray,
Yet does not scorch us with too fierce a Day;
How small a Portion of his Pow'r is giv'n
To Orbs more distant, and remoter Heav'n?
And of those Stars, which our imperfect Eye
Has doom'd, and fix'd to one Eternal Sky,
Each by a native stock of Honor great,
May dart strong Influence, and diffuse kind Heat,
It self a Sun; and with transmissive Light
Enliven Worlds deny'd to human Sight:
Around the Circles of their ambient Skies
New Moons may grow or wane, may set or rise;
And other Stars may to those Suns be Earths;
Give their own Elements their proper Births;
Divide their Climes, or elevate their Pole;
See their Lands flourish, and their Oceans roll;
Yet these great Orbs thus radically bright,
Primitive Founts, and Origins of Light,

MATTHEW PRIOR

May each to other (as their diff'rent Sphere
Makes or their Distance, or their Height appear)
Be seen a nobler, or inferior Star;
And in that Space, which We call Air and Sky,
Myriads of Earths, and Moons, and Suns may lye
Unmeasur'd, and unknown by human Eye.

In vain We measure this amazing Sphere,
And find and fix it's Centre here or there;
Whilst it's Circumf'rence, scorning to be brought
Ev'n into fancy'd Space, illudes our vanquish'd Thought.

Where then are all the radiant *Monsters* driv'n,
With which your Guesses fill'd the frighten'd Heaven?
Where will their fictious Images remain?
In paper Schemes, and the CHALDEAN's Brain.

This Problem yet, this Offspring of a Guess,
Let Us for once a Child of Truth confess;
That these fair Stars, these Objects of Delight,
And Terror, to our searching dazl'd Sight,
Are Worlds immense, unnumber'd, infinite.
But do these Worlds display their Beams, or guide
Their Orbs, to serve thy Use, to please thy Pride?
Thy self but Dust, thy Stature but a Span,
A Moment thy Duration; foolish Man!
As well may the minutest Emmet say,
That CAUCASUS was rais'd, to pave his Way:
The Snail, that LEBANON's extended Wood
Was destin'd only for his Walk, and Food:
The vilest Cockle, gaping on the Coast
That rounds the ample Seas, as well may boast,
The craggy Rock projects above the Sky,
That He in Safety at it's Foot may lye;
And the whole Ocean's confluent Waters swell,
Only to quench his Thirst, or move and blanch his Shell.

A higher Flight the vent'rous GODDESS tries,
Leaving material Worlds, and local Skies:
Enquires, what are the Beings, where the Space,
That form'd and held the ANGELS ancient Race.

For Rebel LUCIFER with MICHAEL fought:
(I offer only what Tradition taught:)
Embattl'd Cherub against Cherub rose;
Did Shield to Shield, and Pow'r to Pow'r oppose:
Heav'n rung with Triumph: Hell was fill'd with Woes.
What were these Forms, of which your Volumes tell,
How some fought great, and others recreant fell?
These bound to bear an everlasting Load,
Durance of Chain, and Banishment of God:
By fatal Turns their wretched Strength to tire;
To swim in sulph'rous Lakes, or land on solid Fire:
While Those exalted to primæval Light,
Excess of Blessing, and Supreme Delight,
Only perceive some little Pause of Joys
In those great Moments, when their God imploys
Their Ministry, to pour his threaten'd Hate
On the proud King, or the Rebellious State:
Or to reverse JEHOVAH's high Command,
And speak the Thunder falling from his Hand,
When to his Duty the proud King returns;
And the Rebellious State in Ashes mourns.
How can good Angels be in Heav'n confin'd;
Or view that Presence, which no Space can bind?
Is GOD above, beneath, or yon', or here?
He who made all, is He not ev'ry where?
O how can wicked Angels find a Night
So dark, to hide 'em from that piercing Light,
Which form'd the Eye, and gave the Pow'r of Sight?

What mean I now of Angel, when I hear
Firm Body, Spirit pure, or fluid Air?
Spirits to Action spiritual confin'd,
Friends to our Thought, and Kindred to our Mind,
Should only act and prompt us from within,
Nor by external Eye be ever seen.
Was it not therefore to our Fathers known,
That these had Appetite, and Limb, and Bone?
Else how could ABRAM wash their weary'd Feet;
Or SARAH please their Taste with sav'ry Meat?
Whence should they fear? or why did LOT engage
To save their bodies from abusive Rage?

MATTHEW PRIOR

And how could Jacob, in a real Fight,
Feel or resist the wrestling Angel's Might?
How could a Form it's Strength with Matter try?
Or how a Spirit touch a Mortal's Thigh?

Now are they Air condens'd, or gather'd Rays?
How guide they then our Pray'r, or keep our Ways,
By stronger Blasts still subject to be tost,
By Tempests scatter'd, and in Whirlwinds lost?

Have they again (as Sacred Song proclaims)
Substances real, and existing Frames?
How comes it, since with them we jointly share
The great Effect of one Creator's Care;
That whilst our Bodies sicken, and decay,
Their's are for ever healthy, young, and gay?
Why, whilst We struggle in this Vale beneath,
With Want and Sorrow, with Disease and Death;
Do They more bless'd perpetual Life employ
On Songs of Pleasure, and in Scenes of Joy?

Now when my Mind has all this World survey'd,
And found, that Nothing by it self was made;
When Thought has rais'd it self by just Degrees,
From Vallies crown'd with Flow'rs, and Hills with Trees;
From smoaking Min'rals, and from rising Streams;
From fatt'ning Nilus, or victorious Thames;
From all the Living, that four-footed move
Along the Shoar, the Meadow, or the Grove;
From all that can with Finns, or Feathers fly
Thro' the Aërial, or the Wat'ry Sky;
From the poor Reptile with a reas'ning Soul,
That miserable Master of the Whole;
From this great Object of the Body's Eye,
This fair Half-round, this ample azure Sky,
Terribly large, and wonderfully bright
With Stars unnumber'd, and unmeasur'd Light;
From Essences unseen, Celestial Names,
Enlight'ning Spirits, and ministerial Flames,
Angels, Dominions, Potentates, and Thrones,
All that in each Degree the name of Creature owns:

Lift we our Reason to that Sov'reign Cause,
Who blest the whole with Life, and bounded it with Laws;
Who forth from Nothing call'd this comely Frame,
His Will and Act, His Word and Work the same;
To whom a thousand Years are but a Day;
Who bad the Light her genial Beams display;
And set the Moon, and taught the Sun his Way:
Who waking Time, his Creature, from the Source
Primæval, order'd his predestin'd Course:
Himself, as in the Hollow of His Hand,
Holding, obedient to His high Command,
The deep Abyss, the long continu'd Store,
Where Months, and Days, and Hours, and Minutes pour
Their floating Parts, and thenceforth are no more.
This ALPHA and OMEGA, First and Last,
Who like the Potter in a Mould has cast
The World's great Frame, commanding it to be
Such as the Eyes of Sense and Reason see;
Yet if He wills, may change or spoil the whole;
May take yon' beauteous, mystic, starry Roll,
And burn it, like an useless parchment Scroll:
May from it's *Basis* in one Moment pour
This melted Earth——
Like liquid Metal, and like burning Oar:
Who sole in Pow'r, at the Beginning said;
Let Sea, and Air, and Earth, and Heav'n be made:
And it was so——And when He shall ordain
In other Sort, has but to speak again,
And They shall be no more: Of this great Theme,
This Glorious, Hallow'd, Everlasting Name,
This GOD, I would discourse——

The learned Elders sat appall'd, amaz'd;
And each with mutual Look on other gaz'd.
Nor Speech They meditate, nor Answer frame:
Too plain, alas! their Silence spake their Shame:
'Till One, in whom an outward Mien appear'd,
And Turn superior to the vulgar Herd,
Began; that Human Learning's furthest Reach
Was but to note the Doctrines I could teach;

That Mine to Speak, and Their's was to Obey:
For I in Knowledge more, than Pow'r did sway;
And the astonish'd World in Me beheld
MOSES eclips'd, and JESSE's Son excell'd.
Humble a Second bow'd, and took the Word;
Foresaw my Name by future Age ador'd.
O Live, said He, Thou Wisest of the Wise!
As None has equall'd, None shall ever rise
Excelling Thee——

Parent of wicked, Bane of honest Deeds,
Pernicious Flatt'ry! Thy malignant Seeds
In an ill Hour, and by a fatal Hand
Sadly diffus'd o'er Virtue's Gleby Land,
With rising Pride amidst the Corn appear,
And choak the Hopes and Harvest of the Year.

And now the whole perplex'd ignoble Crowd
Mute to my Questions, in my Praises loud,
Echo'd the Word: whence Things arose, or how
They thus exist, the Aptest nothing know:
What yet is not, but is ordain'd to be,
All Veil of Doubt apart, the Dullest see.

My Prophets, and my Sophists finish'd here
Their Civil Efforts of the Verbal War:
Not so my *Rabbins*, and Logicians yield:
Retiring still they combat: from the Field
Of open Arms unwilling they depart,
And sculk behind the Subterfuge of Art.
To speak one Thing mix'd Dialects they join;
Divide the Simple, and the Plain define;
Fix fancy'd Laws, and form imagin'd Rules,
Terms of their Art, and Jargon of their Schools,
Ill grounded Maxims by false Gloss enlarg'd,
And captious Science against Reason charg'd.

Soon their crude Notions with each other fought:
The adverse Sect deny'd, what This had taught;
And He at length the amplest Triumph gain'd,
Who contradicted what the last maintain'd.

O wretched Impotence of human Mind!
We erring still Excuse for Error find;
And darkling grope, not knowing We are blind.

Vain Man! since first thy blushing Sire essay'd
His Folly with connected Leaves to shade;
How does the Crime of thy resembling Race
With like Attempt that pristine Error trace?
Too plain thy Nakedness of Soul espy'd,
Why dost Thou strive the conscious Shame to hide
By Masks of Eloquence, and Veils of Pride?

With outward Smiles their Flatt'ry I receiv'd;
Own'd my Sick Mind by their Discourse reliev'd;
But bent and inward to my Self again
Perplex'd, these Matters I revolv'd; in vain.
My Search still tir'd, my Labor still renew'd,
At length I Ignorance, and Knowledge view'd,
Impartial; Both in equal Balance laid:
Light flew the knowing Scale; the doubtful Heavy weigh'd.

Forc'd by reflective Reason I confess,
That human Science is uncertain Guess.
Alas! We grasp at Clouds, and beat the Air,
Vexing that Spirit We intend to clear.
Can Thought beyond the Bounds of Matter climb?
Or who shall tell Me, what is Space or Time?
In vain We lift up our presumptuous Eyes
To what our Maker to their Ken denies:
The Searcher follows fast; the Object faster flies.
The little which imperfectly We find,
Seduces only the bewilder'd Mind
To fruitless Search of Something yet behind.
Various Discussions tear our heated Brain:
Opinions often turn; still Doubts remain;
And who indulges Thought, increases Pain.

How narrow Limits were to Wisdom giv'n?
Earth She surveys: She thence would measure Heav'n:
Thro' Mists obscure, now wings her tedious Way;
Now wanders dazl'd with too bright a Day;

MATTHEW PRIOR

And from the Summit of a pathless Coast
Sees INFINITE, and in that Sight is lost.

    Remember, that the curs'd Desire to know,
Off-spring of ADAM, was thy Source of Woe.
Why wilt Thou then renew the vain Pursuit,
And rashly catch at the forbidden Fruit?
With empty Labor and eluded Strife
Seeking, by Knowledge, to attain to Life;
For ever from that fatal Tree debarr'd,
Which flaming Swords and angry CHERUBS guard.

PLEASURE:

THE

SECOND BOOK.

The ARGUMENT.

SOLOMON *again seeking Happiness, enquires if Wealth and Greatness can produce it : begins with the Magnificence of Gardens and Buildings, the Luxury of Music and Feasting; and proceeds to the Hopes and Desires of Love. In two Episodes are shewn the Follies and Troubles of that Passion.* SOLOMON *still disappointed, falls under the Temptations of Libertinism and Idolatry; recovers his Thought, reasons aright, and concludes, that as to the Pursuit of Pleasure, and sensual Delight,* ALL IS VANITY AND VEXATION OF SPIRIT.

MATTHEW PRIOR

TEXTS *chiefly alluded to in this Book.*

I said in my own Heart, go to now, I will prove thee with Mirth; therefore enjoy Pleasure. ECCLESIASTES, Chap. II. Vers. 1.

I made me great Works, I builded me Houses, I planted me Vineyards. Vers. 4.

I made me Gardens and Orchards; and I planted Trees in them of all kind of Fruits. Vers. 5.

I made me Pools of Water, to water therewith the Wood that bringeth forth Trees. Vers. 6.

Then I looked on all the Works that my Hands had wrought, and on the Labour that I had laboured to do: And behold, all was Vanity, and Vexation of Spirit; and there was no Profit under the Sun. Vers. 11.

I gat me Men-Singers and Women-Singers, and the Delights of the Sons of Men, as Musical Instruments, and that of all Sorts. Vers. 8.

I sought in mine Heart to give my self unto Wine (yet acquainting mine Heart with Wisdom) and to lay hold on Folly, 'till I might see what was that Good for the Sons of Men, which they should do under Heaven, all the Days of their Life. Vers. 3.

Then I said in my Heart, as it happeneth unto the Fool, so it happeneth even unto Me; and why was I then more Wise? Then I said in my Heart, that this also is Vanity. Vers. 15.

Therefore I hated Life, because the Work that is wrought under the Sun is grievous unto me. Chap. II. Vers. 27.

Dead Flies cause the Oyntment to send forth a stinking Savour: so doth the little Folly him that is in Reputation for Wisdom and Honour. Chap. X. Vers. 1.

The Memory of the Just is blessed, but the Memory of the Wicked shall rot. PROVERBS, Chap. X. Verse. 7.

PLEASURE:

THE

SECOND BOOK.

TRY then, O Man, the Moments to deceive,
    That from the Womb attend Thee to the Grave:
For weary'd Nature find some apter Scheme:
Health be thy Hope; and Pleasure be thy Theme:
From the perplexing and unequal Ways,
Where Study brings Thee; from the endless Maze,
Which Doubt persuades to run, forewarn'd recede,
To the gay Field, and flow'ry Path, that lead
To jocund Mirth, soft Joy, and careless Ease:
Forsake what may instruct, for what may please:
Essay amusing Art, and proud Expence;
And make thy Reason subject to thy Sense.

  I commun'd thus: the Pow'r of Wealth I try'd,
And all the various Luxe of costly Pride.
Artists and Plans reliev'd my solemn Hours:
I founded Palaces, and planted Bow'rs.
Birds, Fishes, Beasts of each Exotic Kind
I to the Limits of my Court confin'd.
To Trees transferr'd I gave a second Birth;
And bid a foreign Shade grace JUDAH's Earth.
Fish-ponds were made, where former Forrests grew;
And Hills were levell'd to extend the View.
Rivers diverted from their Native Course,
And bound with Chains of Artificial Force,
From large Cascades in pleasing Tumult roll'd;
Or rose thro' figur'd Stone, or breathing Gold.
From furthest AFRICA's tormented Womb
The Marble brought erects the spacious Dome;
Or forms the Pillars long-extended Rows,
On which the planted Grove, and pensile Garden grows.

MATTHEW PRIOR

The Workmen here obey the Master's Call,
To gild the Turret, and to paint the Wall;
To mark the Pavement there with various Stone;
And on the Jasper Steps to rear the Throne:
The spreading *Cedar*, that an Age had stood,
Supreme of Trees, and Mistress of the Wood,
Cut down and carv'd, my shining Roof adorns;
And LEBANON his ruin'd Honor mourns.

A thousand Artists shew their cunning Pow'r,
To raise the Wonders of the Iv'ry Tow'r.
A thousand Maidens ply the purple Loom,
To weave the Bed, and deck the Regal Room;
'Till TYRE confesses her exhausted Store,
That on her Coast the *Murex* is no more;
'Till from the PARIAN Isle, and LYBIA's Coast,
The Mountains grieve their hopes of Marble lost;
And INDIA's Woods return their just Complaint,
Their Brood decay'd, and want of *Elephant*.

My full Design with vast Expence atchiev'd,
I came, beheld, admir'd, reflected, griev'd.
I chid the Folly of my thoughtless Hast:
For, the Work perfected, the Joy was past.

To my new Courts sad Thought did still repair
And round my gilded Roofs hung hov'ring Care.
In vain on silken Beds I sought Repose;
And restless oft' from purple Couches rose:
Vexatious Thought still found my flying Mind
Nor bound by Limits, nor to Place confin'd;
Haunted my Nights, and terrify'd my Days;
Stalk'd thro' my Gardens, and pursu'd my Ways,
Nor shut from artful Bow'r, nor lost in winding Maze.

Yet take thy Bent, my Soul; another Sense
Indulge; add Music to Magnificence:
Essay, if Harmony may Grief controll;
Or Pow'r of Sound prevail upon the Soul.
Often our Seers and Poets have confest,
That Music's Force can tame the furious Beast;

Can make the Wolf, or foaming Boar restrain
His Rage; the Lion drop his crested Mane,
Attentive to the Song: the Lynx forget
His Wrath to Man, and lick the Minstrel's Feet.
Are we, alas! less savage yet than these?
Else Music sure may human Cares appease.

I spake my Purpose; and the chearful Choir
Parted their shares of Harmony: the Lyre
Soften'd the Timbrel's Noise: the Trumpet's Sound
Provok'd the DORIAN Flute (both sweeter found
When mix'd:) the Fife the Viol's Notes refin'd;
And ev'ry Strength with ev'ry Grace was join'd.
Each Morn they wak'd Me with a sprightly Lay:
Of opening Heav'n they Sung, and gladsome Day.
Each Evening their repeated Skill express'd
Scenes of Repose, and Images of Rest:
Yet still in vain: for Music gather'd Thought:
But how unequal the Effects it brought?
The soft *Ideas* of the chearful Note,
Lightly receiv'd, were easily forgot.
The solemn Violence of the graver Sound
Knew to strike deep, and leave a lasting Wound.

And now reflecting, I with Grief descry
The sickly Lust of the fantastic Eye;
How the weak Organ is with Seeing cloy'd,
Flying e'er Night what it at Noon enjoy'd.
And now (unhappy Search of Thought!) I found
The fickle Ear soon glutted with the Sound,
Condemn'd eternal Changes to pursue,
Tir'd with the last, and eager of the New.

I bad the Virgins and the Youth advance,
To temper Music with the sprightly Dance.
In Vain! too low the Mimic-Motions seem:
What takes our Heart, must merit our Esteem.
Nature, I thought, perform'd too mean a Part,
Forming her Movements to the Rules of Art;
And vex'd I found, that the Musician's Hand
Had o'er the Dancer's Mind too great Command.

P.   T

MATTHEW PRIOR

I drank; I lik'd it not: 'twas Rage; 'twas Noise;
An airy Scene of transitory Joys.
In vain I trusted, that the flowing Bowl
Would banish Sorrow, and enlarge the Soul.
To the late Revel, and protracted Feast
Wild Dreams succeeded, and disorder'd Rest;
And as at Dawn of Morn fair Reason's Light
Broke thro' the Fumes and Phantoms of the Night;
What had been said, I ask'd my Soul, what done;
How flow'd our Mirth, and whence the Source begun?
Perhaps the Jest that charm'd the sprightly Croud,
And made the Jovial Table laugh so loud,
To some false Notion ow'd it's poor Pretence,
To an ambiguous Word's perverted Sense,
To a wild Sonnet, or a wanton Air,
Offence and Torture to the sober Ear.
Perhaps, alas! the pleasing Stream was brought
From this Man's Error, from another's Fault;
From Topics which Good-nature would forget,
And Prudence mention with the last Regret.

Add yet unnumber'd Ills, that lye unseen
In the pernicious Draught; the Word obscene,
Or harsh, which once elanc'd must ever fly
Irrevocable; the too prompt Reply,
Seed of severe Distrust, and fierce Debate;
What We should shun, and what We ought to hate.

Add too the Blood impoverish'd, and the Course
Of Health suppress'd, by Wine's continu'd Force.

Unhappy Man! whom Sorrow thus and Rage
To diff'rent Ills alternately engage.
Who drinks, alas! but to forget; nor sees,
That melancholy Sloath, severe Disease,
Mem'ry confus'd, and interrupted Thought,
Death's Harbingers, lye latent in the Draught:
And in the Flow'rs that wreath the sparkling Bowl,
Fell Adders hiss, and poys'nous Serpents roll.

Remains there Ought untry'd, that may remove
Sickness of Mind, and heal the Bosom?——Love,
Love yet remains: Indulge his genial Fire,
Cherish fair Hope, solicit young Desire,
And boldly bid thy anxious Soul explore
This last great Remedy's Mysterious Pow'r.

Why therefore hesitates my doubtful Breast?
Why ceases it one Moment to be blest?
Fly swift, my Friends; my Servants, fly; imploy
Your instant Pains to bring your Master Joy.
Let all my Wives and Concubines be dress'd:
Let them to Night attend the Royal Feast;
All ISRAEL's Beauty, all the foreign Fair,
The Gifts of Princes, or the Spoils of War.
Before their Monarch They shall singly pass;
And the most Worthy shall obtain the Grace.

I said: the Feast was serv'd: the Bowl was crown'd;
To the King's Pleasure went the mirthful Round:
The Women came: as Custom wills, they past:
On One (O that distinguish'd One!) I cast
The fav'rite Glance: O! yet my Mind retains
That fond Beginning of my infant Pains.
Mature the Virgin was of EGYPT's Race:
Grace shap'd her Limbs; and Beauty deck'd her Face:
Easy her Motion seem'd, serene her Air:
Full, tho' unzon'd, her Bosom rose: her Hair
Unty'd, and ignorant of artful Aid,
Adown her Shoulders loosely lay display'd;
And in the Jetty Curls ten thousand CUPIDS play'd.

Fix'd on her Charms, and pleas'd that I could love,
Aid me my Friends, contribute to improve
Your Monarch's Bliss, I said; fresh Roses bring
To strow my Bed; 'till the impov'rish'd Spring
Confess her Want; around my am'rous Head
Be dropping Myrrhe, and liquid Amber shed,
'Till ARAB has no more. From the soft Lyre,
Sweet Flute, and ten-string'd Instrument, require

MATTHEW PRIOR

Sounds of Delight: and Thou, fair Nymph, draw nigh;
Thou, in whose graceful Form, and potent Eye
Thy Master's Joy long sought at length is found;
And as thy Brow, let my Desires be crown'd;
O fav'rite Virgin, that hast warm'd the Breast,
Whose sov'reign Dictates subjugate the East!

I said; and sudden from the golden Throne
With a submissive Step I hasted down.
The glowing Garland from my Hair I took,
Love in my Heart, Obedience in my Look;
Prepar'd to place it on her comely Head:
O fav'rite Virgin! (yet again I said)
Receive the Honors destin'd to thy Brow;
And O above thy Fellows happy Thou!
Their Duty must thy sov'reign Word obey.
Rise up, my Love; my fair One, come away.

What Pang, alas! what Ecstasy of Smart
Tore up my Senses, and transfix'd my Heart;
When She with modest Scorn the Wreath return'd,
Reclin'd her beauteous Neck, and inward mourn'd?

Forc'd by my Pride, I my Concern suppress'd
Pretended Drowsiness, and Wish of Rest;
And sullen I forsook th'Imperfect Feast:
Ordering the Eunuchs, to whose proper Care
Our Eastern Grandeur gives th'imprison'd Fair,
To lead Her forth to a distinguish'd Bow'r,
And bid her dress the Bed, and wait the Hour.

Restless I follow'd this obdurate Maid:
(Swift are the Steps that Love and Anger tread:)
Approach'd her Person, courted her Embrace,
Renew'd my Flame, repeated my Disgrace:
By Turns put on the Suppliant and the Lord;
Threaten'd this Moment, and the next implor'd;
Offer'd again the unaccepted Wreath,
And Choice of happy Love, or instant Death.

Averse to all her am'rous King desir'd,
Far as She might, She decently retir'd;

And darting Scorn, and Sorrow from her Eyes,
What means, said She, King SOLOMON the Wise?

This wretched Body trembles at your Pow'r:
Thus far could Fortune: but She can no more.
Free to her Self my potent Mind remains;
Nor fears the Victor's Rage, nor feels his Chains.

'Tis said, that Thou can'st plausibly dispute,
Supreme of Seers, of Angel, Man, and Brute;
Can'st plead, with subtil Wit and fair Discourse,
Of Passion's Folly, and of Reason's Force.
That to the Tribes attentive Thou can'st show,
Whence their Misfortunes, or their Blessings flow.
That Thou in Science, as in Pow'r art great;
And Truth and Honor on Thy Edicts wait.
Where is that Knowledge now, that regal Thought,
With just Advice, and timely Counsel fraught?
Where now, O Judge of ISRAEL, does it rove?
What in one Moment dost Thou offer? Love——
Love? why 'tis Joy or Sorrow, Peace or Strife:
'Tis all the Color of remaining Life:
And Human Mis'ry must begin or end,
As He becomes a Tyrant, or a Friend.
Would DAVID's Son, religious, just, and grave,
To the first Bride-bed of the World receive
A Foreigner, a Heathen, and a Slave?
Or grant, Thy Passion has these Names destroy'd;
That Love, like Death, makes all Distinction void;
Yet in his Empire o'er Thy abject Breast,
His Flames and Torments only are exprest:
His Rage can in my Smiles alone relent;
And all his Joys solicit my Consent.

Soft Love, spontaneous Tree, it's parted Root
Must from two Hearts with equal Vigour shoot:
Whilst each delighted, and delighting, gives
The pleasing Ecstasy, which each receives:
Cherish'd with Hope, and fed with Joy it grows:
It's chearful Buds their opening Bloom disclose;
And round the happy Soil diffusive Odor flows.

293

If angry Fate that mutual Care denies;
The fading Plant bewails it's due Supplies:
Wild with Despair, or sick with Grief, it dies.

By Force Beasts act, and are by Force restrain'd:
The Human Mind by gentle Means is gain'd.
Thy useless Strength, mistaken King, employ:
Sated with Rage, and ignorant of Joy,
Thou shalt not gain what I deny to yield;
Nor reap the Harvest, tho' Thou spoil'st the Field.
Know, SOLOMON, Thy poor Extent of Sway;
Contract thy Brow, and ISRAEL shall obey:
But wilful Love Thou must with Smiles appease;
Approach his awful Throne by just Degrees;
And if Thou would'st be Happy, learn to please.

Not that those Arts can here successful prove:
For I am destin'd to another's Love.
Beyond the cruel Bounds of Thy Command,
To my dear Equal, in my Native Land,
My plighted Vow I gave: I His receiv'd:
Each swore with Truth: with Pleasure each believ'd.
The mutual Contract was to Heav'n convey'd:
In equal Scales the busy Angels weigh'd
It's solemn Force, and clap'd their Wings, and spread
The lasting Roll, recording what We said.

Now in my Heart behold Thy Poynard stain'd:
Take the sad Life which I have long disdain'd:
End, in a dying Virgin's wretched Fate,
Thy ill-starr'd Passion, and My steadfast Hate.
For long as Blood informs these circling Veins;
Or fleeting Breath it's latest Pow'r retains;
Hear Me to EGYPT's vengeful Gods declare,
Hate is My Part: be Thine, O King, Despair.

Now strike, She said, and open'd bare her Breast:
Stand it in JUDAH's Chronicles confest,
That DAVID's Son, by impious Passion mov'd,
Smote a She-Slave, and murder'd what He lov'd.

Asham'd, confus'd I started from the Bed;
And to my Soul yet uncollected said:
Into Thy self, fond SOLOMON, return;
Reflect again, and Thou again shalt mourn.
When I through number'd Years have Pleasure sought;
And in vain Hope the wanton Phantom caught;
To mock my Sense, and mortify my Pride,
'Tis in another's Pow'r, and is deny'd.
Am I a King, great Heav'n! does Life or Death
Hang on the Wrath, or Mercy of My Breath;
While kneeling I My Servant's Smiles implore;
And One mad Dam'sel dares dispute My Pow'r?

To Ravish Her? That Thought was soon depress'd,
Which must debase the Monarch to the Beast.
To send Her back? O whither, and to whom?
To Lands where SOLOMON must never come;
To that Insulting Rival's happy Arms,
For whom, disdaining Me, She keeps her Charms.

Fantastic Tyrant of the am'rous Heart;
How hard Thy Yoke! how cruel is Thy Dart!
Those 'scape Thy Anger, who refuse Thy Sway;
And those are punish'd most, who most Obey.
See JUDAH's King revere thy greater Pow'r:
What can'st Thou covet, or how triumph more?
Why then, O LOVE, with an obdurate Ear
Does this proud Nymph reject a Monarch's Pray'r?
Why to some simple Shepherd does She run,
From the fond Arms of DAVID's Fav'rite Son?
Why flies She from the Glories of a Court,
Where Wealth and Pleasure may Thy Reign support,
To some poor Cottage on the Mountain's Brow,
Now bleak with Winds, and cover'd now with Snow,
Where pinching Want must curb her warm Desires,
And Household Cares suppress Thy Genial Fires?

Too aptly the afflicted Heathens prove
The Force, while they erect the Shrines of LOVE.
His Mystic Form the Artizans of GREECE
In wounded Stone, or molten Gold express:

MATTHEW PRIOR

And CYPRUS to his Godhead pays her Vow:
Fast in his Hand the Idol holds his Bow;
A Quiver by his Side sustains a Store
Of pointed Darts; sad Emblems of his Pow'r;
A pair of Wings He has, which He extends
Now to be gone; which now again He bends
Prone to return, as best may serve his wanton Ends.
Entirely thus I find the Fiend pourtray'd,
Since first, alas! I saw the beauteous Maid:
I felt Him strike; and now I see Him fly:
Curs'd Dæmon! O! for ever broken lye
Those fatal Shafts, by which I inward bleed!
O! can my Wishes yet o'ertake thy Speed!
Tir'd may'st Thou pant, and hang thy flagging Wing;
Except Thou turn'st Thy Course, resolv'd to bring
The Dam'sel back, and save the Love-sick King.

My Soul thus strugling in the fatal Net,
Unable to enjoy, or to forget;
I reason'd much, alas! but more I lov'd;
Sent and recall'd, ordain'd and disapprov'd:
'Till hopeless plung'd in an Abyss of Grief,
I from Necessity receiv'd Relief:
Time gently aided to asswage my Pain;
And Wisdom took once more the slacken'd Rein.

But O how short My Interval of Woe!
Our Griefs how swift; our Remedies how slow!
Another Nymph (for so did Heav'n ordain,
To change the Manner, but renew the Pain)
Another Nymph, amongst the many Fair,
That made My softer Hours their solemn Care,
Before the rest affected still to stand;
And watch'd My Eye, preventing My Command.
ABRA, She so was call'd, did soonest hast
To grace my Presence: ABRA went the last:
ABRA was ready e'er I call'd her Name;
And tho' I call'd another, ABRA came.

Her Equals first observ'd her growing Zeal;
And laughing gloss'd, that ABRA serv'd so well.

To Me her Actions did unheeded dye,
Or were remark'd but with a common Eye;
'Till more appris'd of what the Rumor said,
More I observ'd peculiar in the Maid.

The Sun declin'd had shot his Western Ray;
When tir'd with Bus'ness of the solemn Day,
I purpos'd to unbend the Evening Hours,
And banquet private in the Women's Bow'rs.
I call'd, before I sat, to wash My Hands:
For so the Precept of the Law commands.
Love had ordain'd, that it was Abra's Turn
To mix the Sweets, and minister the Urn.

With awful Homage, and submissive Dread
The Maid approach'd, on my declining Head
To pour the Oyls: She trembled as She pour'd;
With an unguarded Look She now devour'd
My nearer Face: and now recall'd her Eye,
And heav'd, and strove to hide a sudden Sigh.
And whence, said I, canst Thou have Dread, or Pain?
What can thy Imag'ry of Sorrow mean?
Secluded from the World, and all it's Care,
Hast Thou to grieve or joy, to hope or fear?
For sure, I added, sure thy little Heart
Ne'er felt Love's Anger, or receiv'd his Dart.

Abash'd She blush'd, and with Disorder spoke:
Her rising Shame adorn'd the Words it broke.

If the great Master will descend to hear
The humble Series of His Hand-maid's Care;
O! while She tells it, let him not put on
The Look, that awes the Nations from the Throne:
O! let not Death severe in Glory lye
In the King's Frown, and Terror of his Eye.

Mine to obey; Thy Part is to ordain:
And tho' to mention, be to suffer Pain;
If the King smiles, whilst I my Woe recite;
If weeping I find Favour in His Sight;
Flow fast my Tears, full rising his Delight.

MATTHEW PRIOR

O ! Witness Earth beneath, and Heav'n above ;
For can I hide it ? I am sick of Love :
If Madness may the Name of Passion bear ;
Or Love be call'd, what is indeed Despair.

Thou Sov'reign Pow'r, whose secret Will controlls
The inward Bent and Motion of our Souls !
Why hast Thou plac'd such infinite Degrees
Between the Cause and Cure of my Disease ?
The mighty Object of that raging Fire,
In which unpity'd ABRA must expire,
Had He been born some simple Shepherd's Heir,
The lowing Herd, or fleecy Sheep his Care ;
At Morn with him I o'er the Hills had run,
Scornful of Winter's Frost, and Summer's Sun,
Still asking, where He made his Flock to rest at Noon.
For him at Night, the dear expected Guest,
I had with hasty Joy prepar'd the Feast ;
And from the Cottage, o'er the distant Plain,
Sent forth my longing Eye to meet the Swain ;
Wav'ring, impatient, toss'd by Hope and Fear ;
Till He and Joy together should appear ;
And the lov'd Dog declare his Master near.
On my declining Neck, and open Breast,
I should have lull'd the lovely Youth to Rest ;
And from beneath his Head, at dawning Day,
With softest Care have stol'n my Arm away ;
To rise, and from the Fold release the Sheep,
Fond of his Flock, indulgent to his Sleep.

Or if kind Heav'n propitious to my Flame
(For sure from Heav'n the faithful Ardor came)
Had blest my Life, and deck'd my natal Hour
With Height of Title, and Extent of Pow'r :
Without a Crime my Passion had aspir'd,
Found the lov'd Prince, and told what I desir'd.

Then I had come, preventing SHEBA's Queen,
To see the comeliest of the Sons of Men ;
To hear the charming Poet's am'rous Song,
And gather Honey falling from his Tongue ;

To take the fragrant Kisses of his Mouth,
Sweeter than Breezes of her native South;
Likening his Grace, his Person, and his Mien
To all that Great or Beauteous I had seen.
Serene and bright his Eyes, as solar Beams
Reflecting temper'd Light from Crystal Streams;
Ruddy as Gold his Cheek; his Bosom fair
As Silver; the curl'd Ringlets of his Hair
Black as the Raven's Wing; his Lip more red,
Than Eastern Coral, or the scarlet Thread;
Even his Teeth, and white, like a young Flock
Coeval, newly shorn, from the clear Brook
Recent, and blanching on the Sunny Rock.
Iv'ry with Saphirs interspers'd, explains
How white his Hands, how blue the Manly Veins.
Columns of polish'd Marble firmly set
On golden Bases, are his Legs, and Feet.
His Stature all Majestic, all Divine,
Strait as the Palmtree, strong as is the Pine.
Saffron and Myrrhe are on his Garments shed:
And everlasting Sweets bloom round his Head.
What utter I? where am I? wretched Maid!
Dye, ABRA, dye: too plainly hast Thou said
Thy Soul's Desire to meet His high Embrace,
And Blessings stamp'd upon thy future Race;
To bid attentive Nations bless thy Womb,
With unborn Monarchs charg'd, and SOLOMONS to come.

Here o'er her Speech her flowing Eyes prevail.
O foolish Maid! and O unhappy Tale!
My suff'ring Heart for ever shall defy
New Wounds, and Danger from a future Eye.
O! yet my tortur'd Senses deep retain
The wretched Mem'ry of my former Pain,
The dire Affront, and my EGYPTIAN Chain.

As Time, I said, may happily efface
That cruel Image of the King's Disgrace;
Imperial Reason shall resume her Seat;
And SOLOMON once fall'n, again be great.

MATTHEW PRIOR

Betray'd by Passion, as subdu'd in War,
We wisely should exert a double Care,
Nor ever ought a second time to Err.

This ABRA then——
I saw Her; 'twas Humanity: it gave
Some Respite to the Sorrows of my Slave.
Her fond Excess proclaim'd her Passion true;
And generous Pity to that Truth was due.
Well I intreated Her, who well deserv'd;
I call'd Her often; for She always serv'd.
Use made her Person easy to my Sight;
And Ease insensibly produc'd Delight.

Whene'er I revell'd in the Women's Bow'rs;
(For first I sought Her but at looser Hours:)
The Apples She had gather'd smelt most sweet:
The Cake She kneaded was the sav'ry Meat:
But Fruits their Odor lost, and Meats their Taste;
If gentle ABRA had not deck'd the Feast.
Dishonor'd did the sparkling Goblet stand,
Unless receiv'd from gentle ABRA's Hand:
And when the Virgins form'd the Evening Choir,
Raising their Voices to the Master-Lyre;
Too flat I thought This Voice, and That too shrill;
One show'd too much, and one too little Skill:
Nor could my Soul approve the Music's Tone;
'Till all was hush'd, and ABRA Sung alone.
Fairer She seem'd, distinguish'd from the rest;
And better Mein disclos'd, as better drest.
A bright *Tiara* round her Forehead ty'd,
To juster Bounds confin'd it's rising Pride:
The blushing Ruby on her snowy Breast,
Render'd it's panting Whiteness more confess'd:
Bracelets of Pearl gave Roundness to her Arm;
And ev'ry Gem augmented ev'ry Charm.
Her Senses pleas'd, her Beauty still improv'd;
And She more lovely grew, as more belov'd.

And now I could behold, avow, and blame
The several Follies of my former Flame;

Willing my Heart for Recompence to prove
The certain Joys that lye in prosp'rous Love.
For what, said I, from ABRA can I fear,
Too humble to insult, too soft to be severe?
The Dam'sel's sole Ambition is to please:
With Freedom I may like, and quit with Ease:
She sooths, but never can enthrall my Mind:
Why may not Peace and Love for once be join'd?

Great Heav'n! how frail thy Creature Man is made!
How by Himself insensibly betray'd!
In our own Strength unhappily secure,
Too little cautious of the adverse Pow'r;
And by the Blast of Self-opinion mov'd,
We wish to charm, and seek to be belov'd.
On Pleasure's flowing Brink We idly stray,
Masters as yet of our returning Way:
Seeing no Danger, We disarm our Mind;
And give our Conduct to the Waves and Wind:
Then in the flow'ry Mead, or verdant Shade
To wanton Dalliance negligently laid,
We weave the Chaplet, and We crown the Bowl;
And smiling see the nearer Waters roll;
'Till the strong Gusts of raging Passion rise;
'Till the dire Tempest mingles Earth and Skies;
And swift into the boundless Ocean born,
Our foolish Confidence too late We mourn:
Round our devoted Heads the Billows beat;
And from our troubl'd View the lessen'd Lands retreat.

O mighty Love! from thy unbounded Pow'r
How shall the human Bosom rest secure?
How shall our Thought avoid the various. Snare?
Or Wisdom to our caution'd Soul declare
The diff'rent Shapes, Thou pleasest to imploy,
When bent to hurt, and certain to destroy?

The haughty Nymph in open Beauty drest,
To-Day encounters our unguarded Breast:
She looks with Majesty, and moves with State:
Unbent her Soul, and in Misfortune great,
She scorns the World, and dares the Rage of Fate.

MATTHEW PRIOR

Here whilst we take stern Manhood for our Guide,
And guard our Conduct with becoming Pride;
Charm'd with the Courage in her Action shown,
We praise her Mind, the Image of our own.
She that can please, is certain to perswade:
To-day belov'd, To-morrow is obey'd.
We think we see thro' Reason's Optics right;
Nor find, how Beauty's Rays elude our Sight:
Struck with her Eye whilst We applaud her Mind;
And when We speak Her great, We wish Her kind.

To-morrow, cruel Pow'r, Thou arm'st the Fair
With flowing Sorrow, and dishevel'd Hair:
Sad her Complaint, and humble is her Tale,
Her Sighs explaining where her Accents fail.
Here gen'rous Softness warms the honest Breast:
We raise the sad, and succour the distress'd:
And whilst our Wish prepares the kind Relief;
Whilst Pity mitigates her rising Grief:
We sicken soon from her contagious Care;
Grieve for her Sorrows, groan for her Despair;
And against Love too late those Bosoms arm,
Which Tears can soften, and which Sighs can warm.

Against this nearest cruelest of Foes,
What shall Wit meditate, or Force oppose?
Whence, feeble Nature, shall We summon Aid;
If by our Pity, and our Pride betray'd?
External Remedy shall We hope to find,
When the close Fiend has gain'd our treach'rous Mind;
Insulting there does Reason's Pow'r deride;
And blind Himself, conducts the dazl'd Guide?

My Conqueror now, my Lovely ABRA held
My Freedom in her Chains: my Heart was fill'd
With Her, with Her alone: in Her alone
It sought it's Peace and Joy: while She was gone,
It sigh'd, and griev'd, impatient of her Stay:
Return'd, She chas'd those Sighs, that Grief away:
Her Absence made the Night: her Presence brought the
    Day.

The Ball, the Play, the Mask by Turns succeed.
For Her I make the Song : the Dance with Her I lead.
I court Her various in each Shape and Dress,
That Luxury may form, or Thought express.

To-day beneath the Palm-tree on the Plains
In DEBORAH's Arms and Habit ABRA reigns :
The Wreath denoting Conquest guides her Brow :
And low, like BARAK, at her Feet I bow.
The Mimic Chorus sings her prosp'rous Hand ;
As She had slain the Foe, and sav'd the Land.

To-morrow She approves a softer Air ;
Forsakes the Pomp and Pageantry of War ;
The Form of peaceful ABIGAIL assumes ;
And from the Village with the Present comes :
The Youthful Band depose their glitt'ring Arms ;
Receive her Bounties, and recite her Charms ;
Whilst I assume my Father's Step and Mein,
To meet with due Regard my future Queen.

If hap'ly ABRA's Will be now inclin'd
To range the Woods, or chace the flying Hind ;
Soon as the Sun awakes, the sprightly Court
Leave their Repose, and hasten to the Sport.
In lessen'd Royalty, and humble State,
Thy King, JERUSALEM, descends to wait,
'Till ABRA comes. She comes : a Milk-white Steed,
Mixture of PERSIA's, and ARABIA's Breed,
Sustains the Nymph : her Garments flying loose
(As the SYDONIAN Maids, or THRACIAN use)
And half her Knee, and half her Breast appear,
By Art, like Negligence, disclos'd, and bare.
Her left Hand guides the hunting Courser's Flight :
A Silver Bow She carries in her Right :
And from the golden Quiver at her Side,
Rustles the Ebon Arrow's feather'd Pride.
Saphirs and Diamonds on her Front display
An artificial Moon's increasing Ray.
DIANA, Huntress, Mistress of the Groves,
The fav'rite ABRA speaks, and looks, and moves.

Her, as the present Goddess, I obey:
Beneath her Feet the captive Game I lay.
The mingl'd Chorus sings DIANA's Fame:
Clarions and Horns in louder Peals proclaim
Her Mystic Praise: the vocal Triumphs bound
Against the Hills: the Hills reflect the Sound.

If tir'd this Evening with the hunted Woods,
To the large Fish-pools, or the glassy Floods
Her Mind To-morrow points; a thousand Hands
To-night employ'd, obey the King's Commands.
Upon the wat'ry Beach an artful Pile
Of Planks is join'd, and forms a moving Isle.
A golden Chariot in the Midst is set;
And silver Cygnets seem to feel it's Weight.
ABRA, bright Queen, ascends her gaudy Throne,
In semblance of the GRÆCIAN VENUS known:
TRITONS and Sea-green NAIADS round Her move;
And sing in moving Strains the Force of Love:
Whilst as th'approaching Pageant does appear;
And echoing Crouds speak mighty VENUS near;
I, her Adorer, too devoutly stand
Fast on the utmost Margin of the Land,
With Arms and Hopes extended, to receive
The fancy'd Goddess rising from the Wave.

O subject Reason! O imperious Love!
Whither yet further would My Folly rove?
Is it enough, that ABRA should be great
In the wall'd Palace, or the Rural Seat?
That masking Habits, and a borrow'd Name
Contrive to hide my Plenitude of Shame?
No, no: JERUSALEM combin'd must see
My open Fault, and Regal Infamy.
Solemn a Month is destin'd for the Feast:
ABRA Invites: the Nation is the Guest.
To have the Honor of each Day sustain'd,
The Woods are travers'd; and the Lakes are drain'd:
ARABIA's Wilds, and EGYPT's are explor'd:
The Edible Creation decks the Board:
Hardly the *Phœnix* 'scapes——

The Men their Lyres, the Maids their Voices raise,
To sing my Happiness, and ABRA's Praise.
And slavish Bards our mutual Loves rehearse
In lying Strains, and ignominious Verse:
While from the Banquet leading forth the Bride,
Whom prudent Love from public Eyes should hide;
I show Her to the World, confess'd and known
Queen of my Heart, and Part'ner of my Throne.

And now her Friends and Flatt'rers fill the Court:
From DAN, and from BEERSHEBA They resort:
They barter Places, and dispose of Grants,
Whole Provinces unequal to their Wants.
They teach Her to recede, or to debate;
With Toys of Love to mix Affairs of State;
By practis'd Rules her Empire to secure;
And in my Pleasure make my Ruin sure.
They gave, and She transferr'd the curs'd Advice,
That Monarchs should their inward Soul disguise,
Dissemble, and command; be false, and wise;
By ignominious Arts for servile Ends
Should compliment their Foes, and shun their Friends.
And now I leave the true and just Supports
Of Legal Princes, and of honest Courts,
BARZILLAI's, and the fierce BENAIAH's Heirs;
Whose Sires, Great Part'ners in my Father's Cares,
Saluted their young King at HEBRON crown'd,
Great by their Toil, and glorious by their Wound.
And now, unhappy Council, I prefer
Those whom my Follies only made me fear,
Old CORAH's Brood, and taunting SHIMEI's Race;
Miscreants who ow'd their Lives to DAVID's Grace;
Tho' they had spurn'd his Rule, and curs'd Him to his Face.

Still ABRA's Pow'r, my Scandal still increas'd;
Justice submitted to what ABRA pleas'd:
Her Will alone could settle or revoke;
And Law was fix'd by what She latest spoke.

ISRAEL neglected, ABRA was my Care:
I only acted, thought, and liv'd for Her.

P.   U   305

MATTHEW PRIOR

I durst not reason with my wounded Heart.
ABRA possess'd; She was it's better Part.
O! had I now review'd the famous Cause,
Which gave my righteous Youth so just Applause;
In vain on the dissembl'd Mother's Tongue
Had cunning Art, and sly Perswasion hung;
And real Care in vain, and native Love
In the true Parent's panting Breast had strove;
While both deceiv'd had seen the destin'd Child
Or slain, or sav'd, as ABRA frown'd or smil'd.

Unknowing to command, proud to obey,
A life-less King, a Royal Shade I lay.
Unhear'd the injur'd Orphans now complain:
The Widow's Cries address the Throne in vain.
Causes unjudg'd disgrace the loaded File;
And sleeping Laws the King's Neglect revile.
No more the Elders throng'd around my Throne,
To hear My Maxims, and reform their own.
No more the Young Nobility were taught,
How MOSES govern'd, and how DAVID fought.
Loose and undisciplin'd the Soldier lay;
Or lost in Drink, and Game, the solid Day:
Porches and Scholes, design'd for public Good,
Uncover'd, and with Scaffolds cumber'd stood,
Or nodded, threat'ning Ruin——
Half Pillars wanted their expected Height;
And Roofs imperfect prejudic'd the Sight.
The Artists grieve; the lab'ring People droop:
My Father's Legacy, my Country's Hope,
God's Temple lies unfinish'd——

The Wise and Grave deplor'd their Monarch's Fate,
And future Mischiefs of a sinking State.
Is this, the Serious said, is this the Man,
Whose active Soul thro' every Science ran?
Who by just Rule and elevated Skill
Prescrib'd the dubious Bounds of Good and Ill?
Whose Golden Sayings, and Immortal Wit,
On large *Phylacteries* expressive writ,
Were to the Forehead of the *Rabbins* ty'd,

306

Our Youth's Instruction, and our Age's Pride?
Could not the Wise his wild Desires restrain?
Then was our Hearing, and his Preaching vain:
What from his Life and Letters were we taught,
But that his Knowledge aggravates his Fault?

In lighter Mood the Humorous and the Gay,
As crown'd with Roses at their Feasts they lay;
Sent the full Goblet, charg'd with ABRA's Name,
And Charms superior to their Master's Fame:
Laughing some praise the King, who let 'em see,
How aptly Luxe and Empire might agree:
Some gloss'd, how Love and Wisdom were at Strife;
And brought my Proverbs to confront my Life.
However, Friend, here's to the King, one cries:
To Him who was the King, the Friend replies.
The King, for JUDAH's, and for Wisdom's Curse,
To ABRA yields: could I, or Thou do worse?
Our looser Lives let Chance or Folly steer;
If thus the Prudent and Determin'd err.
Let DINAH bind with Flowers her flowing Hair;
And touch the Lute, and sound the wanton Air:
Let Us the Bliss without the Sting receive,
Free, as We will, or to injoy, or leave.
Pleasures on Levity's smooth Surface flow:
Thought brings the Weight, that sinks the Soul to Woe.
Now be this Maxim to the King convey'd,
And added to the Thousand He has made.

Sadly, O Reason, is thy Pow'r express'd,
Thou gloomy Tyrant of the frighted Breast!
And harsh the Rules, which We from Thee receive; ⎫
If for our Wisdom We our Pleasure give; ⎬
And more to think be only more to grieve. ⎭
If JUDAH's King at thy Tribunal try'd,
Forsakes his Joy to vindicate his Pride;
And changing Sorrows, I am only found
Loos'd from the Chains of Love, in Thine more strictly bound.

But do I call Thee Tyrant, or complain,
How hard thy Laws, how absolute thy Reign?

While Thou, alas! art but an empty Name,
To no Two Men, who e'er discours'd, the same;
The idle Product of a troubled Thought,
In borrow'd Shapes, and airy Colors wrought;
A fancy'd Line, and a reflected Shade;
A Chain which Man to fetter Man has made,
By Artifice impos'd, by Fear obey'd.

Yet, wretched Name, or Arbitrary Thing,
Whence ever I thy cruel Essence bring,
I own thy Influence; for I feel thy Sting.
Reluctant I perceive thee in my Soul,
Form'd to command, and destin'd to control.
Yes; thy insulting Dictates shall be heard:
Virtue for once shall be Her own Reward:
Yes; Rebel ISRAEL, this unhappy Maid
Shall be dismiss'd: the Crowd shall be obey'd:
The King his Passion, and his Rule shall leave,
No longer ABRA's, but the People's Slave.
My Coward Soul shall bear it's wayward Fate:
I will, alas! be wretched, to be great;
And sigh in Royalty, and grieve in State.

I said: resolv'd to plunge into my Grief
At once so far, as to expect Relief
From my Despair alone——
I chose to write the Thing I durst not speak,
To Her I lov'd; to Her I must forsake.
The harsh Epistle labour'd much to prove,
How inconsistent Majesty, and Love.
I always should, It said, esteem Her well;
But never see her more: It bid Her feel
No future Pain for Me; but instant wed
A Lover more proportion'd to her Bed;
And quiet dedicate her remnant Life
To the just Duties of an humble Wife.

She read; and forth to Me She wildly ran,
To Me, the Ease of all her former Pain.
She kneel'd intreated, struggl'd, threaten'd, cry'd;

And with alternate Passion liv'd, and dy'd:
'Till now deny'd the Liberty to mourn,
And by rude Fury from my Presence torn,
This only Object of my real Care,
Cut off from Hope, abandon'd to Despair,
In some few posting fatal Hours is hurl'd
From Wealth, from Pow'r, from Love, and from the World.

Here tell Me, if Thou dar'st, my conscious Soul,
What diff'rent Sorrows did within Thee roll:
What Pangs, what Fires, what Racks didst Thou sustain,
What sad Vicissitudes of smarting Pain?
How oft from Pomp and State did I remove,
To feed Despair, and cherish hopeless Love?
How oft, all Day, recall'd I ABRA's Charms,
Her Beauties press'd, and panting in my Arms?
How oft, with Sighs, view'd every Female Face,
Where mimic Fancy might her Likeness trace?
How oft desir'd to fly from ISRAEL's Throne,
And live in Shades with Her and Love alone?
How oft, all Night, pursu'd Her in my Dreams,
O'er flow'ry Vallies, and thro' Crystal Streams;
And waking, view'd with Grief the rising Sun,
And fondly mourn'd the dear Delusion gone?

When thus the gather'd Storms of wretched Love
In my swoln Bosom, with long War had strove;
At length they broke their Bounds: at length their Force
Bore down whatever met it's stronger Course:
Lay'd all the Civil Bonds of Manhood waste;
And scatter'd Ruin as the Torrent past.

So from the Hills, whose hollow Caves contain
The congregated Snow, and swelling Rain;
'Till the full Stores their antient Bounds disdain;
Precipitate the furious Torrent flows:
In vain would Speed avoid, or Strength oppose:
Towns, Forests, Herds, and Men promiscuous drown'd,
With one great Death deform the dreary Ground;
The echo'd Woes from distant Rocks resound.

MATTHEW PRIOR

And now what impious Ways my Wishes took;
How they the Monarch, and the Man forsook;
And how I follow'd an abandon'd Will,
Thro' crooked Paths, and sad Retreats of Ill;
How JUDAH's Daughters now, now foreign Slaves,
By turns my prostituted Bed receives.
Thro' Tribes of Women how I loosely rang'd
Impatient; lik'd To-night, To-morrow chang'd;
And by the Instinct of capricious Lust,
Enjoy'd, disdain'd, was grateful, or unjust:
O, be these Scenes from human Eyes conceal'd,
In Clouds of decent Silence justly veil'd!
O, be the wanton Images convey'd
To black Oblivion, and eternal Shade!
Or let their sad *Epitome* alone,
And outward Lines to future Age be known,
Enough to propagate the sure Belief,
That Vice engenders Shame; and Folly broods o'er Grief.

Bury'd in Sloth, and lost in Ease I lay:
The Night I revell'd; and I slept the Day.
New Heaps of Fewel damp'd my kindling Fires;
And daily Change extinguish'd young Desires.
By its own Force destroy'd, Fruition ceas'd;
And always weary'd, I was never pleas'd.
No longer now does my neglected Mind
It's wonted Stores, and old *Ideas* find.
Fix'd Judgment there no longer does abide,
To take the True, or set the False aside.
No longer does swift Mem'ry trace the Cells,
Where springing Wit, or young Invention dwells.
Frequent Debauch to Habitude prevails:
Patience of Toil, and Love of Virtue fails.
By sad Degrees impair'd my Vigor dyes;
Till I Command no longer ev'n in Vice.

The Women on my Dotage build their Sway:
They ask; I grant: They threaten; I obey.
In Regal Garments now I gravely stride,
Aw'd by the PERSIAN Dam'sel's haughty Pride.

310

Now with the looser SYRIAN dance, and sing,
In Robes tuck'd up, opprobrious to the King.

   Charm'd by their Eyes, their Manners I acquire;
And shape my Foolishness to their Desire.
Seduc'd and aw'd by the PHILISTINE Dame,
At DAGON's Shrine I kindle impious Flame.
With the CHALDEAN's Charms her Rites prevail;
And curling Frankincense ascends to BAAL.
To each new Harlot I new Altars dress;
And serve Her God, whose Person I caress.

   Where, my deluded Sense, was Reason flown?
Where the high Majesty of DAVID's Throne?
Where all the Maxims of Eternal Truth,
With which the Living GOD inform'd my Youth?
When with the lewd EGYPTIAN I adore
Vain Idols, Deities that ne'er before
In ISRAEL's Land had fix'd their dire Abodes,
Beastly Divinities, and Droves of Gods:
OSIRIS, APIS, Pow'rs that chew the Cud,
And Dog ANUBIS, Flatt'rer for his Food:
When in the Woody Hill's forbidden Shade
I carv'd the Marble, and invok'd it's Aid:
When in the Fens to Snakes and Flies, with Zeal
Unworthy human Thought, I prostrate fell;
To Shrubs and Plants my vile Devotion paid;
And set the bearded Leek, to which I pray'd:
When to all Beings Sacred Rites were giv'n;
Forgot the Arbiter of Earth and Heav'n.

   Thro' these sad Shades, this *Chaos* in my Soul,
Some Seeds of Light at length began to roll.
The rising Motion of an Infant Ray
Shot glimm'ring thro' the Cloud, and promis'd Day.
And now one Moment able to reflect,
I found the King abandon'd to Neglect,
Seen without Awe, and serv'd without Respect.
I found my Subjects amicably joyn,
To lessen their Defects, by citing Mine.

311

MATTHEW PRIOR

The Priest with Pity pray'd for DAVID's Race;
And left his Text, to dwell on my Disgrace.
The Father, whilst he warn'd his erring Son,
The sad Examples which He ought to shun,
Describ'd, and only nam'd not, SOLOMON.
Each Bard, each Sire did to his Pupil sing,
A Wise Child better than a Foolish King.

Into My self my Reason's Eye I turn'd;
And as I much reflected, much I mourn'd.
A Mighty King I am, an Earthly God:
Nations obey my Word, and wait my Nod.
I raise or sink, imprison or set free;
And Life or Death depends on My Decree.
Fond the *Idea*, and the Thought is vain:
O'er JUDAH's King ten thousand Tyrants reign.
Legions of Lust, and various Pow'rs of Ill
Insult the Master's Tributary Will:
And He, from whom the Nations should receive
Justice, and Freedom, lyes Himself a Slave,
Tortur'd by cruel Change of wild Desires,
Lash'd by mad Rage, and scorch'd by brutal Fires.

O Reason! once again to Thee I call:
Accept my Sorrow, and retrieve my Fall.
Wisdom, Thou say'st, from Heav'n receiv'd her Birth;
Her Beams transmitted to the subject Earth.
Yet this great Empress of the human Soul
Does only with imagin'd Pow'r controul;
If restless Passion by Rebellious Sway
Compells the weak Usurper to obey.

O troubled, weak, and Coward, as thou art!
Without thy poor Advice the lab'ring Heart
To worse Extremes with swifter Steps would run,
Not sav'd by Virtue, yet by Vice undone.

Oft have I said, the Praise of doing well
Is to the Ear, as Oyntment to the Smell.
Now if some Flies perchance, however small,
Into the Alabaster Urn should fall;

The Odors of the Sweets inclos'd would dye;
And Stench corrupt (sad Change!) their Place supply.
So the least Faults, if mix'd with fairest Deed,
Of future Ill become the fatal Seed:
Into the Balm of purest Virtue cast,
Annoy all Life with one contagious Blast.

Lost SOLOMON! pursue this Thought no more:
Of thy past Errors recollect the Store:
And silent weep, that while the Deathless Muse
Shall sing the Just; shall o'er their Head diffuse
Perfumes with lavish Hand; She shall proclaim
Thy Crimes alone; and to Thy evil Fame
Impartial, scatter Damps, and Poysons on thy Name.

Awaking therefore, as who long had dream'd,
Much of my Women, and their Gods asham'd,
From this Abyss of exemplary Vice
Resolv'd, as Time might aid my Thought, to rise;
Again I bid the mournful Goddess write
The fond Pursuit of fugitive Delight:
Bid her exalt her melancholy Wing,
And rais'd from Earth, and sav'd from Passion, sing
Of human Hope by cross Event destroy'd,
Of useless Wealth, and Greatness unenjoy'd,
Of Lust and Love, with their fantastic Train,
Their Wishes, Smiles, and Looks deceitful all, and vain.

MATTHEW PRIOR

POWER;

THE

THIRD BOOK.

The ARGUMENT.

SOLOMON considers *Man through the several Stages and Conditions of Life; and concludes in general, that We are all Miserable. He reflects more particularly upon the Trouble and Uncertainty of Greatness and Power; gives some Instances thereof from* ADAM *down to Himself; and still concludes that* ALL *is* VANITY. *He reasons again upon Life, Death, and a future Being; finds Human Wisdom too imperfect to resolve his Doubts; has Recourse to Religion; is informed by an Angel, what shall happen to Himself, his Family, and his Kingdom, 'till the Redemption of* ISRAEL: *and, upon the whole, resolves to submit his Enquiries and Anxieties to the Will of his Creator.*

TEXTS *chiefly alluded to in this Book.*

Or ever the Silver Cord be loosed, or the golden Bowl be broken, or the Pitcher be broken at the Fountain, or the Wheel broken at the Cistern. ECCLESIASTES, Chap. XII. Vers. 6.

The Sun ariseth, and the Sun goeth down, and hasteth to his Place where He arose. ECCLESIASTES, Chap. I. Vers. 5.

The Wind goeth towards the South, and turneth about unto the North. It whirleth about continually; and the Wind returneth again according to his Circuit. Vers. 6.

All the Rivers run into the Sea: yet the Sea is not full. Unto the Place from whence the Rivers come, thither they return again. Vers. 7.

Then shall the Dust return to the Earth, as it was: and the Spirit shall return unto God who gave it. ECCLESIASTES, Chap. XII. Vers. 7.

Now when SOLOMON had made an End of Praying, the Fire came down from Heaven, and consumed the Burnt-offering, and the Sacrifices; and the Glory of the Lord filled the House. II CHRONICLES, Chap. VII. Vers. 1.

By the Rivers of BABYLON, there We sat down; Yea We wept, when We remembred Sion &c. PSALM CXXXVII. Vers. 1.

I said of Laughter, it is mad; and of Mirth, what doeth it? ECCLESIASTES, Chap. II. Vers. 2.

——No Man can find out the Work that God maketh, from the Beginning to the End. ECCLESIASTES, Chap. III. Vers. 11.

Whatsoever God doeth, it shall be for ever: nothing can be put to it, nor any thing taken from it: and God doeth it, that Men should fear before Him. Vers. 14.

Let us hear the Conclusion of the whole Matter; Fear God, and keep his Commandments; for this is the whole Duty of Man. ECCLESIASTES, Chap. XII. Verse. 13.

MATTHEW PRIOR

POWER;

THE

THIRD BOOK.

COME then, my Soul: I call Thee by that Name,
   Thou busie Thing, from whence I know I am:
For knowing that I am, I know Thou art;
Since That must needs exist, which can impart.
But how Thou cam'st to be, or whence Thy Spring:
For various of Thee Priests and Poets sing.

   Hear'st Thou submissive, but a lowly Birth,
Some sep'rate Particles of finer Earth,
A plain Effect, which Nature must beget,
As Motion orders, and as Atoms meet;
Companion of the Body's Good or Ill,
From Force of Instinct more than Choice of Will;
Conscious of Fear or Valor, Joy or Pain,
As the wild Courses of the Blood ordain;
Who as Degrees of Heat and Cold prevail,
In Youth dost flourish, and with Age shalt fail;
'Till mingl'd with thy Part'ner's latest Breath
Thou fly'st, dissolv'd in Air, and lost in Death.

   Or if Thy great Existence would aspire
To Causes more sublime; of Heav'nly Fire
Wer't Thou a Spark struck off, a sep'rate Ray,
Ordain'd to mingle with Terrestrial Clay;
With it condemn'd for certain Years to dwell,
To grieve it's Frailties, and it's Pains to feel;
To teach it Good and Ill, Disgrace or Fame;
Pale it with Rage, or redden it with Shame:
To guide it's Actions with informing Care,
In Peace to Judge, to Conquer in the War;

Render it Agile, Witty, Valiant, Sage,
As fits the various Course of human Age;
Till as the Earthly Part decays and falls,
The Captive breaks Her Prison's mould'ring Walls;
Hovers a-while upon the sad Remains,
Which now the Pile, or Sepulchre contains;
And thence with Liberty unbounded flies,
Impatient to regain Her native Skies.

Whate'er Thou art, where-e'er ordain'd to go:
(Points which We rather may dispute, than know)
Come on, Thou little Inmate of this Breast,
Which for Thy Sake from Passions I divest:
For these, Thou say'st, raise all the stormy Strife,
Which hinder Thy Repose, and trouble Life.
Be the fair Level of Thy Actions laid,
As Temp'rance wills, and Prudence may perswade;
Be Thy Affections undisturb'd and clear,
Guided to what may Great or Good appear;
And try if Life be worth the Liver's Care.

Amass'd in Man there justly is beheld
What thro' the whole Creation has excell'd:
The Life and Growth of Plants, of Beasts the Sense,
The Angel's Forecast and Intelligence:
Say from these glorious Seeds what Harvest flows;
Recount our Blessings, and compare our Woes.
In it's true Light let clearest Reason see
The Man dragg'd out to Act, and forc'd to Be;
Helpless and Naked on a Woman's Knees
To be expos'd or rear'd as She may please;
Feel her Neglect, and pine from her Disease.
His tender Eye by too direct a Ray
Wounded, and flying from unpractis'd Day;
His Heart assaulted by invading Air,
And beating fervent to the vital War;
To his Young Sense how various Forms appear;
That strike his Wonder, and excite his Fear?
By his Distortions he reveals his Pains;
He by his Tears, and by his Sighs complains;

MATTHEW PRIOR

'Till Time and Use assist the Infant Wretch,
By broken Words, and Rudiments of Speech,
His Wants in plainer Characters to show,
And paint more perfect Figures of his Woe.
Condemn'd to sacrifice his childish Years
To babling Ign'rance, and to empty Fears;
To pass the riper Period of his Age,
Acting his Part upon a crowded Stage;
To lasting Toils expos'd, and endless Cares,
To open Dangers, and to secret Snares;
To Malice which the vengeful Foe intends,
And the more dangerous Love of seeming Friends.
His Deeds examin'd by the People's Will,
Prone to forget the Good, and blame the Ill:
Or sadly censur'd in their curs'd Debate,
Who in the Scorner's, or the Judge's Seat
Dare to condemn the Virtue which They hate.
Or would he rather leave this frantic Scene;
And Trees and Beasts prefer to Courts and Men?
In the remotest Wood and lonely Grott
Certain to meet that worst of Evils, Thought;
Diff'rent IDEAS to his Mem'ry brought:
Some intricate, as are the pathless Woods;
Impetuous some, as the descending Floods:
With anxious Doubts, with raging Passions torn,
No sweet Companion near with whom to mourn;
He hears the Echoing Rock return his Sighs;
And from himself the frighted Hermit flies.

Thus, thro' what Path soe'er of Life We rove,
Rage companies our Hate, and Grief our Love:
Vex'd with the present Moment's heavy Gloom,
Why seek We Brightness from the Years to come?
Disturb'd and broken like a sick Man's Sleep,
Our troubl'd Thoughts to distant Prospects leap;
Desirous still what flies us to o'ertake:
For Hope is but the Dream of Those that wake:
But looking back, We see the dreadful Train
Of Woes, a-new which were We to sustain,
We should refuse to tread the Path again.

Still adding Grief, still counting from the first;
Judging the latest Evils still the worst;
And sadly finding each progressive Hour
Heighten their Number, and augment their Pow'r;
Till by one countless Sum of Woes opprest,
Hoary with Cares, and Ignorant of Rest,
We find the vital Springs relax'd and worn:
Compell'd our common Impotence to mourn,
Thus, thro' the Round of Age, to Childhood We return;
Reflecting find, that naked from the Womb
We yesterday came forth; that in the Tomb
Naked again We must To-morrow lye,
Born to lament, to labor, and to dye.

Pass We the Ills, which each Man feels or dreads,
The Weight or fall'n, or hanging o'er our Heads;
The Bear, The Lyon, Terrors of the Plain,
The Sheepfold scatter'd, and the Shepherd slain;
The frequent Errors of the pathless Wood,
The giddy Precipice, and the dang'rous Flood:
The noisom Pest'lence, that in open War
Terrible, marches thro' the Mid-day Air,
And scatters Death; the Arrow that by Night
Cuts the dank Mist, and fatal wings it's Flight;
The billowing Snow, and Violence of the Show'r,
That from the Hills disperse their dreadful Store,
And o'er the Vales collected Ruin pour;
The Worm that gnaws the ripening Fruit, sad Guest,
Canker or Locust hurtful to infest
The Blade; while Husks elude the Tiller's Care,
And Eminence of Want distinguishes the Year.

Pass we the slow Disease, and subtil Pain,
Which our weak Frame is destin'd to sustain;
The cruel Stone, with congregated War
Tearing his bloody Way; the cold Catarrh,
With frequent Impulse, and continu'd Strife,
Weak'ning the wasted Seats of irksom Life;
The Gout's fierce Rack, the burning Feaver's Rage,
The sad Experience of Decay; and Age,

Her self the soarest Ill; while Death, and Ease,
Oft and in vain invok'd, or to appease,
Or end the Grief, with hasty Wings receed
From the vext Patient, and the sickly Bed.

Nought shall it profit, that the charming Fair,
Angelic, softest Work of Heav'n, draws near
To the cold shaking paralytic Hand,
Senseless of Beauty's Touch, or Love's Command,
Nor longer apt, or able to fulfill
The Dictates of it's feeble Master's Will.

Nought shall the Psaltry, and the Harp avail,
The pleasing Song, or well repeated Tale,
When the quick Spirits their warm March forbear;
And numbing Coldness has unbrac'd the Ear.

The verdant Rising of the flow'ry Hill,
The Vale enamell'd, and the Crystal Rill,
The Ocean rolling, and the shelly Shoar,
Beautiful Objects, shall delight no more;
When the lax'd Sinews of the weaken'd Eye
In wat'ry Damps, or dim Suffusion lye.
Day follows Night; the Clouds return again
After the falling of the later Rain:
But to the Aged-blind shall ne'er return
Grateful Vicissitude: He still must mourn
The Sun, and Moon, and ev'ry Starry Light
Eclips'd to Him, and lost in everlasting Night.

Behold where Age's wretched Victim lies:
See his Head trembling, and his half-clos'd Eyes:
Frequent for Breath his panting Bosom heaves:
To broken Sleeps his remnant Sense He gives;
And only by his Pains, awaking finds He Lives.

Loos'd by devouring Time the Silver Cord
Dissever'd lies: unhonor'd from the Board
The Crystal Urn, when broken, is thrown by;
And apter Utensils their Place supply.
These Things and Thou must share One equal Lot;
Dye and be lost, corrupt and be forgot;

While still another, and another Race
Shall now supply, and now give up the Place.
From Earth all came, to Earth must all return;
Frail as the Cord, and brittle as the Urn.

But be the Terror of these Ills suppress'd:
And view We Man with Health and Vigor blest.
Home He returns with the declining Sun,
His destin'd Task of Labor hardly done;
Goes forth again with the ascending Ray,
Again his Travel for his Bread to pay,
And find the Ill sufficient to the Day.
Hap'ly at Night He does with Horror shun
A widow'd Daughter, or a dying Son:
His Neighbor's Off-spring He To-morrow sees;
And doubly feels his Want in their Increase:
The next Day, and the next he must attend
His Foe triumphant, or his buried Friend.
In ev'ry Act and Turn of Life he feels
Public Calamities, or Household Ills:
The due Reward to just Desert refus'd:
The Trust betray'd, the Nuptial Bed abus'd:
The Judge corrupt, the long depending Cause,
And doubtful Issue of misconstru'd Laws:
The crafty Turns of a dishonest State,
And violent Will of the wrong-doing Great:
The Venom'd Tongue injurious to his Fame,
Which nor can Wisdom shun, nor fair Advice reclaim.

Esteem We these, my Friends, Event and Chance,
Produc'd as Atoms form their flutt'ring Dance?
Or higher yet their Essence may We draw
From destin'd Order, and Eternal Law?
Again, my Muse, the cruel Doubt repeat:
Spring they, I say, from Accident, or Fate?
Yet such, We find, they are, as can controll
The servile Actions of our wav'ring Soul;
Can fright, can alter, or can chain the Will;
Their Ills all built on Life, that fundamental Ill.

O fatal Search! in which the lab'ring Mind,
Still press'd with Weight of Woe, still hopes to find

MATTHEW PRIOR

A Shadow of Delight, a Dream of Peace,
From Years of Pain, one Moment of Release;
Hoping at least She may Her self deceive,
Against Experience willing to believe,
Desirous to rejoice, condemn'd to grieve.

Happy the Mortal Man, who now at last
Has thro' this doleful Vale of Mis'ry past;
Who to his destin'd Stage has carry'd on
The tedious Load, and laid his Burden down;
Whom the cut Brass, or wounded Marble shows
Victor o'er Life, and all Her Train of Woes.
He happyer yet, who privileg'd by Fate
To shorter Labor, and a lighter Weight,
Receiv'd but Yesterday the Gift of Breath,
Order'd To-morrow to return to Death.
But O! beyond Description happyest He,
Who ne'er must roll on Life's tumultuous Sea;
Who with bless'd Freedom from the gen'ral Doom
Exempt, must never force the teeming Womb,
Nor see the Sun, nor sink into the Tomb.

Who breaths, must suffer; and who thinks, must mourn;
And He alone is bless'd, who ne'er was born.

"Yet in thy turn, Thou frowning Preacher, hear:
"Are not these general Maxims too severe?
"Say: cannot Pow'r secure it's Owner's Bliss?
"And is not Wealth the potent Sire of Peace?
"Are Victors bless'd with Fame, or Kings with Ease?

I tell Thee, Life is but one common Care;
And Man was born to suffer, and to fear.

"But is no Rank, no Station, no Degree
"From this contagious Taint of Sorrow free?

None, Mortal, None: Yet in a bolder Strain
Let Me this melancholy Truth maintain:
But hence, Ye Worldly, and Prophane, retire:
For I adapt my Voice, and raise my Lyre
To Notions not by Vulgar Ear receiv'd:
Ye still must covet Life, and be deceiv'd:

Your very Fear of Death shall make Ye try
To catch the Shade of Immortality;
Wishing on Earth to linger, and to save
Part of it's Prey from the devouring Grave;
To those who may survive Ye, to bequeath
Something entire, in spight of Time, and Death;
A fancy'd Kind of Being to retrieve,
And in a Book, or from a Building live.
False Hope! vain Labor! let some Ages fly:
The Dome shall moulder, and the Volume dye:
Wretches, still taught, still will Ye think it strange,
That all the Parts of this great Fabric change;
Quit their old Station, and Primæval Frame;
And lose their Shape, their Essence, and their Name?

Reduce the Song: our Hopes, our Joys are vain:
Our Lot is Sorrow; and Our Portion Pain.

What Pause from Woe, what Hopes of Comfort bring
The Name of Wise or Great, of Judge or King?
What is a King? A Man condemn'd to bear
The public Burden of the Nation's Care;
Now crown'd some angry Faction to appease;
Now falls a Victim to the People's Ease:
From the first blooming of his ill-taught Youth,
Nourish'd in Flatt'ry, and estrang'd from Truth:
At Home surrounded by a servile Crowd,
Prompt to abuse, and in Detraction loud:
Abroad begirt with Men, and Swords, and Spears;
His very State acknowledging his Fears:
Marching amidst a thousand Guards, He shows
His secret Terror of a thousand Foes;
In War however Prudent, Great, or Brave,
To blind Events, and fickle Chance a Slave:
Seeking to settle what for ever flies;
Sure of the Toil, uncertain of the Prize.

But He returns with Conquest on his Brow;
Brings up the Triumph, and absolves the Vow:
The Captive Generals to his Carr are ty'd:
The Joyful Citizens tumultuous Tyde
Echoing his Glory, gratify his Pride.

MATTHEW PRIOR

What is this Triumph? Madness, Shouts, and Noise,
One great Collection of the People's Voice.
The Wretches he brings back, in Chains relate,
What may To-morrow be the Victor's Fate.
The Spoils and Trophies born before Him, show
National Loss, and Epidemic Woe,
Various Distress, which He and His may know.
Does He not mourn the valiant Thousands slain;
The Heroes, once the Glory of the Plain,
Left in the Conflict of the Fatal Day,
Or the Wolve's Portion, or the Vulture's Prey?
Does He not weep the Lawrel, which he wears,
Wet with the Soldier's Blood, and Widow's Tears?

See, where He comes, the Darling of the War!
See Millions crowding round the gilded Car!
In the vast Joys of this Ecstatic Hour,
And full Fruition of successful Pow'r,
One Moment and one Thought might let Him scan
The various Turns of Life, and fickle State of Man.

Are the dire Images of sad Distrust,
And Popular Change, obscur'd a-mid the Dust,
That rises from the Victor's rapid Wheel?
Can the loud Clarion, or shrill Fife repel
The inward Cries of Care? can Nature's Voice
Plaintive be drown'd, or lessen'd in the Noise;
Tho' Shouts as Thunder loud afflict the Air;
Stun the Birds now releas'd, and shake the Iv'ry Chair?

Yon' Crowd (He might reflect) yon' joyful Crowd,
Pleas'd with my Honors, in my Praises loud,
(Should fleeting Vict'ry to the Vanquish'd go;
Should She depress my Arms, and raise the Foe;)
Would for That Foe with equal Ardor wait
At the high Palace, or the crowded Gate;
With restless Rage would pull my Statues down;
And cast the Brass a-new to His Renown.

O impotent Desire of Worldly Sway!
That I, who make the Triumph of To-day,

May of To-morrow's Pomp one Part appear,
Ghastly with Wounds, and lifeless on the Bier!
Then (Vileness of Mankind!) then of all These,
Whom my dilated Eye with Labor sees,
Would one, alas! repeat Me Good, or Great?
Wash my pale Body, or bewail my Fate?
Or, march'd I chain'd behind the Hostile Carr,
The Victor's Pastime, and the Sport of War;
Would One, would One his pitying Sorrow lend,
Or be so poor, to own He was my Friend?

   Avails it then, O Reason, to be Wise?
To see this cruel Scene with quicker Eyes?
To know with more Distinction to complain,
And have superior Sense in feeling Pain?

   Let us revolve that Roll with strictest Eye,
Where safe from Time distinguish'd Actions lye;
And judge if Greatness be exempt from Pain,
Or Pleasure ever may with Pow'r remain.

   ADAM, great *Type*, for whom the World was made,
The fairest Blessing to his Arms convey'd,
A charming Wife; and Air, and Sea, and Land,
And all that move therein, to his Command
Render'd obedient: say, my Pensive Muse,
What did these golden Promises produce?
Scarce tasting Life, He was of Joy bereav'd:
One Day, I think, in PARADISE He liv'd;
Destin'd the next His Journey to pursue,
Where wounding Thorns, and cursed Thistles grew.
E'er yet He earns his Bread, a-down his Brow,
Inclin'd to Earth, his lab'ring Sweat must flow:
His Limbs must ake, with daily Toils oppress'd;
E'er long-wish'd Night brings necessary Rest:
Still viewing with Regret his Darling EVE,
He for Her Follies, and His own must grieve.
Bewailing still a-fresh their hapless Choice;
His Ear oft frighted with the imag'd Voice
Of Heav'n, when first it thunder'd; oft his View
A-ghast, as when the Infant Light'ning flew;

325

And the stern CHERUB stop'd the fatal Road,
Arm'd with the Flames of an Avenging GOD.
His Younger Son on the polluted Ground,
First Fruit of Death, lies Plaintif of a Wound
Giv'n by a Brother's Hand : His Eldest Birth
Flies, mark'd by Heav'n, a Fugitive o'er Earth.
Yet why these Sorrows heap'd upon the Sire,
Becomes nor Man, nor Angel to enquire.

Each Age sinn'd on ; and Guilt advanc'd with Time :
The Son still added to the Father's Crime ;
'Till God arose, and great in Anger said :
Lo ! it repenteth Me, that Man was made.
Withdraw thy Light, Thou Sun ! be dark, Ye Skies !
And from your deep Abyss, Ye Waters, rise !

The frighted Angels heard th'Almighty Lord ;
And o'er the Earth from wrathful Viols pour'd
Tempests and Storm, obedient to His Word.
Mean time, His Providence to NOAH gave
The Guard of All, that He design'd to save.
Exempt from general Doom the Patriarch stood ;
Contemn'd the Waves, and triumph'd o'er the Flood.

The Winds fall silent ; and the Waves decrease :
The Dove brings Quiet, and the Olive Peace :
Yet still His Heart does inward Sorrow feel,
Which Faith alone forbids Him to reveal.
If on the backward World his Views are cast ;
'Tis Death diffus'd, and universal Waste.
Present (sad Prospect !) can He Ought descry,
But (what affects his melancholy Eye)
The Beauties of the Antient Fabric lost,
In Chains of craggy Hill, or Lengths of dreary Coast ?
While to high Heav'n his pious Breathings turn'd,
Weeping He hop'd, and Sacrificing mourn'd ;
When of GOD's Image only Eight He found
Snatch'd from the Wat'ry Grave, and sav'd from Nations
     drown'd ;
And of three Sons, the future Hopes of Earth,
The Seed, whence Empires must receive their Birth,

One He foresees excluded Heav'nly Grace,
And mark'd with Curses, fatal to his Race.

ABRAHAM, Potent Prince, the Friend of GOD,
Of Human Ills must bear the destin'd Load ;
By Blood and Battles must his Pow'r maintain,
And slay the Monarchs, e'er He rules the Plain ;
Must deal just Portions of a servile Life
To a proud handmaid, and a peevish Wife ;
Must with the Mother leave the weeping Son,
In Want to wander, and in Wilds to groan ;
Must take his other Child, his Age's Hope
To trembling MORIAM's melancholy Top,
Order'd to drench his Knife in filial Blood ;
Destroy his Heir, or disobey his GOD.

MOSES beheld that GOD ; but how beheld ?
The Deity in radiant Beams conceal'd,
And clouded in a deep Abyss of Light ;
While present, too severe for Human Sight,
Nor staying longer than one swift-wing'd Night.
The following Days, and Months, and Years decreed
To fierce Encounter, and to toilsome Deed.
His Youth with Wants and Hardships must engage :
Plots and Rebellions must disturb his Age.
Some CORAH still arose, some Rebel Slave,
Prompter to sink the State, than He to save :
And ISRAEL did his Rage so far provoke,
That what the God-head wrote, the Prophet broke.
His Voice scarce heard, his Dictates scarce believ'd,
In Camps, in Arms, in Pilgrimage, He liv'd ;
And dy'd obedient to severest Law,
Forbid to tread the promis'd Land, He saw.

My Father's Life was one long Line of Care,
A Scene of Danger, and a State of War.
Alarm'd, expos'd, his Childhood must engage
The Bear's rough Gripe, and foaming Lion's Rage.
By various Turns his threaten'd Youth must fear
GOLIAH's lifted Sword, and SAUL's emitted Spear.

MATTHEW PRIOR

Forlorn He must, and persecuted fly;
Climb the steep Mountain, in the Cavern lye;
And often ask, and be refus'd to dye.

For ever, from His manly Toils, are known
The Weight of Pow'r, and Anguish of a Crown.
What Tongue can speak the restless Monarch's Woes;
When GOD, and NATHAN were declar'd his Foes?
When ev'ry Object his Offence revil'd,
The Husband murder'd, and the Wife defil'd,
The Parent's Sins impress'd upon the dying Child?
What Heart can think the Grief which He sustain'd;
When the King's Crime brought Vengeance on the Land;
And the inexorable Prophet's Voice
Gave Famine, Plague, or War; and bid him fix his Choice?

He dy'd; and Oh! may no Reflection shed
It's poys'nous Venom on the Royal Dead:
Yet the unwilling Truth must be express'd;
Which long has labor'd in this pensive Breast:
Dying He added to my Weight of Care:
He made Me to his Crimes undoubted Heir:
Left his unfinish'd Murder to his Son,
And JOAB's Blood intail'd on JUDAH's Crown.

Young as I was, I hasted to fulfill
The cruel Dictates of My Parent's Will.
Of his fair Deeds a distant View I took;
But turn'd the Tube upon his Faults to look;
Forgot his Youth, spent in his Country's Cause,
His Care of Right, his Rev'rence to the Laws:
But could with Joy his Years of Folly trace,
Broken and old in BATHSHEBA's Embrace;
Could follow Him, where e'er He stray'd from Good,
And cite his sad Example; whilst I trod
Paths open to Deceit, and track'd with Blood.
Soon docile to the secret Acts of Ill,
With Smiles I could betray, with Temper kill:
Soon in a Brother could a Rival view;
Watch all his Acts, and all his Ways pursue.

In vain for Life He to the Altar fled:
Ambition and Revenge have certain Speed.
Ev'n there, My Soul, ev'n there He should have fell;
But that my Interest did my Rage conceal.
Doubling my Crime, I promise, and deceive;
Purpose to slay, whilst swearing to forgive.
Treaties, Perswasions, Sighs, and Tears are vain:
With a mean Lie curs'd Vengeance I sustain;
Joyn Fraud to Force, and Policy to Pow'r;
'Till of the destin'd Fugitive secure,
In solemn State to Parricide I rise;
And, as GOD lives, this Day my Brother dies.

Be Witness to my Tears, Celestial Muse!
In vain I would forget, in vain excuse
Fraternal Blood by my Direction spilt;
In vain on JOAB's Head transfer the Guilt:
The Deed was acted by the Subject's Hand;
The Sword was pointed by the King's Command.
Mine was the Murder: it was Mine alone;
Years of Contrition must the Crime attone:
Nor can my guilty Soul expect Relief,
But from a long Sincerity of Grief.

With an imperfect Hand, and trembling Heart,
Her Love of Truth superior to her Art,
Already the reflecting Muse has trac'd
The mournful Figures of my Action past.
The pensive Goddess has already taught,
How vain is Hope, and how vexatious Thought;
From growing Childhood to declining Age,
How tedious ev'ry Step, how gloomy ev'ry Stage.
This Course of Vanity almost compleat,
Tir'd in the Field of Life, I hope Retreat
In the still Shades of Death: for Dread and Pain,
And Grief will find their Shafts elanc'd in vain,
And their Points broke, retorted from the Head,
Safe in the Grave, and free among the Dead.

Yet tell Me, frighted Reason! what is Death?
Blood only stopp'd, and interrupted Breath?

MATTHEW PRIOR

The utmost Limit of a narrow Span,
And End of Motion which with Life began?
As smoke that rises from the kindling Fires
Is seen this Moment, and the next expires:
As empty Clouds by rising Winds are tost,
Their fleeting Forms scarce sooner found than lost:
So vanishes our State: so pass our Days:
So Life but opens now, and now decays:
The Cradle and the Tomb, alas! so nigh;
To live is scarce distinguish'd from to dye.

Cure of the Miser's Wish, and Coward's Fear,
Death only shews Us, what We knew was near.
With Courage therefore view the pointed Hour;
Dread not Death's Anger; but expect his Pow'r;
Nor Nature's Law with fruitless Sorrow mourn;
But dye, O Mortal Man! for Thou wast born.

Cautious thro' Doubt; by Want of Courage, Wise,
To such Advice, the Reas'ner still replies.

Yet measuring all the long continu'd Space,
Ev'ry successive Day's repeated Race,
Since Time first started from his pristin Goal,
'Till He had reach'd that Hour, wherein my Soul
Joyn'd to my Body swell'd the Womb; I was,
(At least I think so) Nothing: must I pass
Again to Nothing, when this vital Breath
Ceasing, consigns Me o'er to Rest, and Death?
Must the whole Man, amazing Thought! return
To the cold Marble, or contracted Urn?
And never shall those Particles agree,
That were in Life this Individual He?
But sever'd, must They join the general Mass,
Thro' other Forms, and Shapes ordain'd to pass;
Nor Thought nor Image kept of what He was?
Does the great Word that gave him Sense, ordain,
That Life shall never wake that Sense again?
And will no Pow'r his sinking Spirits save
From the dark Caves of Death, and Chambers of the Grave?

POEMS ON SEVERAL OCCASIONS

Each Evening I behold the setting Sun
With down-ward Speed into the Ocean run:
Yet the same Light (pass but some fleeting Hours)
Exerts his Vigor, and renews his Pow'rs;
Starts the bright Race again: His constant Flame
Rises and sets, returning still the Same.
I mark the various Fury of the Winds:
These neither Seasons guide, nor Order binds:
They now dilate, and now contract their Force:
Various their Speed, but endless is their Course.
From his first Fountain and beginning Ouze,
Down to the Sea each Brook, and Torrent flows:
Tho' sundry Drops or leave, or swell the Stream;
The Whole still runs, with equal Pace, the Same.
Still other Waves supply the rising Urns;
And the eternal Floud no Want of Water mourns.

Why then must Man obey the sad Decree,
Which subjects neither Sun, nor Wind, nor Sea?

A Flow'r, that does with opening Morn arise,
And flourishing the Day, at Evening dyes;
A Winged Eastern Blast, just skimming o'er
The Ocean's Brow, and sinking on the Shore;
A Fire, whose Flames thro' crackling Stubble fly;
A Meteor shooting from the Summer Sky;
A Bowl a-down the bending Mountain roll'd;
A Bubble breaking, and a Fable told;
A Noon-tide Shadow, and a Mid-night Dream;
Are Emblems, which with Semblance apt proclaim
Our Earthly Course: But, O my Soul! so fast
Must Life run off; and Death for ever last?

This dark Opinion, sure, is too confin'd:
Else whence this Hope, and Terror of the Mind?
Does Something still, and Somewhere yet remain,
Reward or Punishment, Delight or Pain?
Say: shall our Relicks second Birth receive?
Sleep We to wake, and only dye to live?
When the sad Wife has clos'd her Husband's Eyes,
And pierc'd the Echoing Vault with doleful Cries;

Lyes the pale Corps not yet entirely Dead?
The Spirit only from the Body fled,
The grosser Part of Heat and Motion void,
To be by Fire, or Worm, or Time destroy'd;
The Soul, immortal Substance, to remain,
Conscious of Joy, and capable of Pain?
And if Her Acts have been directed well,
While with her friendly Clay She deign'd to dwell;
Shall She with Safety reach her pristine Seat?
Find her Rest endless, and her Bliss compleat?
And while the buried Man We idly mourn;
Do Angels joy to see His better Half return?
But if She has deform'd this Earthly Life
With murd'rous Rapine, and seditious Strife;
Amaz'd, repuls'd, and by those Angels driv'n
From the Ætherial Seat, and blissful Heav'n,
In everlasting Darkness must She lye,
Still more unhappy, that She cannot dye?

Amid Two Seas on One small Point of Land
Weary'd, uncertain, and amaz'd We stand:
On either Side our Thoughts incessant turn:
Forward We dread; and looking back We mourn.
Losing the Present in this dubious Hast;
And lost Our selves betwixt the Future, and the Past.

These cruel Doubts contending in my Breast,
My Reason stagg'ring, and my Hopes oppress'd,
Once more I said: once more I will enquire,
What is this little, agile, pervious Fire,
This flutt'ring Motion, which We call the Mind?
How does She act? and where is She confin'd?
Have We the Pow'r to guide Her, as We please?
Whence then those Evils, that obstruct our Ease?
We Happiness pursue; We fly from Pain;
Yet the Pursuit, and yet the Flight is vain:
And, while poor Nature labors to be blest,
By Day with Pleasure, and by Night with Rest;
Some stronger Pow'r eludes our sickly Will;
Dashes our rising Hope with certain Ill;

And makes Us with reflective Trouble see,
That all is destin'd, which We fancy free.

That Pow'r superior then, which rules our Mind,
Is His Decree by Human Pray'r inclin'd.
Will He for Sacrifice our Sorrows ease?
And can our Tears reverse His firm Decrees?
Then let Religion aid, where Reason fails:
Throw loads of Incense in, to turn the Scales;
And let the silent Sanctuary show,
What from the babling Scholes We may not know,
How Man may shun, or bear his destin'd Part of Woe.

What shall amend, or what absolve our Fate?
Anxious We hover in a mediate State,
Betwixt Infinity and Nothing; Bounds,
Or boundless Terms, whose doubtful Sense confounds
Unequal Thought; whilst All We apprehend,
Is, that our Hopes must rise, our Sorrows end;
As our Creator deigns to be our Friend.

I said;——and instant bad the Priests prepare
The ritual Sacrifice, and solemn Pray'r.
Select from vulgar Herds, with Garlands gay,
A hundred Bulls ascend the Sacred Way.
The artful Youth proceed to form the Choir;
They breath the Flute, or strike the vocal Wire.
The Maids in comely Order next advance;
They beat the Tymbrel, and instruct the Dance.
Follows the chosen Tribe from LEVI sprung,
Chanting by just Return the Holy Song.
Along the Choir in Solemn State they past.
——The Anxious King came last.
The Sacred Hymn perform'd, my promis'd Vow
I paid; and bowing at the Altar low,

Father of Heav'n! I said, and Judge of Earth!
Whose Word call'd out this Universe to Birth;
By whose kind Pow'r and influencing Care
The various Creatures move, and live, and are;
But, ceasing once that Care; withdrawn that Pow'r;
They move (alas!) and live, and are no more:

MATTHEW PRIOR

Omni-scient Master, Omni-present King,
To Thee, to Thee, my last Distress I bring.

Thou, that can'st Still the Raging of the Seas,
Chain up the Winds, and bid the Tempests cease;
Redeem my ship-wreck'd Soul from raging Gusts
Of cruel Passion, and deceitful Lusts:
From Storms of Rage, and dang'rous Rocks of Pride,
Let Thy strong Hand this little Vessel guide
(It was Thy Hand that made it) thro' the Tide
Impetuous of this Life: let Thy Command
Direct my Course, and bring me safe to Land.

If, while this weary'd Flesh draws fleeting Breath,
Not satisfy'd with Life, afraid of Death,
It hap'ly be Thy Will, that I should know
Glimpse of Delight, or Pause from anxious Woe;
From *Now*, from instant *Now*, great Sire, dispell
The Clouds that press my Soul; from *Now* reveal
A gracious Beam of Light; from *Now* inspire
My Tongue to sing, my Hand to touch the Lyre:
My open'd Thought to joyous Prospects raise;
And, for Thy Mercy, let me sing Thy Praise.
Or, if Thy Will ordains, I still shall wait
Some New *Here-after*, and a future State;
Permit me Strength, my Weight of Woe to bear;
And raise my Mind superior to my Care.
Let Me, howe'er unable to explain
The secret Lab'rynths of Thy Ways to Man,
With humble Zeal confess Thy awful Pow'r;
Still weeping Hope, and wond'ring still Adore.
So in my Conquest be Thy Might declar'd:
And, for Thy Justice, be Thy Name rever'd.

My Pray'r scarce ended, a stupendous Gloom
Darkens the Air; loud Thunder shakes the Dome:
To the beginning Miracle succeed
An awful Silence, and religious Dread.
Sudden breaks forth a more than common Day:
The sacred Wood, which on the Altar lay,

Untouch'd, unlighted glows——
Ambrosial Odor, such as never flows
From ARAB's Gum, or the SABÆAN Rose,
Does round the Air evolving Scents diffuse:
The holy Ground is wet with Heav'nly Dews:
Celestial Music (such JESSIDES' Lyre,
Such MIRIAM's Timbrel would in vain require)
Strikes to my Thought thro' my admiring Ear,
With Ecstasy too fine, and Pleasure hard to bear.
And lo! what sees my ravish'd Eye? what feels
My wond'ring Soul? an opening Cloud reveals
An Heav'nly Form embody'd and array'd
With Robes of Light. I heard: the Angel said:

Cease, Man of Woman born, to hope Relief
From daily Trouble, and continu'd Grief.
Thy Hope of Joy deliver to the Wind:
Suppress thy Passions; and prepare thy Mind.
Free and familiar with Misfortune grow:
Be us'd to Sorrow, and inur'd to Woe.
By weak'ning Toil, and hoary Age o'ercome,
See thy Decrease; and hasten to thy Tomb.
Leave to thy Children Tumult, Strife, and War,
Portions of Toil, and Legacies of Care.
Send the Successive Ills thro' Ages down;
And let each weeping Father tell his Son,
That deeper struck, and more distinctly griev'd,
He must augment the Sorrows He receiv'd.

The Child to whose Success thy Hope is bound,
E'er thou art scarce Interr'd, or he is Crown'd;
To Lust of Arbitrary Sway inclin'd,
(That cursed Poyson to the Prince's Mind!)
Shall from thy Dictates and his Duty rove,
And lose his great Defence, his People's Love.
Ill Counsell'd, Vanquish'd, Fugitive, Disgrac'd,
Shall mourn the Fame of JACOB's Strength effac'd.
Shall sigh, the King diminish'd, and the Crown
With lessen'd Rays descending to his Son.

335

Shall see the Wreaths, His Grandsire knew to reap
By active Toil, and Military Sweat,
Pining incline their sickly Leaves, and shed
Their falling Honors from His giddy Head.
By Arms, or Pray'r unable to asswage
Domestic Horror, and intestine Rage,
Shall from the Victor, and the Vanquish'd fear,
From ISRAEL's Arrow, and from JUDAH's Spear:
Shall cast his weary'd Limbs on JORDAN's Floud,
By Brother's Arms disturb'd, and stain'd with Kindred-Blood.

Hence lab'ring Years shall weep their destin'd Race
Charg'd with ill Omens; sully'd with Disgrace.
Time by Necessity compell'd, shall go
Thro' Scenes of War, and Epocha's of Woe.
The Empire lessen'd in a parted Stream,
Shall lose it's Course——
Indulge thy Tears: the Heathen shall blaspheme:
JUDAH shall fall, oppress'd by Grief and Shame;
And Men shall from her Ruins know her Fame.

New ÆGYPTS yet, and second Bonds remain,
A harsher PHARAOH, and a heavyer Chain.
Again obedient to a dire Command,
Thy Captive Sons shall leave the promis'd Land.
Their Name more low, their Servitude more vile,
Shall, on EUPHRATES' Bank, renew the Grief of NILE.

These pointed Spires that wound the ambient Sky
Inglorious Change! shall in Destruction lye
Low, levell'd with the Dust; their Heights unknown,
Or measur'd by their Ruin. Yonder Throne,
For lasting Glory built, design'd the Seat
Of Kings for ever blest, for ever great,
Remov'd by the Invader's barb'rous Hand,
Shall grace his Triumph in a foreign Land.
The Tyrant shall demand yon' sacred Load
Of Gold and Vessels set a-part to GOD,
Then by vile Hands to common Use debas'd;
Shall send them flowing round his drunken Feast,
With sacrilegious Taunt, and impious Jest.

Twice fourteen Ages shall their Way complete:
Empires by various Turns shall rise and set;
While Thy abandon'd Tribes shall only know
A diff'rent Master, and a Change of Woe:
With down-cast Eye-lids, and with Looks a-ghast,
Shall dread the Future, or bewail the Past.

Afflicted ISRAEL shall sit weeping down,
Fast by the Streams, where BABEL's Waters run;
Their Harps upon the neighb'ring Willows hung,
Nor joyous Hymn encouraging their Tongue,
Nor chearful Dance their Feet; with Toil oppress'd,
Their weary'd Limbs aspiring but to Rest.
In the reflective Stream the sighing Bride,
Viewing her Charms impair'd, abash'd shall hide
Her pensive Head; and in her languid Face
The Bridegroom shall fore-see his sickly Race:
While pond'rous Fetters vex their close Embrace.
With irksome Anguish then your Priests shall mourn
Their long-neglected Feasts despair'd Return,
And sad Oblivion of their solemn Days.
Thenceforth their Voices They shall only raise,
Louder to weep. By Day your frighted Seers
Shall call for Fountains to express their Tears;
And wish their Eyes were Flouds: by Night from Dreams
Of opening Gulphs, black Storms, and raging Flames,
Starting amaz'd, shall to the People show
Emblems of Heav'nly Wrath, and Mystic Types of Woe.

The Captives, as their Tyrant shall require,
That They should breath the Song, and touch the Lyre,
Shall say: can JACOB's servile Race rejoice,
Untun'd the Music, and disus'd the Voice?
What can We play? (They shall discourse) how sing
In foreign Lands, and to a Barb'rous King?
We and our Fathers from our Childhood bred
To watch the cruel Victor's Eye, to dread
The arbitrary Lash, to bend, to grieve;
(Out-cast of Mortal Race!) can We conceive
Image of ought delightful, soft, or gay?
Alas! when We have toyl'd the longsome Day,

MATTHEW PRIOR

The fullest Bliss our Hearts aspire to know,
Is but some Interval from active Woe;
In broken Rest, and startling Sleep to mourn;
'Till Morn, the Tyrant, and the Scourge return.
Bred up in Grief, can Pleasure be our Theme?
Our endless Anguish does not Nature claim?
Reason, and Sorrow are to Us the Same.
Alas! with wild Amazement We require,
If Idle Folly was not Pleasure's Sire:
Madness, We fancy, gave an Ill-tim'd Birth
To grinning Laughter, and to frantic Mirth.

This is the Series of perpetual Woe,
Which Thou, alas! and Thine are born to know.
Illustrious Wretch, repine not, nor reply:
View not, what Heav'n ordains, with Reason's Eye;
Too bright the Object is: the Distance is too high.
The Man who would resolve the Work of Fate,
May limit Number, and make Crooked Strait:
Stop Thy Enquiry then; and curb Thy Sense;
Nor let Dust argue with Omnipotence.
'Tis GOD who must dispose, and Man sustain,
Born to endure, forbidden to complain.
Thy Sum of Life must His Decrees fulfill:
What derogates from His Command, is Ill;
And that alone is Good, which centers in His Will.

Yet that thy Lab'ring Senses may not droop,
Lost to Delight, and destitute of Hope;
Remark what I, GOD's Messenger, aver
From Him, who neither can deceive, nor err.
The Land at length redeem'd, shall cease to mourn;
Shall from her sad Captivity return.
SION shall raise her long-dejected Head;
And in her Courts the Law again be read.
Again the glorious Temple shall arise,
And with new Lustre pierce the neighb'ring Skies.
The promis'd Seat of Empire shall again
Cover the Mountain, and command the Plain,
And from Thy Race distinguish'd, ONE shall spring,
Greater in Act than Victor, more than King

In Dignity and Pow'r, sent down from Heav'n,
To succour Earth. To HIM, to HIM 'tis giv'n,
Passion, and Care, and Anguish to destroy.
Thro' HIM soft Peace, and Plenitude of Joy
Perpetual o'er the World redeem'd shall flow.
No more may Man inquire, nor Angel know.

Now, SOLOMON, rememb'ring Who thou art,
Act thro' thy remnant Life the decent Part.
Go forth : Be strong : With Patience, and with Care
Perform, and Suffer : To Thy self severe,
Gracious to Others, Thy Desires suppress'd,
Diffus'd Thy Virtues, First of Men, be Best.
Thy Sum of Duty let Two Words contain ;
O may they graven in thy Heart remain !
Be Humble, and be Just. The Angel said :
With upward Speed His agile Wings He spread ;
Whilst on the holy Ground I prostrate lay,
By various Doubts impell'd, or to obey,
Or to object : at length (my mournful Look
Heav'n-ward erect) determin'd, thus I spoke :

Supreme, Allwise, Eternal Potentate !
Sole Author, Sole Disposer of our Fate !
Enthron'd in Light, and Immortality,
Whom no Man fully sees, and none can see !
Original of Beings ! Pow'r Divine !
Since that I Live, and that I Think, is Thine ;
Benign Creator, let Thy plastic Hand
Dispose it's own Effect. Let Thy Command
Restore, Great Father, Thy Instructed Son ;
And in My Act may THY great WILL BE DONE.

NOTES

A = the 'unauthorised' edition of 1707; B = the edition of 1709; C = the 'unauthorised' edition of 1716; D = the text of 1718, adopted in the present edition; E = the version as it first appeared in Dryden's *Miscellanies*.

When necessary, words from the present text are attached to each variant to indicate where the difference begins or ends. Titles of poems and numbers of verses are included in numbering the lines.

p. xxv, l. 10. D *misprints*] tbe.

p. 1, ll. 4—7. Published in Dryden's *Miscellany Poems*, Part 3, 'Examen Poeticum,' 1693 (second edition, 1706), where it is divided into six stanzas only.   l. 5. A and E] A Pindaric Ode.   l. 15. A] Yet much cans't thou discern.   A and E] and much impart.   l. 18. B and E] art Dust.   l. 19. A and E] Wisdom her Oars, and Wit her Sails may lend.   l. 26. A and E] Loses itself, and its increasing Way.

p. 2, l. 3.   A and E] You boast your Doubts resolv'd.   l. 8.   A] That Nothing, less than Nothing, you.   l. 12.   A] delightful.   l. 13.   A] of his.   l. 16.   B and D] Command.   ll. 16—20.   A and E]
    Prepar'd to meet his [E its] High Command [E Commands];
    And with diffus'd Obedience, spread
    Their op'ning Banks [E Ranks] o'er Earth's submissive Head;
    And march, thro' diff'rent Paths, to different Lands?
l. 21.   A] shou'd the.   l. 22.   A] Journey.   l. 26.   A and E] And, filling A] her wan'd.   l. 27.   E] Power.   l. 29.   A and E] Why shou'd.   l. 30.   A] it's Sphere.   l. 31.   A and E] Why shou'd.   ll. 33, 34.   A and E] To keep in Order, and gird-up the Regulated Year?

p. 3, l. 11.   E] Lines, new Circles.   ll. 12—17.   A and E]
    On t'other's Ruin rears his Throne:
    And shewing his Mistakes, maintains his own.
    Well then! from this New Toil what Knowledge flows!
    Just as much, perhaps, as shows,
    That former Searchers were but Bookish-Tools [E Fools].
    Their Choice Remarks, their Darling-Rules,
    But Canting Error all, and Jargon of the Schools.
l. 19.   A and E] Thro' the Aerial-Seas, and Watry-Skies.   l. 31.   A and E] And tell us how.   ll. 32, 33.   A and E]
      Vain Man! that Pregnant Word sent forth again,
        Thro' either Ocean.
l. 35.   A] And for each Drop call forth a Sea, a Heav'n for ev'ry Star.

NOTES

p. 4, l. 6. B] Sustaining how.   ll. 6—9.   A and E]
  By telling thee, Perfection suffer'd Pain,
    An ETERNAL ESSENCE Dy'd!
  Death's Vanquisher, by Vanquished *Death* was Slain;
  The *Promis'd Earth* Prophan'd with *Deicide.*
l. 16. A and E] And to see HEAV'N.   l. 20. A] And *Grace's* Preference.
l. 21. A and E] shall know.   ll. 25—30. A and E] So fit as Jacob's *Ladder*
was, to Scale the distant SKY.

  p. 5, ll. 1—3. Published in E, 1693, where it is called 'To a Lady of
Quality's Playing...' A] On Celia's Playing upon the Lute.   l. 6. A and E]
the Subject of our Daring Song.   ll. 7 and 8 *are omitted in* A and E.
ll. 9—11. A and E]
  But when you pleas'd to show the Lab'ring Muse,
  What Greater Themes your Music could produce,
  Our Babling Praises we repeat no more.
l. 19. A and E] That You in *Beauty* and in *Birth* excel.

  p. 6, l. 2. A and E] Our Inmost Thoughts and sanctifies.   l. 5. A
and E] beyond both.   l. 18. A and E] So, whilst.   l. 23. A and E]
Viewing your.   l. 24. A, B and E] The Reigning.   l. 25. A] Celia's.
l. 28. A and E] had rais'd.   l. 29. A and E] a fairer Town.

  p. 8, l. 1.   Published in E, 1693. A] To His Mistress.   l. 4. A and E]
In all thy Looks and Gestures Shine.   l. 6. A and E] To Rule this destin'd
Heart of Mine.   l. 7. E] what your.   l. 8. E] and you.   l. 10. A and E]
then rely.   l. 12. A and E] 'Tis but a.   l. 13. A and E] To do.   l. 15.
A, B and E] and but.   l. 18. A and E] Time equally with Love is.   l. 28.
A and E] Even Kindness then too.   l. 29. A and E] the Ghost of my
Departed Love.

  p. 9, l. 16. A and E] whilst Love invites.   l. 17. A] Obey soft Cupid's
gentle Voice. E] Obey the Godhead's gentle Voice.   l. 21. E] art Kindness
all.   l. 24. A and E] Your...your...your.   l. 32. E] And thinking.   l. 35.
A and E] we'll wake.

  p. 10, ll. 1—5. For the earlier Epistle, see the companion volume to the
present text. This poem was published in 'Miscellany Poems upon Several
Occasions: Consisting of Original Poems by The late Duke of *Buckingham*,
Mr *Cowly*, Mr *Milton*, Mr *Prior*...Printed for Peter Buck, at the Sign of the
Temple, near *Temple-Bar*, in *Fleetstreet*, 1692.' Variations in this version are
lettered F, below. It is also printed in Dryden's *Miscellany Poems*, 1702
(= E below), where it is dated Burleigh, Aug. 10, 1690. A] A Second Epistle
to Sir Fleetwood Shephard. E] A Letter to.   l. 8. A, E and F] Whom
some call Pope, some Antichrist.   l. 9. F] Spanish Monarch sends a.
l. 18. F] the Sea.   l. 23. A and E] bump one's.

  p. 11, l. 12. A] he shou'd.   l. 28. A] A Beau.   l. 34. A] prompted.
l. 36. F] Pettys.

  p. 12, l. 14. F] in the Belly.   l. 22. F] form'd all.   l. 29. A] ty'd
[possibly correct, though in both authorised editions it is altered to 'try'd'].

  p. 13, l. 5. F] a Writer.   l. 8. F] Authors.   l. 13. F] I thought at
first.   l. 14. F] since that.   ll. 19, 20. A and F]
  So when [F where] I've with my Granam gon,
  At Sacred Barne of pure Noncon.
l. 19 is omitted in E.   l. 21. A and F] has sitted.   l. 23. F]
  The Rogue has cough'd up to'ther Hour,
  And to apply, etc.

NOTES

l. 24. **A, E and F]** Villain Stuff.   ll. 25, 26. **A, E and F]**
first, I hear [F then, I hear]
A very good Account of Her.
ll. 33—38. **A, E and F]**
For if their fame be justly high, who
Wou'd never treat the Pope's *Nuncio*.
That his is higher, we must grant,
Who will treat Nuncio's Protestant.

p. **14,** l. 15. A] I rise to read. E and F] I rise to Read, perhaps to
Breakfast. l. 26. A] Ceylon. l. 29. A] Lauzone. F] Better, perhaps,
than Count Lausune.

p. **15,** ll. 11—13. **A, E and F]**
Thus, far from Pleasure, Sir, or Grief,
I fool away an Idle Life,
Till Mr. *Maidwell* cease to Teach,
Then I'll Jerk [A and E ferk] Youth, and say *In speech*;
Or *Shadwell* from the Town retires.
l. 15. A and F] Woods.

p. **16,** ll. 1—3. Published in E, 1694 (second edition, 1708), where it is
entitled 'To my Lady Dursley On her Reading Milton's Paradise Lost.'
l. 7. E] Small is that part. l. 9. E] your Race. l. 10. E] the Features
took. l. 11. E] Heavn's own Work, in Eve's. l. 13. E] Whilst scarce
one actual Guilt. l. 14. E] your Mind vain Triumphs. ll. 16—19. E]
With equal Virtue had frail Eve been arm'd,
In vain the Fruit had blush'd, the Serpent charm'd:
Our Bliss by Penitence had neer been bought;
Adam had never faln, or *Milton* wrote.

p. **17,** ll. 1—4. Published in Dryden's *Miscellany Poems*, Part 5, 1703/4,
where it is called 'To a Boy Playing with his Cat.' ll. 11 to end. E]
And potent of his Vows and Joys,
He thank'd the Gods, and blest his Choice.
Ah! Beauteous Boy, take care least thou
Renew the fondness of his Vow,
Take care to think the Queen of Love
Will e're thy Fav'rites Charms improve;
Shoud'st thou prefer so rash a Pray'r,
The Queen of Love wou'd never hear.
Ah! rather from her Altars run,
Least thou be griev'd and she undone.
The Queen of Love will quickly see
Her own *Adonis* live in thee;
And glances thrown upon a Beast,
Which well might make a Goddess blest,
Will lightly her first Love deplore,
Will easily forgive the Boar,
And on her Tabby Rival's Face,
Enrag'd will mark her new Disgrace.

p. **19,** l. 1. Published in Dryden's *Miscellany Poems*, Part 5, 1703/4.
The Despairing Shepherd was reprinted in 1717 in 'A Collection of the
Best English Poetry, by Several Hands,' in two 8vo. vols. 'Printed and
Sold by *T. Warner*, at the *Black Boy* in *Pater-Noster-Row*,' the imprint of

343

that part of the book in which the poem occurs being ' *H. Hills*, in *Black Fryars*, near the Water-side, 1709.' ll. 16, 17. Published in Dryden's *Miscellany Poems*, Part 5, 1703/4 (=E). l. 19. E] and sprightly.

p. 20, l. 2. E] She too a kind. l. 21. E] But yet. ll. 22, 23. E] Provided you will ne'er again Declare your, etc.
ll. 25, 26. Published in E, 1693. A] Heraclitus. E] In a Letter To, etc. l. 29. A and E] Fate's Fantastick Mazes. l. 31. A] real Fears.

p. 21, l. 2. A and E] we pursue. ll. 4, 5. A and E] And like the doating Artist, woo The Image we our selves have wrought. l. 7. A and E] we believe. l. 8. A] Argue against. E] And argue. l. 9. A and E] Pleased, that we can our selves deceive. l. 10. A and E] our...our. l. 18. A and E] former fled. l. 20. A and E] he's dead. l. 24. A and E] But all the Pleasure. l. 25. A and E] Is a-far-off to. ll. 27—35. A and E]

VII.

The worthless Prey but only shows,
The Joys [E Joy] consisted in the Strife;
What-e'er we take, as soon we lose;
In Homer's Riddle, and in Life.

VIII.

So whilst in Feverish Sleeps, we think
We taste, what waking we desire:
The Dream is better than the Drink,
Which only feeds the Sickly-Fire.

IX.

To the Mind's Eye, Things will [E well] appear
At distance, thro' an Artful-Glass;
Bring but the Flattering-Object [E Objects] near,
They're all a Senseless-Gloomy-Mass.

p. 22, l. 2. A and E] Seeing aright, we. l. 5. B] And Sorrow from our being wise. l. 9. A and E] but stinking. ll. 11—14. A] An Ode to the Returning Sun, Intended to be Sung before Their late Majesties, on New-Year's-Day 169¾, (but here Printed with Alterations; as it was performed lately at a Consort of Musick, by the most Eminent Masters.) E 1694, second edition, 1708] For the New Year: to the Sun. Intended to be Sung... 1693/4. Written by Mr. Prior at the Hague. ll. 18, 19. A and E]
And as the Radiant Journey's run,
Where e'er thy Beams are spread, where e'er thy Power is known,
Thro' all the distant Nations own.
21. A] The Mildest Prince. l. 22. A and E] That ever Sav'd a *People*, ever Grac'd a *Throne*. l. 28. A, B and E] Its. l. 29. A] Marlbrô's.

p. 23, l. 1. A, B and E] Its. l. 2. A] round Anna's. E] Mary's. l. 3. A] From thy blessings she shall know. E] They shall know. l. 5. A] She governs and enlightens. l. 13. A and E] with all. l. 18. A and E] From Ancient Times, Historic Stores. l. 20. A and E] All that with. l. 22. A and E] All that with. ll. 23—26. A and E]
His Great Fore-Fathers Pious Cares;
All that story have Recorded;
Sacred to Marlbrô's [E Nassau's] long Renown,
For Countries Sack'd, and Battels Won.
l. 31. A] Marlbrô's Fame.

NOTES

p. 24, l. 4. A] for Anna's sake. E] for Mary's Sake. l. 6. A and E] with lucky. l. 8. A and E] have glad. l. 10. A and E] many Lustres. l. 14. A] which Anna should. E] The fuller Bliss which Mary should. l. 16. A and E] the Graver. l. 19. A and E] the Eastern. A, B and E] Travel. ll. 22, 23. A and E]

> To ease the Cares, which for Her Subjects sake,
> The Pious Queen does with Glad Practice [E Patience] take.
> Cho.   *To let her all the Blessings know,*
> > *Which from those Cares upon Her Subjects flow.*

l. 28. A] Marlbrô's Name. l. 30. A and E] Take Anna's [E Mary's] goodness for their Theme. l. 32. A] Anna's…Marlbrô's. E] Mary's Praise. l. 33. A and E] Subjects. ll. 36, 37. A and E] 'Till thou shalt shine no more.

p. 25, ll. 1, 2. Published in Dryden's *Miscellany Poems*, Part 5, 1703/4 (= E), where its sub-title is 'in Imitation of a Greek Idyllium.' ll. 9—14. E]

> The Prospect and the Nymph were gay,
> With silent Joy I heard her say,
> That we shou'd walk there ev'ry Day.

l. 15. E] grew. ll. 21, 22. E] she…Will press the Shore or see the Main. l. 23. E] Look back at least once more, said I.

p. 28, ll. 1—4. Published in Dryden's *Miscellany Poems*, Part 5, 1703/4 (= E). l. 7. E] Corinna's *and so throughout.* l. 18. E] Heart beat. l. 21. E] May Cytherea make her Conquest sure. l. 22. E] And let. ll. 25—27. E]

> Yet, if amidst the Series of these Joys,
> One sad Reflection should by chance arise,
> Give it, in Pity, to the wretched Swain.

l. 29. E] Felt. l. 30. E] And dy'd.
The version of Mrs Singer's Pastoral, given in Dryden's *Miscellany Poems*, differs considerably from the text printed by Prior in 1718 and reprinted here, but I have not thought it needful to give a list of these variations.

p. 29, ll. 1—4. Published in Dryden's *Miscellany Poems*, Part 5, 1703/4 (= E), where it is entitled 'Disputing with a Lady, Who left me in the Argument.' l. 22. E] On Force thus formidably join'd?

p. 30, verses v.—viii. E]

> But quicker Arts of Death you use,
> > Traverse your Ground to gain the Field,
> And, whilst my Argument pursues,
> > With sudden Silence bid me yield.
> So when the *Parthian* turn'd his Steed,
> > And from the Hostile Camp withdrew,
> He backward sent the Fatal Reed;
> > Secure of Conquest as he flew.
> Daunted, I dropt my useless Arms,
> > When you no longer deign'd to Fight,
> Then Triumph deck'd in all its Charms,
> > Appear'd less beautiful than Flight.
> Oh! trace again the Hostile Plains,
> > My Troops were wounded in the War,
> But whilst this fiercer Silence reigns
> > They suffer, famish'd by Despair.

NOTES

Capricious Author of my Smart,
Let War ensue, or Silence cease,
Unless you find my Coward Heart
Is yielding to a separate Peace.

l. 7. B] the Gift.   l. 11. B] she shuns [probably a misprint in D].

p. 31, l. 9. B] half-clos'd.   ll. 20—22. Published in Dryden's *Miscellany Poems*, Part 5, 1703/4 (=E).

p. 32, l. 5. B and E] from its.   l. 19. E] Great Minute.   l. 32. B and E] some Beauty.   l. 33. B and E] little Lustre.   l. 38. E] And with indented Furrows mark his sad extent of Sway.

p. 33, l. 10. E] And Custom call you forth to distant Arms.   l. 18. E] with Jolly.   l. 23. E] Honour fills.   l. 25. E] find you landed on. B] my Lover.   l. 26. B and E] Fill'd with new.

p. 34, l. 12. E] from its.   l. 23. B and E] and soon the.   ll. 25, 26. E] Must *Celia* be undone for loving you?

p. 35.   Published separately in 1695, title-page as follows:—
To the King, an Ode on His Majesty's arrival in Holland, 1695. By Mr Prior. *Quis desiderio sit pudor aut Modus Tam Chari capitis?* Hor. London, Printed for *Jacob Tonson* at the *Judge's-Head* near the *Inner-Temple-Gate* in *Fleetstreet.* 1695.
The following are readings from the 1695 text, which consists of 40 verses instead of 41 as in the later and considerably altered text.   ll. 10—23]
On Mary's Tomb thrô rowling Years,
The Mournful Graces all shall weep;
And, with fresh Lamps and flowing Tears,
The Virtues endless Vigils keep.
For Mary distant Lands shall Mourn
When late Records Her Deeds relate,
Ages to come, and Men unborn,
Shall Bless Her Name, and Sigh Her Fate.

l. 25] watchful Trust.   l. 28] To Cloath it in its full.

p. 36, l. 2] King forsake.   ll. 7—10]
The Lovely Dead, whom He regrets,
Can know no Fear, can feel no Grief;
The living World, whom He forgets,
Would perish without His Relief.
In vain the British Lyons roar,
While prest by Grief their Monarch stoops;
The Belgic Darts will wound no more,
If He, whose Hand sustain'd them, droops.

l. 15] Europe's.   ll. 27—35]
Oh! give the Mourning Nations Joy,
Break forth, great Sun with usual Light:
And let thy stronger Beams destroy
Those Clouds, which keep Thee from our sight.
Advance in thy Meridian Course,
And, since thy Mary's Light is gone,
Rejoyce the World with double Force,
Thy Beams all fixt in Thee alone.

NOTES

p. 37, ll. 7—10]
Her fair Delight, Her softer Half,
Cold in the Grave with Mary lies,
Unless in Thee her strength is safe,
The frighted Nation wholly dies.

l. 12] our Land.　　ll. 14, 15]
Lest rais'd and rescu'd by thy Hand,
She bend and sink beneath thy Woe.

l. 22] is Britain's.　　l. 24] where that excess.　　l. 28] Thee...thy.　　l. 32] gone...chang'd.

p. 38, l. 2] Martial Sounds.　　l. 13] her Darts.　　l. 14] That she could strike.　　l. 16] But that with which she struck the Queen.

Between verses xxi. and xxii. the 1695 text has verse xxx. of present text and then adds]
Envy shall calm that useless Rage,
By which Thy Glory brighter grows,
And Death, Thy Sorrows to asswage,
Shall turn her wrath, and wound Thy Foes.

ll. 19, 20]　　She hated Hope, She scorned Relief,
And triumph'd, Proud in full Despair.

ll. 22—28]　　Her echo'd Wailings pierc't the Skyes,
To Earth her bended Forehead bow'd,
The Tears unbounded from her Eyes,
As Waters from her Sluices flow'd.
But soon as Thou her Lord return'd,
Her Head is rear'd, her Eyes are dry'd,
She smiles, etc.

pp. 38, 39, between verses xxv. and xxvi.]
Dissembling Ease, and forcing Joy,
She begs her Lord his Tears to dry:
Did Belgia e're her prayers employ,
And Orange stand regardless by?

p. 39, l. 10] pious Father.　　ll. 12—15]
A second William's Bloom could tell
How Heroes rise, how Patriots set:
As Theirs did Others Deeds excel,
Excelling Theirs be Thine compleat.

l. 20] As glorious as thy Mary died.

pp. 39, 40, ll. 21 et seqq.　For stanza xxx. see note to p. 38 above.　Verses xxxi.—xxxvii. of the present text take the place of the four following verses in 1695]
That Thou canst live for Belgia's sake,
Pierc'd by her Griefs forget Thy own;
New Toyls endure, new Conquests make
To give her Ease, thô Thou hast None.
To keep from treach'rous Foes Her store,
Thô all Thy Wealth be robb'd by Death;
To vanquish, thô She lives no more
Whose Hands prepar'd the Victor's Wreath.
Oh, could Thy Griefs obdurate prove
To Belgia's Cries, to Britain's Fears,
Yet let them yield to Mary's Love,

347

NOTES

To Nassau's Glory joyn'd in Her's.
If Mary could so well command,
It was by long obeying Thee;
Her Scepter, guided by Thy Hand,
Preserv'd the Isles and rul'd the Sea.

p. 40, l. 5.   B] turn'd aside.   l. 30] To fix His Name amidst the Stars.
l. 34] Glories.

p. 41, ll. 7—10]
And to Thy Fame alone 'tis given
Unbounded thrô all Worlds to go,
While Mary reigns a Saint in Heaven,
And Thou a Demi-God below.

p. 47, ll. 23 et seqq.   Published in 1695 under the following title: 'An
English Ballad: In Answer to Mr. Despreaux's Pindarique Ode On the Taking
of Namure.   Dulce est desipere in loco.   London, Printed for *Jacob Tonson*,
at the *Judge's Head* near the *Inner Temple Gate* in *Fleetstreet*.'   The variants
that follow are, unless otherwise indicated, from the 1695 edition.

p. 47, ll. 30—33, p. 48, ll. 1—4]
Was you not drunk, and did not know it,
When you thought *Phœbus* gave you Law?
Or was it not, good Brother Poet,
The chaste Nymph *Maintenon* you saw?
   She charm'd you sure, or what's the matter,
That Oaks must come from *Thrace* to dance?
If Stocks must needs be taught to flatter,
You'll find enough of them in *France*.

p. 48, ll. 12—17]
Des Preaux, a Vulture only flies
Where sordid Interest seeks the Prey.
   When once the Poet's Conscience ceases,
His Measures soon from Truth will rove;
Give *Boileau* but Five Hundred Pieces,
And *Louis* takes the Wall of *Jove*.

ll. 22—26]
At *Trianon* the wondrous Plan.
   Such Walls these three wise Gods agreed
By Human Force could ne'er be shaken;
But, *Boileau*, we who *Homer* read,
Find Gods as well as Men mistaken.

ll. 35—39]
Yet they march'd but like other Men.
   Cannons above and Mines below
Did Death and Tombs for Us contrive,
Yet William order'd matters so,
That few were there but are alive.

p. 49, verse v.]
Why is *Namure* compar'd to *Troy*?
Are we then braver than the *Greeks*?
Their Siege did Ten long Years employ,
We've done our bus'ness in Ten Weeks.
   What Godhead does so fast advance?
What Power Divine those Hills regain?

348

NOTES

'Tis *Britain's* King, the Scourge of *France*,
No Godhead, but the first of Men.
   His Arm shall keep your Victor under,
And *Europe's* Liberty restore;
Your *Jupiter* must quit his Thunder,
And fright the injur'd World no more.

l. 3. B] excell.   ll. 15—22]
   Whilst William trembles at Namure,
Great *Villeroy* who ne'er afraid is,
To *Bruxels* marches on secure,
To Bomb the Monks and scare the Ladies.
   Add to this Glorious Expedition
One more, and then thy Fame is Crown'd,
Perform thy Master's high Commission,
For *William* ne'er will stand his Ground.

Verse vii.]   He comes, this mighty Marshal comes,
But finds a River in his way;
He waves his Colours, beats his Drums,
Yet thinks it Prudence there to stay.
   Ban and *Arriereban,* all appear
Great Armies, would they march but faster;
But *Vill'roy* moves so slowly here,
One would have thought it was his Master.

   p. 50, ll. 3, 4]
   Disguise a General's Disgrace;
No Torrents swell this low *Mehayne.*
ll. 6—13]   The Water-Nymphs are all unkind,
We hope the Land-Nymphs are not so:
Or Fortune sure with Love has join'd
To fail a General and a Beau.

l. 10. B] are all.   l. 12. B] These Ebb alas! fly they?
ll. 17—26] Nations combin'd may bless his Name,
And *France* in secret own his Glory.
   Yet, *Boileau,* we'll take t'other Strain
In Honour of that greater Prince,
Who lost *Namure* the same Campaign
He bought *Dixmuyd,* and conquer'd *Deynse.*

Verse x.]   Tis done, Great *Louis,* Troops advance,
Mars speaks thro' Cannons Mouths in Fire;
That is, one Mareschal of *France*
Tells t'other, he dare come no nigher.

   p. 51, ll. 3—12]
   For you that saw it best can say
The Steps by which *Namure* was lost.
   Think not what Reasons to produce
From *Louis* to conceal your Fear;
He'll own the Strength of your Excuse,
Tell him that William was but there.

Verse xii.]   But where is now great *Louis* Feather,
That wav'd so glorious from afar?
The Generals could not come together,
Without the Lustre of that Star.

NOTES

Ah, **Poet**, thou hadst been discreeter,
Since thou would'st hang his Hat so high,
If thou had'st call'd it but a Meteor,
That blaz'd a while, and then God b'y.

ll. 23—28]

To animate the doubtful Fight,
The World in vain expects that Ray;
In vain *France* hopes the Sickly Light
May equal William's fuller Day.
Safe *Louis* shines, knows his own Station,
He likes not any Foreign Sphere.

l. 27. B] He likes *Versailles*, his.　　l. 33. B] William left an open way.

p. 52, ll. 10—14; verse xiv. was added later]

Of Death, Pikes, Rocks, Arms, Bricks, and Fire,
We'll play three Stanza's, and have done;
The Castle yields, the *French* retire,
So keep your Powder in your Gun.
Namure by William's Arms is freed.

l. 19 to end]

March, Foes of France, march on thro' *Flanders*,
Divide to *Bruxelles*, or to *Liege*;
Nor fear the least these fierce Commanders,
Who neither fight, nor raise the Siege.
Losing *Namure*, *France* gains a Peer;
Let William's Armies but advance,
Bouffler's shall lose *Dinant* next Year,
And be made Constable of *France*.

The following additional French verse is given in the 1695 edition:—

Pour moy, que Phebus anime
De ses transports les plus doux,
Rempli de ce Dieu sublime,
Je vais, plus hardi que vous,
Montrer que sur le Parnasse,
Des bois frequentés d'Horace
Ma Muse dans son declin,
Sçait encor les avenuës
Et des sources inconnuës
A L'Auteur du Saint Paulin*.

* Poem Heroique du sieur F***.

p. 53, l. 16. B] bid alternate.　　l. 19. B] dread you.

p. 55, l. 18. B] mark, and surly Drums.　　ll. 20, 21 transposed in B, which also reads] Behold the Soldier.　　l. 21. D] A full-stop replaces a comma at the end of the line.　　l. 23. B] your pristin.

p. 56, l. 5. B] But drop the Head, and hang the Wing.　　ll. 20—23] not in B.　　l. 26. B] Mistress to the Painter sat.

p. 57, l. 18. B] O Howard.　　l. 24. B] unhappy Youth.　　l. 27. B] to evince.

p. 59, l. 27. B] Banks.

p. 62, l. 2. B] keener Darts.　　l. 18. B] Aimed at his.　　l. 19. B] With certain Speed the Arrow.

NOTES

p. 64. The Dove, A Poem, was published in 1717, 'London: Printed for J. Roberts, near the *Oxford-Arms* in *Warwick-Lane*.' The following are variations noted in a copy of the 1717 issue. l. 7] dares. l. 29] Subaltern Loves.

p. 68, l. 12] But O, l. 20] I'm sure I touch the.

p. 69, l. 7. D] Lethe'.

p. 76, l. 21. D] XII.

p. 78. Pallas and Venus. Published in 1706, 'London: Printed for *John Nutt* near *Stationers-Hall* (*Price 2d.*).' The following are variations noted in a copy of the 1706 issue. ll. 23—26]

> From Head to Foot she view'd, etc.
> And tauntingly the wanton Goddess said;
> Alas, since naked I cou'd vanquish Thee,
> How more successful Pallas, shall I be.

l. 27] When to...I come. l. 29] with a Smile. l. 33] To be more Strong abandon ev'ry Dress.

p. 79, ll. 1—4. Published in Dryden's *Miscellany Poems*, Part 5, 1703/4 (=E). Sub-title in A] A Poesy for a Wedding-Ring. l. 7. A, B and E] Chloe or Cloe, and so throughout. l. 14. A] Th' uneasie. l. 21. A] hated Head.

p. 80, l. 4. A] since were. l. 7. A] shall find. ll. 12—17. A and E]

> Can suffer Shipwreck [E Racks and], run thro' Flame,
> Still contented, still the same.
> Then trace me some unheard-of Way,
> How I thy constant Ardour might repay;
> [E Thy constant Ardour to repay]
> For I my Sense of it wou'd shew,
> In something more than Woman e'er cou'd do.
> [E In more, etc.]

l. 30. A and E] Happy these. l. 31. A and E] But Oh! how soon. l. 37. A and E] As soon as ever he. l. 39. A] all the while.

p. 81, l. 4. A and E]

> Our Sex will be inur'd to Lye,
> And their's instructed to Reply.

l. 10. A] The. l. 12. A] The forward Dame, when fair and young. l. 19. A] And acted Vigorous and. l. 31. A] less Owners.

p. 82, l. 1. A and B] who does. A] does the Fair One. l. 9. A and B] has that. l. 14. A] She wishes, she. l. 19. A] Darling see. ll. 31—34. A]

> I lock her fast, I keep the key;
> The key-hole,—Fool! That take away.

l. 35. A] what may.

p. 83, l. 4. A] A Steeple. l. 5. A] False Fears. l. 14. A] those monstrous ills. l. 15. A] She should. l. 23. A] Then clap. l. 24. Published in Dryden's *Miscellany Poems*, Part 5, 1703/4 (=E). A, B and E] Monsieur De La Fontaine's Hans Carvel Imitated.

p. 84, l. 3. A and E] To spill a hated Rival's. l. 9. A] first in. l. 12. A] Slipt often out to Mistress Hoddy's. l. 14. A and E] What else o' [E in] God's Name could she mean? l. 31. A, B and E] Wives... Husbands. l. 32. A] rowl in. l. 33. A] durst not. l. 35. A] to's Wife.

NOTES

p. 85, ll. 3, 4. E] Cares...Pray'rs.   l. 6. A] While Taylor, Scot and.
l. 7. A] us to.   l. 8. A, B and E] Lay unmolested.   l. 11. A] The Trade
continued still the same.

p. 86, l. 10. A] down some.   l. 17. A] about a.   l. 21. A] Nice
Ratafia for. E] Modish Ratafia for.   l. 24. A] Dame went.   l. 33. E]
view the.

p. 87, l. 1. A] But such.   l. 9. A] says.   l. 17. A] beyond the.

p. 90, l. 35. B] all which.

p. 91, l. 11. B] Those beat.

p. 92, l. 4. B] Up from her Ladyship to.

p. 93, ll. 1, 2. Published in Dryden's *Miscellany Poems*, Part 5, 1703/4
(=E). Sub-title in A] In Imitation of Mons. De la Fontaine's Hans Carvel.
l. 10. A and E] from pleasure as from.   l. 13. A] or rise.   l. 16. A and E]
dangerous and.

p. 94, l. 13. E] no Medium.   l. 14. A full-stop has been supplied at
the end of the line.   l. 28. A and E] might please.

p. 95, l. 3. A and E] For Hills before and Woods behind.   l. 4. A]
Kept off the Rain, and broke the Wind.   l. 5. A and E] Fat Oxen.
l. 11. A] live so.   l. 17. A] Sometimes, My Rogue! sometimes, My
Darling!   l. 22. A] The Farmer.

p. 96, l. 5. A and E] Wou'd gloriously in verse appear.   l. 7. A]
'Twou'd grieve me should I have.   l. 9. A and E] my Epic very.   l. 32. A]
Is all.   l. 36. A] arse.

p. 97, l. 14. A and E] Some Parts.   l. 19. A and E] dare. E] the gotten.

p. 99, ll. 8, 9. B] Reading Mezeray's.

p. 100, l. 8. B] the Book called.

pp. 100, 101. 'Adriani Morientis, etc., Imitated' was published in Dryden's
Miscellany Poems, Part 5, 1703/4 (=E below).   l. 4. E] thy doubtful.
l. 7. E] Lyes interrupted and forgot.

p. 102, ll. 1—5. Published in E, 1693, where Dr Sherlock is described as
'Dean of St Paul's.'   l. 12. E] her Numbers to that blest.   l. 16. B and E]
Who, like...wert sent.   l. 17. E] To be the Voice, and bid.   l. 24. E]
Philip's Son, shall sit and view.   l. 25. E] This sordid.

p. 103, l. 1. E] to that height.   l. 6. B and E] beyond the.   l. 12. E]
various Deaths.   l. 13. E] kind Works.   l. 30. B and E] dreaded.
l. 33. E] their hidden way.   l. 37. E] and Worlds.   l. 38. B] those
that.

p. 104. Carmen Seculare was published in 1700, 'London, Printed for
Jacob Tonson, at *Grays-Inn-Gate* in *Grays-Inn-Lane*.' The following variants
are from a copy of the 1700 issue, save where otherwise noted.   l. 12] Call
out the.   l. 20] comely order march each.   ll. 21, 22]
> Mark ev'ry Act with its intrinsic Worth:
> Then hast the Mighty Parallels to bring.

p. 105, l. 2, *omit*] Thy Native.   l. 6] Turn hither the fair.   l. 8] of the.
l. 10] let fair Proof my bold Affection grace.   l. 12] If Mars son reduc'd.
l. 14, *omit*] But yet.   l. 16] Strict Religion Numa knew.   ll. 20, 21]
> Sealing his Justice with his Childrens Blood
> Stern Brutus was with too much Horror good.

352

NOTES

l. 26] How dang'rous Lusts must be.   l. 28] But scarce.   l. 33] Too many Patriots.   l. 34] And tho'.   l. 37] Let their Deserts with mighty Praise be drest.   B] With equal.

p. **106**, l. 1] rowling like.   l. 2] Its rapid Force design'd their.   l. 5. B] So with.   l. 6] Some small allaying Tincture.   l. 20] And in fierce Battels Bloody Laurels won.   l. 23] Illustrious Heroes.   l. 31] Afflicted Britain. l. 35] The fruitful...Great Nassaw's Race.

p. **107**, l. 1] Next see.   l. 5] Then call the.   l. 23] forth *altered to* fresh. l. 27] blooming Life.   ll. 28—30]

> His Infant Patience calming Factious Strife,
> Quelling the Snakes that round his Cradle ran,
> For William thus, *Alcides* thus began.

l. 34] Vanquish'd, not.   l. 36.   1700 and B] Maria.

p. **108**, l. 10] And happy Pow'r.   l. 16] By Moderation greater than. l. 18] His Life enforcing what.   l. 22] By equal Virtues all the Piece is. l. 36] To future.   l. 37] Bid Her.   l. 38] Trace every Toil and mention (*i.e. omit* To).

p. **109**, l. 2] In shining Characters.   ll. 3—27]

> Fair to be read, when all that we can give
> To make our Master's Glory live,
> Does of its self insensibly decay,
> When Time the Marble and the Brass devours,
> And envious Winters in sure Ruin lay
> The Pride of *Namur's* Towers.
> Namur's Towers which War had arm'd,
> Against what human Force cou'd do,
> By William's Valour were alarm'd,
> Were subdu'd by William's Blow:
> William mounted *Namur's* Towers,
> Second him *Jove*, and *Pallas*, Mighty Powers;
> He flew like *Perseus* thro' the Air,
> The utmost dreadful height to gain.
> William and the God of War
> Can only Toils like these sustain;
> Rocks, Rivers, Mountains, Armies, Fire,
> To stop his Glorious Course conspire:
> Why will they conspire in vain?
> What can William's Force restrain?

l. 31] France dismay'd.   l. 32] William from...survey'd.   l. 33] He order'd War and Rage to cease.

p. **110**, l. 3] how Grace made Clemency.   l. 4] And how.   l. 6] Confessing him less Great than Good.   l. 7] fair Glory.   l. 10] Virtue proclaim'd...and Fame the Best of Kings.   l. 12, *add*] Whither is wild Fancy brought? Whither, etc.   l. 26] pursues her Godlike King.   l. 33] his adventrous.

p. **111**, ll. 2—4] Anon in *Irish* Camps she finds her Theme.   ll. 11—24]

> She thence to *Albion* does the Victor bring,
> Albion with Iö's greets her happy King;
> But he declines the Altars she wou'd raise,
> Accepts the Zeal, tho' he rejects the Praise.
> Again she follows him thro' *Belgia's* Land,
> And Nations often sav'd by William's hand,

NOTES

Ranges Confederate Armies on the Plains,
And in pitch'd Battles bleeding Conquest gains;
Thence to the Points of armed Rocks aspires,
O'er hollow Mountains bellowing hidden Fires,
Beholds the Rocks submit, the Mountains bow,
And willing Nations Crown the Common Victor's Brow.

l. 34. 1700 and B] Eastward, to Danube.

p. 112, l. 4] To Him.   l. 6] Him all Religions, Him all Nations trust.
l. 16. 1700 and B] his violent.   l. 17] meets its.   ll. 19—21]
Serene, yet Strong, exempt from all Extreams,
And with fair Speed devolving fruitful Streams.

ll. 24—27]
Round either Bank the Vales their Sweets disclose,
Fresh Flowers for ever rise, and fruitful Harvest grows.
Whither wou'd the Goddess go.

l. 31] Her daring.   l. 35, *omit*] Yet.

p. 113, l. 3] in ample.   ll. 10, 11]
Too bold the Strong, the Hero was too Great;
She chuses rather thus to die.

l. 18. B] his bolted. 1700 and B] Temples.   l. 32] Rampart.   l. 34]
The Oaken.   ll. 35—38]
Can to Victorious William's Name
Augmented Honours give:
His is an ample Plenitude of Fame,
Incapable Addition to receive.

p. 114, l. 1. B and 1700] Mystic Gate.   l. 10] Command the laughing
Hours.   l. 12] Distribute Years.   l. 13] And Times from better.   l. 17]
From other.   l. 19] Of which no portion she shall bear.   l. 22] with ripen'd.
l. 26. B and 1700] And let Eternal Sweets.

In the 1700 version, verses xxvii.—xxxii. of the present text follow, with
many variations, verse xxxv.

pp. 114, 115, verses xxvii. to l. 4, inclusive, of verse xxx.]
From the wild Ruins of the Ancient Court,
Let a new Phœnix her young Columns rear,
As may the Greatness of this Reign support,
An Object worthy William's Care;
Open, yet Solid, as the Builder's Mind,
Be her spacious Rooms design'd;
Let every Sacred Pillar bear
Trophies of Arms, and Monuments of War:
Then shall the King in *Parian* Marble Breath,
His Shoulder bleeding fresh, and at His Feet
Disarm'd and Stopt shall lie the threatn'd Death,
(For so was saving *Jove's* Decree compleat)
His Genius plac'd behind defends the Blow;
Disembled Waters from the Basis flow,
And *Boyn's* Triumphant Flood is known,
For ever in the Wounded Stone.
Before the Palace, *Thames* shall softly glide,
With dear Affection forming long delay,
Unwilling to be forc'd away,
Tho' all the Sister-Rivers chide,
Fond of Her Lord, forgetful of Her Tide.

NOTES

And thou Imperious *Windsor* stand enlarg'd,
With all the Stores of *Britain's* Honour charg'd:
Thou the fair Heaven that dost the Stars enclose,
Which William's Bosom wears, His Hand bestows,
To the Great Champions that support His Throne,
    And Virtues nearest to His own;
Round *Ormond's* Knee, thou tyest the Mystic String
That makes the Knight Companion to the King;
Returning Glorious from the Foreign Field,
In Thee he pays his Vows, and hangs his Shield.
Thou smiling see'st Great *Dorset's* Worth confest;
Transcendent Goodness in just Honours drest,
The Ray distinguishing the Patriot's Breast.

p. 115, l. 16.   B and 1700] To the...that support.

p. 116, verses xxxi., xxxii.]
    In Thee Great *Cavendish* Name shall long be known,
    The Father's Light transmitted to the Son.
    In Thee the *Seymours*, and the *Talbots* Line,
    With high Preheminence shall ever shine.
    And if a God these lucky Numbers guide,
    If sure *Apollo* o'er the Song preside,
    Jersey, Belov'd by All as well as Me
    Shall at thy Altars bow, shall own to Thee
    The fairest Mark of Favour and of Fame,
        Familiar to the *Villiers* Name.
Verses xxxiii.—xxxv. follow xxvi. in the edition of 1700.   l. 26] By hardy
Feats.   l. 27] To stimulate Desert with Thirst.   l. 36] Give all the...and
midst the.   l. 37] Draw the sure Sword (*omit* To).

p. 117, ll. 2, 3]
    To plant Societies for peaceful Arts,
    Increase our Learning and unite our Hearts.
l. 10. 1700 and B] That distant Realms may from our Authors know.   l. 17]
guard Great Agamemnon's.   l. 24] The mutual Obligation hide.   l. 28.
1700 and B] The Song with Him.   l. 32] shall ever chase the.

p. 118, l. 10] and William's Fleets.   ll. 30, 31]
    His own Stupendious Victories restrain'd,
    And o'er the Righted World Eternal Triumph gain'd.

p. 119, l. 3] a perfect.   l. 7] calls our.   l. 19] And Man, that knows
his Course, adores his Light.   l. 23] That (*omit* Above) Sun shou'd cease his
Destin'd Way to go.   l. 24] to Govern all below.   l. 26] were born.   The
1700 version, from this line, concludes as follows:
    Her absent Lord *Britannia* once must mourn,
    And of the Demi-God the Earthly-half must die:
    Yet if our Incense can excite your Care,
    If Heavenly Wills relent to Human Pray'r,
    Exert Great God thy Interest in the Sky,
    Gain ev'ry Tutelary Deity;
    That Conquer'd by the Public Vow,
    They keep the dismal Mischief long away,
    And far as lengthn'd Nature may allow,
    Reject with happy Power the threatn'd Day.

NOTES

Into the Ocean for his Life design'd,
Throw, bounteous Heav'n, innumerable Hours,
And that stern Fate its strict Account may find,
Make up that loss by taking them from Ours.
Deep in this Age let Him extend His Sway,
And our late Sons with chearful Awe obey.
On His sure Virtue long let Earth rely,
And late let the Imperial Eagle fly,
To bear the Hero through His Father's Sky.
 To Great *Æneas*, to *Themistocles*,
 To *Pollux*, *Theseus*, *Hercules*,
 And all the Radiant Names above,
 Rever'd by Men and Dear to *Jove*;
 Late let the New-born Nassaw-Star
 With dawning Majesty appear,
 To Triumph over vanquish'd Night,
 And Guide the *British* Mariner,
With everlasting Beams of Friendly Light.

l. 34. B and 1700] long away. l. 35. B and 1700] far as.

p. 121, l. 5. The date does not appear in B. l. 29. B] directs the.

p. 124. Published in 1704. 'London: Printed for Jacob Tonson.' The 1704 version is identical with the version in the 'unauthorised' edition of Prior's poems, 1707, save that on p. 124, l. 31, of the present edition it agrees with the later reading 'a Woman,' and in (ll. 8, 9, p. 125 of) the 1707 version quoted below it reads 'execute' for 'exercise' and 'meantime' for 'meanwhile.' l. 1. A] A Prologue. l. 9. A] kind Star, whose Tutelary. l. 10. A] Guided the future Monarch's. l. 12. A] Only less bless'd than Cynthia. l. 17. A] For what can Virtue more to man express. l. 19. A] What further thought of Blessing can we frame. l. 20. A] Than that, that Virtue should be still. l. 31. A] a Female.

p. 125, l. 1. A] Gives Glorious. ll. 7—10. A]
 Told him how Barb'rous Rage should be restrain'd,
 And bid him exercise what she ordain'd.
 Meanwhile, the Deity in Temples sat,
 Fond of her native Grecian's future Fate.

l. 13. A] Thus whilst the Goddess did her Pow'r dispose. l. 15. A] and Athens rose. ll. 16 et seqq. This 'Letter' was published in 1704. 'London. Printed for *Jacob Tonson*, within *Grays-Inn-Gate* next *Grays-Inn Lane*.' The variants of the 1704 are those given below save where otherwise stated. l. 19. B *omits*] Despreaux. l. 29] thy servant. l. 30] a happy.

p. 126, l. 8] Must certainly be Fortune's lasting Fault. l. 11] And darted Rays. l. 12] Some erring Deities disturb'd the. l. 13] And Fate. l. 25] Louis or. ll. 30—34]
 Hamilton, Lumley, Palmes, or *Ingoldsby*,
 May tolerably well with Verse agree.
 And Marlbrô, Poet, Marlbrô has a Name
 Which thou and all thy Breth'ren may proclaim,
 Elected to immortal Lays, and sure of endless Fame.

p. 127, l. 2] And generous Sylvius stand. ll. 3—6]
 And Churchil if that rough Sound offend the Strain
 Be true to Glorious Worth, and sing the Dane.

NOTES

l. 23—p. 128, l. 9]
> Ave Apollo !—Sir—one Moment's Ease.
> Tell me, is this to reckon or rehearse?
> A Commissary's List or Poet's Verse?
> Why Faith Depreaux there's Sense in what you say,
> I told you where my Difficulty lay;
> He that can make the rough Recital chime,
> Or bring the Sum of Lewis' Loss to Rhime,
> May make Arithmetic and Epic meet,
> And Newton's Books in Dryden's Stile repeat.
> O Boileau, had it been Apollo's Will
> That I had shar'd a Portion of thy Skill,
> Had this poor Breast receiv'd the Heav'nly Beam,
> And were my Numbers equal to my Theam,
> To noblest Strains I'd raise my serious Voice,
> And calling ev'ry Muse to bless my Choice,
> Arms and a Queen I'd sing; who Great and Good.

l. 32. B] Louis' Loss.

p. 128, l. 13] To vindicate a sinking Empire's Cause.   l. 15] I'd place the Queen in.   l. 18] These prompt to fix Her Joys, those to.   l. 20] And as Her Looks may dissipate their.   ll. 21, 22] With active Dance shou'd please Her Eye, with Vocal Shells her Ear (*one line*).   l. 27] With Pious Speech the River shou'd.   l. 28] blesses Anna's careful.

p. 129, l. 2] Nor names Her Bounty, nor proclaims his Worth.   l. 18] Counted by Men below, and bless'd by Gods above.   l. 26] 'Tis Anna's Glory, and Thou shalt be Great.   l. 29] I'll visit Thee again.   ll. 30, 31] And sit propitious on Thy Helm in Blenheim's glorious Plain (*one line*).
l. 34] Commission thro' the land is known.   l. 35] thronging Countries.

p. 130, l. 1] her Coast.   ll. 2—8]
> And almost ceases to weep William lost.
> Since that Great *Hercules* resign'd to Fate,
> The Atlas This, who must support her State;
ll. 10—12]
> He sees half Germany combin'd with France;
> Combin'd in vain—He draws the fatal Sword,
> The Troops obedient wait the Master Word.
l. 11. B] English General.   l. 13] charging Gen'ral.   l. 16] threat'ning Armies.   ll. 22—25]
> The *Roman* Eagle on the *Danube* Shoars
> Hears how the *British* Lion Victor roars,
> She claps her joyful Wings, and high to *Julian* Glory soars.
l. 28. B] British Muse.   l. 31] But, Goddess, change.   l. 38] As we have Victors.   l. 39 *omitted*.

p. 131, ll. 7—11]
> Our Muses as our Armies can agree,
> To humble Lewis, and reply to Thee.
> Nor shall we want just Subject for our Strains,
> Whilst Marlbrô's Arm eternal Lawrel gains,
> And in the Land where Spencer sung, a new Elisa reigns. }
l. 15. B] The Queen's Effigies on a.

p. 132, l. 13. B] (G—d knows) is fit.

p. 133, l. 12. B] writ on.

357

NOTES

p. 134, l. 29. A] in this.   l. 31.   A] turns.

p. 139, l. 22. B] Had brought.   l. 27.   B] softly past.

p. 140, l. 17. B] Deed.

p. 144, l. 11. B] Spirit which does closest.

p. 146, l. 5. B] Behold me fix'd.   l. 27.   B] Censure.

p. 147, l. 9. B] Cheek.

p. 148, l. 3. B] Will...Will.

p. 151, l. 19. B] and my Hands shall tear.

p. 152, l. 33. B] all the.

p. 154, l. 6. B] An useless.   l. 37.   B] A pious.

p. 155, l. 31. B] Herds.

p. 156, l. 33. B] Treasures.

p. 157, ll. 5, 6. B] Pow'r...Hour.

p. 159.   Published in 1706.   'London: Printed for *Jacob Tonson*, within *Grays-Inn-Gate* next *Grays-Inn Lane.*' The following variations are from the 1706 version, save where otherwise noted.   l. 6] Late Glorious.

p. 160, l. 9. 1706 and B] writ in.   l. 13. 1706 and B] and add variously. l. 13] as my Subject and Imagination.   l. 14] the matter of Style.   l. 19. 1706 and B] Numbers.   l. 19] only chang'd one Verse in his.   l. 20, *omit*] which...Harmonious.   ll. 20, 21] and avoided his Obsolete Words.   l. 30. 1706 and B] Ode I.

p. 161, l. 6. 1706 and B *omit*] if not.   l. 7. 1706 and B] Monmouth and the.   ll. 7, 8] yet Our Great Cambden does not reject it, and Milton tells it. l. 10. B and 1706] It carries, however.   l. 13. B] writ.   l. 13] Virgil writ one of the best Poems.   l. 14] Elizabeth one of the greatest Compliments. ll. 15—20 inclusive are not in 1706.   l. 21] Spencer, do I think, in.   l. 29] So leaving our.   l. 31. 1706 and B] to add, as to my own part.   l. 32, *omit*] at least.   l. 34] self obliged.   After l. 35 B adds] *Now if the* Reader *will be good enough to Pardon me this Excursion, I declare I will not trouble him again in this kind, 'till my Lord Duke of* Marlborough *gains another Victory, greater than those of* Blenheim *and* Ramillies. The 1706 version ends as follows:
And hereupon I declare, that if the Reader will be good enough to Pardon me this Excursion, I will neither trouble him with Poem or Preface any more, 'till my Lord Duke of Marlborough gets another Victory greater than those of Blenheim and Ramillies.

p. 162, l. 7.   1706] Troops to.   B] his Legions forth to.

p. 163, l. 3] and Victories rehearse.   l. 4] By story yet untold, unparal- lell'd by Verse.   l. 13] would raise.   l. 18] Nor seeking Battel, nor intent on Harms.   Verse vi.]
> In Council Calm and in Discourse Sedate,
> Under his Vineyard in his Native Land,
> Quiet and safe thus Victor *Marlb'rough* sate,
> Till *Anna* gives Her Thunder to his Hand;

NOTES

Then leaving soft Repose and gentle Ease
With swift Impatience seeks the distant Foe;
Flying o'er Hills and Vales, o'er Rocks and Seas,
He meditates, and strikes the wond'rous Blow;
Quicker than Thought he takes his destin'd Aim,
And Expectation flies on slower Wings than Fame.

p. 164, ll. 2, 3]
      Untam'd Bavar, when on Ramillia's Plain
      Afar he did the British Chief behold.
l. 25] tempt thy Rival.   l. 28] That Laurel Grove, that Harvest of.
ll. 32, 33]
      Must shed, I ween, its Honours from thy Brow
      And on another Head another Spring must know.
l. 38] In thy ill Conduct seek thy ill Success.

p. 165, ll. 5, 6]
      Jove's Handmaid Pow'r must Jove's Behests pursue,
      And where the Cause is Just, the Warrior shall subdue.
l. 9] sprung from.   ll. 11—17 and verse xii.]
      With an Intrepid Hand and Courage draws
      That Sword, Immortal *William* at his Death
      (Who could a fairer Legacy bestow?)
      Did to the Part'ner of his Arms bequeath:
      That Sword well *Louis* and his Captains know;
      For they have seen it drawn from William's Thigh,
      Full oft as he came forth, to Conquer, or to Die.
      But brandish'd high, and waving in the Air,
      Behold unhappy Prince, the Master Sword,
      Which perjur'd *Gallia* shall for ever fear:
      'Tis that which Cæsar gave the *British* Lord.
      He took the Gift; Nor ever will I sheath,
      He said, (so *Anna*'s high Behests Ordain)
      This Glorious Gift, unless by Glorious Death
      Absolv'd, 'till I by Conquest fix your Reign.
      Returns like these Our Mistress bids us make,
      When from a Foreign Prince a Gift Her *Britons* take.
l. 36] The Two great adverse Chiefs unmov'd abide.

p. 166, l. 2] The Shock sustain'd, the Friendly Pair.   l. 6] Fix'd on
Revenge.   l. 11] their Deeds.   l. 13] But oh! while mad with Rage
Bellona.   ll. 15—22]
      While with large Steps to Conquest *Britain* goes,
      What Horror damps the Strong and quells the Great?
      Why do those Warriors look dismay'd and pale,
      That ever Dreadful, never knew to Dread?
      Why does the charging Foe almost prevail,
      And the Pursuers only not recede?
      Their Rage, alas! submitting to their Grief,
      Behold they weep, and croud around their falling Chief.
l. 26] that Thunderbolt.   l. 27] I saw their Marlb'rough stretch'd along the.
l. 28] Vain Hope...for Marlb'rough mounts.   l. 35] And lo! the dubious
Battel.   l. 38] And Liberty must live and Gallia yield.

NOTES

p. **167**, ll. 5, 6]
> The Foe retires, the Victor urges on,
> And Blenheim's Fame again is in Ramillia known.

l. 13] We wish'd Thou wou'dst no more those.   l. 14] Gallia's.   l. 19] of Rest.   l. 26] To lift Great Anna's Glory further on.   l. 28] Nothing was done, He thought, while.

p. **168**, l. 3] as he sees the Eagle cut.   l. 4] and fearful.   l. 6] Why then did.   l. 7] To dare the British Foe.   l. 25] his azure.

p. **169**, l. 13] Still breaking...still.   l. 14] usual Bane.   l. 24. 1706 and B] And to...they must.

p. **170**, l. 11] and spend.   l. 19] Intomb'd I'll Slumber, or Enthron'd I'll Reign.   l. 28] from the Rival.

p. **171**, l. 8] There Brabant clad.   l. 9] In decent.   l. 11] Laying her. l. 12] Flanders.   l. 16] Her Sister Provinces from her shall.   l. 22] with Marks.   l. 24] Types of.   l. 31. 1706 and B] should see.   l. 33] sweet pow'r.   ll. 36—39]
> And Ireland's Harp, her Emblem of Command,
> And Instrument of Joy, should there be seen.
> And Gallia's wither'd Lillies pale, and torn,
> Should, here and there dispers'd, the lasting Work adorn.

l. 37. B] should there.

p. **172**, l. 9] will, appointed Marlb'rough's hand.   B] Thy Marlbrô's Hand.   l. 10] To end those Wars, and make that.   l. 11. 1706 and B] to Everlasting Peace.

p. **185**, ll. 23, 24. Published in folio 2 pp., undated, 'Printed for Bernard Lintott, at the *Cross-Keys*, between the two *Temple-Gates* in *Fleet-street*. (Price one Penny.)' C] 'To the Right Honourable Robert Harley, Esq.'

p. **188**. Erle Robert's Mice, etc. Published in 1712 in 'Two Imitations of Chaucer, viz. I. Susannah and the Two Elders. II. Earl Robert's Mice. By Matthew Prior, Esq.' There are two versions of Susannah and the Two Elders given in this issue, the second one being a rendering 'attempted in a Modern Stile,' as follows:
> When Fair Susannah in a cool retreat
> Of shady Arbours shun'd the Sultry heat,
> Two wanton Lechers, seiz'd the trembling Dame.
> What Female Strength could do, her Arms perform,
> And guarded well the Fort they strove to Storm.
> The Story's ancient, and if rightly told,
> Young was the Lady, but the Lovers Old.
> Had the Reverse been true, had Authors Sung,
> How that the Dame was *Old*, the Lovers *Young*,
> If She had then the blooming Pair deny'd,
> With tempting Youth and Vigour on their side,
> Lord! How the Story would have shock'd my *Creed*!
> For that had been a Miracle indeed.

A copy of a 1712 version is catalogued in the Locker-Lampson Collection. 'By M——w P——r, Esq; London. Printed for A. Baldwin, near the Oxford Arms in Warwick-Lane. Price Three pence. Folio.'

The two imitations of Chaucer were reprinted in 'A Collection of Original Poems, Translations, and Imitations, By M^r. Prior, M^r. Rowe, Dr Swift, And

NOTES

other Eminent Hands. London: Printed for E. Curll, at the *Dial and Bible* against St. *Dunstan's* Church in Fleet-street 1714. (Price Five Shillings).' They also occur in the 'unauthorised' edition of 1716=C below. There are many differences of spelling in these versions, but the following variants are the only ones that need be noted.

l. 28. 1712] could wish.

p. 189, l. 2. 1712] the Mice. l. 18. 1712] or any. l. 25. 1712] Godes. C] unworthy Godis. l. 30. 1712] in the. l. 37. 1712] rack.

p. 190, l. 6. 1712] from the. l. 16. 1712] be done. ll. 18 et seqq., not in 1712. l. 25. 1712 and C] Susannah and the Two Elders. l. 29. 1712 and C] The Paramours were Olde, the Dame was Yong. l. 32. 1712 and C] Sweet Jesu! that had bene much.

p. 195. Published in C. l. 25] Walter Danniston, To his Friends.

p. 196, l. 14. C] And Death's.

p. 204, ll. 12—17. Published in Dryden's *Miscellany Poems*, Part 5, 1703/4 (=E). l. 12. A] Faith, Hope, and Charity. Being a Paraphrase, etc. l. 19. E] men. A and E] Angels.

p. 205, l. 12. A] and as much believes.

p. 206, l. 3. A and E] With all His Robes. l. 11. A] And still.

p. 209, l. 9. D] Stobœum.

APPENDIX A

CONTENTS OF THE EDITION OF 1707.

(Copies of this edition are very rarely to be seen.)

Advertisement from the Publisher.

The Name of Mr. Prior, is a more Satisfactory Recommendation of the following Sheets to those Gentlemen who are Judges of Poetry, than whatever can be offer'd in their Behalf.

All that I here endeavour'd, (and which by the Assistance of some Friends, I have accomplish'd) is, that the several Pieces herein contain'd, should appear more Perfect and Correct by this Publication, than they have hitherto done elsewhere; and that no Copy should be inserted, 'till I was assur'd of its being Genuine.

APPENDIX B

CONTENTS OF THE EDITION OF 1716.

'A Second Collection of Poems on Several Occasions. By Matthew Prior, Esq; [Device] London: Printed for J. Roberts near the *Oxford Arms* in *Warwick-Lane,* 1716. Price One Shilling.'

INDEX OF TITLES

INDEX OF TITLES

INDEX OF FIRST LINES

INDEX OF FIRST LINES

INDEX OF FIRST LINES

CAMBRIDGE: PRINTED BY W. LEWIS, M.A., AT THE UNIVERSITY PRESS